The Liberating Power of Emotions

By Riet Okken

PO Box 754, Huntsville, AR 72740
800-935-0045; fax 479-738-2348; www.ozarkmt.com
ISBN: 90-807368-1-3

Published in Dutch by: Astarte Publishing House
Also available in all bookshops in the Netherlands and Belgium.
E-mail: uitgeverij.astarte@orange.fr   Translation: Shannon Davidson

Library of Congress Cataloging-in-Publication Data
Okken, Riet, 1948-
The Liberating Power of Emotions, by Riet Okken
A concrete path that will enable readers to free themselves from ego and banish depression, jealously, burnout, shame, guilt and addiction.

1. Emotions 2. Healing 3. Psychotherapy 4. Metaphysics 5. Soul Growth
I. Okken, Riet, 1948- II. Healing   III. Metaphysics
IV. Title

Library of Congress Catalog Card Number: 2012936034

ISBN: 978-1-886940-56-7

Cover Art and Layout: www.enki3d.com
Book set in: Times New Roman, Apple Chancery
Book Design: Julia Degan

Published by:

WWW.OZARKMT.COM
Printed in the United States of America

I dedicate this book to my mother who was so in need of emotional healing but got only the doctors' advice to drink a good cup of milk.

Table of Contents

Part V: Frequently Discussed Subjects

Preface

The liberating force of emotions has been a *leitmotif* in my life, both along my own road to liberation and in my therapeutic work with others. Emotions have motivated me and given me a free and fulfilling life. I am very happy to share my vision of this path with you. The path consists of abandoning the fruitless denial of emotions and giving them a loving welcome instead. It is a way of achieving fundamental health. I am not describing yet another therapy method but rather a way of life in which healthy emotional management is a part of your daily routine.

I suggest that when you read this book, you keep one eye on the page. With the other eye, look into your heart, for this book is only useful when it moves your heart. I sincerely hope that this book begins or intensifies this process within you and stimulates you to enrich the quality of your life. Emotions can free you from old fixations and patterns if you manage them well. They set you free and give you joy and fullness of life. They can point you to your destination in life and your truth. Put simply: true feelings make you *feel* your truth, and this truth will set you free.

You can read this book from beginning to end or read chapters individually, depending on what appeals to you most. Each part is complete. It does mean, however, that there are a few repetitions, but I can't see how this can be avoided and actually feel it is useful in a workbook such as this. Initially, I wrote each chapter separately, depending on what I felt like on that day. After I had completed the writing, I placed the chapters in sequence. This allowed me to keep up the creative flow from which this book was born. It is the fruit of thirty years of very intense work, but I wrote it in a three-month period with great joy and an unprecedented amount of energy.

This book is suitable for reading and using on your own but also for discussion groups, self-help groups and therapy training.

Several people have been of great help in the writing process. They shared my enthusiasm, contributed their stories and gave me the feedback I needed. First and foremost, I want to mention my friend Janet Emmelkamp who was always by my side. Without her, my work would only have been half complete.

Also, I want to thank the many Spark of Light Workers for their enthusiastic contributions and corrections.

And last but not least I would like to thank my parents. My mother has always been there for me with an open heart and mind, and my father gave me his confidence and fatherly blessing when I had to make big decisions. They gave me space and freedom to live my life the way I wanted. It certainly was a good base to realize my freedom.

This book is my contribution to the emotional liberation of this planet. May it help you, dear reader, and inspire you in your path of liberation. I wish you courage and good Work.

Introduction: Our Emotions

True feelings will show us our truth and this truth will set us free.

In this day and age people are beginning to realize that man is not the rational being he has always pretended to be. *Homo rationalis* has played the dominant role, and in our human society we have always turned to our "common sense" in times of difficulty and continue to do so even today. We slowly find out, however, that this reasoning might have helped us to make the world a highly technical and sophisticated place, but that it cannot help us to solve the enormous problems of hatred, war, racism and the overwhelming problems of physical and mental health which we face today.

It is time to acknowledge that within *Homo rationalis* there is a *Homo emotionalis* faced with a huge "backlog of emotional maintenance" caused by centuries of neglect. This neglect of our emotions runs parallel with centuries of degrading women to second-class citizens. Emotions were attributed to the weaker sex and because of these emotions they were considered inferior. Coinciding with the emancipation of women, realization has been growing that even though our emotions are often subconscious and hidden, they ultimately determine our society and culture. The time has come for us to clear our sister's name because she is a fundamental part of our own rich humanity. In order for us to heal the planet, we will have to address the root of the problem—the war between this brother and sister within us. The great challenge we face today involves harmonizing our emotional and rational choices and qualities. Without sister emotion, there is no heart in a technical and rational world. Without brother reason, there is no head and no organization. Both are fundamental instruments with which to live on this planet in peace and joy.

This inner war which is reflected in our external wars is the reason we have not learned to cope with our emotions. The only thing we have been doing for centuries is trying to control emotions. This is the very foundation of our constitutions and religions, our family upbringing, our schools, and our health services. Our collective drama is that over and over again we fail to keep our emotions under control. At unguarded moments, when brother reason nods off to sleep, our emotional pressure cooker blows its top, and we lash out, usually at people who have nothing to do with the issue. Due to this control and these unconscious emotional outbursts, we have not found ways of establishing a conscious relationship with our emotions. We just do not know how to deal with them. Children are not taught how to deal with them nor are they told how to express these emotions in school, and in our institutions of physical and mental health, the language of technology and reason has become more and more prominent. Psychology, which should really be a representative of sister emotion, is trying to respond to this but is a child of its time, too. It competes with ever-higher levels of abstraction in the scientific competition of brother reason, and, in doing so, it drifts further and further away from peoples' concrete experiences. It also gets carried away by the modern tendency of a "quick fix" and tries to reintegrate people whose souls are wounded into today's society. With our power of reason, we cleverly divided man into different compartments. You consult a doctor for your physical body, you see a psychologist for your psyche, and you visit your vicar, priest, rabbi, or imam for your soul. For the mind, such compartmentalization is easy and clear and also perhaps for the practicality of life—we do not know any better—but for true peaceful cohabitation, we need something else. In order to fully recover from wars and conflict, we need to heal ourselves and undo the fruitless compartmentalization of man. For us to be complete once more, we need a whole approach, one which honors and respects all aspects of our humanity. Medicine, psychology, and spirituality should work together in their efforts of helping man become aware of his totality. In other words, we need an integral program with an integral approach.

As sister emotion has been the most neglected, she can and must take the lead on this path. She has determined our ups and downs for centuries. She can lead us to a new path and a new paradigm. Paradigm means "example." Let the path of emotion be the one to set a new example this time. She should have the chance to give this world the heart it so yearns for. We need to let emotional development go hand in hand with physical, intellectual, and spiritual development. Our emotions carry the power to heal ourselves and the world at large if we handle them in the right way. This means that, first and foremost, we should respect our emotions. We subsequently need a concrete method to clear up the backlog of maintenance which causes our current emotional problems. This approach can help us to not subconsciously lash out or project our emotions at the wrong people. It will become apparent that once we find the way of dealing with this emotional backlog, it will be easier to develop good emotional management. This emotional management is the harvest of a lot of hard Work (written with a capital W). Because hard Work it will be, integrating this new paradigm into everyday life.

The enormous problem we face on this planet is how to undo this control while we deal with our emotions—and each other—in a healthy and non-damaging way. How do we clean up the mess caused by centuries of repressing our emotions? We all have a backlog of unresolved traumas because we have denied and controlled our emotions for so long. Suppressing emotions creates violence and chaos. Suppressed and denied emotions are the basis of the world as it is now.

How do we heal this world, for God's sake? The only approach that I can see is to liberate ourselves and our emotions from the long denial they have suffered. And that is no small task. It will not be a "quick fix;" we have strayed too far from home for that. We now face the choice of either keeping on inventing more tricks for survival or opting for healing our damaged and hurt sister.

With this book I wish to contribute to this path of emotional liberation and maturity. My observations and ideas have developed over my many years of practice. I have experienced the liberating power of emotions myself, and in my role as a psychologist and therapist, I have helped many others to experience that power within them and to transform it into a wholesome and creative life.

This book is about finding our essence again through emotional cleaning. Ultimately it is not about emotions as such but about the light—and that is essentially awareness—that surfaces once we have cleaned our "emotional pressure cookers." This light can appear in many different ways: emotional freedom, a sense of peace that goes beyond all reason, joy, feeling satisfied, and knowing your purpose in life, a sense of worth and above all connection with the Loving Light, which began our path of evolution a long time ago and of which we are part, a Spark of Light. This is why I call this path Spark of Light Work.

Part One:

"Homo Emotionalis"

Chapter 1

Control

Everything we shut our eyes to, everything we run away from, everything we deny, denigrate, or despise, serves to defeat us in the end. What seems nasty, painful, evil can become a source of beauty, joy, and strength if faced with an open mind.
~Henry Miller

Emotions essentially rule our entire existence. Looking at the world around us, we can see that emotions are the driving force in human interaction. We might think we are in the driver's seat, but it is the unconscious emotions in the back seat that actually steer and make the decisions. There is a lot of fear, anger and pain, a lot of emotionally charged discussions and interactions between partners, parents and children, colleagues, and between management and so-called "subordinates." Emotions are rife in road traffic, relationships, the arts, schools and in politics. Even our whole economic system is ruled by emotions and stands or falls with the fear and emotional chaos in world politics. When we are optimistic and hopeful, the financial markets do well, and when we fear for the future, the stock market crashes as does the economy.

At crucial times emotions determine how we act and in times of danger our emotions lead the way. The choice of a partner and the decision to have a family are other important goals that are largely determined by emotions.

Emotions rule—and by these, we also define the biggest problem of our society. We are governed by our emotions instead of us managing them and being in touch with them. This is just like the horse before the cart: is there someone sitting on the box ready to lead the horse, or do we let the horse, which in this example represents our emotions, just gallop away wildly?

Carl Jung, the famous psychiatrist, spoke about "*anima* and *animus-besetztheit*." In this case, we speak of *emotional obsession*. Emotions largely control us; in other words, we have been hijacked by them. Hijacking and obsession are opposites of connection and freedom. In the case of hijacking and obsession, there is no leader, no management, and no governing body to manage and rule in wisdom. The only thing we can do when we are controlled by our emotions is to try and control them—in turn, an eye for an eye, a tooth for a tooth! Who is controlling whom?

When growing up the message was "behave yourself, control yourself, and keep intense emotions under wraps." Freudian psychology is a continuation of this misconception and neurotic development that the Ego should control the Id with all its dark instincts and emotions. Here the "I" is the great neurotic, who has everything neatly under control, so that the Id and all that is subconscious does not flood the "I." Freud certainly contributed a great deal to the development of psychology and human society as a whole. However, his psychology is partly a phenomenon of its time and period. Human evolution continues, and we now need to take the next step forward. We need a new psychology in which the "I" no longer leads the horse but our soul instead—a new psychology in which control of our emotions is no longer the most important and in which connection, freedom, and healthy management are the new ingredients in dealing with our emotions.

We could call "control" the first path in coping with our emotions. But this has not proven to be the adequate way of making our society more pleasant and liveable. In our collective inner world, we seem to harbor more depressions, anxiety, fear, and feelings of meaninglessness than ever before even though we are better off materially. Why is this? The most important cause is that what you keep under control always resurfaces. An example to clarify this: when you feel angry but you do not know why, you will try to restrain your anger when you interact with others. The reason for doing this is that we have been taught to do so because we are afraid of conflict; because if we did not, we would face too much rejection; and because we want to be loved by others and so on. Nevertheless from time to time, especially when we are tired or under stress (for example when we are in a traffic jam and are on our way to an important meeting), we lose our temper and lash out. We might curse at the driver overtaking us from the slow lane, make gestures, perhaps even chase others, or cut them off.

Another example about grief: when you suffer deep down from a depression which you have suppressed or forgotten the cause of, you are likely to be moody, tired and apathetic at times. You will not look happy even though you try really hard. Depression can express itself in many different ways—from anger to crying without knowing why to sarcasm and sentimentality. We could say that control causes distortion, and that is a good definition of neurosis.

Anger which is controlled causes bitterness or sarcasm, contempt, hatred, prejudice and irritation. When we control sadness, we become depressed, anxious, tired, or we start feeling like a victim. Controlling fear causes all kinds of anxiety for all sorts of things and people. This leads to avoidance behavior, leading a petty and minimal life and to seeking false security in things that do not really matter. Joy which is controlled on the pretext of "act normally, anything else is too much" makes life dull and boring. It kills the fun in life and makes you unable to feel real joy.

Control just does not work! Why is that the case? Because, as Einstein said, everything is energy, and energy cannot be removed or extinguished. It can only be *transformed*. When we control something, we try to sweep it under the carpet and replace it with something else, a different kind of behavior. This is, however, not transformation, but s*ubstitution*. It is a subconscious juggling of feelings and emotions. And as you would expect, juggling is a way of fooling yourself and others. Truth is the only thing that lasts and sets you free. The road of transformation is very different than that of substitution. Before we explore this road a bit further, let us look a little closer at the schools of thought from the past, the old "seekers of truth." How did they deal with emotions?

Control in Religion

Most religions, spiritual schools, and spiritual movements advocate control as the path to fulfilment and God. Asceticism and abstinence, control and self-improvement are all highly regarded on many spiritual paths. Because we have denied our emotions for centuries, we have become cut off from our origins, we do not sense God anymore, and do not know what the true fulfilment of human existence means. We have replaced it with exercises, rules, Judgments, theories, dogmas, theology, moralism, and ritualism.

Emotions have been execrated in a lot of spiritual and philosophical literature. These emotions—mainly anger—were seen as a diabolical force. One day, a boy came to me for therapy who had joined the Jehovah's witnesses. He had a lot of problems at home and suffered from serious emotional neglect. I noticed by the way he talked that he was in fact very angry. However, he did not want to acknowledge this anger, let alone express it. He kept quoting from the Bible, for example:

6

James I 19:20. "My dear brothers, do not forget this: every man should be quick to listen, slow to speak, and slow to be angry. When a man is angry, he does not do what God says is right." This boy might be an extreme example and many people will not be as familiar with these texts as he was, but such words have greatly influenced many Christians and continue to do so perhaps even today.

Religions often speak in terms of imperatives: "Thou shalt ..." and "Thou shalt not." "Love thy neighbor as thyself," "Be perfect, as your heavenly Father is perfect," "Let go of your ego," "Be humble," "Be detached," or "Be compassionate." That which should come from within is dictated or presented as a virtue to be attained. What happens deep down inside of you when someone says, "Be spontaneous"? Exactly. You tense up! When spontaneity, compassion, and friendliness are real, they come from within just as love does, and they cannot be dictated by others if you want them to be authentic.

The influence of denial and control of emotions is clearly recognizable here—because the road from inside to outside is blocked and has become clogged up, man has had to follow the path leading from the outside to the inside. This has resulted in religious upbringing, indoctrination, and the following of teachers and gurus. The original meaning of religion, namely connection, has been reduced to morality. If we listen carefully to certain quotes by the Pope or other religious leaders, we notice that the majority of these quotes are of an ethical rather than religious nature: "Thou shalt ..." and "Thou shalt not." In my opinion, spiritual leaders should not only tell us, but especially show us *how* we can reaffirm and feel our connection with God. That is what people long for! If we can feel God, Loving Light, in our own heart once more, then there will be no more need for external ethics. All will then be able to take the measure of their own actions in a mature and responsible way against what Loving Light tells their heart of hearts to do. Morality and theology were born because the path to our feelings was blocked. We need new ethics that are based on emotions and integrated emotionality again. Once the connection with the heart is re-established, everyone will know how to act in full awareness in a responsible and honest way. I will not deny that on the road to such new ethics we will also need "external ethics" for as long as our emotions have not fully been integrated.

Religions usually focus on striving for that which has been realized by certain saints or spiritual leaders. This then becomes the virtue or ideal to which people aspire. The ideal of perfection, whether it is called compassion, friendliness, humility, or love, has to be realized within most religious systems by eliminating the opposite of what is considered to be negative. The way this is done is by control on a conscious level, called suppression, and on a subconscious level, called repression in psychology. Suppression is when we consciously try to suppress or eliminate tendencies and characteristics. Discipline and asceticism are the most well-known forms of conscious suppression. Abstinence from sexuality is a well-known example, seen in both Christianity and Eastern religions. Vows of poverty, chastity, and obedience have long been the disciplines with which to obtain the inner experience of God through detachment. Again, this is following the path from outside to inside rather than inner growth and the development of our emotions from within.

However, efforts to achieve this inner detachment were only successful if the initiate or novice stayed safely within the boundaries of the cloister or their own culture. The current failure of the Christian cloister culture teaches us that striving for the ideal of perfection based on control usually results in spiritual slavery and inner poverty. It is very sad to see how many seekers of God have become lost within the church.

The derailments of many Eastern gurus and lamas, who came to the West over the last few decades in order to teach their path to enlightenment, show us how quickly their control falls short. Vows of celibacy and abstinence of alcohol, wealth, or power were sometimes broken in a flagrant manner leaving the bewildered students asking what Enlightenment really is.

The teachers appeared to be spiritually enlightened but were certainly not at an emotional or relationship level. One can ask what such "Enlightenment" really is when it does not include the whole person and is based on suppression and control. Many people have become disillusioned by these stories and by experiencing the shortcomings of their guru with regards to emotions and relationships and have returned to everyday life. Is this throwing out the good with the evil? I believe it is. I think we need a more complete understanding and experience of Enlightenment, one that comprises the transformation of the person on all levels, including the emotional level. This means a transformation and liberation of a controlled emotionality, which leads to freedom and an open heart in which a true and full realization of one Self becomes possible.

Chapter 2

Venting Emotions: The Second Way of Dealing with Emotions

As long as we are emotionally tied, we will always be the disappointing disappointee.
~C.G. Jung

Control and venting/acting out usually follow one other. When control weakens, we vent subconscious emotional reactions. Our world suffers from the dilemma of subconscious emotional responses. Venting or acting-out behavior has two characteristics: it is subconscious and wrongly aimed. This is called projection.

These projective and subconscious emotions might give temporary solace and relief but will not help us in the long run. A burst of anger aimed at your children because they are too lively or have a mind of their own, might temporarily release the tensions which have been pent up but will make you feel guilty because you know that what you are doing is not right. You know that a large part of your emotional charge has nothing to do with them. A good cry after a fight with your partner might help you to reconnect with each other, but if the reasons for the

11

conflict remain unclear, the conflict will repeat itself. Being jealous of your partner and the subsequent emotional conflict will not transform your life unless you realize that those feelings of jealousy belong to the child within you. Another sign that healing is not taking place is feeling scared over and over again without knowing what you are actually afraid of. Similarly, cursing at other drivers in traffic will not make you feel any better. We often "transfer" old emotional pain to new events. Not only does this not solve anything, it also adds to the emotional pollution of this planet. It will make you feel more guilty and will add to the sense of insecurity and heaviness surrounding you.

Your relationships become poisoned by these subconscious old emotional charges. The things you do and say in an "unguarded" moment of emotional overreaction usually stay around for a long time, despite reconciliation rituals.

The Ten Commandments and ethics arose from this kind of venting. It was a good effort to try and minimize this flow of emotional pulp. We have internalized ethics and social rules and regulations to a certain extent so that our society remains somewhat governable. However, it remains a very precarious balance between control and venting, as the core and causes of the emotional reactions are not being solved. This is why we need a new approach, a third path. For us to climb out of our emotional deadlock, this path should be like a root canal treatment.

This third approach means exceeding the paths of control and venting/acting out. It involves descending into the dark recesses of our emotions. It means deep emotional Work with a capital W. From these depths we can perhaps learn how to handle our emotions healthily. We will then be able to create a healthy emotional management in a healthy society together.

Chapter 3

Emotional Management: A New Approach

Remain true to yourself, child. When you know your own heart,
you will always have at least one friend.
~Marion Bradley

*E*motional management means becoming the shepherd of your emotions. Good management has nothing to do with control but is all about good stewardship. Imagine a good shepherd who is counting all his sheep. The sheep represent the resources we are born with, such as our bodies, our mind, our feelings, and our willpower. The sheep could also stand for our entire wealth of feelings and emotions. We should count all of them and appreciate them the way a good shepherd does. To be more precise, good emotional management means this:

1. That you are **connected** to all of your emotions and feelings and that you can feel them. Connection is created step by step when you become aware of your mechanism of denial and control and when you digest

13

your emotions. In doing so, you heal and liberate yourself. The road to connection with the present consists of becoming aware of these mechanisms and emotional digestion of old pains.

2. Through emotional digestion, you can **integrate and transform** your emotions into positive qualities of life, such as creativity, joy, wisdom, inner peace, and freedom, sense of purpose in life, and last but not least, being capable of loving.

3. Emotional Work is an aid for balancing body, mind, emotions, and spirituality. There are many inner battles between these aspects. Until now, the mind has had the conscious supremacy here on earth. One could even say that this is the cause of all our problems. I would rather say that the basis of all problems is the **subconscious dominance of emotions**. There is nothing wrong with our minds. It is just that our minds have had to work overtime because we have learned to fear our emotions. When we become aware of our emotions and when we integrate them, the head can take a break and can be used solely for what it was created to do.

4. The **center of your feelings** moves from your head to your heart and abdomen. When you become the custodian of your emotions, you can clearly feel this center in your abdomen and your heart and no longer in your head. Emotional integration means learning how to live from the center in your abdomen and your heart—that is where the guidance and the warmth are.

5. Finally, good emotional management means taking full **responsibility for your emotions**. It means accepting that your emotions are your own creation. You are then no longer a victim of the emotions that rest heavily on your shoulders. You take full responsibility for everything you feel and experience as being your lessons in life. Every now and then you let the child

14

within you scream and shout and blame parents and educators in a safe therapeutic setting to free yourself from old emotional baggage. In this way you take fundamental responsibility for your emotions. What you experience in the outside world is a perfect mirror of your inner world. There are no coincidences and everything is right, whether you like it or not. If you experience rape, then it is a theme in your life in one way or another.

In Spark of Light Work, I often see that people who experience sexual violence in this life have also experienced it in past lives. The purport of events is different for everyone. It can be learning to set boundaries, mobilizing your anger, gaining respect for yourself, learning the right value of sexuality and so on. By looking for a possible explanation, by mobilizing your emotions, rather than primarily analyzing them, you start taking full responsibility for your own ups and downs. This is not always easy, but it does increase the possibilities you have of being the answer to your own life.

If control and venting are the key words for the old paths, *digesting emotions* is the key word for this new approach to emotional management.

Emotional Intelligence: A New Form of Control?

How do we arrive at what Daniel Goleman calls "emotional intelligence"?[1] Goleman also advocates a vision of human nature, which takes the power of emotions into account. I will discuss his viewpoints in detail to make it clearer what my own vision is and to explain the differences between the two. Emotional intelligence concerns skills which differ from purely intellectual capacities, ones that can be measured by an IQ-test.

We will have a look at how he defines emotional intelligence: "It refers to the ability to recognize your emotions and those of others, to distinguish and regulate them and express them adequately." The field of emotional intelligence is divided into several main areas:

- Self-awareness: knowledge of your own emotions. This involves recognizing a particular feeling when it arises.

- Regulating emotions: Goleman mentions the ability to calm yourself down.

- Self-motivation: how to use your emotions to achieve your goal. This is the ability of emotional self-control and the suppression of impulsiveness in order to achieve a certain goal.

- Empathy: recognition of and empathy for other people's emotions.

- Relationship skills: the ability to regulate other people's emotions.

At first sight, you might think this looks quite good. It is certainly very valuable that the traditional understanding of intelligence is supplemented by the understanding of emotional intelligence. The abilities Goleman refers to are indeed very necessary and valuable skills. He also searches for a balance between the head and the heart. But how do we achieve this balance and emotional intelligence? This is where Goleman and I part ways.

Influence and Digestion: Two Different Things

Goleman and the rest of the emotional-intelligence movement, including NLP (Neuro Linguistic Programming), work on *influencing* emotions rather than *digesting* them. Goleman even claims that we have little or no control over our emotions, which can flood us, and that we also lack the

16

necessary knowledge of how to do this. He claims that we can only determine *how long* an emotion lasts. According to Goleman, when an emotion surfaces, we should be able to influence it in the following ways:

- Use of self-awareness. Being aware of certain emotions can in itself have a restraining effect.

- Use of cognitive reconstruction, which means trying to see the cause of the emotion in a different light. Anger can be defused by overcoming and contesting the thoughts which bring about the bursts of anger. For example: instead of immediately becoming angry at the driver who cuts off your path, you can think of why he might be in such a hurry, perhaps there is a medical emergency. Worries can be contested effectively by critically examining your own assumptions.

- Use of diversion tactics. Goleman speaks of relaxation techniques and counting to ten, jogging, avoiding the people in question, taking your mind off things, and looking for "boosters."

What we see here is that Goleman's method of achieving emotional intelligence is based on cognition and behavior. It is a mental approach which uses mental techniques to influence the layer of emotions. In this book I will show you that we can take the next step in our joint evolution, a step which goes beyond influencing. The influencing methods suggested by Goleman and cognitive behavioral therapies, such as NLP, an approach to effective communication and changing of patterns of behavior by way of awareness of the connections between the neurological processes, language, and behavioral patterns in which we are programmed by way of experience/s, are ultimately a new, smart way of control.

Let us look at the three influencing techniques one by one. Naturally I have nothing against the first step of self-awareness. It is good to be at least aware of your emotions and to recognize them. Cognitive therapies can do a lot of good in that respect. Many people lack this fundamental awareness and are not able to get beyond noticing that they are miserable, vaguely unhappy, or easily annoyed. What is the next step, once you know that you are actually angry or sad? Awareness is a step in the right direction, but it is hopelessly insufficient for good emotional management.

The use of techniques such as cognitive reconstruction and different kinds of distraction indicate that people do not know what to do with the emotions themselves. You have to use tricks of the mind and ways of taking your mind off your emotions. That is very similar to what our neurotic little self has been trying to do for centuries: "Look at other people. They are worse off than me. He or she didn't mean it like that. Take a deep breath, count to ten. Go and do something nice." Master yet another relaxation technique, stop seeing certain people, and so on.

Looking at our earlier example of anger which surfaces when someone cuts off your path in traffic, I think it is important to ask yourself why you react so emotionally and whether you also react very strongly to other unimportant things. You could look at the reasons behind your emotional charge. In subsequent chapters, we will look at this way of working more closely.

Emotional Control and Impulse Control

Another difference between the two approaches becomes clear when we read about the "marshmallow test," which is by now quite well-known. Goleman uses it to illustrate the importance of impulse control. That is why he calls an impulse "the medium of the emotion." In a study by psychologist Walter Mischel, a number of four-year-olds were given the following options: "I have to run an errand. If you wait until I get back, you will get two marshmallows. If you can't wait that long, you will only get one, but you can have it right away."

There was a follow-up study twelve to fourteen years later. Goleman describes the results: "The emotional and social differences between the toddlers who grabbed the marshmallow immediately and ones that waited for their reward were dramatic. People that were able to resist temptation at four years of age grew up to be more socially skilled adolescents: on a personal level they were more effective, more self-aware, and able to deal better with disappointments in life. They had less chance of breaking down under pressure, stagnating or showing regression. When under pressure, they were less stressed or disorganized; they accepted challenges and even in times of difficulty they stuck with it instead of quitting; they were independent, self-confident, and reliable; they took the initiative and threw themselves into many different undertakings. And more than ten years later, they were still capable of postponing a reward to achieve their goals."[2]

In short, children who were able to control their impulses (Goleman considers emotions to be impulses of action) showed signs of emotional intelligence. This places Goleman close to Freud. He says, "It is possible that there might not be a more fundamental psychological skill than the control of impulses. Impulse control is the basis of all emotional self-control because every emotion is known to cause an impulse of action."[3]

Does this research show that these children are emotionally more intelligent because they are able to postpone their desires? I think it can mean two entirely different things. It could be that these children were able to postpone eating the marshmallow because they were fundamentally more fulfilled and had experienced more love in childhood. That is also the reason why they functioned better in later life. Another explanation could be that these emotionally intelligent children had better control over themselves because they had had a stricter upbringing which resulted in them being more socially adjusted later on in life. Social adjustment and success play an important part in Goleman's ideas. The subtitle of his book is "Emotions as a Key to Success." That is very different goal as my "Emotions as a force of liberation."

Control or Cleaning

Goleman mainly bases his "regulation of emotions" on neuro-scientific research. It becomes apparent that Goleman's method has to do with controlling emotions by thinking, a very old method indeed. With respect to regulation of emotions, he uses terms such as control, calm down, tame, dominate, enfeeble, and cool off.

Goleman speaks of "emotional hijacking" when we lose control and are overwhelmed by an emotion. Neuroscientist Joseph LeDoux believes its origin can be found in the amygdala or almond-shaped gray matter, which is located above the brainstem and, in evolutionary terms, is the oldest part of our brain. The amygdala is the reservoir of emotional memory. The thinking brain is the neocortex, a relatively young part of the brain. LeDoux discovered that there are two routes through which sensory signals fire us into action. One of these goes from the amygdala via the neocortex; this means that emotions are controlled by thought. The other route is faster because the thinking brain is bypassed. The second route causes flooding by an emotion without giving a chance for controlling of thought. This fast road was necessary for survival in the course of evolution: "fight or flight." This fast route, however, is also responsible for emotional acting-out behavior.

The amygdala is associative and causes emotions from the past to be "triggered" by events in the present. A powerful woman can remind you of your dominant mother, and you fly emotionally off the handle at the slightest implication. Goleman alleges that emotional intelligence has to do with good cooperation between the amygdala and neocortex, our feeling and thinking, in which thought governs. With Goleman it is all about controlling the fast route. "Emotions which are no longer controlled hinder the intellect."[4] The idea of emotional intelligence is used for improving the mental level, which should be in charge and have control.

We have already seen that, in my opinion, emotional management is about integrating our physical, mental, emotional, and spiritual skills and qualities. Goleman may focus on the slow route; I focus on the fast route. I believe we should directly address our reservoir of emotional memory, which is seated in the amygdala. In my method of working with emotions, which I explain in this book, we clean the reservoir by emotionally digesting our past.

This is a very different path. Where Goleman works with cognition and behavior, I work directly with the emotions themselves.

Control, Venting, and a Third Approach

I agree with Goleman that acting-out behavior is not the answer. It is apparent from his book that he only knows the road of control and venting. He is negative about "catharsis," the venting of an emotion. This proves that he does not know the difference between venting and taking responsibility for one's own emotional digestion. In the next chapters I will describe the road of digestion as a third road to arrive at a healthy emotional management. Seen from Goleman's cognitive perspective, it is logical to assume that emotional intelligence is something that can be taught. After publication

21

of his books, emotional intelligence courses were being given everywhere, especially for the business community and in the field of education.

Schools which offer emotional training to their students do, indeed, report that, for example, there are fewer fights during lunchtime. Goleman adds that he is against training in conformism, where children learn how to give emotionally desirable responses. A discussion in *Time Magazine* states: "The author [Goleman] assumes that we know exactly which correct emotions to teach to children. We don't even know which ones to teach adults." The article continues: "The problem is that there is one ingredient missing. Emotional skills like intellectual skills are morally neutral. In the same way as a genius can use his mind to cure cancer or develop a deadly virus, someone with a lot of empathy can use this empathy either to inspire his colleagues or to take advantage of them. When people do not have a moral compass to guide them in using their gifts, they can use their emotional intelligence for doing good or bad."[5]

We see here what happens if we try to get a grip on the sphere of emotions from the outside. To get ourselves out of trouble, we then have to fall back on morals. That is a well-worn track. Changes in convictions very seldom help in generating different behavior. Emotions are just too powerful for that. They largely determine our behavior. Trying to change our behavior without deep emotional Work is like driving a car with the hand brake on. Our current emotional problems started in our childhood. However, it often happens that we do not remember them. The only things that remain are our emotional charges, which subconsciously determine our current life in which we might focus on the wrong people. It is possible that you were not acknowledged enough in your childhood by people important to you. If you have not emotionally digested this, your behavior could be primarily focused on achievements and you could pass this behavior on to your children. I would like to show to you that the problem of morality does not occur

22

when we approach our emotional work from the inside and deal with our emotions directly. When we find our heart under a layer of the old dirty washing of repressed emotions, we no longer need morality. We have found the place of love and love will be our compass.

Erich Fromm's Understanding of Emotional Maturity

My description of healthy emotional management is closer to Erich Fromm's definition of "emotional maturity." In his book *The Sane Society,*"[6] he states that emotional maturity is characterized by "the ability to love and be creative." In the same publication, written in 1955, he remarks that the Western world has come to a point were it has become mentally unhealthy. People have started identifying themselves with their race, religion, country, and careers, instead of developing themselves. He says that in such an unhealthy society, the majority mistakenly consider people who adapt to unwholesome lifestyles and standards as emotionally mature. He quotes from Strecker's book, *Their Mothers Sons*, which defines emotional maturity as follows: "I define maturity as the ability to persevere in a profession, giving more than is asked of you, being reliable, persevering, continuing with a plan despite difficulties, being able to cooperate with others in an organization and under an authority, being able to make decisions, having a will to live, being flexible, independent and tolerant."

Fromm reacts to this definition: "It is clear that what Stecker describes as maturity here, are, in reality, the virtues of a good worker, employee, or soldier in the great companies of our time. They are qualities which are usually mentioned in job advertisements for managers." Is not this definition very similar to Goleman's, in which he describes the successful adolescents from the "marshmallow test"?

23

Chapter 4

Defining Emotions

Your vision will become clear
Only when you look into your own heart.
Who looks outside, dreams.
Who looks inside, awakens.
~C.G. Jung

here is a lot of uncertainty about what emotions are exactly. We come across an astonishing collection of contradicting and confusing theories and definitions when we study psychological literature looking for information about emotionality. The experts mainly agree that emotions are a collective name for a complex phenomenon. American psychologist and author James Hillman carried out an extensive study of the literature, and he concluded, "Emotions will forever be a problem and the solution cannot be put into words."[1] This was in 1961. Luckily, things have changed since then. Nowadays the subject of emotions has become fashionable. Emotional intelligence has become a household name in a short period of time and people are diligently looking for applications. However, in practice and in recent literature, both in the field of traditional psychology as in that of more "alternative" psychology, I still see a great deal of confusion about what emotions are precisely and how to handle them in a healthy way.

In daily life, many people are confused about emotions. There seems to be a lot of estrangement, guilt, and shame regarding emotionality. But mainly, I see ignorance and fear. We experience daily the consequences of our restrictive upbringing and constrained spirituality in which control and keeping a grip on the situation is highly regarded. We have learned to fear our emotions because emotion means loss of control, and showing what you feel to the outside world is something we are not used to.

First, we will look at emotions themselves:

- Emotions are the principal cause of consciousness-raising. Without our emotions we would sleep and lead a sleeping life in a subconscious state of being. Emotions are the foundations of our psychological and spiritual maturity. Without the driving force of a healthy emotional life, there is no growth and no maturity.

- Without emotion, there is no evolution.

- Without emotion, life is dull and sterile. Emotions give us passion and color.

- Without the intensity of emotions, there are no exciting and enriching relationships.

- Without emotion, there is no creativity. Without emotional depth, we humans are merely well brought-up and trained robots.

- Without emotion, there is no spontaneity.

- And finally, without a healthy emotional life, religion is not possible in the original meaning of "connection" (*religare* in Latin) with Loving Light, and the only things that remain are a sterile religion of dogma and laws.

Emotions are in fact the motor behind all movement! This is the literal meaning of the word "emotion." Emotion comes from the Latin word *emovere* which means "to cause movement" or "to move outward or onward." It is a very active word. An emotion moves us, something moves within us. In psychology this refers to the fact that emotions go hand in hand with strong physical sensations, such as crying, perspiring, shaking, or screaming. These are, indeed, the most obvious and visible changes. However, the changes go much deeper than that! Emotions carry the power to digest things life throws at us and, therefore, set us in motion in all possible ways and may speed up our lives.

Emotion: A Natural Digestive

Let us take a look at children: when a child is emotionally or mentally hurt, he or she cries or screams in anger. In other words, there is a signal to the outside world saying "Stop! This is my limit." By giving out this signal, the child also releases the shock of being hurt. In doing so, the child digests the situation and a few minutes later happily plays again. This means that emotion is communication, as well as expression.

The most important characteristic of emotion is that it helps us to cope with life's ups and downs. Once we have digested issues, we can move on and focus on other things. A healthy emotionality introduces action and movement in our lives. A direct emotional reaction to the outside world means a release of shocked energy which starts to flow again once it is expressed. Through our emotions, we "unshock" ourselves. We could call them "shock breakers"!

A healthy digestion of our emotions also helps us to stay connected to our basic energy flow. The movement does not stagnate and, therefore, we stay healthy. I actually believe that true emotions are, by definition, always expressed.

27

Otherwise, I would not call them emotions. For the true meaning of the word is "to move us."

Does the above mean that you should always express your emotions and direct them at whoever happens to pass by? Definitely not! So how do we do it? This has always been the great dilemma resulting in the controlling of our emotions. But control proved not to be a good solution. Control is a neurotic, artificial solution which is used all over the world in all cultures and religions and which has caused centuries of old emotional charge to build up. What you control does not really go away and is not really solved. It is conscious and subconscious suppression and denial. Everything suppressed, resurfaces, either in a different shape or in a different direction. If you have not emotionally digested your anger towards your aggressive father or addicted mother, you will sooner or later aim this anger towards others (projection) who remind you of your parents because of their behavior or status—for example, a figure of authority. Without noticing it, you will also aim this anger towards yourself in the form of negative and destructive behavior, such as smoking and drinking. On a more subconscious level, this anger will be embedded in your body as a hardening or weakening of the muscles or as a cramp in your organs.

How can we express our emotions without venting them at each other? In this book I will give an answer to that question. I will use many examples of emotions and their fixations to illustrate how you can address your own 'backlog of maintenance' and how you can set yourself free. This is a way which does not involve control and does not harm others, as this is the combination that is essential. This is the solution of an apparently unsolvable problem of either control or venting. We will learn to find answers for our emotions. Clarity and knowledge can reduce the fear and help us befriend our emotions.

Emotion: Moving Towards Spontaneity

You lose your ability to express yourself naturally when your emotions are too pent up. You lose your spontaneity. You can only be totally spontaneous if you fully accept yourself. You do not have to worry about what other people might think of you; then you can be spontaneous and yourself. This spontaneity is the fruit of self-acceptance, which is the fruit of good emotional Work. Good emotional Work has to do with letting go of the control you have over yourself, the control that hinders your spontaneous expression. In doing so, you will encounter guilt, shame, and self-hatred. The liberation of such fixations is what emotional Work has to offer you. Underneath, all these fixations your spontaneous inner child is buried.

Spontaneity is on a higher level than impulsiveness. It is heightened because in comparison to impulsiveness, it goes together with consciousness. In a safe environment where you can return to your natural impulses, you can become spontaneous again. This is a different path to that of impulse-control, the path of Freud, and the current movement of emotional intelligence.

Chapter 5

Emotions, Feelings, Moods and Fixations

> *Men go abroad to wonder*
> *at the heights of mountains*
> *at the huge waves of the sea,*
> *at the long courses of the rivers,*
> *at the vast compass of the ocean,*
> *at the circular motions of the stars;*
> *and they pass themselves by without wondering.*

> ~Saint Augustine

O nce you were natural, and you responded naturally. That was when you were a child. A lot has changed since then. Because of the way you were raised and because of the trials and tribulations of life, you began to control and distort yourself. You have become fixated in your natural manner of expressing yourself. You have become depressed when you were originally sad and angry. You have started to feel guilty when you were angry to begin with. You have started hating because you had to control your anger, and you have become scared because you have not known enough security. You have started to feel ashamed because there was not enough love for you. You have become scared because you have been through too much which you could not emotionally digest. You have become weak because fighting was not an option and because your dignity was trampled on. You have become proud because the only defense from so much incomprehension and cold-heartedness was to decide to "do it yourself." How do you annul this distortion and stagnation in natural energy? How do you straighten what has become crooked? The only fundamental approach is to imagine you are traveling back in time to when things went wrong. That will mean going back to many places and times because life is complex and problems often have multiple causes. It is exactly at that place within you and your experiences that you can heal yourself. You heal by finding your original, natural response within that situation again. Here are examples of natural emotions:

- Crying when you are sad;
- Stamping your feet, beating a pillow with a carpet-beater, or yelling when you are angry;
- Looking for safety when you are scared; and
- Laughing when you are happy.

Let us take a brief look at these phases of natural emotions from fixation to regaining your natural response.

Natural Emotions on a Subconscious Level

These are most clearly seen in children. When a baby feels discomfort because of a wet diaper, hunger, or loneliness, it will cry with sadness or scream with anger, depending on the temperament of the baby and the level of frustration. This is a primary way of communicating with its surroundings. When a newborn baby is exposed to bright lights and loud noises, it will scream with fear. It is not a reflex response but clearly an emotional way of reacting and communicating. When there is fear, the facial expression and the sound of the voice will alter and the pulse will change too. Similarly, we can see joy in various levels of intensity in the emotional repertoire of the baby.

Unfortunately, we drift away from this natural and direct emotional expression by experiences in life and due to the phenomenon called upbringing.

If you are often left alone when you are sad—it used to be said that it was good to let the child cry and "not to spoil it too much"—you will give up crying because you know there will no response. You then start to know feelings of hopelessness.

If you have tantrums, and punishment was your parents' only response, then you will control your anger and, in doing so, you will develop hatred and fear deep inside of you. When you are not comforted in worrying situations, the fear will be imbedded inside of you and will flood you later in similar situations.

It all depends on whether there is a loving welcome for your natural emotions. That is the deciding factor of whether you stay natural or become neurotic. Unfortunately, very few people on this planet remain completely natural, as we collectively seem to be caught in neurotic and loveless behavior. Our ignorance about genuine love has been so immense up to now that all of us are emotionally damaged to a certain extent in our childhood. We can see this as the emotional drama of this earth. But we can also view it as the experiment we once started together, an experiment in which we learn to study ourselves fully, feel our emotions and get to know ourselves. And in doing so, learning to know what love is.

Fixations

Natural emotions become unnatural when you are not lovingly welcomed enough by key figures in your childhood. The result is that a whole spectrum of fixations comes into being in which the original hurt is forgotten, suppressed, and denied. Why? Because at a young age, it is usually too painful to fully feel this hurt on our own, so we have no other option than to suppress these feelings. A characteristic of a fixation is that its content is mostly subconscious.

You learn, subsequently, through imitating and identifying with important people, such as your parents, to deny your natural emotions a loving welcome. A neurosis has been created. What is a neurosis? A neurosis is recurrence and fear of recurrence: history repeating itself.

It is usually this unnatural and subconscious emotionality—which I call "fixation"—which we encounter in our daily interactions. They make up the often-negative image which many people have of emotionality. We cannot really call unnatural emotions, emotions, as they are a *contradicto in terminis*, a contradiction in terms. We have already seen that emotion means movement, and unnaturalness means stagnation. Thus, helplessness, bitterness, cynicism, shyness, jealousy, hatred, depression, distrust, and envy are unnatural fixations of natural emotions. That is why I would rather call them "fixations of emotions." I choose to go against the common terminology in view of the much-needed clarity. These fixations are the icebergs in our sea of emotionality.

This form of emotionality usually finds its expression in projection. It is, in fact, subconscious and misplaced emotionality. It usually consists of old charge which belongs in the past but is expressed in the present and aimed at people or situations which play no part in the cause of the emotional reaction. They are used as a stepping-stone, something that resembles the previous, repressed situation. Let me clarify this with a few examples.

Sarcasm is a fixation of an original, natural anger which has been repressed and denied. A characteristic for a subconscious fixation is that the energy is projected. In the case of sarcasm, it is directed at just about anybody even though the anger was originally aimed at a particular person. This is usually a key person from childhood.

John's story.

John was 35 years old when he was killed in a car crash. He had a lovely wife and three daughters. A nice family. He worked hard and was fully involved in several clubs in his small town. He clearly had one nasty habit, which often caused trouble at home and at work. He was often sarcastic and very critical towards other people and also made critical comments about them. His employer sent him to a psychologist because his communicative problems started to interfere with his professional relationships. It became clear during these sessions that he worried a lot that his dad never paid him a compliment and never gave him the feeling that he was proud of his son. John discovered that he was, in fact, very angry with his father and that he really missed his love. He could acknowledge this fear and became milder in his interaction with others. Unfortunately, he was not really able to express his anger in this short counseling course. He directed the anger inwards and towards himself. Six months later, he was killed in a car crash.

Bitterness is likewise a fixation of old anger and so is irritability. Repressed fear can be expressed by different phobias from fear of being alone to fear of spiders, avoidance behavior, seeking false security in relationships and other forms of security that do not really provide a safety net, and in control and power. Repressed joy—yes, it exists—may express itself in dullness, boredom, living a minimal life, and blocked creativity.

Natural Emotions on a Conscious Level

The third phase consists of regaining your natural responses to all your fixations and repressions. In order to become natural again, we need to find our emotions under the thick layers of fixations and distortions. We can bring them back by connecting ourselves to who we once were as children—but in full awareness this time. That is the true meaning of Jesus' words: "If you don't become like children, you cannot enter my Kingdom." The kingdom of love can only be reached when you are emotionally connected to who you once were as a child. This book is about finding this natural and healthy emotionality again. We will show you how to work with your emotions in a way that is liberating and transforming and will ultimately lead to those qualities of the soul that religions and spiritual teachers speak about. This regained natural emotionality is rare on this planet. Many people are searching for it and have started to tread the path of emotional cleaning. It is an intense and long process to clean up all the emotional rubble and transform it. We all have a huge emotional maintenance backlog, especially if we are also dealing with emotional baggage from past lives, but to my knowledge, this is the only Work we have all come here to do! All other activities can be of help in becoming aware of this true Work.

Feelings: Differentiated and Undifferentiated

There is a whole range of feelings at the basis of emotions. Emotions are a more intense and more externally focused reaction to the outside world—there where it affects us. Feelings are the calmer, unexpressed forms of sadness, joy, anger and fear, being in love, mistrust, despair, pity, being annoyed, humility, love, insecurity, hatred, bitterness, excitement, disgust, a feeling of haste, etc.

Feelings can be differentiated but sometimes also undifferentiated. Why is this? Feelings can be differentiated and refined with people who are emotionally well- integrated and who are very aware of their own feelings.

36

Feelings can also be a much-undifferentiated mix of subconscious and indistinct awareness. Unfortunately, this is often the case and will occur in varying degrees when you find it hard to cope with your emotions, if you cannot express them well, and if you have little awareness of your feelings.

Feelings which are subconscious and do not know the richness of expressing an emotion are crude and undifferentiated. These feelings are largely subconscious in origin, direction, and meaning. For example, when you are feeling miserable—one big mess of subconscious feelings—you do not know where those feelings come from, who they are meant for, and what they are trying to tell you. We could call such feelings "neurotic." We could give them the qualification "pre-emotional" while we could call healthy, differentiated feelings "post-emotional." But this is only of real interest to theoreticians. For the actual Work, it is important to transform your vague, unclear feelings by intensifying them into emotions. Your emotions will automatically become clearer, more positive, and calmer.

Moods

A mood is a state of mind. It lasts longer than an emotion and is less intense. Sometimes it is a long-drawn-out emotion, such as a happy mood or an angry or scared mood. It can also be a mix of several fixations or feelings, like a miserable mood. In this case suppressed anger and sadness are the key players.

When you are emotionally well-integrated, a mood is clear and conscious. If you are not, it can worry you and be subconscious. A mood can then catch you unawares. In that case, it is called "being susceptible to moods." In fact, it is an expression of subconscious emotionality. It is a tense atmosphere that surrounds someone and which can lead to an emotional outburst. It can be threatening and full of indefinable charge.

Emotional Integration

Your feelings in interaction with others and the world around you are calm and differentiated when you are emotionally well-integrated. There is no emotional charge. Emotional charge stems from the past and from other situations. When you have emotionally digested old hurt in regards to loneliness, you can calmly say good-bye to people who are no longer a source of inspiration and nourishment, without a great deal of emotional charge. You can feel sad about saying good-bye but not be burdened by old emotional charge. When you have expressed and emotionally digested anger with former authority figures, you will, as an adult, no longer have an authority conflict even though you do not appreciate authoritative behavior.

This emotional integration is a result of deep emotional Work in which you have learned to deal with your emotions in a healthy way. Later on in this book, I will explain the meaning of this in all its facets. This learning process has many different aspects:

- Getting to know your feelings and emotions;
- Getting to know their background ; and
- Learning to express emotions without venting on others.

Chapter 6

Overview of Transformation

*There can be no transforming of darkness into light and of
apathy into movement without emotion.*
~C.G. Jung

any feelings are called emotions although
technically, they are not according to the definition
of emotion: "that which brings about movement." I
do not call jealousy or envy emotions because they do not set
things in motion but instead cause stagnation. Depression is not
an emotion either. It is nothing more than pain and anger that
have not been expressed. It is a fixation. In the same way, hate
is a fixation of anger, as are guilt, revenge, and feelings of
bitterness. In Part II, I will discuss various fixations and
explain how to set them in motion.

In practice, I have only come across four emotions,
which are capable of setting us in motion. These are anger,
sadness, fear, and joy. In Part II, I will explain these in more
detail, and I will indicate how we can express them in a healthy
and responsible way, so that ultimately joy is all that remains.
It is a long road but not an impossible one!

By way of illustration, I have made an overview that
shows the development of fixations and neuroses, which I call
the "pool of stagnant water," from the expression of the

"stream of emotions" to the "ocean of essence," where the soul as an expression of who we essentially are, reaches the light. At that level, we will have become entirely natural once more.

The Pool of Emotions and the Treasures at the Bottom

We could see ourselves and our society as a huge pool of emotions, in which we do not know our way around. There is a lot of splashing around on the surface, often undifferentiated, without regard for the people involved. Venting is the key word here. Besides acting-out behavior, we often see control. One of the characteristics of a pool is that there is no movement in the water. As we have learned before, the word emotion means movement, action. An important characteristic of emotion is that it brings about movement. The key question is "How?" How can emotions move from a pool to a stream and from stagnation or repetition to movement and fundamental change?

For the past thirteen years, I have lived in France on the banks of a river. The source of this river is only six miles from our house. It is a quagmire. However, in the depths of this quagmire there is a large spring. From here the stream of water develops within a short time and distance into a wild river which eventually flows to the sea.

The source is in the quagmire... and at the bottom of your quagmire of emotions and misery you will find a source, a treasure-trove.

First, in order to find this treasure-trove, we will have to start by looking at the quagmire of emotions. What does yours look like? Which feelings does it contain? Depression, anxiety, jealousy, shame, hardening, weakening, cynicism, bitterness, fighting, apathy? And how do you cope with this? How do you judge emotions? Are you afraid of your emotions, and what is your personal history with these emotions?

Second, we will have to discover how we can enter into the depths of our emotions. I will give you a concrete guideline with tips and aids or, in other words, with life jackets and buoys.

Third, we will harvest in stages. Let us take a brief look at a possible harvest. That might help you, should you decide to take the plunge!

You will only find the treasure if you truly dare to feel the depths of your emotions, which means feeling them completely in all their intensity. This mainly means two things: movement in your body and making sounds. This is only possible in a safe place and preferably having a safe other person there with you. It means crying from the bottom of your heart when you are sad, kicking and hitting (a pillow or bed) when you are angry, and breathing fast and screaming when meeting the fear inside of you. And, of course, laughing when you are happy! It is a way of becoming a natural human being again.

The hidden treasure at the bottom of your pool will appear, depending on how deep you have gone (and once is not enough!). Regained emotionality can bring you:

- Self-knowledge and a feeling of identity—knowing who you are and realizing how unique you are;
- Being an individual, that is, being undivided, a whole human being;
- Emotional freedom—no more old charges to bother you and your relationships;
- Inner peace and joy;
- Being capable of relationships and of intimacy with an open heart;
- Experiencing real life joy and enjoying it;
- Being creative in shaping your own life;

- The capability of taking full responsibility for your life, which means answering the call of your existence;
- Find your true power;
- Feeling the motivation to dedicate yourself to something;
- Emotional and mental clarity;
- A healthy sense of self-worth; and
- Realizing your meaning and destination; an answer to the question: why am I here on this earth?

The most important pearl is that your pool of emotions becomes a flow of living water full of movement and clarity, finding its way to the sea of All-that-is!

From Emotion to Essence

The table shows that when we set our fixations in motion by allowing space for the emotions underneath, we ultimately step by step, arrive at the realization of soul qualities referred to by all religions and religious schools. We move from emotional fixation through emotional expression and consciousness to essence. In this understanding, our human feelings and problems are the base material for the highest mystic experience. We could say that the depths make the highs possible. This is a completely different path than that in which emotions and the connecting ego are released or avoided. From our point of view, we go through the neurotic mud. We bring the light of consciousness to it by mobilizing emotions, and by doing so, we free our neurotic selves of our neurotic layers. What remains is an "I," a person who can serve as an instrument for living one's life on this earth. This is the same work as that which takes place in good psychotherapy sessions. We take it one step further. Because of the depths of the emotional Work, which I call Spark of Light Work, we arrive at the layers that lead us to our essence.

In the following chapters I will elaborate on the table and show you how to use it. Here is an overview:

- When you overcome your fears by placing them where they belong in your experience, you develop courage, faith, and inner freedom. (Chapter 10)
- When you transform your chronic hate and bitterness into acute anger, you learn love and respect and find your true power. (Chapter 11)
- When you transform your depression into tears and anger, you can once again experience joy. (Chapter 12).
- When you tackle boredom and blocked creativity at its source, you meet joy and can become a playful human being again. (Chapter 13)
- When you learn how to transform your feelings of guilt into anger, you get to know freedom and tolerance. (Chapter 15)
- When you trace your problems with authority back to the feelings of powerlessness and anger you experienced as a child, you will experience true power. (Chapter 16)
- When you start to feel the source of your pride, and you mobilize the underlying anger, you learn how to live with dignity. (Chapter 17)
- When you bring your experience with shame into motion, your personal freedom will increase. (Chapter 18)
- When you melt your deep-rooted feelings of being a victim into anger and pain, you start to tap into creative powers. (Chapter 19)
- When you dare to become aware of your longing for death and when you again experience your old despair, you learn what it is to embrace life. (Chapter 20)

- When you mobilize the anger beneath your auto-mutilation, you start to feel love for yourself and your body. (Chapter 21)
- When you tackle jealousy at its source, you learn what fulfilment is. (Chapter 22)
- When you deal with addiction at its root, you get to know love. (Chapter 23)

In order to realize Loving Light in your life, you do not have to be anyone other than who you are. You can start with the ingredients you have now—that is, your personal pool of emotions. Nothing has to go—it is not even possible—and no more books will be closed. The only thing we have to do is introduce movement to our pool by emotional Work. This movement brings liberation, healing, and transformation.

Transformation

In our New Age, transformation has become a well-known and almost common word. Many good therapies and creative ways have been developed with the aim of transformation. But what does it really mean? In the dictionary it is defined as "the act of transforming, or the state of being transformed, change of form or condition (metamorphosis)." This meaning makes it clear that we do not have to become different or better people as is preached in many religious and spiritual schools. We are all beautiful, just as we are. The only problem is that we find it difficult to see this beauty within ourselves and others. This is caused by the subconscious and stagnant pool of undigested emotions. This is where our feelings of worthlessness and self-hatred live. We use it to make ourselves ugly. The Work we must do is to transform this self-hatred into self-love. That is the Work of transformation. In doing this, we deny nothing nor do we close any books. The latter is not always the case in the field of therapy and spirituality. There is a lot of denial in the name of personal and spiritual growth. The word "trans" then becomes "skimming over" instead of "going through." The path to true transformation accepts all materials, knowing energy can never be negated and can only be transformed into something else. The motto here could be that a sweet-smelling rose seems to grow best on the manure heap.

Some Remarks Regarding the Table

- A table can never completely do justice to reality. There are many combinations. Depression, for example, usually consists of both suppressed anger and suppressed sadness. The natural emotion with insecurity is fear, but underneath, there is very often anger. Fixations are combinations of several emotions, which are stored in various "layers" within us. The order of these layers is different for everyone. Generally speaking, we can state that under fear there is very often anger and under anger we find fear. In order to fully experience joy, we need to work first through a layer of sadness.

- The movement in the table is from left to right but is not strictly linear. I would rather call it circular. We can, at times, be at the stage where we have already set a few fixations in motion and transformed them into soul qualities, but in other areas, we will still be stuck in a fixation. We can have largely transformed our depression into joy and vitality but still have some work to do in the field of abuse of power or sarcasm.

- The movement also means a movement from a cramped solar plexus to the heart. The solar plexus or third chakra is the domain of the emotional body. This is where the exchange of energy takes place between inside and outside and from outside to inside. This is the fire that enables emotional

45

digestion; it is analogous to the detox function of the liver and the digestion in the stomach. It is the center of our vitality, our emotional openness, and receptiveness. If our life's experiences are not emotionally digested, our solar plexus becomes cramped during the course of our lives. We are emotionally fenced off, shut down, and constricted. Our entire emotional control is expressed in this area, even though we can find the control in our entire body. By the cramping of our emotional body, we become fundamentally closed off from our spiritual nourishment, both horizontally in relation to other people and also vertically, in relation to our soul, our higher self, and God. We become a closed circuit, hardly able to connect with other people and with God. The result of this barrier between us and that which feeds us is exhaustion or "burnout," as it is called these days. Our life energy becomes a survival strategy. I will go into more detail in Chapter 33. It is all about finding the heart again. This heart will gradually see the light in the extent to which we do our Work on the solar plexus. The more we regain our healthy emotionality, the more we find our essence again, the light that we essentially are.

Table 1: **Overview of Transformation**

Unnatural: Fixations *"Pool of Stagnant Water"*	Natural: Emotions *"Stream of Emotions"*	Essence: Soul *"Ocean of Essence"*
Depression Feelings of unease Feeling miserable Despair	Sadness	Peace Joy Compassion Vitality Connection
Hatred, contempt Bitterness, resentment Revengefulness Feelings of guilt Feeling a victim Sarcasm, aggression Being annoyed Power Pride Jealousy Being suicidal Disgust	Anger	Love Strength Sincerity Sense of destiny Identity
Fear of . . . Shyness Worry Distrust Insecurity Arrogance Shame	Fear	Courage Trust Freedom Intuition Living in the here and now Surrender Susceptibility Spontaneity
Boredom Blocked creativity Dullness Living a minimal life Seriousness	Joy	Gratitude Being joyful Creativity Having an abundant life Playfulness Humour

Chapter 7

Experiencing the Depth of Emotions

In order to find pearls, one has to dive deep.

eople often say, "I am very emotional" or "I know everything about emotions" when they burst into tears over the slightest thing or if they frequently have tantrums. They shed a tear watching something on television, grumble when the cake turns out to be a disaster, or get sentimental when they have a few drinks too many. Usually these are projected and subconscious forms of emotionality. Others may be more aware of their true feelings but feel that expressing them is not very beneficial. A good cry now and then might make them feel better, but they do not feel that it actually improves things. What is missing here?

Experience of the Depths of Emotion

What does this mean? Using the metaphor of our overview of transformation and the pool of emotions; we can only reach the treasure which lies at the bottom of the pool if we dive down into its depths. Exploring the depths of our emotions means four things:

- Intensity—feeling your emotions entirely, in all their intensity;
- Feeling the depths of your emotions in your body;
- Depth of content;
- Depth of time and space—this means that we look at the deeper background of emotions and experience traveling back in time and place.

Intensity and Expression

First of all, this means learning to express the emotions of fear, sadness, anger, and joy through tears, intense breathing, your voice, and beating a pillow with a carpet-beater. This means allowing yourself to feel the intensity of your emotions. If you are not used to this, it might be a little scary at first. I advise you to find a good therapist, who can teach you to do this in a safe environment. Take your time to find out if the therapist is comfortable with this kind of intense Work. When I met fellow mainstream psychologists with whom I had not been in touch for a long time, I was requested to do so in view of assurances of the Exceptional Medical Expenses Act—I was shocked to see that even they were scared of intense emotionality. When I was quite open with them and told them I did breathing work and emotional therapy with people, I started getting phone calls from colleagues asking me if I was not worried about psychosis. Later on, I was called before the needs assessment committee. It took a lot of diplomacy to safeguard my contract for myself and my clients. In Chapter 26, I will indicate when intensive breathing is useful and which contraindications apply.

Expressing your emotions under your own responsibility, in your own home, or within your own therapy is essential on this path. In the New Age Movement, many people distinguish between positive and negative emotions. This is a pitfall really. Anger is often seen as negative and love and joy as positive. Love and joy are not anymore positive than anger and sadness. It is our mind—and with that our fear—which labels reality. A negative emotion is an emotion which is not expressed, and a positive emotion is one which is expressed in an effective, aware, and non-projected way. Not expressing your feelings recurrently makes you ill and could literally kill you. Many accidents probably happen because people are angry within. The intensity is there, but pent-up inside. We need to transform it in a non-damaging, healing way. I remember, a long time ago, not giving way at a junction and was hit by another car. I was on my way back from the dentist who had just made an irreparable mistake with one of my molars. My own unvoiced anger came back to me subconsciously, just like a boomerang.

Releasing the Emotions in Your Body: The Physical Depth

Our suppressed emotions are embedded in our bodies. In order to release them from the depths of our system, bodywork is needed. Different kinds of massage, Postural Integration and Rolfing, Shiatsu, Bioenergetics, Reichian bodywork, and breathing work are good for bringing lodged emotions to light. When doing bodywork, it is important to get to know the message and emotions of your body. More about this is found in Chapter 28.

It is of no real help to you when somebody else does the work for you. There are many rescuers in the land of therapy, but they are really after power. They want you to believe they can heal and rescue you. If you surrender to them, you are the helpless, powerless one and will not be able to regain your own power. Breathing work is a good technique which you can do yourself, and it makes you less dependent on therapists. I will discuss this in Chapter 26.

Good therapists are people for whom the work with others is also an initiation and learning path for themselves during which they continue to work on themselves in a client situation. Therapy does not serve to cover up personal pools of emotions in that case. Good therapy knows a functional inequality—it is client orientated—but essential equality. Essentially there is brother and sisterhood in the joint Work. Fundamentally, what you need is someone who can offer safety and experience. In this New Age there are fortunately various possibilities for growth by means of courses, therapies, training, and books.

The Correct Message: Depth of Content

It is important to find the correct message from your emotions. Crying and being angry without knowing why is simply not enough. When you fully recognize your feelings, the message automatically becomes clear, and you will find words to describe it. This clarity is a necessary ingredient for liberation. It is important to know why you are crying or why you are angry. Very often people do not know the reason. My experience is that when you surrender to emotions and let them be there fully, the message becomes clear. First the emotion, then the nuance. However, we usually ask ourselves too soon why we feel the way we do. That is often a repetition of what our educators did in the past. When we are asked the question why, we are made to think and emotion disappears. The head should know its place, and that is a secondary place!

It helps to enlarge vague feelings and to exaggerate when you feel vaguely miserable, nothing seems to be going your way, or you are wandering around, grab a pillow and tell all your worries to it. Take out all the unhappy feelings on the pillow. Say anything that comes to mind and use the carpet-beater if you feel like it. Your life will become more fun if you clarify your vague feelings and moods as quickly as possible by setting your emotions in motion. I remember that I was often "bored" as a child and that I used to say, "Mum, I am so bored." I always got the same reply, "Go and stand on your head and shoot tuppenny [two penny] pieces." So what did I do? I stood on my head on a chair and called out again, "Mum, I am so bored." I spent a great deal of time standing on my head instead of playing. It was not really boredom, but vague feelings of dissatisfaction. Now when I am "bored"—luckily this doesn't happen very often—I enlarge this feeling to see what message it has for me.

A lot of our behaviour is subconscious. Sometimes we do not know why we do certain things. Often it is just out of habit. But beyond this habit, there is a deeper meaning; otherwise we would not do it! The behaviour is transference from something else. Sexual behaviour, for example, without connection with one's heart and emotions, does not bring satisfaction, let alone transformation. It tends to become a repetition or a search for technical variation. Sexuality can become an addiction unless it is connected to a deeper need for love. When love and affection are not received emotionally, sexuality becomes routine and is empty.

The Correct Address: Depth in Time and Space

Subsequently, it is important to find the correct address of your emotions. Many emotions originate in your past. Many irritations between husband and wife come from past situations. A lot of authority conflicts on the work floor can be traced back to authority problems with your mother or father in early childhood or to problems with older brothers or sisters or with teachers or priests. As long as we continue to vent our emotions in a projected way, there will be no liberation and no healing. Only by accessing the deeper layers of our emotions can there be a fundamental change within us.

I do not advocate literally dropping all of our old pent-up emotions at the correct addresses. Our parents and educators gave us the best they had and did the best they could. Emotional Work with a pillow is a good way of getting rid of your emotional garbage!

Chapter 8

Spark of Light Work

Depth gives you a foundation for experiencing highs.

There are already many schools and many names for the work called "know thyself." Why do we need yet another name? The words light, liberation, and emotions have always been key to my own inner path. I always look at emotional work against the background, or better still, the foreground of the realization of the light of consciousness. Emotional work involves bringing to the light that which is dark and hidden within us. It is also called "shadow work," but you could just as well call it "light work." Without light, there is no darkness, and without darkness, there is no light. That is the way it works on our polarized planet. We are working with shadow, knowing that all shadow is basically light. Spark of Light Work is all about the true realization of the light. We have chosen this new name because it has to do with psychology and spirituality as one path for the whole person. It is about integral psychology and integral spirituality. I see this division between psychology and spirituality as fruitless. By keeping these areas separate, we continue this separation within ourselves. The difference with "normal therapy" is that in Spark of Light Work, we focus on core-healing. Adjusting to societies' status quo is not our goal. Moreover, we see Spark of Light Work as an integral part of normal life. Why Spark of

Light Work? We have given it this name because the Work is about the individual realization of light as consciousness and sparks of the one big Light and Consciousness. There is a lot of misunderstanding about "lightwork." Many people think that the greatest goal is to merge into the light. I wish to look at this from three perspectives: 1) the soul and personality in its search for the connection; 2) height and depth—spiritual psychotherapy with our feet on the ground; and 3) awareness and memory—without the past, there is no basis for the present.

Soul and Personality: Searching for the Connection

Our "I" or personality is that part of our greater soul that incarnates on earth in order to gain experience in this physical world of duality. As Gary Zukav says in his book, *The Seat of the Soul,* "The lifetime of your personality is one of the myriad of experiences of your soul."[1] He sometimes compares the soul to the mother ship which shows a large number of ships (your personalities) the way in the fleet. This personality loses in the course of its life, to a larger or lesser extent, its connection with this mother ship. This mother ship is our essence, the one we essentially are, in connection with the universal Consciousness or Light. Our "I" is our instrument in this world of polarity and concrete matter. At the same time, our "I" is that part of our soul that needs healing and liberating where it is damaged. Spiritual growth is about increasing consciousness. Our limited thinking, coming as it does from the personality focused on material things, often hinders the flow of consciousness. That is why many spiritual schools see the ego as the evildoer and the biggest obstacle. Often not enough distinction is made between a healthy "I" as instrument and the damaged "I" which has had to survive hurt, and as a result wants to control things in life and manipulate them. We need to heal our personality, our "I" from its fixating and controlling behavior, so that it can once again follow the wake

56

of the big mother ship, the soul. Then we actualize the Spark of Light we essentially are, as this personality we become lighter and brighter.

This is a completely different path than that in which emotions and the connecting ego are released or avoided. In this viewpoint, we go through our "neurotic mud" and in doing so we connect with our divine core, our Spark of Light.

Height and Depth: Spiritual Psychotherapy with Our Feet on the Ground

Much "Light Work" involves dissolving entirely into the light or the universal consciousness, like "a drop in the ocean" without addressing your personal and emotional healing. That is a premature goal, an unhealthy avoidance of the part of you that is damaged. Many seekers on the spiritual path want to attain new heights, but avoid descending into the depths. Without the depth of shadow work, the heights of the light become unreal, sentimental, and superficial. The basis of a healthy personality is then lacking. We have to realize the light within us. We need to "earth the Light." There is a reason we are here on earth. By floating up to the Light, we avoid doing what we came here to do, namely realizing our essence, our Spark of Light, here on earth. Only after we have created a good solid base in ourselves, will there be space for the vertical axis of connection with the light. Depth gives us the foundation for experiencing Heights.

Awareness and Memory: The Past as the Basis for the Present

Everything depends on the way we define consciousness. Do we only see it as being aware or as a memory too? We could describe memory as a storage area for the experience of awareness. Spiritual teacher Lama Govinda believes that this latter function of consciousness is "infinitely more important than awareness. The latter is only quick and more or less limited to one object, but the first is universal in nature and is not influenced by time. It even remains after we are no longer aware of it."[2] He believes that the meditation systems which claim to practice "pure awareness" are a form of self-cheating, as it is impossible to be fully aware of something without a link to a past experience. When we acknowledge memory as an important function of our awareness, the depth-axis of our past must be included on the path to self-realization. Without the past, there is no basis for the present. Spark of Light Work is the inner Work for people who want to realize and express their essential being, their Spark of Light. In that light, we address everything that blocks the realization of the light and awareness. These obstacles are of a mental, emotional, and physical nature. They can be undigested traumas and experiences, negative patterns of thought and suppressed emotions from this life and past ones. This means Work(ing) on the personality as the reincarnated part of our soul. In Spark of Light Work the "I" or personality is respected as an essential part of our soul and as an essential part on the path of becoming conscious.

As a Spark of Light we are part of the great Light, which we traditionally call God. Our soul has the answer to the three great questions in life:

- Who am I?
- Where do I come from?
- Why am I here?

A grounded connection with our inner Spark of Light is not possible without cleaning our personality. There no healthy spirituality without a thorough therapeutic cleansing. Spark of Light Work is an integral psychology and integral spirituality without artificial mental divisions.

Spark of Light Work is about wholeness. Nothing is excluded, and nothing is denied. We can allow everything we are to come to the light. It is about transformation and enlightenment in the meaning of making that which we already are, lighter. This form of enlightenment goes hand-in-hand with wholeness. It serves Loving Light. We need to lovingly agree with ourselves and, in doing so, with each other.

Spark of Light Work's Four Important Aspects:

1. Focusing on your deepest desire for freedom, light, healing, and permanent joy;
2. Expressing suppressed emotions and their integration into your current life;
3. Being aware of old emotional imprints and getting to know your blockages; and
4. Becoming susceptible again to that which you essentially need: the connection with Loving Light.... in yourself.

Part Two:

Four Basic Emotions and Many Fixations

Chapter 9

Four Natural Fundamental Emotions

What a curious phenomenon it is that you can get men to die for the liberty of the world who will not make the little sacrifice that is needed to free themselves from their own individual bondage.
~Bruce Barton

In practice, I have only observed four natural emotions which can be divided into two pairs: sorrow and joy, anger and fear. These four emotions can be seen as analogous to the four elements: water, fire, earth and air. Sorrow and joy are as water, and fire and anger and fear are as earth and air.

- Sorrow is a damp emotion that goes together with tears and shaking or jerking movements in the gastric region, also called the solar plexus or emotional body.

- Joy encompasses the element fire and expresses itself in exuberant laughter and ecstasy.

- Anger has to do with being grounded. If we are angry, we draw a line, stomp our feet, hit, and

63

shout—all of which come from our abdominal region as fitting ways of expressing this.

• Angst (anxiety) comes from the Latin "angustia," meaning narrow and has to do with lack of oxygen. We hold our breath when we are scared, or we breathe minimally. Fear as a natural emotion is a danger signal and can help us to survive by being alert and taking to flight or fighting for our lives. Neurosis is the energy of fear that has become constricted and rigid. It belongs in our first category—still water. To be able to live fully, the "fear energy" should be set in motion and brought to expression.

It is evident that sorrow and joy are opposites. It does not immediately become apparent with regard to anger and fear. Yet there is strong bond between anger and fear. If you have good anger management skills, for example, you can stand firmly on your own two feet. Anger is just a question of showing where you draw the line. If you can do that properly, one of the consequences will be that you experience less fear. In reverse, fear, which always originates somewhere in the past, carries an image of the enemy. Being frightened of somebody means that you have branded him an enemy beforehand, and anger is smouldering subconsciously inside you.

In Goleman's book, I unexpectedly found support for these four basic emotions. He mentions a study by Paul Eckman, who discovered that the specific facial expressions of the said four emotions are recognized by people from different cultures all over the world. This proves that they are universal emotions.

In the next chapters, we will study these four basic emotions in depth and relate them to fixations.

Chapter 10

Fear as a Teacher

Fear is one of the greatest forces in the life of a warrior. It spurs him on to learn.
~ Carlos Castaneda

In this chapter we will describe as many aspects of the phenomenon of fear as possible. We will look at fear in general, at the background of phobia, and at the connection between fear and anger. Fear of emotions is subsequently an important subject as fear often keeps other emotions firmly in its grasp. Step by step, we will look at how we can set fear in motion. Further on, we will discuss separate subjects, such as hyperventilation, fear of failure, shyness, fear of commitment, fear of separation, and fear of death. We will, finally, have a look at the fear of freedom, of God, and of love.

Three Paths: Fear as a Disorder, an Illusion, and a Teacher

The starting point of this chapter is fear as a teacher. This point of view is at odds with accepted ideas (from conventional to New Age) that people have about fear. Conventional medicine and psychology view fear as a disorder that has to be combated by medicine, relaxation exercises, and talks. In a large part of the New Age circuit, fear is seen as opposed to love and people have to simply let go of fear on the pretext of "All fear is a thing of the past; now there is only love," and "Fear has nothing to offer us because it is nothing."[1] I read somewhere else about the extent to which fear is denied: "We must expose fear as a lie," and "The theme of fear has a pure spiritual dimension, namely the divine that cannot express itself creatively in this world."[2] And I found the next sentence by another spiritual writer: "Say softly, in your heart of hearts, that you are not afraid." My commentary: you are by definition what you do not want to be. It is a clever way to deny fear. Will fear go away like this? Both ways deny fear or see fear as an enemy. You have to defeat an enemy and that means war. The one fights openly, often with medicine or a plastic bag at hand, the other secretly by declaring that fear is an illusion. Both methods are based on denial. In conventional psychological literature, fear and phobia are often portrayed as non-realistic fears. Expressing it in this way, leads to confusion. People experience their fear as real fear, but they are told that it is not real. They say to you: "If a certain situation does not frighten you normally, but you panic, block, or show physical tension reactions anyway, you have a non-realistic fear." We should learn to distinguish between true and real. You can really be frightened of birds, for example, while it is not true that they will attack you at this moment. By being careful in the way we express ourselves, we do not need to deny anything.

Thankfully, there is a third way that does not argue fear away spiritually nor fight it but listens and takes it seriously. That way is the way of love that encompasses everything, even unpleasant things, such as fear. Fear has something to teach us, and fear can guide us back home again by taking us to those parts that need the most healing and love. We can make fear our friend by acknowledging it, bringing it to the light, and transforming it to courage and trust.

Defining Fear

Having said this, we can look at fear itself. What is fear? As a natural phenomenon, fear is a warning signal for danger. It protects us. Fear is the cause of the fight or flight response, which means we can survive if we are lucky. The problem with fear is that there are situations in which we cannot fight or take flight. These situations take place during times of great power inequality, such as in our childhood and during periods of war and violence.

What is the consequence? We become overwhelmed and paralyzed or petrified by fear. This paralyzing, terrible fear, together with having nowhere to go to, means fear can only go one way and that is inwards: fear lodges inside us, in our breath, in our muscles, in our organs, in our feelings, and in our thinking. This paralyzing, petrifying anxiety poisons our natural fight or flight response, crushes our energy, our trust, and our openness. It makes us live minimally and on alert. It is not about "fight or flee" anymore but about "paralyze or petrify." There is no other choice.

Can fear still be our teacher? Yes it can, if we dare to look lovingly at the origin of our fear and at the bearer of this paralyzing, petrifying fear: namely ourselves. We, poor little frightened lambs, were pushed violently out of the womb straight into the hands of strangers who washed us, weighed us, and dressed us. If you were lucky, you were not held upside down by the heels and hit on the bottom. If you were lucky, you were not immediately put in a cot all on your own.

And then, later on in life, there were many other moments when there was nowhere to go—only inwards. The times that your parents quarreled and shouted at each other while you listened at the top of the stairs, petrified with fear. The times your father hit you, or your mother threatened to leave you or wished you were in a children's home. The time you almost drowned, and your father just managed to save you.

The time you wanted to touch your mother, and you were tensely rejected, the times the neighbor put his hand in your panties. The times... you can fill it in yourself this time, then look lovingly and compassionately at your fear, at that frightened child.

All that old fear that has been turned inwards is the real cause of most of your present anxiety.

It is important to learn to make a connection between the past and the present, between past and present fear—that is where friendship with your fear starts. Before giving a number of instructions on how to make that connection, I will first give you a quote from an informative website about fear. This is typical of current, conventional ideas about fear, about what happens when that connection is not made.

> *Some people are scared even when there is no reason for it. They dare not leave their houses without checking at least ten times if the gas has been turned off. Or they break out in a sweat at the thought of having to make a phone call. People who have such excessive anxiety are inclined to avoid situations that are often quite ordinary because they associate these with fear. That avoidance starts to dominate their lives, and their anxiety does not lessen. A person with this kind of fear has an anxiety disorder.*

It is incomprehensible that you are suddenly scared of going out into the street when there is nobody threatening you or that you are scared of crossing a sturdy bridge. You must be going mad! It is incomprehensible that you wake up one morning and without apparent reason start to shake with anxiety. Without the connection, you will find it strange that you start breathing fast (hyperventilating), turn red when a man or woman talks to you, or feel scared stiff when you have to stand in front of the class and hold a talk. Or perhaps you are a stutterer or you act childishly or are a scaredy-cat. We judge people when we do not understand their behavior. In official jargon this is called a diagnosis. A DSM IV system looks impressive with its boxes and phobias all neatly arranged according to type, length, and symptoms, generalized or not, single or plural.[3] Of course, classifications can help us understand reality better, but if an in-depth insight into the classification is omitted, this insight becomes superficial and nothing is gained from it. A person suffering from anxiety will gain nothing from knowing in which box his fear belongs. He needs a connection between his original fears and his present ones, which are a derivation.

The Degeneration of the Fight or Flight Response: Phobia and Hatred

When we are unable to react in a healthy way to our environment by taking to flight or fighting when necessary, situational taking to flight becomes chronic avoidance behavior and situational fighting becomes hate because of the original situation of powerlessness. By this, I mean that it is healthy to consider each situation in freedom and decide whether to fight or take flight. It becomes unhealthy when we constantly have an attitude of avoidance or hate, whatever the situation is.

We will begin with *avoidance behavior*. In jargon, this is called a *phobia,* a fear. The acute flight mechanism, originally biologically well-advised in certain dangerous situations, has been extended to a continual attitude of avoiding anything difficult. Avoidance, that is, of that which the subconscious associates with the original, frightening situation. It is time for an example:

An originally frightening situation from which you wanted to flee but could not: you were two years old, you were feeding the ducks in the park, and you fell into the pond and almost drowned. You survived, but because of fear, you disassociate from your feelings and from this situation. Later you will not remember what has happened, but what remains is avoidance of water.

69

Another example:

An originally frightening situation from which you wanted to flee but could not: you were five years old. You had been "naughty" and had to sit out your punishment in a dark cellar. In this situation, you again isolate yourself from your feelings; it is too frightening to keep feeling. After all, emotion minus loving reception is too hard to take. You forget the whole hellish experience; what remains is a fear of small spaces. You avoid those. In psych-jargon, this is given the label claustrophobia.

Characteristic of avoidance behavior is that it becomes worse and the anxiety grows. For this reason, behavior therapy advises you to repeatedly transform avoidance into approach. And that certainly does help. In this way, you experience that your avoidance behavior is not necessary in the here and now. It would be splendid if you could supplement this working method with insight into the original background. Not only would your attitude change to your advantage, but you would also widen your awareness and learn to have compassion with that frightened child somewhere inside you. But you will have to make contact with your anger about the misuse of power with regard to being locked up in a dark cellar.

With a phobia there is a kind of mutation from the original anxiety to fear. Depending on what the original fear situation looked like, the fear forms and directs itself. There are so many phobias: fear of stains, fear of open places, fear of birds, fear of spiders and.... fear of people. I will not discuss them all here. They can all be traced back to avoidance of the original, fearful experience that will have to be lived through again if you want to become free of fear. Becoming free of your specific fear can usually be done with behavior therapy, but you will not be able to get rid of your deeper-lying anxiety.

Avoidance will make your life petty and minimal. When fundamental anxiety is not treated, you search for false security in unimportant things, such as externals, gadgets, and fashion. The other side of fear is courage. To develop courage, you must extract your avoidance behavior by the roots—that is anxiety with, possibly, underlying anger.

Another option when there is danger is ***fighting behavior.*** Fear can turn into hate if we remain fixed in this. This type of behavior is not easily recognized. For this reason, behavioral therapy will not be able to accomplish much. This type of fear can be resolved by setting the underlying fear in motion. I will try to illustrate this with an example:

Harry is a 16-year-old boy who starts hitting people as soon as he thinks that he is hard-pressed. However, he feels hard-pressed very quickly. The original situation: when he was six years old, he was cornered by a group of boys, pestered, and kicked. Afterwards, he did an inward turnabout. Instead of being a shy, scared boy, he became a tearaway/hothead so he could survive in the asphalt jungle. When he was a teenager, you only had to point at him for him to start hitting out at you. He is, in reality, scared stiff but has banished this completely from his repertoire of feelings and turned it into the opposite. Flight is not tough, so he has "chosen" fight.

Anger and Fear: The Best of Friends

In all these examples, we see that anger and fear are really good friends. In the past, they used to be friends in the original situation, too, but they were then called "fight or flight." They stood next to each other as two possibilities to choose from. Now they are under and above each other. If anger is above, fear will be underneath—they cover each other. An example of the latter type:

Margaret is an anxious woman, who lives a very withdrawn life. If we were to put her on the scale of the DSM IV system, she would belong to the social phobia category. In this category we find people who are very shy, scared of not doing the right thing or of people finding them odd. They have trouble making contact. On the face of it, it seems that this is a continuation of a flight impulse. But there is a repressed fight impulse inside. This comes to the surface quite clearly when Margaret visits her elderly mother and reacts testily to every little remark. She packs it in when her mother becomes needy. She does not want to look after mother and without saying a word, she breaks off the contact.

Essentially, fear gives the object of fear the label enemy. You would not have to be frightened of it otherwise. The cooperation with anger can be seen clearly here. In the case of being locked up in the cellar, we see that the small space, the original cellar becomes the object of hatred. One step further would be to direct the anger properly and in this case at the ignorant parents who had forgotten their own childhood fears. In reverse, the horror of fear is often to be found under anger as can be seen in the example of Harry. A safe contact could help him to come face to face with his fears after which he could vent his anger on a cushion. Anger that is expressed in a safe environment gives strength and courage and allows fear to melt like snow in summer. I remember Anne from the Spark of Light weeks in our house in France where we Work according to the principles of this book. She started the week as a timid, oversensitive woman, but at the end she was a strong and brave lass. She had used the carpet beater often and with a great deal of pleasure.

Fear of Emotions: The Greatest Fear

Our greatest fear is the fear of our emotions. This keeps all other fears and emotions firmly in their place. As soon as you set your emotions in motion, you become aware of your fears. You will start to feel them and that is scary. Fear is an emotion that is often denied. It is a taboo. Many people are not aware of their fears. I have noticed that people who are extremely anxious (but have it well under control) remark that they are not scared at all. You recognize them by their control

72

behavior. There is a lot of hidden fear and a lot of fear that is masked. We should learn to recognize these first.

I often notice that people are very scared of starting on the path of emotional digestion and spiritual awareness. Most people are forced to start on this road by the blows life deals them: problems with relationships, illness, loss, depression, and so on. This is the chance that difficulties offer us. It is the hidden blessing in a crisis. In the Chinese language, crisis also means chance. However, people often stop the process of awareness as soon as the difficulties are over. They are then forced by the next crisis or loss to set out on the Path again. It seems that we have things to learn on this planet. The only choice we have is to learn voluntarily or be forced to learn! There is so little culture available in which to get to know ourselves (the only way to start to understand something about life) that we have learned to project learning outside ourselves. We learn all about the outside of things, but what about the inside?

Due to centuries of neglect, we are encrusted with a lot of darkness and dirt, ignorance and undigested experiences inside. Because of this, the light hidden under this darkness cannot be felt or seen. Because of this, we can no longer feel that we are light. Everybody would love to have that light, you only have to look at the enormous hunger within the New Age Movement, but not everybody wishes to fight the way to that light through all the old muddle and darkness.

Why is this? I think it is probably because of the fear of emotions. Fear is part of every step to awareness; fear of something new, fear of change and especially fear of pain. Everybody recognizes this. The difference lies in what you do with that fear; do you stand still because of it, or do you set foot on the Path to awareness and to the recovery of your emotional management (even though you may break out in a cold sweat). In other words: do you take to flight or do you go for it?

73

Let us look at this fear of emotions more closely. Clarity with regard to fear can be the first step to reducing the fear. The path to emotional liberation starts with awareness of your fear of emotions.

Judgments about emotions.

Fear often disguises itself as a judgment. You could say there are just as many fears in this world as there are opinions. Judgments about emotions abound. They can be found in religions and in certain philosophies of life that have greatly influenced the way we think and the way we behave. Emotions have been declared taboo in many philosophies of life. In Christianity, anger was seen as the first mortal sin. Bible texts have greatly influenced the attitude towards anger and have declared it a mortal sin. For example Ephesians 4.26, "Be ye angry, and sin not, let not the sun go down upon your wrath."

In the popular *Course in Miracles* (a kind of Christian New Age book of beliefs) we can find the following text: "God's peace can never come where anger is because anger inevitably denies that peace exists. Whoever sees anger as justified in any respect or situation, declares that peace has no meaning and has to believe that it cannot exist. In this situation, peace cannot be found."[4] Whatever way you look at it, the reality of people being full of old anger is denied here! It is, however, a reality that cannot be swept away by spiritual ideas.

In some of the other New Age schools of thought, anger is found under the so-called negative emotions. Anger was once called a sin; nowadays it is called negative. I cannot see the difference. By labeling anger as negative, you take the fundamental ability to cope with life's problems away. It is said that anger and fear are not spiritual. All these judgments stem from the fact that no difference has been made between healthy emotionality that helps us to digest life's experiences and neurotic emotionality that is subconscious and misplaced in time, space, and with regard to people. It is in other words, projected.

The idea that we cannot heal everything is also an obstacle on this path to liberation. It is a way of masking the fear of emotions.

Negative opinions about our emotions have the greatest influence in our situations of upbringing. We have all learned, to some extent, not to be too emotional. "Don't act so emotionally," "Don't act so childishly," and "Why are you crying?" are expressions many of us know. From these expressions we have learned that we are not lovable if we express ourselves too much. Later in life, it becomes simply frightening to show your emotions. We say we are scared of being vulnerable. Sensibility is often branded "hypersensitivity." Public figures are still ridiculed or called "a Wally" (overly sensitive), if they cry in public. Being sensitive is seen as a weakness.

Especially men were not and sometimes are still not allowed "to be weak." A lot of men were told that they were "a sissy" if they cried. Now that people are more tolerant, many men who have lost the ability to cry have to learn how to do so. After all, we can only fundamentally digest the things we experience in life if we can combine tears with insight. Thankfully, nowadays boys are allowed to cry more, at least inside the house. Outside in the street and at school, the culture of tough boys still exists.

It is also a fact that only the so-called "positive emotions" are tolerated in the spiritual part of the New Age circuit (not so much in the therapeutic and creative schools).

We are used to keeping our emotions under wraps. The saying "He learned it at his mother's knee" plays an important role here. For example, how many of the age group of forty years and over, have ever seen their father cry? And what kind of impression did it make on you when he did? I remember, during my first therapy training (Gestalt), crying along with the men in the group when they cried. It affected me because I was not used to seeing men cry. I thought it was wonderful! It does women in our current Spark of Light group a lot of good when men dare to melt. And the men find it liberating!

How often do you swallow hard when something on television affects you? And how often do you call yourself emotional and hypersensitive?

I often come across a well-known way of thinking, namely: "I don't really want to feel sorry for myself." Why would that not be good for you? I advise you to feel really sorry for that little child who is inside you and who is still carrying a lot of old hurt and feelings of guilt. The words "feeling sorry for yourself" are an indoctrination and often used by parents and educators who were once under the spell of control and fortitude.

The first step is becoming aware of your opinions about emotions. After all, they have become your opinions. We treat ourselves in fundamentally the same way as significant others used to treat us. This is as constant as the northern star, but we can change it by awareness. In our group we sometimes do that by playing a game; we walk around and introduce ourselves as a little girl or boy with the messages we used to receive in the past about ourselves and our emotions. It goes something like this: "I'm Mary, and I must stop being silly" or "I'm little Joyce. I'm a cry-baby" or "I'm Pete and I'm Mummy's big boy" and "I'm Martin and I act like a girl." Having fun with a game like this helps you to laugh about these old imprints and become aware of them and let them go. You can, subsequently, work out how much these ideas still influence your present life.

Fear of pain.

Fear of pain is often a reason to deny emotions. You do not want to feel, as feeling can be painful. It is not the emotions that create pain, but the revealing of existing pain.

With regard to old pain, the only choice you have is between the chronic pain of resistance and the acute temporary pain of going through the emotion. You can compare it to an abscess under the skin, it will hurt for a short while if you puncture and clean it, but eventually it will be able to heal. If you do not, the pain will continue. Pain that has not been dealt with continues in the form of depressions and anxiety. The reason is that you do not really want to feel the pain.

Fear of the unknown.

An important fear for the depths of your emotions is the fear of what you will encounter. What kinds of things can you encounter in your age-old pools? There will be intense anger, hatred, sorrow, of course, many old frustrations and disappointments, many painful memories of this life and past ones. Many illusions and blinds will be unmasked. Perhaps you always thought you had a wonderful childhood, but it turns out that there is an experience lying at the bottom of your pool that proves that the fairy tale is false.

Perhaps we are frightened the most by positive emotions and feelings, such as love and joy. People are constantly talking about love, peace, and freedom. But I do not believe that the old saying "Out of the abundance of the heart, the mouth speaketh" is often right. It is usually "The heart speaketh of the abundance of fear." Receiving love, confronts you with all the old pain of not being loved that you can find in your soul's history. That is the profound reason for there being little or no love in your life. You are afraid of it and have learned to isolate yourself from it because of old, unpleasant experiences of not being loved. Many people find it strange when I say that what you long for the most often frightens you the most. ***Accepting love confronts you with old loveless situations***. That is why the confrontation with somebody who has completely become Love, is huge. The masses were opposed to a person such as Jesus because they were not able to cope with his love.

When I, myself, stood eye to eye with an enlightened Master, I could only cry. I saw the possibilities of realization in his eyes and cried because of my own lack of Love.

Fear of change.

Another fear in your heart of hearts is the fear that life will change if you feel completely. And that can mean anything! If you clear away your old anger, you know what you stand for and that can mean that you are no longer able to adjust to old systems and patterns, be that a marriage that is in a rut or a relationship that has gone cold, a job or an area of work that is no longer close to your heart. If you digest old pain, you may exchange your role of victim for one in which you make sure that you get what you need in life. It is possible that you will no longer put up with a partner who shuts himself off emotionally. It is possible, for example, that you will finally start studying to become a teacher, something you could not do earlier as your parents were poor or even worse perhaps, thought that you were aiming too high (or not high enough) for somebody of your class. If you can surmount your fears, what will your life look like? What would you do? And what would you not do? Let your fantasy loose; that is where many desires are hidden! My experience is that if you follow the path of your heart, you will receive everything you need. Liberation of old pain frees a lot of creativity to form your own life as you think best. In any case, inner change and renewal challenges your courage to take risks and align your outer world with the change in your inner world. You could start "fantasying" and ask the hidden, free child inside you, how it would like life to be. Children are often very wise!

Fear of losing control.

Loss of control is one of the greatest fears you will meet on this path, especially if you are used to controlling yourself. Control has often come to mean safety. "As long as I don't show anything, as long as they don't see me, as long as I don't feel any thing" are all strategies for survival. However, surviving is not living.

We are often scared of showing the depth of our emotions. The following are examples of widespread fears.

- *The fear of going mad.* With regard to most of the people reading this book—if you bottle up your emotions, you will go mad sooner! There is, however, a category of people who have not built up enough sense of self in their young lives and that means that the confrontation with their own emotionality must be slow and careful. Experiences should be integrated and the loss of control must not deteriorate into being completely swamped. It is, therefore, important to decide for yourself which steps and which type of therapy you can handle at this moment in your life. It is also important to distinguish between real fear and true fear. With this, I mean that it is possible that your fear of beginning to feel is real, but it does not have to correspond with the present. What you could not handle once, you can now, while the feeling of fear has stayed the same. It is good if you can do what you think you ought to do, namely develop yourself, even though you break out in a cold sweat.

- *The fear that people think you are odd* if you show your emotions. You have become ashamed of

79

showing them, perhaps because once your sister pestered you when you cried or were called a hothead when you got angry. The best way to get over this, is to do what you are ashamed of in a safe environment in the company of safe others. Once you have experienced a loving reception for your feelings, you will not be ashamed anymore. The criterion of safety is very important when you choose a therapist, especially if you suffer from feelings of shame.

- *The fear that nothing will remain of you.* You have let yourself become so identified with survival strategies and control behavior that it seems that nothing of you will remain if you let go. Being conscious of this helps you to set a step into the unknown. You are, after all, not your survival strategies. You can find out step-by-step who you really are, when you dare to pass beyond these false selves.

- *The fear that you will not be loved anymore.* This fear is the effect of deep imprints that we have picked up in the course of our lives. "If I show my true self, mummy and daddy will no longer love me." "If I show emotions, they'll reject me." "If I don't behave nicely, control myself, they won't like me." "If I cry, other children will think I'm stupid," etc. You may fill in your own imprints here.

It is good to realize that emotions determine your whole life even though you think that you have everything under control. It is important to get to know your emotional boss, step by step, if you want to start a good cooperation. Control is, in reality, a no-confidence motion against this boss. For centuries you were taught to distrust your emotions. You can learn the path of friendship with regard to all aspects of your personality. What a chance you have!

Working Step by Step with Fear

> *Where there is fear, there lies a task.*
> ~C.G.Jung

Here are some steps that you can used to work with your fears:

1. ***Becoming aware of your fears.*** Discover your masks and uncover the hidden. Make a list of your present fears. I am afraid...of criticism, of rejection, of pain, of the anger of others, of being alone, of men, of women, of violence, of confinement, of sexuality, of blushing, of independence. Why not make your own list? Do not trivialize but write everything down that comes to mind. Make a party game of it with your partner, your friends, and your children. Help each other to list all fears.

2. Make a list of all the ways in which you ***mask your fears;*** your compensation mechanisms. Consider fixed behavior patterns, such as these:

   - An urge to control;
   - Talking a lot in company so you will not feel how scared you are;
   - Leading a petty life according to an established pattern;
   - Working hard so you will not feel how scared you are of shortage;
   - Doing your best for fear of "not doing it properly;"
   - Putting yourself out for your husband because you are afraid he might otherwise
   - grumble or abandon you;

81

- Kissing somebody three times on the cheek to avoid eye contact and real intimacy;
- Etc., etc.

3. Make a *list of the consequences* that these fears have in your life. Realize that fears restrict your life and make you "unfree." Know that fears have an affect on your life and on your freedom of movement. Realize that fear prevents you from having the relationships you long for. Check what your "shopping list" does to you and your life. What are the consequences? How does each specific fear stand in your life? You have, for example, filled in "Fear of losing control." Write down in which spheres of life that comes to the fore and what the consequences are. For example, with regard to sexuality, what is missing because of this urge to control. Or, what does your urge to control, as manifestation of fear, do in the upbringing of your children. And what does it do in relation to God? Or have a look at fear of change. What are the consequences for your life? Which of your desires is not given a chance? With each fear, ask yourself what you are missing because of it. And how would you like it to be?

4. *Choose* which fear you want to be rid of and which type of freedom you wish to obtain. Do you really want to be rid of your fears? If the answer is yes, decide "to go for it." For example, say to yourself, "I want to become a free person" or "I am going to clear up all my old fears" and "I'm going to make time for it." After all, it is a Work!

5. *Investigate the past history of each fear.* An indication: *what you are frightened of has happened and has not been emotionally digested.* It is possible that you cannot place this past history,

but that is the Work—remembering. There is always a past history, however distant and far back in time. Sometimes you will have to remember a past life with regard to a certain fear. There will be more about this in Chapter 35. Take out your list now and write behind each fear where you felt it for the first time, with whom and in which circumstances. You will establish the lost link between your past and present fear in this manner. If you have filled in that you are frightened of criticism, go and meditate about that fear (sometimes that works better than a beautiful piece of writing!). Perhaps you will see the face of your brother before you who thought you were a silly little girl and who you were of no consequence at all. Or perhaps you are afraid of letting love into your life. Imagine what would happen if you were to melt and let what you long for into your life. Are you afraid of old feelings of pain and hurt in connection with love? With whom? When?

6. *Relive past experiences.* Aids to that end:

- *Breathwork.* With breathwork I mean intensive breathing to set your emotions more easily in motion. In the part about hyperventilation, directly after this, you will find more information. Furthermore, breathwork will be discussed extensively in Chapter 26. An aid is speaking sentences *aloud* that occur to you. Or saying what you do not feel as yet, but know is there. You could, for example, repeat saying, "I'm scared." During breathwork there may be additions to this sentence, such as "I'm scared of you when..."

- *A safe buddy,* preferably one who is more experienced than you. Fear is one of the most difficult emotions to relive and to really feel. It can be scary to feel frightened. But remember, what you were not able to handle as a child in an unsafe situation, you can handle now as a grown up. Moreover, what you relive has already happened. Only your emotions have remained behind. You can create your own safety now, and that makes a world of difference. You need safety if you are to work on releasing fear. You will, furthermore, notice that if you do breathwork, your fear can turn to anger, and that can be an important way to release your fear. Of course, grief and sorrow can be released, too. Fear can be expressed by shaking or by panting. Go along with the quickened breathing, you will breathe the fear out of your system in this way.

- ***Gestalt work.*** Dialogue and active contact is the core issue of Gestalt work. If you suddenly think of your mother, talk to her. Tell her what you have possibly never told her. She need not be there in the flesh; it is even better if she is not. If, for example, you get a cramp in your leg or it starts to shake, talk to it and let it give an answer. Say whatever occurs to you. If you feel resistance against this kind of work, say so by declaring aloud that you do not feel like doing it. You repeat this and exaggerate it until you perhaps start to feel that you are, in fact, frightened. You then declare this aloud until you start to feel fear and fear-related experiences, as well as other emotions. More about Gestalt work in Chapter 27.

- ***Bodywork.*** Feel where fear is fixed in your body. Put your hand there or let somebody else do it for you. Breathe in that spot. Fear is often to be found in the chest; give yourself more room by breathing so the emotions that have accumulated there can be brought to light. You will notice that you become lighter physically. Emotions are fixed where you feel pain in your body. Breathe towards the pain and try to breathe through it. More about body work in Chapter 28.

- *Music* is a wonderful aid to finding your emotions. Use music that touches you. If there are other emotions, such as anger and sorrow, welcome them. Other emotions are usually to be found where there is fear.

- Finally, **comfort** the fearful child inside you. Or seek comfort with your helper. Realize that the loving welcome your emotions receive now is very different than that of the past. Look with compassion at the child that has survived in spite of fear and pain. You may thank your clever survival tactics. They have helped you to remain standing and surviving. You could tell them you are now taking another path......that of *Living.*

Hyperventilation: Fear of Emotions and an Aid to Release

Nowadays, hyperventilation is generally seen as a difficult phenomenon to combat. I will, first of all, describe what hyperventilation is. A larger stream of oxygen is created when people breathe too quickly and excessively and when they breathe more in than out.

In the case of fear, this is completely normal. When I came across a wolf in a wood in Romania once, my body went into a state of stress, and I automatically started to breathe quickly. That helped me to flee. But when old fear and other emotions have been turned inwards, chronic stress builds up in your body. The adrenalin level is, as it were, constantly in a state of alarm. With other emotions that have turned inwards, the physical stress can lodge itself everywhere in your body.

In the case of fear, the stress will be aimed at breathing. It is possible that breathing becomes stressed even though there is no real state of alarm in the outside world and not a wolf to be seen. What does this stress, called hyperventilation, look like? With regard to hyperventilation (stressed breathing) there are two opposite forces at work: there is pressure from the subconscious to express suppressed emotions, and at the same time there is a fear of emotion that wants to confine it. This kind of stress sometimes causes you to breathe shallowly and too quickly, which means that you pump too much oxygen through your body. This often happens at impossible moments. This causes complaints, such as dizziness, tingling, dry mouth, sweating, and false heart attacks.

It is handy to use tricks recommended by doctors and associations for these moments in the super market or in the street: hold your hands in a cup before your mouth so you can inhale your own exhaled air, breathe into a plastic bag, make body movements to recover the balance of your oxygen and carbon-dioxide levels. There is, however, another way of combating hyperventilation.

In the above-described manner, hyperventilation will come as a thief in the night. It is like a shadow in your system. What you are now going to do is what I have been singing the praises of in this book; you are going to meet your shadow. If there is a shadow and if there are old problems, you only have two choices: the shadow is master and will catch you unawares whenever he wants, or you are master and you go forward and meet your shadow with attention and love. In previous chapters I have called that healthy emotional management.

Towards your shadow: Breathwork.

Go somewhere safe and start to breathe more quickly with awareness and love. Breathe just like you do when hyperventilation catches you unawares. It is nice if you can do this work with a hands-on-expert for the first couple of times. It helps you over your initial fear. You should start to breathe more in than out in a very conscious manner; a more linked breathing will come about as a matter of course. You are now doing this with the intention of releasing yourself from your fears. And that makes a world of difference. You might have the same symptoms for a time, but by lying down and actively working at accepting your emotions, it will become less scary. Hyperventilation is, in fact, fear of your emotions. From the moment you accept your emotions—and that can be anger or sorrow—your hyperventilation symptoms will vanish into thin air, sometimes from one moment to the next! I will mention the most important symptoms and put them in a different light:

- *Dizziness.* One of the first symptoms that may appear is dizziness. It is, in fact, an impulse to walk away from your feelings. "I don't want to be part of this!" By becoming aware of this and by saying aloud, "I'm frightened of my emotions," you transform the dizziness into conscious fear. For a moment you can breathe more quietly, then subsequently more quickly but now with full awareness of your fear. It is not necessary for your body to subconsciously express what you are aware of.

- *Muscle tension.* Tension in your muscles points to an inner conflict between two forces withstanding each other. This is usually the struggle between an emotion and the fear thereof. Depending on how much you dare to actuate your emotions, you will find that your body becomes more relaxed and tension lessens step by step.

- ***Tingling around your mouth and a dry mouth.*** Sometimes your mouth can become so cramped that you can no longer talk. That is, in fact, the message; it is a symptom of your inability to say something. This has more to do with an old situation of impotence than with your situation in the here and now. It is usually a subconscious expression of the child within you that in the past could not say what it had to say because there was no loving welcome, or you were too small to articulate your message. Now it is all about saying what is on your mind. You will then find that the symptoms disappear quickly. Yell your message aloud and direct it in your imagination at the person it is meant for. Perhaps you want to tell your mother that you felt stifled by her fear and worry. Perhaps you want to tell your parents that you cannot stand their quarrels and that they frighten you. Perhaps you want to tell your uncle that he should keep his hands to himself. Perhaps after you have done this work, you will realize that as a grown-up you still hold back messages to others, your partner, your employee, or your colleagues.

- ***Tingling in hands and feet.*** This is a signal from your body that energy is being charged that cannot escape. It is usually accumulated anger. It is anger that you could not express. As a child you did not have the power to bang your fist on the table or kick something or someone. You should do so now, but with a cushion or mattress. You will transform the tingling into anger and in this way not only release yourself from hyperventilation complaints but also from old anger.

- *Shaking and trembling.* This can mean a number of things: it can be an expression of anger. Convert it into language. Tell your helper that you are frightened. Perhaps you need to hold a hand or feel somebody's arm around you. However, it is good to realize that it is old fear and that you need to get through it. If you are comforted too early, it can cover up fear. Shaking can also mean shivering with cold. That is usually old cold that your body is trying to make you aware of. Do not cover this experience up either, by using a blanket or by premature human warmth. Live through the cold and feel it and find out to which old situation this cold is related. Speak the sentence "I'm cold" aloud. If nothing becomes clear, continue by saying "I was so cold when I was with you." See which reaction that sentence provokes, make a slight distinction, and think to whom and when you would like to say that sentence.

- *Transpiration.* We use the term "cold sweat" to mean a state of nervousness or fear. This fear is just the fear of emotions with regard to things that happened in your past. The fact that symptoms disappear when you understand your body language and turn it into emotion applies here, too. Have you ever noticed that you can measure the extent of your subconscious fear by the way your sweat smells? The stronger the smell, the more subconscious your fear is. Your body can put you on the track of awareness!

- *Having to go to the toilet often.* If I do breathwork in the above-mentioned manner with a group, there are often frequent visits to the toilet. This is, in fact, a manifestation of fear.

- ***Fear of loud noises.*** People who are very tense are sometimes afraid of loud noises. This can go back to traumatic experiences with loud noises. It could also have to do with an experience in childhood in which you experienced a bombardment in a war. It can also date back to a previous life. But it is often that you are frightened of your own sound. Perhaps there is a kind of primal scream inside you, which you find frightening to express and project outside of you.

- ***A fake heart attack.*** Perhaps we should say that your heart attacks you with a message. This Work is, after all, about finding the message of your heart and understanding it. If you understand the physical attack of your heart and transform it into emotion, the physical complaints will disappear. You loosen the stress around your heart by crying, and the tears soften the hardening.

- ***Fear of dying*** is a feeling that sometimes occurs during hyperventilation attacks. This is really the fear of letting go of the control over fear and feeling what you feel.

- ***The urge to control is a way of hiding your fear.*** You try to control your surroundings so as not to feel how scared you are. Ways in which this can manifest itself are recurrent counting, hand washing, cleaning, and other obsessive-compulsive disorders.

All of this has to do with getting to know your body language. Do not be afraid to seek help. It is often difficult to see your blind spot and two see more than one, especially if one is more experienced than you are in this field.

Fear of Failure: A Fight with Your Expectations

*Expectation is the greatest impediment to living. In
anticipation of tomorrow, it loses today.*
~Seneca

Fear of failure is a common symptom. Fear of failure
has to do with so-called catastrophic expectancy. You expect
the worst because you have no self-confidence. The expression
"fear of failure" indicates that something has to be achieved.
Fear of failure has to do with taking action. It happens in
situations in which something is expected of you, or you expect
something of yourself. Expectations are a nuisance. It is a kind
of projection into the future that takes away freedom in the
present. You can fail your exams by being occupied by the
thought that you have to succeed. If you could set yourself free
from the result of your work, be that an exam or writing a
book, you could enjoy the work itself. This ability has to do
with self-confidence and with the ability to live in the here and
now. Let me start with self-confidence.

Self-confidence.

Self confidence is a quality that is often undermined at
a young age by critical educators [parents are included in this
category], educators who do not affirm, expect too much, or
who compare children to one other. We all experience a
mixture of this, and that makes it difficult to keep on believing
in ourselves! We have all, more or less, been mangled by this
jumble.

1. *Critical educators* When parents or educators are
not happy with themselves, they will pass that
dissatisfaction on to their children. The
dissatisfaction of parents is passed on unwittingly to
their children. The dissatisfaction of parents will
probably have to do with their upbringing, and thus

91

we have, as always, the continuing relay race of human shortcomings. Constant criticism at a vulnerable age leads to the feeling of not being good enough and later to self-criticism. After all, the way we have been treated by key figures is the way we will treat ourselves later in life.

2. ***Educators who are not affirmative*** When parents and educators are unsure of themselves and not conscious of it, they will not be inclined to affirm their children in what they do well. People who are unsure of themselves find it very difficult to give someone else a compliment. They need it so badly themselves.

3. ***Educators and parents who expect too much*** Educators and parents who are not fulfilled in their lives will be inclined to expect their children to realize what they did not. The housewife who was not allowed to become a teacher hopes her daughter will become one. The man who was not allowed to study hopes his son will do so. The man who is musical but never had the chance to play an instrument expects his son to play the violin. Where there is expectation, disappointment lies in waiting. Where there is expectation, there is insufficient contact with the reality of the other. Your child is another person and has other talents than his father or mother. Another example stems from a negative expectation. Somebody told me:

> *I'm from a working background, and we had the device [belief] 'If you're born poor, you'll remain poor all your life'... and lots of accompanying stories. I was about thirty when I'd gathered enough courage to study. I managed to succeed for the exams, notwithstanding sleepless nights and growing*

tension. The only way to calm down enough to do the exam was to accept that I would, of course, fail.

4. ***Educators and parents who compare.*** Drawing a comparison from the background of old emotional charge is often top sport in human society. By drawing a comparison, one will always be more and the other less. We run the risk of nobody's unique qualities being acknowledged if we compare. Fear of failure and pride will then alternate. Nobody will really be seen.

In Spark of Light work, everything revolves around actively winning back your self-confidence. How do you go about this? You do this by remembering your history and by consciously going back in time. You remember how the four above mentioned aspects played a role in your life and how they still do. In second place, you ensure your emotions accompany your memories.

Feel how it was for the child in you and release the child from the expectations you still have of yourself. After all, you are the one who can flip the light switch! If you manage this, you will notice that you will become less frightened of failure. You will acquire more self-confidence. You will not care about expectation at all because you know that expectation leads to disappointment. You will accept yourself as you are with all your specific qualities. That will create room for decisiveness and creativity and that will make your undertakings successful.

Living in the here and now.

A second element which can free you from fear of failure and disengage you from the result of your acts has to do with living in the here and now. This is one of the most difficult tasks on your path to liberation. Being able to live in the here and now is an attainment achieved by conquering your fear of failure. You can live fully in the here and now when your past has been emotionally digested. When the power of the here and now has become strong in you, you do not project your life into the future anymore. You are then free.

Shyness

Shyness is a mild form of fear of people. You are not quite at ease with people. You are scared of showing yourself in all your vulnerability. By calling it shyness, you mask the fact that it is really a fear. Why not call a spade a spade? You are frightened of people. It is possible to find its source by translating it into what it really is and magnifying it a bit further. I have always been slightly shy. With my gift of the gab, I could often mask my shyness, but it felt uncomfortable inside. An important process of reliving helped me to get rid of it. I will relate it here as it was a surprising revelation and because it was an explanation for the reason of my shyness. Of course, all have their own stories, and sometimes the cause of things is not what is expected. Shyness is often the result of many unpleasant experiences with other people in the past. This is my personal story:

> *During a ritual of the Santo Daime movement where we drunk ayahuasca to cleanse us of everything that stands in the way of freedom and the light and also to heighten our awareness, I heard a voice saying the following to me, 'Did you know that you were a completely different child before your third birthday than afterwards? And do you know that what happened has to do with your shyness?'*
>
> *I said, 'I don't know anything about that' and I felt that I really wanted to add, 'and I don't want to know either.'*

94

But before I could say that, the voice went on, 'We will bring you to a painful experience that is hardly bearable for you, but know that we will be with you.'

I started to become really frightened and had the inclination to concentrate on something else—on what was happening to others, for example. But through this fear, I started to think about the tonsil operation I had when I was three.

I did not have happy memories of it. But I could not remember many details. I know that I had to wait a whole day in a bare ward together with my friend without any toys and that my mother had gone home. There were women with black gowns (I later realized that they were nuns) who told me to stop crying and acting so childishly. That is all I remember.

But now I felt afraid as never before in my life. I asked somebody to hold my hand, and I looked fear in the face. What I saw then, I had believed to be impossible: I saw the operating theater, I saw them putting a mask over my mouth, and I saw them going into my throat with a knife or scissors. At that moment, during the ritual, I screamed my head off. Thank goodness people were singing and that drowned out my screaming. I understood that the anesthetics had not worked properly and that I had been conscious throughout. My fear of people had been born in mere minutes. And now, in a couple of minutes, I was set free from that fear.

Contemporary cognitive psychology holds the view that shyness is innate. In a fruitless cooperation with neurobiology "evidence" is given that the amygdala is stimulated more quickly in the brains of shy people.[5]

Of course, the next step will then be the drug Seroxat, which also has the name of being "a pill for shyness." This is what happens when we dampen down the human soul and refuse to look any deeper or see beyond the end of our scientific noses. I think that it is obvious that shyness and fear become visible in our brains. But there is something very wrong with science when these symptoms are seen as cause. We call something "science" when the process of procuring information goes via certain controllable protocols. The presumption preceding a scientific process usually defines its outcome to a large extent. These presumptions are just as unscientific as every other human observation. We cannot conclude from observations that one in five babies is shy or that it relates to "an inherited chronically high level of the neurotransmitter noradrenalin."[6]

This kind of conclusion shows that the outcome of scientific research is highly subjective. Only the part "in-between," between presumption and conclusion, meets the criteria of science. It is possible that shy babies have a heightened level of noradrenalin, but that is not the cause of shyness! The cause of shyness stems from emotional experiences that the baby has brought with him or her from previous lives and/or from the experiences that the individual has had during birth and/or in contact with his or her parents. If we only look at behavior and at neurotransmitters in the brain, we get "dampened down psychology," "dampened down psychological assistance," and a shallow view of mankind. Further information can be found in Chapter 31, Early Emotional Imprints.

Besides shyness as a fear, there is also a mild form of shyness that has to do with intimacy. Shyness is then the identifying mark. It shows that you no longer have any role-play at your disposal and that you are genuine. You then show your insecurity and vulnerability.

Shyness is sometimes nothing else but false modesty and fear of accepting and showing your magnificence. We do not exactly affirm this kind of behavior in our culture. There is a difference between false modesty and true modesty. True modesty is a manifestation of respect and self-knowledge.

Concern: Love Mixed with Fear

Concern is usually seen as positive by the person who is feeling concerned. It is seen as an expression of love, but the object of concern usually sees it as a nuisance. It is also necessary to call a spade, a spade here. It is love mixed with fear and power. The person who is concerned does not place enough trust in life. When my mother, after I had just left home, kept on telling me to look after myself and be careful, I told her to have more trust in my life. If it was my time to die, I would die, and nobody would be able to do anything about it. She told me later that that had helped her to let go of her concern.

Worry

Worrying is a form of cognitive fear. It consists of worrying thoughts that go round and round in one's head and keep many people from sleeping. In actual fact, fear is expressed on a mental level instead of being lived through. By worrying, you do not feel the fear. Thinking is often used as a means of not feeling. To free yourself from fear, you need to let it "sink in." You must start by feeling the fear in your body instead of in your head. Feel your palpitations and your sweat drops. See which fears your worrying is hiding. Go and do something about it, as I described in the beginning of this chapter.

Fear of Bonding and Separation Anxiety

Fear of bonding and separation anxiety are both usually mentioned in one breath. They belong together. I would rather speak of the fear of commitment. I do not see bonding to someone as positive; to commit is a different matter and is positive. You cannot emotionally commit yourself to somebody when you carry an old fear of being deserted. This fear of separation means you avoid committing yourself to another person because of the fear of pain—and the pain of recurrence. We have already seen that things that scare you have already happened in a distant past of which you have no memory. We can, in actual fact, trace this problem of commitment and separation back to an ***old history of being deserted***. This does not necessarily mean that another person has actually deserted you. It is often affective desertion by one of your parents. It can mean that your mother has not formed a symbiotic bond with you of that she broke this bond too early because of another pregnancy. You can also develop separation anxiety, for example, when you recurrently had to move from house to house as a child because of your father changing jobs. Another example is, of course, being separated from one of your parents because one of them died when you still needed him or her. By experiencing these old histories of separation again emotionally, your fear of commitment and separation can disappear in the here and now.

The Fear of Death and the Fear of Living: Two Sides of the Same Coin

Because I am free, unconditioned, whole, not the part, not dependent on anything but the whole Truth that is eternal, I desire those who seek to understand me to be free, not to follow me, not to make out of me a cage which will become a religion, a sect. Rather should they be free from all fears—from the fear of religion, from the fear of salvation, from the fear of spirituality, from the fear of love, from the fear of death, from the fear of life itself.
~Krishnamurti

The fear of death and the fear of life are closely intertwined. Fear of life often has it origins in old fears of dying that are subconscious and have not been dealt with. These can be experiences from this life, but they can also originate in past lives. I know somebody who has suffered from phobia all her life and leads a solitary existence, too frightened to take part in the fullness of life. I know that she was born with the umbilical cord around her neck and that she had a blue tinge to her skin when she was born. Is there a connection between this fear of dying and her fear of living?

Somebody told me **the following story** about his research into his fears:

> *Finally, I reached a fundamental fear of living that never went away, despite all the therapy I followed and despite all the attempts at accepting myself as I am. I suddenly had the impulse to go to the municipal archive of my native town and look at the history of 1942, the year I was born in. I received a booklet and found out that the town had been on the front with planes constantly flying back and forth from Germany. The population spent practically three years in cellars with constant air raid alarms. After reading it and comparing it to what I knew about our own personal history from my mother, I burst into tears. I now understand what my father and mother went through and what I, myself, experienced as an unborn child and later as a baby.*

> *My parents went through so much fear; frightening noises and fleeing from danger. After being in the womb for ten months, my birth was a terrible event. Mother and father did not know how children were born. They thought I would be 'shat out'...! Father was seized by panic and sent to the cellar by my mother. While she waited for the doctor (who could not be reached), she laid bathing in her own blood for two*

99

hours, with me between her legs. In the meantime, there was one air raid alarm after the other. The umbilical cord was cut very late and directly afterwards, according to the anecdote, I peed straight over the bed onto the round iron stove that stood in the upstairs flat. Was it a manifestation of fear? Fear played a major role from the moment I was fathered. Three months after my birth, a grenade hit our house, and we were miraculously spared because we were at my grandmother's. A week after, we took up temporary residence in a garage (where people were hiding). My sleeping-place was hit by a grenade, and we again lived to tell the tale because we were visiting my grandmother. A year later, my parents and I were in the cellar of a house together with other residents when a bomb fell on it. Again wonder of wonders, we were saved. I now understand my fear of embracing life and never daring to take part fully. I could only shout something about those rotten Krauts and that rotten war. I feel really sad and it's all so long ago...'

When you notice a reserve towards life and you cannot embrace it, you should have a good look at your fears. There is always a reason to be found that usually lies in your past. The old platitudes "Let bygones be bygones" and "Bury the past" will not help you any further. We carry our past with us till we have emotionally digested it. We can then live, as free as the wind, in the present—not because it is a closed book but because we have freed ourselves emotionally from the past.

Fear as a Teacher

In the preceding, I portrayed fear as a friend, which you can accept by regarding it as a teacher. Is fear "an instrument of evil" as a vicar asked me recently? Is fear a denial of love, and thus an enemy, as people in the New Age Movement think? If fear stops you doing what you really want to do, it really seems to be your enemy. Fear is your enemy when it petrifies you and keeps you back, when it restricts your freedom and spoils your life. But...then you live as a victim of your own fear. There is only an enemy when you feel you are a victim. If you take matters into your own hands and claim full responsibility for your life, you will find a way to conquer all your fears. And you can only do that when you stop thinking of enemies and start to think inclusive. Inclusive thinking means that you enwrap everything in Love, also fear and so-called evil. Fear will become parts of yourself that have not been liberated, evil [will become] goodness that has not been liberated, and darkness [will become] light that has yet to be kindled.

Start to make contact with your fear; ask "him" if he will become your friend. A characteristic of friendship is getting to know each other well.

In this case, knowing well means feeling the depths of your fear and taking the root of it back to where it belongs: in your past. If, in this sense, you know your fears well, fear will be transformed into courage and trust—just like the frog that turned into a prince once the princess had kissed him. That is the Work of transformation and the alchemy of Love.

Fear of God

Many people have been brought up "in the fear of the Lord." They are often still afraid of the God of their youth when they are adults and have sometimes been separated from church and faith for a long time. Sometimes the theology is already different in their minds, but the old God still lives on in their hearts. Deep inside, they are still afraid of "Judgment." Certainly the strict Protestant followers of Jesus accept as axiomatic that people are "prone to all evil, adverse to all good." For this reason, the fear of oneself came into existence at the same time as the fear of the judgment of God, and this self was seen as sinful. Likewise, fear of the "tempting world" and the "veil of tears" were born. Fear became the basis of the relationship with God and permeated people's whole existence. It is enough to make you weep. Telling people like this that they should become friends with their fears is difficult. Fear has been connected to love in a pact with the devil. Love became corrupted. And fear? Fear was considered to be of paramount theological importance but become the soul's enemy number one. An awful disunity came from this. A vicar I am friendly with wrote this text as reaction:

> *Amen—and thank you. Ouch. It's awful, isn't it? And because I've been wrestling with this for thirty years, I often meet people who have been badly damaged by this. Ouch. Ouch. Many people still swear by this, you know—they find fear an excellent characteristic, the more God-fearing, the better, of course! I am always surprised that you can prove almost anything with the Bible in the hand...*

Freeing yourself from anger.

Next to insight into the mechanisms of such a belief system, it is important to set your emotions in motion. When you start to really feel, you will find that under all that fear there is a huge amount of anger. It will be difficult for many to express anger towards this God. After all, this God is intermingled with love. Perhaps He comforted you, or the atmosphere of togetherness and singing comforted you. It is then important to divide this God from the other for a while, just like you can do with your parents during this Work. Leave the good intact. Put the good God in the corner for a while! You can ask Him for help in freeing yourself from the neurotic God who is, in reality, a neurotic church and a neurotic belief. You address yourself to the God, as representative of the parental and religious authority, with whom you have a bone to pick. It helps to become angry with this God. The real God will help you heal.

You put the neurotic God, minister, vicar, or priest on a cushion, and you start talking to him. Tell him how he spoiled your youth and how much he frightened you. Let all the images, experiences, and emotions come to the light. Do not spare the rod or save your tears for later. By letting you tears flow liberally during this Work, you make sure your life does not become a veil of tears.

If you are part of this group, the key to friendship with "all that is" will be opened by the friendship with your anger. If you accept this totally and express it, fear will disappear, and you will find your own way to Loving Light. Your fear will melt away in the fire of your anger. There will then be room for your own experience of God. If this affects you, you can have a look at Chapter 47 Liberation of "God" to find God.

Fear of Freedom

Freedom will cost you the mask you have on, the mask that feels so comfortable and is so hard to shed, not because it fits so well, but because you have been wearing it for so long.
~Florinda Donner

Fear of freedom is probably one of our greatest fears. It is not very visible, for we have masked it in various ways. By looking at how we mask it, we can look fear in the face:

Seeking refuge in power relations.

If you are frightened of the breathtaking freedom of forming your own life on this planet of free will, you may give your freedom away to an institution, such as a state or church, a philosophy of life, a guru, a Pope, or another religious leader. This will stop you developing your own power and authority. Your choice is that of impotence and electing to become a follower. You prefer hierarchical and authoritarian relations above brotherhood and sisterhood. I invite you to look at the fears linked to this choice.

Seeking refuge in established structures and fixed patterns.

Fixed patterns and certain regularity can be helpful in making life easier and simpler. If you have a large family, it is handy to set a fixed time for dinner. It is also easier and more economical to do certain jobs according to a certain routine. If routines are subconscious and recurrent, it is best to look at the underlying fear. We are often not aware of being caught in certain patterns. I will give a few examples.

Many people in our modern society are used to working from nine to five for their so-called "daily bread." They find it completely normal to work for most of their lives to earn an income. It is a pattern in which people seem to be locked. If you have opted for that choice and like your work, then that is all right. But how free is that choice? How much has it been influenced by cultural, social, and parental expectations? Are you courageous enough to choose what you really want? Perhaps you really want, as the old philosopher said, to go fishing in the morning, to go hunting in the afternoon, and to sit and read in the evening. Or do you want something completely different?

How much room do you allocate yourself to, at least, fantasize about it? Another example of fixed patterns is to be found in families and partner relationships. We can think of the fixed patterns in male-female relationships, of the invariable sitting together on the sofa after work to watch television and the fixed patterns of who does what. Fixed structures can mean that everything becomes deadly boring, and life deteriorates into a gray dullness of certainty. That is what it is meant for: safety in a changing world even if you feel inside that it is a false security. The other side of fixed patterns means having the courage to do things differently, the courage to change one's tack and see what that way has to offer.

Seeking refuge in conformism.

You adapt to the group you belong to. You adapt to the codes of conduct of your culture and to everyday routine because you are frightened of being alone, of being ostracized, of not being loved, or of people finding you strange. Due to these fears, we have made essential equality into uniformity, and we have all been swept along by the maelstrom of conformity. We only have to look at fashion. When I was a child, my mother could really make me angry by telling me when I did not like the clothes in a shop, that they were fashionable! Even the color is determined by fashion. Right from childhood, we are taught to listen to the expectations of people in our surroundings.

We might, otherwise, be ostracized and disowned. It is not for nothing that the great of this earth, found the courage to be at odds with the beliefs of their surroundings. The great renewers/visionaries/prophets were always renegades and heretics. In our worship and fear of freedom, we often lose sight of this aspect. They had the courage to grasp freedom. We could follow them not by following their path, as we are taught in many religions but by courageously following our own path. This is where we touch on the fear of being unique and different, of being an individual. Why is this? People who dare to express their uniqueness are not predictable and, therefore, not controllable. They slip through the hands of those in power.

Rulers have an interest in those who are powerless and predictable. Rulers merely exist by the grace of those who are powerless and afraid. They maintain each other. The ruler is finished from the moment the powerless become powerful. That is the "law of complementarity."

It is also possible that when you do not conform anymore, your circle of acquaintances will not accept you and will sever relations. People have a need for safety, and part of

105

that is that you remain the same. The other side of the flight into conformity is the need for adventure and originality. It is courageous to express your own uniqueness and originality in your own way even if it costs you the approval of your surroundings. You can only do this when you have more or less solved your own basic neurosis and are no longer dependent on parental and social approval.

Seeking refuge in the other.

This form of the fear of freedom is not always easy to recognize. But it has to do with complementarity, with halves that complement each other and with dependency. Marriage has often been described in this way. The other person represents the part you miss. In black and white, we could say that it is about the frightened little woman who marries the strong man and the immature boy who marries the caring mummy figure. You flee to the other because you are scared of standing on your two feet and realizing your potential. If you did, marriage would not be about two halves, but about two individuals who find it inspiring and enjoyable to spend time together. The underlying fear in seeking refuge in the other is being afraid of yourself and all your possibilities.

Seeking refuge in orgasmic experiences.

This can mean sex, amusement, and peak experiences. These areas have tension and relaxation as theme and are a means to avoid freedom. The loss of freedom is obvious in themes such as sexuality. By being dependent on the tension-relaxation mechanism, you lose freedom. You are a slave of your own sexual needs if you experience sexuality in accordance with this main theme. It means that you will want more sex than usual if you are feeling stressed. We speak of freedom when your sexuality is integrated in love and in your relationship and when it is independent of tension and relaxation. If we look at amusement and especially at excitement and kicks, we see that the same thing is happening there. You need tension to become relaxed. Practicing sports obsessively could also belong to this category. You need exertion to relax. In all these examples, we see dependency on the curve of tension and relaxation. In general, this means that where there is dependency; there is lack of freedom.

Seeking refuge in numbness.

This can be refuge in alcohol, drugs, and food, and various kinds of addiction: gambling, constant buying, computing, but also work.

These are all ways of restricting and numbing your freedom of feeling and awareness. Addiction is the ultimate lack of freedom. You are on a constant treadmill of the same old thing because you have to mask fear. You keep on doing the same thing, gambling, buying, eating, or drinking. It is usually a fear of really feeling. The best way to put a stop to your addictions is by setting your emotions in motion. Under the food addiction, lies the fear of not getting enough because you did not get enough once. You did not want for food, but for love. And because you do not want to feel that pain, you keep on eating. Alcoholism is also a way of not feeling, a refuge. The woman who buys one gadget after the other and collects cupboards full of things is covering up the pain of the love she missed and trying not to feel the emptiness. These are all short-term palliative measures that will not really do any good.

Fear and Love

Emotions are often reduced to love and fear in New Age thinking. Love is seen as a polar opposite of fear. This way of thinking is to be found in the ideas of Gerald Jampolsky and Marianne Williamson in imitation of *A Course in Miracles*, as well as in the ideas of many others. One of the most important principles in Jampolsky's work with children and adults is choosing for love instead of hate. "If you look straight into your fears," Jampolsky says, "you will see that they are not realistic." In the name of love, that is known as the essence of all that is—fear is spirited and visualized away. On the cover of the Dutch translation of his book *Love Is Letting Go of Fear* [7] we see somebody letting go of a balloon. The word 'Fear' is written on this balloon. By saying that this fear is not real, only love remains. It is spiritual brainwashing, however well meant. Fear is too deeply rooted in us to disappear in this magical, spiritual way. If we say that love is antipodal to fear, we place fear outside love. Fear can teach us things and is a very powerful teacher.

It is true that fear is an indication that we are not completely rooted in love, but it is not the opposite. "There is no fear in love, but perfect love casts out fear" is found in the first epistle of St. John. But that does not mean that fear is not real. It is important to distinguish between true and real. We can say that at spiritual levels only love is true, but that fear is, indeed, real at psychological and experiential levels. These fears demand healing and liberation at the level in which they belong, and that is the level of human experience.

Fear is a reaction to the absence of love, and love means healing fear. With this in mind, Jampolsky does splendid work with critically ill children. However, the opposite of love is hatred and not fear. Love is, after all, the core of acceptance, and hate is the core of denial. Hate and denial cause pain, love and acceptance cure.

A thorough way of freeing yourself from hate is looking at your fears with love, getting to know them through and through and then transforming them into courage and trust. This transformation needs healing work and is at odds with spirituality that can all too easily be argued away as being the opposite of love.

Love will become complete if we have transformed our neurotic emotionality and become completely natural. Along the way, we experience love in less perfect forms, and this functions as a school of learning.

Fear of Love as the first and last fear.

The fear that is embedded in all fears and that is the source of them all is love. We can ask ourselves how this is possible; love is what we all long for the most! The reason is that if you have gone without unconditional love for years and perhaps even centuries, and most of us have on this planet, accepting love means feeling the old lack of love.

After a session during training with Elisabeth Kübler-Ross in which my past life in Auschwitz came up, I felt the hunger and cold again. When I sat down, someone gave me a few pieces of an orange. I will never forget that gesture of love for which I was really thankful and which made me break down and cry. Accepting love reminds us of lack of love—and we would rather not feel that pain. The denial of love is the most fundamental reason for not knowing enough love on this planet and for us going out of our way to avoid it. But the point is that the pain is there anyhow. It is disguised as physical pain and as the emotional pain we keep on causing each other because we do not want to feel our original pain. Pain will never go if we do not deal with it and bring it to the light. It moves from one person to the next, from one illness to the next, and from one war to the next.

A symptom of shutting out love is to be found in the saying: "It is better to give than to receive." This has been and still is emphasized in Christianity. The New Age Movement sometimes advocates this, too. These sayings and philosophies maintain the lack of love on this planet. Only when we actively work at our susceptibility will love grow among us. To become susceptible, we must create room by clearing away old pain. If we sort out old experiences of lovelessness, we can welcome love and build a house of Love.

I end this long chapter about fear with a quotation by a courageous man whom I hold in high esteem, Nelson Mandela. He made this text by Marianne Williamson famous:

> *Our deepest fear is not that we are inadequate.*
> *Our deepest fear is that we are powerful beyond*
> *measure.*
> *It is our light, not our darkness, that most frightens us.*

Chapter 11

Anger: Transformation from Hate to Love

Jesus said, 'When you bring forth that which is within you, what you have will save you.'
~Gospel of Thomas

In one of the Spark of Light weeks, Carina remembers being driven away from her home by the Nazis together with her parents and brothers and sisters when she was six years old. She tells the story of how they all, mother, father and six children, walked through the bitter cold of the winter of 1944 to friends of her parents. She remembers her mother crying the whole way. When they arrived, she thought of her little scooter and became very indignant. Without saying anything, she went back and saw that the Germans had already occupied the house. Nevertheless, she crept along, under the kitchen window, and got her scooter out of the shed. She tells the story quietly. When I invite

111

*her to show her emotions, she says she has not got any.
'I just hate those people' she said unemotionally.*

*By getting her to say this to the Nazis in her
past, her blood starts to boil and she starts to fume with
anger. This is a great relief, and anger is replaced by
respect for that brave girl.*

Becoming aware of hate is the regal road to love. A statement like this seems shocking as hatred is taboo. Because of this taboo, we often think that we do not know hatred. We tend to soften our feelings and to tone them down so as not to come in contact with the taboo. We often have no idea how much hatred we carry inside ourselves. More often it is toned down forms of hate that we experience: irritation, contempt, indifference, sarcasm, and depression. We know hate in its retroflected form: we hate ourselves. We can compare retroflection to a boomerang. For this kind of hatred, we also use soothing words to alleviate the problem. You do not like yourself, you feel you are not pretty enough, not good enough, not nice enough, etc., etc. The strongest type of self-hatred can end in suicide. Softer types are begrudging yourself things, not listening to your needs, living a minimal life, adapting to what is expected of you, always being capable, always going on with working, achieving, doing your best—in other words, being hard towards yourself. By taking away the verbal softening and seeing things in a sharp light, you can help yourself to learn the truth about yourself step by step and permit yourself to feel and express emotions. The truth about yourself will liberate you. Language that covers up and conceals will not do you any favors here.

Hate as Behavior

Hate can also exist in the way you live. Your behavior can be an expression of hatred if, for example, you wear yourself out completely during your duties. This self-hatred can also be aimed at others. In this case, we can think of behavior, such as careless driving, prostitution (both parties), pornography, children that are hit by adults, animal abuse, etc.

In a wider perspective, we can think of the pollution of the earth, arms traffic, traditions such as circumcision in many African and Islamic countries, the deforestation of the rain forests, violence on television appearing as amusement, and computer games which allow you to kill somebody every other minute if you play well.

Hate is a Fixation

That I feed the hungry, that I forgive an insult, that I love my enemy in the name of Christ - all these are undoubtedly great virtues. But what if I should discover that the least among them all, the poorest of all the beggars, the most impudent of all the offenders, that these are within me, and that I myself stand in need of the alms of my own kindness - that I myself am the enemy who must be loved?
~C.G. Jung

I do not call hate an emotion. Hate is anger that has been stuck fast for too long and has become hardened. Hate is a fixation and stagnation occurring in contact with others and also with yourself. If you hate another, there will always be a part of yourself that you hate, too. And this is elemental. If I hate myself or a certain part of myself, I will always encounter something in the outside world that reflects this self-hatred. When you are very critical towards yourself, it is possible that you are often criticized by somebody else. As it is within, so it is without. On this third-dimensional planet, we often see ourselves in each other's mirrors. What we encounter in the

113

outside world is a perfect mirror of our inside world, our consciousness, and our patterns. If I hate somebody else, that person mirrors an unfinished story of hatred within myself. Hate is anger that has never been expressed; it is compressed anger that has never had a loving welcome and has, therefore, been hoarded. Underlying the hatred, there is usually terror, pain, and sadness that has never come to light.

The Problem of Violence

As everyone knows and experiences, violence is a gigantic problem in our world. Violence and war occur within families and schools, in the streets, between races and tribes, and between peoples and states. In 1932 Albert Einstein wrote a letter to Sigmund Freud asking if there is a way to liberate humanity from war. Einstein suspected, as Freud did, that within man there is "a need to hate and destroy."

"Wouldn't it be possible," he asked Freud, "to influence people's behavior in such a way that they can withstand hate better?"

Freud said, "Man is not a gentle creature that needs love and can only defend himself when he is attacked, but he is endowed with impulses which have huge components that are formed by aggressive tendencies."[1]

According to Freud, the conscience of many people never develops to full maturity. It remains stuck at the level of social fear. As long as culture compels people to constrain themselves, there is nothing wrong. However, when a certain type of social aggression becomes acceptable, the floodgates are opened. That explains the aggression of the pious Crusaders and the decent family men who commit war crimes and take on the role of respectable civilians afterwards. During a short time, it was possible for them to give their aggression free rein under the cloak of elevated cultural or religious ideals.

114

This explains the "surpluses" of aggression during revolutions and wars.

I do not agree with Freud and Einstein that hate is inborn. Hatred is a gigantic planetary rubbish dump of pent-up anger that has not been dealt with by billions of hurt people whose pain has never had a loving welcome. Control has never really helped; it leads to despair and pessimism to which Einstein and Freud could also bear witness after the First World War.

Just after I wrote this, I read an article in the newspaper about Freud's book and the new discontent in our 21st century culture. The points of view of two contemporary European philosophers of culture are also discussed in this book. The French philosopher Edgar Morin writes about a new discontent in culture, which is not caused this time by repression of human instincts but by giving it free rein. Technological and materialistic development has gone hand in hand together with psychological and moral underdevelopment. The German thinker Peter Sloterdijk wonders if we can still control the present tendency of lawlessness. He writes about the constant battle between the tendencies of bestiality and taming and fears that the "brutified human animal" who is looking for kicks and has been freed of his "iron cage of rationally organized bureaucracy" will not want to listen to the voice of reason any longer. The newspaper article ends with the question of what we are to do with the growing sense of disaster and finally with the lament: "Who or what can tame the human as yet?"

This article implicitly refers to two possible solutions: taming or controlling. This is old wine in new bottles, as my teacher Jesus would say. We know that control does not work, and listening to reason is only part of the story. The average person's behavior is driven and governed 80% by subconscious emotions. We often have good intentions and do our best to be reasonable, but our subconscious emotional contents are in the driving seat. Freeing these subconscious emotional contents is what we must do if we want to save our culture and lives from a possible decline. As long as we have not yet delivered ourselves from hate, attempts will be made to keep the spiral of violence in hand by laws, punishments, and peace talks. That is all very necessary. Yet it is important to start, in all possible ways and on all possible fronts, with fundamental depth work if the horizontal measures are to be really effective. With depth work, I mean work as described in this book. Our planet needs a root-canal treatment for violence. Chronic hate should be transformed to acute hate and so to love.

The following areas really need this Work:

1. *Help with bringing up children.*

> There are many people who, so every now and then, take out their own irritations and pent-up anger on their children. An educationally responsible rap on the knuckles seems innocent enough and is understandable. However, parents should think about their own behavior first. If a child tries your patience to the limit and is exasperating, you have already let things go too far, and you ought to have a look at your ability to draw the line. Certainly nowadays children are brought up as little princes and princesses. If they are not taught where the limits lie, they change from princes and princesses into horrible little nuisances who have no respect for other people's limits. Love means saying "No" as well as "Yes." By saying "No" to unwanted behavior there will be more room for "yes." There are many people who do not know the difference between person and behavior. You can say a complete "Yes" to your child, yet a "No" to a certain kind of behavior. I find it very sad that these children receive less and less love due to the consequences of their limitless behavior. It becomes a vicious circle, and the children are always the

116

victims. I think that the hitting of children by grown-ups ought to be forbidden, and there should be a law against it. The government should give the example. Psychologists and educationalists should stop saying that a so-called educationally responsible smack is understandable and can be allowed. Where does the limit lie? My old mother always said that hitting a child is low, and I agree with her wholeheartedly. There should be courses for parents that clarify the above principles. Parents can be taught to use the cushion and the carpet beater to mutual benefit. Perhaps you find using the carpet beater a silly idea and have difficulty getting used to it. I know no better way! I know that you do get used to it quickly and that it saves you from a lot of trouble, especially in your family. A boxing ball or a gunnysack filled with sand is perhaps an easy way to introduce it. As long as it is hit using noise or words in a way that is not harmful. If you come to the agreement that only the cushion can be hit and sworn at, you will see what a beneficial result that has. If emotional charge is expressed in this way, it will be easier to talk afterwards. And that is necessary, too!

2. *Emotional education at school.*

I am not at home in modern education. What I know, I hear from parents and teachers. From this I get the picture that there is increased tolerance and room for children nowadays, but teachers have to deal with a greater degree of complexity. According to the Central Statistical Office in The Netherlands, burnout is highest in teachers. I will discuss the increased aggression and "difficult behavior" in children here. Nowadays behavior is very quickly labelled ADHD (Attention Deficit Hyperactivity

Disorder) and autism. A label is not a solution, and I wonder if the giving of labels is a positive contribution to behavioral problems. A teacher who is a friend of mine told me the following story.

Walter is a little boy of nine who has received the diagnosis ADHD. He is lively, demanding, and often openly aggressive. When he kicks another child, he defends himself: 'I've got ADHD. Even the other children spare him and let themselves be hit by him, and they say: 'Walter can't help it, he's got ADHD.'

Group discussion and endless conversations with Walter and his parents, in which he is told that he is not allowed to hit and kick others, do not help at all. After all, this is asking for control and that has never really worked. Perhaps it would help Walter, the teacher, and the whole class if Walter received lessons in carpet beating or boxing? And would it not be a good idea if children received lessons in handling emotions, such as fear, anger, and sorrow? Courses in emotional interactive skills in which children learn to express their emotions in a beneficial way would be a good alternative for the wholesale doping of children with Ritalin nowadays. There will be more on this subject in Chapter 41.

3. *Emotional work in prisons.*

I will now tell the story of David Mason, who was executed in the state of California in 1991. He had committed a four-fold murder when he was twenty-three.

David was lonely and depressed as a child. His mother had tried to abort him. From the day of his birth, she let him feel he was not wanted. Older sisters described the family as one in which laughing and touching was forbidden, and little David was almost daily beaten with his father's belt and by his mother with anything she happened to be holding. When he was only five years old, he tried to commit suicide by taking a whole pot of pills and setting fire to his clothes. When he was eight, he started to project his anger outwards by committing arson all over the place. His pent-up anger culminated in a four-fold murder of four older men and women in the neighborhood. He confessed later that he 'had always wanted to do something like that.

We can see the direct connection between pent-up anger, terror, and violence here. If we were able to do Spark of Light work in the prisons and take the emotional sting from violence, we would be able to make an enormous step into love. Of course, this is not a cure, but with motivation we are already halfway there. Violence may be infectious, but Love is, too. Violence is also a cry for attention, and if we realize that this lies behind all the terrible murders which should, of course, be punished, we can then do something—namely depth work with the damaged child. Then we recognize the deep emotional distress without accepting it as an excuse for the wrong that is done. The person can be loved—but not his behavior.

To free yourself from feelings of hatred, you must convert hate into acute anger and take this back in time and place to the right persons. What does this mean? If you have feelings of hatred in the present, it is advisable to ask yourself who it is that you hate. It is often not your boss or your colleague or your partner with whom your relationship is not as good as it once was. Most hate stems from your childhood. The difference in power was too great then, and most of your key figures on whom you were utterly dependent are to be found there. If you find the question of hate too direct, you can ask yourself who did not give you enough love, who hit you when you were little, who showed no respect towards you because you were only a child, etc. Not long ago, I read the following in the newspaper:

> *Five men, aged between twenty and thirty-five talk, about what they think of when they hear the word "aggression:" impotence, violence, driving too fast, relationship, fear, pressure, police. But what is aggression? 'That's when your blood begins to boil,' one of them says. The others nod their heads in agreement.*

> *These five men are not here for nothing. They are sitting in this small room in the 'DTC' (Training Center of the Dutch Salvation Army) because the judge thinks they should because they have used violence. They have been sentenced to follow this violence control training. It is remarkable how out-spoken they dare to be, how easily they talk about 'the offense' which has caused them to be here.*

> *They are quite surprised at themselves as it turns out afterwards. 'Great to be able to talk like that; you don't do that at home'. One of them 'hit a junk in his mug'[hit a druggie in his face], the other beat up a taxi driver, yet another the dog. How they came to do this, they do not know.*

> *The youngest members of the group seem to look for causes outside themselves: 'the wrong kind of women', alcohol. One of the men knows he bottles up irritations till he blows up at some futility. 'I'm not really a mean-tempered bastard,' analyzes another.*

'It's those other aggressive people that make me aggressive. They all want to get rid of the aggression, damn it.'

Aggression control is one of the community services at the Dutch Salvation Army's Day Center for probation and after-care service. They were established at the beginning of 1990 and The Netherlands now has nine. Their device is '(Good) behavior can be learned.'

A day center like this is, I think, a wonderful initiative. From the above conversation it becomes clear that the men appreciate such talks. To my alarm, however, I read that it is once again about learning control. Improving various ways of repression is what is really brought about by such behavior therapy. Repression will not work—it never has. Why is this? The reason is that which you repress and suppress will not go away and has to be curbed. Energy is never lost. Something that is constantly under pressure will, sooner or later, start to seethe because of a shock, a trauma, or something that resembles what has been suppressed. Perhaps you relax a little and slacken the reins and all of a sudden.... pop, what has been repressed for years or centuries comes to the surface. It would be good if these men could be helped to find out what they are angry about—with the carpet beater ready.

The above described cognitive behavioral therapy has also been described by the already mentioned Dan Goleman. He describes anger as "the most tempting, negative emotion."[2] He chooses a mental way in which to take the edge off anger and cool it down. My experience proves that a method in which we look anger straight in the face, express it, and let it consciously and harmlessly exist in its entirety brings about a fundamental liberation from pent-up anger. At the same time, an ability to cope with anger in a good way will then be developed. Eventually, we do not get angry easily anymore but are able to draw the line in a friendly but clear way and define our own space.

121

Anger as a Positive Emotion and a Contribution to the Path of Transformation

There are people in the New Age Movement who categorize anger under the negative emotions. It is sometimes described as a psychological cancer that stops us living in accordance with our true soul. I have, during my quest, come across various peculiar arguments from teachers. A well-known yoga teacher said, "You're on thin ice, be careful! Your aura will tear!" A kinesiology therapist told me that if you express your anger, even in a therapeutical manner, your anger will remain in the cosmos. You will contribute to the pollution of the cosmos. When a clairvoyant client came into my room, she was struck by the wonderful atmosphere. She asked if I often purified my room with incense or something similar. To her surprise, I said that I did not find that necessary and that the intense expressing of emotions—including a lot of carpet beating work—purifies the air beautifully.

Recently I read in a New Age magazine that anger is blind and that by expressing it, we lose our senses. This is really a New Age face-lift for an old Christian story: anger is the first mortal sin. There are, in fact, no negative emotions. All emotions are good; they are the original reasonable answers of our system to the outside world. The suppression of emotions makes them negative. They escape from "nooks and crannies" and are then projected, often randomly, at things at which they should not be projected. A negative emotion is, in reality, an emotion that is repressed and that has not been expressed. When you know how to transform your hate to anger in a good and therapeutic way, you do not have to suppress your emotion. But as long as you do not know how to do so, repression and denial have their value. After all, expressing hate can have negative consequences if you do not know about the therapeutical transformation of hatred. It will then lead to acting-out behavior and to expressing hate subconsciously, and we know about this so well because of the many spirals of violence on our planet.

Anger That Leads to War and Anger That Leads to Transformation

There is no faster way of healing the lack of love on earth than to feel your own hating and reproaching fury and to set it in motion till you understand it.
~Ceanne deRohan

It is not for nothing, of course, that we have all become scared of anger and have come to disapprove of it. Most anger that is expressed has been so mixed with old emotional and repressed charge that it is hard to swallow and leads to war. Because of the overloading, the recipient feels attacked and rebuffed. The content may be correct, but because of this overloading we pull out. Overloading is typical of projected anger. Our world is full of it. Because we are full of unfinished, repressed stories of anger, we strew these around randomly without respect to others. The anger we have with regard to unjust treatment in the past is projected on people in our present, usually people who are close to us, such as our partner and our children. These are people from whom you expect just as much as you used to from your parents. Undigested anger towards figures of authority in the past is now aimed at figures of authority in the present, etc.

Anger is often expressed to mask fear and vulnerability. Because feeling fear is such an overwhelming emotion, we try to drown it with anger. We subconsciously use the device "Offense is the best form of defense." Somebody wrote on a personal website:

> *I was sometimes disproportionately angry with my partner. After a quarrel, I often didn't know why I had become so angry. He had had a rotten day at the office and was grouchy when he got back home. The*

children were demanding, and I thought that he was angry with me for not keeping them quiet. I was scared that he would leave me. But he wasn't allowed to know because he could misuse that knowledge. So by frightening him and not letting him see that I'm vulnerable, I could become so angry that we had a fight that stopped him from recognizing my vulnerability. Now that I am further in my emotional development, it works differently; I am more independent of him and can stand on my own two feet. That means that it does not matter for my further life if he stays with me or not. I would, of course, mind terribly if he left me, but I would survive, and that wasn't the case in the way I used to feel. That means that I'm not so scared when he's angry with me. I don't see his anger as having anything to do with me because I'm more independent now. If he comes in with an angry face, I understand better now that it has nothing to do with me.

Anger that has transforming power is completely different than projected, overloaded anger. Transforming anger is anger that is vented in a conscious way under your own responsibility and supervision, preferably on a cushion and with the carpet beater. This anger is of service in a great release and in our growing towards love and peace.

Venting Anger as Drawing the Line

Anybody can become angry—that is easy, but to be angry with the right person and to the right degree and at the right time and for the right purpose, and in the right way is not easy.
~ Aristotle

The whole point is to become conscious of your anger and to learn to vent it with noise and movement in a safe environment and that will not harm anybody. Digesting your old load of hurt in this way does not lead to losing your senses but to becoming more rooted. Anger is just a way of drawing a line: "Stop! That hurts, and that's going too far." Since we were not able to do this as children, we are all more or less troubled by it. We need a lot of "overdue maintenance." That is why we find it difficult to indicate where our limits lie when we are adults. Being able to clearly define and indicate our limits with regard to our personal space is a deed of love for us and also for the other. After all, the way I treat myself, is the way I treat the other. If we tackle overdue maintenance well, anger will be the quickest way to love and strength. But what is a good way to approach it? In my opinion, insight is not enough. Anger should be felt deeply and expressed in a safe environment where it will not do anybody any harm—where the anger cannot only be expressed, body and soul, but where the anger can be clarified.

There are four main ingredients in this process. Ask yourself the following:

1. **Where** is the anger localized in your body? In German there is a saying *"Wut im Bauch"* (anger in the abdomen). The abdomen is the place where a lot of anger accumulates. Hands and arms are just such places; make a fist to help you express your anger.

2. **How** do you bring your anger to the light? You do this by venting your anger completely—by using a carpet beater and a cushion in an environment where you feel safe.

3. **What** makes you angry? Become aware of the message and get rid of your blindness. Talk to whomever you have projected on the cushion. Be as exhaustive as possible.

4. **Who** are you angry at? Become aware of whom your anger is meant for. Look and see if there is another face behind the face you see in your mind's eye. Perhaps you will first see the face of that nasty

colleague who is always trying to outdo you. Then have a look whose face emerges behind it. Perhaps it is that of your older brother who always knew everything better than you. It is extremely important for the effectiveness of the Work to aim your anger anew at who it is really meant for. Just being angry without knowing at whom, does not help at all.

You will find more and more inner strength if you do your Work properly and comprehensively with regard to the anger and underlying fear which is often there, too.

A person who has found his inner strength has overcome his childish powerlessness and with that, his negative power. In a degrading and outrageous situation, he will be able to use his strength and confidence to react with love. His *yes* will be *yes* and his *no, no*.

You will notice that the more you do overdue anger-work, the less tense you are when you are not happy with a situation. Your ability to say, in a quiet and friendly way, what you want to say will grow as will the ability to define your limits. There will be more space in your life and also more self-respect. You will notice that when you have self-respect and respect for your own space, others will have, too.

Anger's Role in Making You Stand Firmly on Your Own Two Feet

If you complete well your overdue maintenance work with regard to anger, you will notice that you stand more firmly on your own two feet and that you will be able to give yourself a solid backing in various situations. It was a liberating experience when I came in contact with my repressed anger for the first time during Scream Therapy when I was about thirty. I noticed that I became less defensive in contact with others and that I conformed myself less to what others expected of me. I started to go my own way and to make my own decisions more often. My *no* was more clearly *no*, but my *yes* become more clearly *yes*!

By eliminating my overdue anger, I not only became less timid and scared in contact with people, but I also had fewer conflicts with the colleagues and management of the psychiatric institution where I worked.

The digestion of old anger makes you strong, which means that you have the nerve to be more vulnerable. The combination of strength and vulnerability makes you tough when and where you need to be. You will, moreover, develop a natural authority.

Discovering Love Beneath Anger

You will often find your original love underlying your old anger when you set this anger in motion and express it under your own emotional supervision. The unexpressed anger kept the love hidden. Here is a great example from somebody who does Spark of Light work intensively:

We have just come back from an evening of playing cards at my parents' house.

>*It was quite enjoyable. I didn't feel like it though I had just done a lot of Work about my father yesterday. I cried because of a film in which a father offered his excuses to his daughter because he had not been the Daddy he had wanted to be. I wept and wept. I think I was crying because 'it' was more about him than me (although I would love to hear that from my Daddy, of course). It seems that he always places his own emotional needs above those that I have, and I did that, too. I was usually busy making things just the way Daddy wanted them, and I did not feel what I really needed from a father. This evening I noticed that he has, more or less, the same kind of humor as I have and that he is a kind and warm-hearted man. He has,*

127

however, his own shortcomings and neuroses, and that's why he can't see me as the person I am.

The Twins: Anger and Fear

It is obvious that sorrow and joy are each other's opposites. It is not as clear with anger and fear. As I have written before, there is a strong bond between anger and fear. If you have good anger management skills, you can stand firmly on your own two feet. Anger is just a question of showing where you draw the line. If you can do that properly, one of the consequences will be that you experience less fear. In reverse fear, which sometimes originates in the present but is usually somewhere in the past, carries an image of the enemy. After all, if you are scared of somebody, you have already branded him an enemy, and anger is smouldering subconsciously inside you. In Spark of Light Work, it is important to perceive the inextricable connection between anger and fear. If there is anger, there is usually underlying fear, and if there is fear, it is important to find the anger underneath and become aware of it. If, for example, you notice that you keep repeatedly exploding with fury without having the feeling that you are getting somewhere with your development (even if it does give temporary relief), you will have to look at the evasion of the underlying fear. In reverse, if you keep on feeling scared while you are conscious of your fears and keep on reliving them, you will have to set to work with the underlying anger to reach complete healing of the traumas concerned. Anger and fear should both be freed from their strongholds. They should be seen in their connection to each other. Then there will be room for true strength and true freedom.

In the Middle East, we have seen for years that anger and fear are carried to the extreme. The real Work, namely working under your own responsibility and in your own safe place at the expression of old and present pain and thus healing wounds, is avoided there. It is a lesson to us all—do we let our emotions subconsciously and in a projected form have free rein, or do we work in our soul of souls at healing ourselves on the principle that to "enlighten the world, begin with yourself."

The following is a letter from a forty-year-old woman:

> *I was always angry and in revolt ever since my early youth. I kicked against everything and everybody. Only since recently have I been able to find out with whom I'm really angry. Since I started doing my emotional work with you, I have found out that my anger constantly shifts to different people: my father and mother, my brother and sister, primary school, church authorities, lodgers, therapists, myself, welfare workers, ministers, and last but not least: Jesus and God. So I'm really angry at the whole world. If something happens that's not to my liking, I blow my top. It's a nuisance, but it's true.*

> *By using the carpet beater at home again and again and beating and shouting out my fury, I often arrive at a horrible desolation and emptiness. I feel very much alone and abandoned, and I really have the feeling [that] now I'm going to end my life. I think that under all my anger lies the fear of being abandoned. A feeling I'm of no account and don't belong. I feel imperfect, bad, not worthy of love, angry at Life. Angry that I had to come back to this earth, while I probably would rather have stayed with my brothers and sisters Elsewhere. Shame and sorrow because the young girl I once was has been damaged because I let myself be abused so I could belong one way or another. Prostituted myself, more or less, just did what I did for love and attention.*

> *I'm not sure what to do with God. I find that frustrating because I want to feel and understand*

His/Her will and intention with my life. Theoretically and intellectually, I can follow Him/Her quite well, but there is still no Flow. My feeling of joy towards God keeps on being blocked off, but my feeling of anger is doing very well. And I experience that my feeling of anger towards God takes me to the feeling of being abandoned by God. Perhaps that is my resistance to taking my chance with Him/Her. Forgive God—does that sound arrogant? I feel quite a resistance when I tell people I'm angry with God. You are not allowed to—God is Love! God does his best for you! And now that I'm writing this down, I feel another wave of anger. How? Why! And yet, I believe that this lost daughter can only get back home again by constantly ploughing on and working with what there is. I will feel what is underneath my anger, dare to face it, and trust that part of my soul will be healed again.

The Transformation of Hate in Steps

1. Becoming conscious of the ***disguises of hate.*** Become conscious of euphemisms and veiled terms in your linguistic usage. Make a list of people and things you dislike. Exaggerate the irritation which keeps on coming back. Enlargement makes things clear. The hate towards others is part of the process of discovering how much you hate yourself.

2. ***Set your hate in motion.*** Tell yourself that you do not hate—but are very angry. Verbally, you are already setting the hate in motion. Now you must do so!

3. ***See who you are really angry at.*** Put those people on a cushion and tell them what's on your mind. It is possible that the people on the cushion will shift; you might begin with your ex-husband and end with

your father or mother. An example by way of explanation:

A young man came in for therapy and told me that he was very angry with a girlfriend. He had courted her recently, but his love for her was not reciprocated because she felt swamped by him. He grabbed the carpet beater and hit the cushion with a lot of energy. He felt relieved for a while, but did it help him get rid his anger? Only for a little while—until he was rejected again. I invited him to have a look at who it was that he really felt rejected by. We finally arrived at the very first woman in his life—his mother. His anger came out and with that, the tears of a little boy who tried so hard to win his mother's love that she apparently could not give him.

4. ***Find out how much anger from others you encounter in your life.*** If everything is a mirror, it is important to look in that mirror consciously. Do you receive a lot of irritation and anger from your circle of acquaintances? This means that you should look at your own anger.

5. ***Find out about your hidden desires.*** You can accept that you long and yearn for the love of the key figures in your life if you have expressed your anger in the above manner and have perhaps let your tears flow. Your love lies hidden under this yearning! If chronic hate is transformed into acute anger, energy can be freed for more gentle feelings that have been hidden for years and perhaps centuries underneath the hate. In this way, we follow the path to love. If we cope with shadow, light remains. If we cope with hate, love remains. For love is original. Hatred is only love that has been denied, and darkness is light that has been

denied. By rectifying our denied emotions, we free energy and change hate to love. That is the Alchemy of this Work.

Love

A loving person lives in a loving world. A
hostile person lives in a hostile world.
Everyone you meet is your mirror.
~Ken Keyes

Love is often called an emotion. In our earthly reality, hate is the opposite of love. But in the greater cosmic reality, there is no opposite to love, and love is not an emotion but far more than that! It is a state of being. Erich Fromm describes love as "an attitude of the personality acquired by experience," and "Love is not a higher power which descends upon man nor a duty which is imposed upon him; it is his own power by which he relates himself to the world and makes it truly his"[3] Love is an ability and a power that develops to the extent that you digest old pain. Love belongs in the third phase of our outline—there where our soul comes home and where we speak of essence. Love is the harvest after hard Work! On this level, love is the complete acknowledgement of who you are.

This is realized step by step. There is no sudden transition from phase two to three of our model. There is a gradual realization from conditional love to unconditional love, from neurotic love to really free love. While we walk this path of realization of love, we can distinguish different aspects.

From object to ability and from need to love.

Many people think that they love if they have someone to love. If we ask a random selection of people about love, most think of the romantic love between two people. This has usually more to do with gratification than with love. Love is an ability that can be developed and learned by inner Work. It has got nothing to do with an object. It is not even important if there is someone to love. Love is or is not. It is autonomous and wells up from inside as "a source that never dries up," as Jesus once said. The more we create room for it in our overcrowded inner worlds, the more we get to know this love that comes from within, step by step.

We are usually so full of needs which originate in old loss and in experiences that have not been dealt with that there is no place for love. Until now we did two things: we repressed these needs, and we mixed up needs and love. We no longer know what is what. We can only unravel this by getting to know ourselves and by seeing how needy we are and by complete truthfulness with regard to love. For the time being, we should talk about our needs and not too much about love. That has been done so often. Love has to be proven. Love becomes clear when we have cleared out our junk room of old needs and old pain.

Conditional and unconditional love.

In our world, most love is conditional: I love you, if you are nice to me, fulfil my needs, live up to my expectations, do what I say, be who I think you are, etc. We could call this neurotic love based on twisted emotionality and on being unfulfilled affectively. A lot of what people call love is mutual need gratification. There is nothing wrong with this, but by calling it love, we obscure the perception of what love can be, and we miss the necessary differentiation and clarity. Maslow, the founder of humanistic psychology, once distinguished between *deficiency love*, love based on your own emotional deficiency, and *being love*, love from the fullness of Being. This fits in with the third phase of our model. These concepts have not really taken hold.

Most of us received conditional love as children. We had to meet certain conditions to be well liked and deny certain

133

aspects of ourselves to deserve love. This was the way we learned to suppress our vulnerability, our tears, and also our sexuality. If we do not become aware of the path to healing and liberation, we will pass on this story of conditional love, not only to our children, but also to our partners and friends and even to others. After all, as key figures treated us in the important imprint years of childhood, so will we treat ourselves and others. How, in heaven's name, do we stop this process that has been passed on from generation to generation? The only fundamental way I can see is the way I have described in this book and with which I am part of an old mystical tradition that says: chasten, chasten, and yet again chasten. This time chastening will not be an exercise in moral virtue, but a loving clean up.

Prostitution: A cry for help.

In effect, we learn to prostitute ourselves by giving conditional love. We behave as we believe people expect us to behave. If you learned in the past that people loved you if you were not a nuisance and were obedient and helpful towards mother, you will later be inclined to lean over backwards to please your partner and your children. For reasons of clarity, this sounds a bit harsh, but you could say that you prostitute yourself towards your husband and children (and at school and work). You hope to receive real love by acting as you were conditioned to act in the past. As conditional love is never really fulfilling—it is not real love—you could put yourself out for love till doomsday—unless you wake up and realize why you are putting yourself out so much. Someone once said, "There are only two kinds of love on this planet: love and a cry for love." Your step on the path to unconditional love is becoming aware of your cry for love. This unconditional love starts with you. It is important to rectify an upbringing where things were messed up and went awry. This starts by realizing where things went amiss, how you prostituted yourself, and by feeling how this feels.

Professional prostitutes and their clients are an extreme example of love that goes awry. Women's bodies are literally sold for so-called love. Others usually only sell their souls. Professional prostitutes are a good example of how anger is retroflected, which means directed back at themselves. They have usually been wounded at a sexual level. Their repressed anger because of vulnerability in the past is so great that their anger and contempt becomes aimed towards themselves and their customers.

The only way you can cure things that have gone amiss is by loving your whole self, and that includes those aspects your parents did not accept. Only unconditional love has healing power. You may ask how you can feel unconditional love for yourself if you have only known conditional love. If you take the path of emotional clearance and liberation, you will learn, step by step, the path of love for your whole being because you are willing to get to know yourself. It is the path of dismantlement of the conditions that you have learned to put between you and yourself. What you learn, you can unlearn again. Unconditional love is a learning process just like conditional love.

Giving and taking love.

It is often said that giving is easier than receiving. Of course, it is easier; you are in an unassailable position of power when you give. Receiving means opening yourself and being vulnerable. For the neurotic, hurt child within us, this is an alarming and threatening position to have. History could repeat itself! That is what neurosis is: fear of repetition. As a child, you were open and willing to receive. This openness has, alas, often been violated unwittingly. Your childhood has not only brought you beautiful things but also less beautiful ones. Your openness depends primarily on healthy, non-neurotic love you received as a child. What parents think of as love can be experienced by the child as overwhelming and suffocating. Everything depends on the level of emotional health of the parents. If parents are affectively unfulfilled, they might need the child too much for themselves. Under the pretext of love for the child, they win love from the child. There is even a phrase for it: *cuddle to death*. The child then becomes *parentified*: in the emotional sphere, it becomes the parent of the parent. It is very difficult to recognize later on because you have been cuddled so much, it seems that you had a lot of love. As a child, you did not know you were really cuddling your father or mother. You can possibly recognize this by the feeling of emptiness and want that you have. It is confusing for a child and will influence its degree of openness. In adulthood, it will lead to restraint and to the tendency to withdraw when others show their affective feelings. Fear of emotional swamping by a partner can be caused by emotional swamping by the mother or father. Being able to receive love is a learning process that starts very early on at conception. It is susceptible to imprints and experiences during your whole childhood, which can be more or less conscious. It is usually subconscious; neither did you have a mental framework when you were child nor were you in the position to become aware of what was happening.

An emotionally healthy person will be able to not only receive, but also to give love. The loving exchange is on different levels:

1. *Emotional level:* you are able to give your love and receive it instinctively.
2. *Physical level:* you feel at ease with physical manifestations of affection, both in giving and receiving towards men, women, and children. A lot of people have a fixed repertoire in their physical contact with others: kissing each other on the cheek is a well-known one. If you observe yourself and

other people well, you will see and feel how because of a pattern like this, real contact is avoided. The (Dutch) ritual of giving three kisses, in turn, on the cheek really hinders just looking at each other or perhaps just having certain feelings. Real contact is never ritualistic or according to fixed patterns but is original and free of fixed conventions.

3. *Verbal level:* this is about being able to verbalize your love. I love you, I like having you around me, etc. It is important that you can use these words in a non-sexual context.

4. *Sexual level:* the ability to express your love sexually with your partner. That is easier said than done! It means combining sexuality and love within your relationship. Sometimes something is lacking in that sphere, especially with the ones who are the least conscious of this fact! We often see that women react from their heart chakra and that they have difficulty with the chakras in lower regions. With men, it is the other way round. It is important for both to realize the connection between the heart center and the sexual center.

Loving reception.

You, yourself just as much as anyone else in the whole universe, deserve your love and affection.
~Buddha

The loving reception of emotions is the central point under and behind every Work described in this book. Because of the lack of loving reception, things have gone wrong, and because of a loving reception all will be healed again. With loving reception, I mean that all emotions are allowed to be and can come to light if expressed in a harmless way and with wise emotional care. Just carpet beating because of impotent vexation does not help. What helps is saying yes to anger as a way to love and also knowing that there is a great difference between emotion and behavior. You can love your emotion completely but not allow yourself to express it in practice. The person who raped you can be *killed* with great conviction on the cushion, without you doing this in reality. It is also not important if the other notices it or hears it. What is important is that you release your anger, heal, and learn love—not only for yourself, but also for whomever you meet. We can stop the relay race of hate in this way. If we do, we can move forward in our collective evolution. It is all about finding the original love with which this beautiful blue planet was created. We can extract this love from under the dust of our ignorance and hurt. All can be healed and all can be learned by those who want to walk the path of love.

Respect.

I suggest that we have a look at the concept of respect since love is a very difficult concept that is filled in so many different ways. Perhaps we can bring love a bit closer by doing this. We could describe respect as taking the needs, thoughts, ideas, wishes, and preferences of somebody else into account. We take them seriously and value them. This is a much more concrete interpretation than that of love. It also serves as a solid handle for learning. Maslow calls respect "one of the basic needs of humans," together with the need for care, safety, and belonging.

In our current society with its decline in traditional standards and values, respect has become an important topic. Especially in such a busy and overcrowded country as The Netherlands, the demand for respect is not only understandable but also urgent. There is a great demand for respect in the public health services where doctors are sometimes treated in an aggressive manner by their patients on the shop floor, in the street, in the contact between different communities, and especially in schools. Of old, respect was connected with awe—the respect for authorities, for example. Now that that fear is disappearing, respect must come from within. And that is where the shoe pinches: to be able to give respect to someone, you must have received it yourself. If we receive a respectful reception in childhood, we learn to respect ourselves and with that, others. This leads us to the three-fold iron rule: as key figures have treated us, we will treat ourselves and others, too. The most fundamental way to learn respect is by emotionally ploughing through the lack of respect you have had. You can only respect yourself when you have digested all your experiences with lack of respect. In the mean time, we can remind each other what the ingredients of respectful behavior are and teach our children what respectful behavior is. Both ways together will help us further on the way to a respectful society.

Love, Once More

Finally, it becomes clear that Love is the sum of all qualities of existence of the third phase of our transformation model. Sincerity, respect, strength, patience, connection, joy, gratitude, devotion, creativity, and more; together they form Love. It is, therefore, difficult to describe and grasp.

Emotional Work leads us step by step to this Love which can be experienced completely from within and can no longer be put into words. It has become a state of existence that we can experience as moments of intense gratitude or happiness, as a connection with "all that is," or as a deep realization of "being in our truth." Sister emotion can bring us to this love; she is the fuel and motivation is our motor. We need both on the path of realization of love. The 13th century Dutch mystic poetess, Hadewych [4] was forgotten but put this beautifully into words in the following poem:

Whoever strives for the fruition of Love
Shall conquer all his distress;
He whom Love touches cannot die—
Her name is amor, 'delivered from death'—
If he has done what Love commanded
And in this has failed in nothing.
She is the wealth of all things;
Love is that living bread
And above all sweet in taste.

Chapter 12

Sorrow: The Liberation of Depression

*Despair can only be fully conquered, if you live through it
fully.*

Sorrow is the third universal emotion. When you mobilize
the layer of anger within yourself, you will often find
sorrow underneath. Sorrow is, after all, the result of being
hurt. When someone hits you, your first reaction is "Ouch!"
before you, perhaps, hit back. This experience of allowing pain
to be brought to the light is another step on the path to
emotional liberation. But let us begin with the status quo, and
this consists of a hefty fixation.

Depression: Stagnation on Your Path

Depression means a large stagnation in our
development, in our creativity, and in our energy. If we realize
that according to a recent survey, sixteen per cent of the
European population suffers from one form of depression or
another, we can imagine how great a loss of energy, creativity,
but also joyfulness this means to our society. And then we are
not even speaking of all the alcoholics and drug users, whose
addiction is mainly based on feelings of depression. The people
who have their depression neatly under control and are

functioning reasonably are not included in this sixteen per cent. The World Health Organization sent out a warning recently that depression, on a worldwide scale, is becoming public enemy number one. Even more threatening was the conclusion of the WHO that in a few decades, depression will belong to the top three causes of death because fifteen per cent of the patients commit suicide. It is very important to give depressives a good treatment. A health report of the European Union states that ten per cent of young people see themselves as depressed. There are also many symptoms to be found in children that can be recorded as depression. It is time for this fixation to be dealt with. Depression is usually defined as a mood disorder that lasts for a longer period of time and that is characterized by symptoms, such as gloominess, apathy, and lack of interest. As secondary symptoms, we find loss of concentration, sleeping problems, tiredness, irritation, worrying, inability to enjoy things, a feeling of emptiness, and lack of emotion. With more serious forms of depression, we see symptoms such as loss of weight, reduced appetite, constipation, suicidal tendencies, strong feelings of worthlessness, and various vague complaints about pain.

Depression as a Brain Disease

Most dominant schools in the mental health care view depression nowadays as a psychological disorder or a brain disease. Especially the last opinion is gaining ground. The medical school of thought still dominates the field of mental health care. The biological psychiatry is gaining more ground with its assumption that depression is a brain disease.

People are often told by their doctor that they miss a chemical in their brain, namely serotonin, and that when they take a pill, their complaints will soon disappear. The assumption with such theories is that our psyche coincides with our brains, which is a contestable proposition. Our brain is, indeed, the organ with which we think, talk, remember, and feel. Without our brains, we would not be able to do any of that and could not even be robots. Does this mean that thinking and feeling coincide with what is in our brains? Brains have to do with abilities and functions while our psyche has to do with content and consciousness.

As for the pills, the depression comes back quickly when you stop taking them. I once had a woman in therapy who had been taking Valium for ten years; she had started when her eldest son died. When she decided to stop ten years later, the undigested grief came back in all its intensity. Pills are part of the system of repression that we all know too well inside ourselves. Pills are in league with our inner enemy. They help to suppress and dull emotions. The current pill culture is also in league with a society fixated on money and economy, which has its interest in a low sickness absence and quick social readaptation.

Using psychopharmaca for emergencies is fine, for example, for people who have gone berserk and lost all contact with reality and for whom there is no other method. They can also be of help to older people who no longer have the vitality to do intense emotional work or as temporary help in time of need. But besides this, other alternatives should be sought which have an effect on a more fundamental layer. And that is, according to me, the emotional level.

Depression as a Disorder and Problem

The other line of approach in treating depression is usually employed by psychologists. Various large therapy schools can be distinguished in the regular circuit where cognitive behavior therapy is popular at the moment. The latter lends itself to study more easily than other schools and is, according to studies, the most effective. As a consequence of this, it is gaining more ground within the regular mental health care. This method sees depression as a thought and behavior problem. Cognitive therapy consists of a collection of discussion and behavior techniques that are geared towards changing ideas and thoughts. It influences people's (underlying) thoughts and behavior in this way. Originally, behavior therapy was only aimed at behavior that could be observed; however, since the mid-1970's, under the influence of therapists, such as Ellis, the emphasis has been put more and more on the (underlying) thoughts of people. It is mainly about learning to regulate and control emotions. According to this approach, people learn to gain insight into the kinds of emotional reacting, thinking, and feeling that cause depression. This approach also has its shortcomings, since behavior and thinking are rather a derivative of the underlying emotional problems than the problem itself. With methods like these, we do not have enough opportunity to look sorrow in the face. The aforementioned Dan Goleman mentions various strategies to manage feelings of depression. He declares that "depressing thoughts are automatic and penetrate unasked into a person's state of mind. Distraction is a good way of preventing this."[1] This kind of therapeutical advice is a continuation of survival strategies, but I believe that they are not very beneficial to fundamental liberation. Next to observing feelings, he argues for relaxation techniques, distraction maneuvers, pick-me-ups, undermining of underlying thought patterns, and cognitive reconstructing. The latter means trying to see things in a different light. What is missing is emotional digestion.

Insight is a good beginning for a therapy but hardly ever enough to resolve depression and getting blocked energy flowing again. A therapy that only brings insight can, I believe, make the depression worse. Somebody in a support group for the bereaved parents of children who had committed suicide told me that on the one hand, she had received a lot from the sharing of experiences; on the other, she had become more depressed. Emotionally, a lot had been touched upon during talks, but there had not been any room to express intense emotions.

A twofold policy is fashionable: talking and pills. It seems to be a treatment compromise between physicians and psychologists. By doing this, are psychologists renouncing themselves and their own handicraft of the soul more and more? Are they letting themselves be intimidated by fine studies where serotonin deficiency is, indeed, found in people who are depressed? But what came first: the chicken or the egg? Is it possible that due to stagnated emotionality, in this case depression, our whole chemistry changes, including the aforementioned serotonin?

Depression is also seen from the angle of problem-solving. In this case, the actual contents of life's problems are examined: problems with work, problems with relationships, money worries, and problems with the rearing of children. Insight and help with specific problems in life can be a great help in lessening depression. But it is also important that the mechanism of emotional digestion improves so that problem-solving abilities grow and people are less dependent on assistance. Incidentally, this approach is not dependent on intelligence or social class as is often the case with, for example, insight-giving therapies. In this chapter, I give my view of the treatment of depression from the angle of emotions. This is aimed at the qualitative improvement of the mechanism of emotional digestion that lies at the basis of the entire physical and psychological well-being. If our digestion mechanism is optimal, we will not be confronted by problems but by challenges that will shape life according to our own taste and pleasure.

Depression as Stagnated Emotionality

From my point of view and from that of many schools in the alternative circuit, depression is stagnation in the flow of emotional expression. Minor to serious depression stems from years of repression of emotions, such as sorrow, fear, and anger. Emotions have stayed behind for centuries in our

145

evolution. Doing and thinking have taken center place. Emotions were a nuisance and put into suspended mode. We have learned to "close the book" on the past, and devices, such as "what is done, is done" are often used as excuses to by-pass emotions. You can close the book on many things, but not on emotionally undigested issues. It remains as Fritz Perls, the founder of the Gestalt Therapy, called it: "unfinished business."

Briefly and to the point: that which has not been digested emotionally will sooner or later take its toll and demand attention. With emotional digestion, I do not mean just insight into our emotions but finally accepting repressed emotions by crying and expressing anger and fear, as described in other chapters.

Even though emotions, such as fear and anger, have as much to do with depression as sorrow, I will mainly occupy myself with the transforming of depression into sorrow in this chapter. With some people, sorrow will predominate, with others, anger. It is important that both emotions come to light when dealing with depression.

Attachment to Depression

You are the only one who has the key to free yourself from your own prison.

It may sound slightly strange, but attachment really does play a role in depression. There is a certain liking for suffering. We can see this attachment in the theories people have about life: "resign yourself to your lot" or "that's my character" or "that's the way I am." They are, in fact, bromides that betray our attachment to suffering and to things we are familiar with. With this, we really say that "there is nothing to be done about it." We can understand this attachment when we realize that it gives us an old, familiar feeling of safety even if it is false safety. Somebody who had been depressed for a long time put it into words as follows:

"I'm nice and depressed which means; I don't have to live, take steps, show who I am. I'm nice and heavy, nice and guilty, just nicely hanging around."

Usually you can only really feel that attachment when you are on the path to liberating yourself from it. As long as you are not emotionally free, renewal and change will always go hand in hand with fear and insecurity. To come out of your shell of depression, you should stand back from the old and familiar and recognize your attachment to suffering. We can easily see the attachment to suffering at work in the continuation of old pain in a later relationship with a partner. Former experiences may initiate a vicious cycle. A woman who has been sexually abused by her father may marry a man who also sexually abuses her. The old pain is repeated although it is done unwittingly. A man with a mother, who is dominant or emotionally blackmailing, marries the same kind of woman. And so we take our past with us into the present until we become aware and choose something new until we really choose for the here and now. But then it will really start to hurt! After all, only when you become aware, will you feel old pain. This choice will help you further. Only by letting go, can you free yourself from past histories and old pain.

Steps in Moving from Chronic Depression to Acute Sorrow

The only thing you should do with depressive feelings is set the depression in motion. Talking and gaining insight help, but setting your depression in motion is crucial. I have outlined the necessary steps as follows:

1. *You have your own responsibility for your own depression.*

In the first place, you should reclaim your own responsibility for your own fixations and emotions. No longer believe in the accepted paradigm that you are suffering from a disorder or illness. We create everything ourselves. Subscribing to this viewpoint or at least giving it a chance is a big step but also an important 'light switch.' The quality of your life depends on it and perhaps the quantity of your life, too. If you have created your depression, this can be undone—with a little help perhaps, but primarily through your own motivation and efforts. Taking responsibility does not mean that "you've made your bed; now lie in it" but responding to your existence and to the challenges it offers. This first step can remove the first weakening layer of your depression. Then you can rise like a phoenix from the ashes!

2. *Being motivated to liberate yourself*

Declare that you will and shall free yourself from depression, whatever the cost in tears. I do not know if it has been studied, but I do know from practical experience that people who are the most motivated to really change their lives, have the most success.

You could say that lack of motivation lies at the core of the depression and that a call for motivation will be very difficult—probably difficult but not impossible! Under every depression lies enormous energy. Tapping that energy is the trick. Depression is, in actual fact, wrongly aimed energy—everything has turned inwards and is aimed at yourself. You can learn to aim that energy outward in a manner that is not harmful to anyone, and you can learn to make use of it yourself.

3. ***Doing it yourself is not the same as doing it on your own.***

   A lot of people do not know the difference between the word "self" and the word "alone." If you say to people that it might be a good idea to ask somebody to help them, they say that they have to do it on their own. Insight into the difference between the two can help you out of the impasse and spur you on to ask for help. Most people, including myself, need a safe relationship and somebody who is more experienced in this emotional work. It is not easy to see one's own blind spots; however, you will find that once you have learned to set your emotions in motion and to express them in a safe way, the emotions themselves will make a lot clear. A good therapist is someone who makes himself/herself superfluous as soon as possible and gives people tools to work with at home, under their own steam. Once you have had a taste of the power of emotional Work, you can do it on your own.

   It is great when you have friends or a partner who can do this work with you. You do it yourself, but it is nice when a safe other is in the vicinity who can lovingly keep an eye on you and take care of you, so you can let go of all control.

4. ***Take your time and make room for this inner Work.***

   As with all activities, this work will need time and care. Resolve to start as soon as you feel bad tempered, dejected, down, bitter or incomprehensibly tired. Liberation will not come of its own accord. It involves a lot of hard work. You must realize that what you have built up during years and perhaps centuries cannot be undone rapidly. My life companion and I ensure that we tackle our fixations every day. As soon as one of us starts feeling cantankerous, listless, or piqued, the other calls for inner Work. We make room for this in between duties and have a look at what is going on. In this way, we do not lose one precious moment on unnecessary depressions. And we have always been able to earn our daily bread! We have experienced that we receive everything we need if we chose this work. Moreover, so much energy and creativity is released by this Work that we are more and more able to create our whole life as we wish to. Freedom from...gives freedom for..!

5. *Setting your depression in motion*

The key question is, of course, how to transform your depression into acute sorrow and acute anger. Emotion is expression and communication. Here are a few suggestions for setting your depression in motion:

- Go and lie down comfortably: that gives the necessary relaxation and helps you to yield to your inner flow. Focus on your physical sensations, pains, and discomforts. Where physical pain and stress are felt, there you will find repressed emotions. Imagine that you are enlarging the pain and talk to it. Find your body's message.

- Lay one hand on your solar plexus (abdomen) and the other on your heart chakra. Ask the Loving Light your guides or guardian angel to send you energy by means of your hands so your solar plexus can relax and no longer be

150

cramped. If you learn to relax in that area, emotions that are stuck will come to the light more easily.

- Let someone give you a massage and allow yourself to melt. I do not mean primarily the work of a physiotherapist or a sports masseur/masseuse, but somebody who can help you transform your tension into emotion. Doing this with your partner is not only good for this emotional Work but may also help to put your relationship and your sexuality on a higher plane.

- Using muscle tests or a biotensor is a very handy tool if you want to know quickly what is happening in the inner self. With a muscle test, also called kinesiology, you can test what is still subconscious. Kinesiology is based on the fact that although we already know everything inside us, but we have lost the memory of it. A difference in muscle tension can indicate what is going on. It is a simple technique that, in principle, anyone can learn. It is a pity that many kinesiology courses are so technical and extensive that they are only of interest to people who wish to work therapeutically with others. It would be good if there were more courses where basic techniques are taught and where these are geared as much as possible to emotional work at home. This could be a great tool for everyone! There is more on this subject in Chapter 25.

- Put music on that moves you and can help you in this Work. I have always been enormously helped by music. Sometimes it was Verdi, sometimes Bach or opera, and sometimes

Russian Folk music, which is very emotionally charged.

• The quickest way to set your emotions in motion is breathwork. During our lives we have learned to restrain our emotions and to suppress them by holding our breath and making it shallow. By intensifying your breath, you will undo the restraint step by step and transform your fixations into emotions. If it is done properly, a lot of old pain will surface, long forgotten memories and painful moments that you could not cope with as a child or did not want to know about as an adult.

• A practical way to feel more is to enlarge your vague feelings and give them a name. You feel bad-tempered and down; you don't say to your partner that you are just a bit grouchy, but you enlarge the feeling. You tell yourself or your partner, who functions as therapist for the moment, that you are really fed up, hate everything and everybody, the whole world, etc. If you have to, go and get a carpet beater, and have a nice go at the sofa! By allowing yourself to fly into a rage, you may burst into tears and feel that every thing is too much for you and realize how much you force yourself to do. Perhaps, eventually, your exacting father or mother will turn up or you will see images of yourself as the eldest in a large family where you were overburdened and did not have enough time to play or do what you wanted. Starting from this emotion, you may be able to make a different choice in life and make sure that that overburdened girl learns to enjoy herself!

• This brings me to a different point: almost all of us have been taught as children to prematurely explain our feelings at a time in which we still were not able do so. Because of this, many adults wonder, as soon as they feel tears, why they are crying. And because the answer is not always immediately clear, they turn off the waterworks. A "why" always leads to a "because." It leads you towards using your brain while you were trying to get a bit "lower down." It is a trick to teach yourself to feel again without immediately having to know why you are crying: "I'm sad and I'm crying, and I don't know why and that's all right." Only when you feel the depth of your emotions will you notice that images and sentences emerge that give an indication and clarification of these emotions. Clarification is really important because it is about both tears and awareness. There are people who say they cry a lot without knowing why. Quite often they feel no relief whatsoever. This can mean two things: you cry because you are angry and cannot express this anger, or you do not cry properly. Tears start to flow, but the area of your emotional body, the area of the abdomen, does not begin to move. A lot of my therapeutical work was about teaching people to cry properly, to cry their hearts out because that would help them further!

6. *Learn to love your tears.*

Your tears are an aid and a sign that you are going to melt. Tears help you to become mild and compassionate for yourself. Tears are the ultimate tool to cope with life's pain and tribulations. Realize how you call your tears and how often you use the negative word "blubber" instead of crying or say the phrase: "Crying is feeling sorry for yourself."

This is a message a lot of us carry with us. I think that you ought to feel sorry for the sad child inside yourself that never had the room to emotionally digest his/her experiences of life. Give that child room and a loving reception now!

"Big boys or girls don't cry." "Crying is weak." This imprint has been given to many by parents and educators who found tears too much of a nuisance and too much of a confrontation. "Keep your tears for later" is another phrase, and you can fill in the ones you have heard yourself. Ignatius van Loyola, the founder of the Jesuit Order and a great mystic was so happy with his tears that the notes in his diary got shorter and became more and more abbreviated to: "Tears, tears in abundance!" Good mystics always called it the "gift of tears" in those days. I think that we are probably only really emotionally healthy when we cry as easily as we laugh. We do not really know how emotionally deadened we have all become.

Through the centuries we have become so used to this dulling and numbing effect that we have started to think that we and life itself are like this. But that is not true at all! We must start to learn, and that it is possible in this day and age. This age is unique in its possibilities to come to terms with our emotionality and with ourselves.

And remember that joy and sorrow are opposites. This means that there is only joy to the extent that you have a connection with your sorrow and have digested it emotionally. Many people may be familiar with this; after a fit of weeping that brings emotional digestion and clarity, it is good to have a laugh again. During our Spark of Light weeks, there is a lot of crying, a lot of carpet beating, and a lot of laughter. By doing this work of liberation with humor and with laughter and tears, "the joy of clearance work," as we call it within the Spark of Light Work, comes into being. Depressions do not remain depressions but become transformed to a flow of inner experiences and feelings that make us, step by step, a freer and happier people who understand what life is about. Coping with sorrow makes us compassionate and mild. It helps us chose what we really want. "This is what I want, not that." We choose whatever fulfils us. We become the creator of our life!

7. *Finally* it is good to remember that when you relive old pain you have four advantages that you did not have before:

   1) You can now lovingly receive your feelings;

   2) There are now two of you: your inner child and your adult self;

   3) You can now choose with whom to share your experiences;

   4) Your sadness is about things that happened long ago. It is all about overdue maintenance work. It is all about what I sometimes jokingly call "plumbing work"—the opening up of blocked water pipes.

Denial and Projection of Sorrow

Next to the denial of sorrow that leads to depression, there is also another type of sorrow, namely the projection towards another person. One form expresses itself in

155

sentimentality. When you see a touching scene on television, you wipe away a tear. You do not allow it to seep into your consciousness and then realize that the images you were touched by have anything to do with you. You leave the sadness outside of yourself and deny that it is your sadness.

You can find a second type of denial of sorrow in *indifference.* Indifference is a hardening and a denial of your own vulnerability; it is a survival strategy that came into existence due to an abundance of pain.

Another type is often seen within the current spirituality of the New Age. They speak simply about *taking over sorrow* from another person. It is said that it is possible for you to be so sensitive and open that you take over another person's energies. There are all kinds of visualization methods from roses to glass partitions to protect you from the negative energies of another—a denial with a New Age veneer. What emerges from the large sales figures of books with tips for similar energetic safeguards is the need for an excuse for not having to take responsibility for one's own feelings and energies.

In actual fact, what is happening is an attempt to stop the flow of energies between people. We could also learn from this "flow" and take responsibility for what we, ourselves, feel. When you are in a group of people, and you feel yourself becoming sad when another person talks about something sad or when they express sadness, there is always a "click" with your sadness—even if it is not yet clear which sadness that is. People who want to stay unaware and who deny their own sadness will say that they feel or "take over" the sorrow of the other person. In almost a hundred per cent of the cases, there is denial and projection of one's own sorrow. Only those who have digested their own sorrow emotionally, can, for a moment, take over the sadness of another in full awareness. They can weep on behalf of the other when the other cannot weep as yet. There is no question here of taking things over unawares but of conscious emotional management in the service of the other. This kind of mastery is thin on the ground and can seldom be found, especially in the case of people who say they are sensitive. Emotional mastery is the result of profound and thorough emotional Work that has a healthy, well-founded basis with which you can stay within your own energy and in connection with the energy of others in all situations. It that case, nothing is denied—not of yourself or another person.

Identification with Gravity: The First and Last Depression

A song of regained Lightness:

I am made of stardust. Ultimately I am Light.

I walk this earth, but I am not heavy.

Down in the depths of our personal, individually colored depression lies one mutual depression: our separation from the Light. It is the consequence of our identification with gravity. As spiritual beings, we once came from the cosmos to live here on earth. We wanted, each from our own background, to take part in the material possibilities earth had to offer. In this process of becoming denser and more compressed, we lost contact with the cosmos and its inhabitants. We lost the emotional connection with our source and with our higher self. We only experienced gravity within the atmosphere of our earth to which we acclimated after many lives. The gnawing feeling that something was missing, remained.

All religions originate from this feeling of the loss of connection. Religion became an expression of our longing for connection, for our true home. All kinds of rituals and theologies were devised to build this lost bridge again. Only one thing was forgotten which is very important to the success of the bridge—the reliving of the original depression. This "reliving" gives us what no other ritual or dogma can offer: the liberation of the identification with gravity. A depression is, after all, a fixation that keeps all energy around certain subjects in its dark hold. Where there is a depression, there is no room for light. If you dare to relive this fundamental depression of being cut off from your source, you can exchange identification with gravity for identification with light. And that will not be easy! This fundamental depression goes further and deeper than all the depressions at the level of your personality. It lies at the basis of all other depressions. The eventual gold of your liberation is held within the process of living through this depression—the enduring and real connection with Loving Light.

Chapter 13

Joy: The Harvest of the Work

Will it come, or will it not
The day joy increases,
The day sorrow lessens?
~Gunnar Ekehöf

Joy and sorrow are polar forces. Without joy, there is no sorrow, and without sorrow, there is no joy. They belong together so they can find out about themselves. If you have never known sorrow, you will never feel the depth of joy. If you do not know joy, a contrast with sorrow will not exist. Without these two, there will be a grey middle area without any ups or downs. Many people live in that grey area. The primary reasons for this are denial and repression of sorrow. To the extent that sorrow is denied, joy will also be denied. I will explain this by using a diagram. In life there are fluctuations, wave-like motions. The highs are joyful moments; the lows are sorrowful ones. If we level off the lows because we do not want to feel sorrow, the highs will be levelled, too. The highs and lows disappear in this way. Does this sound familiar? Perhaps not if you are used to the grey middle area and think that it is normal. Perhaps you have a lot of fun with your colleagues at work or with your family, but is that really joy from within, without any outward cause?

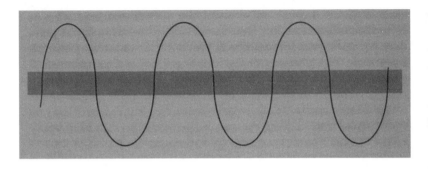

If you level off the lows, you level off the highs and end up in a grey middle area.

Connecting with Your Joy

There are many ways to connect with your joy. Here are a few of the ways:

1. ***Liberation of your sorrow.***

    To feel more joy in your life, you will have to work with your sorrow. A connection with joy will come into being when you let your sorrow come to the light. Usually people try to experience more joy by tinkering with joy: doing more fun things, going out more, going to amusement parks, and looking for more entertainment. More, more, more...it will not work because joy is then connected to something in the outside world which creates dependency and does not satisfy us within ourselves.

    "Wherever you go, you always take yourself with you" is an often-used expression. Real joy is won from the experience of sorrow. Joy is transformed sorrow and has hardly anything to do with the outside world.

2. *Ferreting out your inner child.*

During breathwork people often scream with laughter, a sign that repressed fun is coming to the surface. Many of us take life too seriously. There is usually a great divide between life as a child, where playing is the main thing, and life as an adult, where working and toiling is what we should be doing. The real art of a free and joyful life is connecting the freedom and responsibility of the adult to the playfulness of the child. And that is where the problem lies. We have lost a healthy emotional management together with the connection to our inner child. After all, when you repress unpleasant emotions, such as fear, sorrow, and anger which stem from your childhood, not only does your joy die, but you also lose contact with your inner child. I regard the saying: "Unless ye become as little children, ye cannot enter the kingdom of heaven" as one of the most important messages from Jesus. There is a great difference between remaining a child and becoming a child once more. You remain a child when you cannot emotionally digest old sorrow from your childhood. You will then remain emotionally dependent on other people and expect them to fulfil your affective needs. This childishness is often not seen because of the mask of adulthood. You become a child when you do inner emotional work thoroughly and in the proper way. You heal your traumatized, hurt child so the free, playful, and pure child is given room again and can live. Life becomes one big game, which can be played, as an adult, in a serious and dedicated way. This seriousness is not heavy, but enlightened by a light-hearted spirit. In this way, child and adult live life hand in hand. Profound joyfulness is what results.

161

3. *Following your senses.*

A third way is following your senses. Your senses are organs that enable you to have direct contact with your environment. They allow you to feel, hear, see, smell, and taste. Because of the loss of your childlike, direct way of dealing with reality, the contact with your environment, which is also your breeding ground, goes via mental processes. And that is an enormous detour! A lot of immediate joy is lost because of this detour. You cannot smell the fresh northerly wind or the sultry southern breeze. You do not register the beauty of a butterfly but think "That's a swallowtail." You do not really feel the other person anymore because of your anxieties and associations. You do not hear the birds singing due to all the thoughts in your head. You can hardly listen to music without your reason interfering annoyingly. And this interference does not seem annoying anymore. You are used to it. Because of upbringing and school, you have been taught to primarily use your mind, and you do not even realize that another way of making contact is possible.

With your mind, you can solve problems and puzzles. Your senses are meant for enjoyment. Your senses will bring you in contact with beauty. When you learn enjoyment again, the possibility of feeling profound joy for "what there is" will present itself.

Following your senses can also mean *sensing* what is good for you and doing what you want to do. Most people get up on their hind legs when they hear this: "That's impossible!" and "But what will it lead to?" Yet I challenge everybody to try it! I have tried it out on almost everything. There will always be a moment when you feel like tidying the room because it has become an enormous mess. And then it's time to doubly enjoy the big difference. You can start with simple things and see if it suits you and then expand this "doing what you want to do" further. Many things are not that important. Formulating a new hierarchy of values and choices will help to create more room to sense what is good for you. This does not mean that you will be able to reap rewards quickly. During my time at secondary school, I did not always feel like going there but I wanted my freedom, so I knew that after my exams, I would be able to study and that was what I really did find interesting. Realizing to which extent you live your life according to the expectations of others instead of doing what you want to do, can be an eye opener for "joie de vivre."

I notice in our Spark of Light work that although people have been made neurotic, an important part is still undamaged and pure. Recognizing that pure part of yourself offers the chance to live that part. This pure inner child may ask you which joy is above all external influence. Deep inside, you know what that joy is.

Chapter 14

The Entwining and Stratification of Emotions

A
s I have stated earlier, it is actually not possible to neatly separate our emotions as I have done in the four preceding chapters. In this short chapter I will indicate the various hybrids and how you can liberate yourself from them. As long as feelings stay entwined, they will paralyze you. It is, therefore, important to unravel the entwining of two feelings and allow them into your consciousness *next* to each other and usually one *after* the other.

Nausea and Revulsion: The Entwining of Fear and Anger

Fear and anger that have become entangled in a ball of pent-up emotions are often expressed as revulsion and aversion. Nausea and headaches may accompany this. You may come into contact with revulsion that is enclosed in the stomach area when you mobilize your nausea by putting your fingers in your throat and bringing the peristaltic movement about (the constriction and relaxation of the wall of the stomach and intestine). Vent your feelings in words and see for what or whom you feel revulsion. If you follow this path, you usually end up with anger that was held in the grip of fear.

Express this anger by using the carpet beater and the cushion as described elsewhere.

Ambivalence: The Entwining of Love and Hate

We all know ambivalence. The ones from whom we expect the most, have disappointed us the most. The one we love, we also often hate the most. We say that love and hate are close to each other. We use an important escape route so as not to have to set old anger towards our parents in motion— namely, the inclination to put the emphasis on the good. But it is impossible to cross off the sweet against the bitter. As long as you do not allow the knowledge that you have two feelings, one of love and one of hatred to penetrate your consciousness, you will remain paralyzed. It is important to let both feelings in, one after the other, within the Work. I often invite people to put all the feelings of love and the good things your parents have done in a corner of the room. Nobody needs to touch that; it was real and good, and it can stay. In this way you can create room to completely accept the feeling of anger and indignation about the things that were not right. You will notice that you will love your parents more when you liberate yourself from your old pain. That is one of the rewards of Spark of Light Work; we can feel the love that was snowed under by old cold, anger, and sorrow. Many people visit their parents in a nursing home out of a sense of duty. If you notice that this is what you are doing, it is good to mobilize your old anger under your own responsible supervision and find love again.

The same entanglement between love and hate is also to be found in other relationships, especially in the relationship with your partner. Here it will help, too, if you keep both feelings separate and let them both be: "I love you, and sometimes I'm really angry with you..."

Wavering Between Longing and Anger

Another entangled ball is to be found with your little inner child that was so disappointed that it has decided: "I'll do it on my own. I don't need anybody anymore." You have closed off the fulfilment of your affective longings because of this anger. Once, it was the only way to survive and now, as an adult, you want it to be different. But when you are not conscious of this inner tangle of anger and longing and have not unraveled it, the closing off will carry on and with it the feeling of being unfulfilled, of fundamental loneliness. The tangle will be taken with you into all your further relationships, especially your intimate ones, even if you would like it to be different. It is clear that something can only be healed where it went wrong. For that reason going back in time is an essential part of the Spark of Light Work. Within the Work, you will again let the anger and longing in, one after the other. Usually anger will be first because anger is stopping the longing from being allowed in.

Intermingling of Sorrow and Anger

There are two possibilities here: ***sorrow covers up the anger*** or the anger covers up the sorrow. Let us first look at the case in which sorrow represses anger. We often see that both repressed sorrow and anger play a major role in depression. As sorrow is less of a taboo, anger is transformed into sorrow. Women have this version more often than men. Women take on the role of victim more often than men; this stems from their second-class position. It is important to be able to distinguish properly between sorrow and anger—between when are you sad and when are you sad while you are really very angry. Recognizing and acknowledging anger is a good first step. Becoming strong is the key word here.

The second version: ***anger covers up the sadness.*** This intermingling is to be found in people for whom it is easier to

167

become angry than to become sad. They have a problem with vulnerability and transform this easily into irritated and angry behavior. This version is, I believe, found more often in men. Men, in our culture, have often been denied soft manifestations of their feelings. Boys are not allowed to cry and are supposed to function well as men. They also show more macho behavior among themselves. Liberation from certain patterns is, once again, about learning to distinguish between what anger really is, and which anger is sorrow. Melting and becoming soft are the key words here.

The Sisters Called Arrogance and Shyness

Arrogance is a masking of shyness and really covers up fear. You put yourself above others because you feel that you are really below them. The latter is difficult to live wit,h so you cover up your behavior with the opposite. Another version is grinning while you really want to cry. Or you stare at somebody intently so you will not feel your shyness. The first step is to recognize this; the second is to set the underlying anger in motion.

The Stratification of Emotions

We can picture our warehouse of emotions as a space with a large rack with various drawers and boxes. Everyone has a different warehouse. The rack has many layers and subdivisions that are connected to life experiences. One person may have fear at the top with anger underneath and sorrow underneath that again with joy as the bottom drawer. With a different experience, there will be anger at the top and fear and sorrow underneath. Fixations are usually at the top. There will be a sequence from contempt to anger with a feeling of liberation or power underneath. Or there may be one from shame and fear to anger, after which a feeling of strength emerges. It is a very complex rack that is not classifiable with our power of reason. The emotions make a natural

168

classification that fits the person you are. To put in order, change, and arrange this warehouse anew, we need the emotions themselves. They will make the necessary shifts where we set our emotions in motion. This organizing is called emotional digestion and causes all drawers, even the hidden ones, to become known, step by step.

The picture I am painting is meant to make the process of digestion and the resulting emotional management visible— a complex matter where emotions lead us and help us put things in order. We shall now open the drawers one by one.

Chapter 15

The Curse of Guilt and the Blessing of Emotional Digestion

*The feelings underneath the guilt must move because the
feelings must move the guilt out.*
~Ceanne deRohan

Guilt is one of the greatest barriers in your development. You will be stagnated by it and kept in the grasp of smallness and fear. Guilt restrains and stops you from living fully. It paralyzes your spontaneity. It is the death of life. Guilt stems from the inner confrontation with parental do's and don'ts. It is the voice of your parents, educators, priests, and ministers that you hear in your mind. Freud called that the Super-ego. Not obeying the voice of the Super-ego from which the conscience stems, makes you feel guilty. The most important consequence of guilt is that it stops you developing a healthy feeling of self-respect and love for yourself. With love, there is no room for guilt.

171

If we were to interview people about guilt, perhaps most would say that they are not troubled by it. Yet, this earth is riddled by guilt. We shall have a look if we can clarify this a bit more.

Three steps are needed to liberate us from this curse:

- Recognition
- The intent to free yourself
- Experiencing the underlying emotions

Step One: Recognition of the Feelings of Guilt

Everyone who has ever done thorough therapy discovers how much guilt he or she carries. Many may not have had any knowledge of this beforehand, but it subconsciously played a part in complaints, such as depression. Why are we hardly aware of this feeling of guilt?

Lack of awareness of guilt.

Guilt is stagnation. Feelings of guilt only become clear when you examine your emotions and bring them to light. An example may illustrate this: a young woman found out during Spark of Light work that she was a disappointment in the eyes of her father because she was a girl and not the boy he had wanted. After working through the sorrow and anger, she realized how much this subconscious attitude of her father's had made her timid and shy and that, in all reality, she felt guilty because she was a girl.

Another reason why we have so much trouble recognizing the guilt in us is because our whole human society has become so *moralistic* that we no longer recognize how artificial it is. Religion, as a natural need to connect people with their origin, has become a belief that is connected more with morals and dogmas than with religious inspiration. When a man with a strict Reformed background happens to see beautiful women passing by when he is at an outdoor cafe, he hardly dares to openly enjoy the sight. According to his religious upbringing, even thinking about these women is a sin. This is the way guilt is cultivated. Many people remember from their childhood how guilty they felt if they bit the host by accident or had something to eat before Holy Communion. As adults, we may be able to laugh about it, but the child within us was brought up on emotional imprints that gave us those nonsensical guilty feelings. It started a trend of being careful and looking at the expectations of others. It has affected our spontaneous way of reacting and our love for ourselves.

If a child is proud of himself/herself and shows that spontaneously, mother often reacts, "You are getting too big for your boots." That is guilt at work. You are offered a tasty chocolate and when you accept, somebody says, "Think of your figure." That is where guilt is born. You do not feel like cleaning up after a meal, and your mother says in a resigned voice, "I'll do it." You visit your parents regularly and they say, "You haven't been here for a long time." Guilt is being bred here. Exclamations such as "What kind of daughter are you?", "How could you do that to me?" and "How do you think I feel?" are all the same kind of thing.

Non-verbal, subtle, and indirect accusations are sometimes worse, especially those we experienced as children. This made one person exclaim, "I wish they had beaten me. At least I would have known what was wrong." The next story may clarify the atmosphere of indirectness.

> *I could feel my mother's unspoken reproach if I was boisterous. She was not happy. If my mother ever happened to be elated, my father started to look mean because of the anger he was restraining. He expressed it by belittling remarks, so the fun was soon over for my mother.*

There are many expressions that lead us to the disclosure of our guilty feelings. For example, we hear things like "If you are born poor, you will remain poor all your life," "He that will not stoop for a pin will never be worth a pound," "Little pigs have big ears," "One good turn deserves another," "Promise is debt." It has all so subtlety become part of our language that we do not notice the accusations anymore. Moreover, it is often said with a smile, and that puts us on the wrong track. Another thing, have you noticed how often you unnecessarily say "Sorry"? I received the following message:

> *Now that think about it, I realize how often I felt guilty as a child when I had done something that was not allowed, and I had apparently not thought about it. When I stayed out playing too long and had really forgotten the time, I was punished and was told that I had probably forgotten on purpose and that it was my own fault that I was punished. My own brothers and sisters could heighten the effect by saying that it was my fault we were not allowed outside after dinner for a week. When I was married, I once knocked something off the wall, and my husband was startled by the frightened expression on my face. I suddenly realized that I was full of guilty feelings.*

Step Two: Intention and Focus

Freedom from the power of guilt.

The second step is the intention to free yourself from the power of guilt. With Spark of Light Work, the firm decision to become a free person is of paramount importance. You really have to want to do it. Perhaps the knowledge that life will present lessons anyway will help you. That is the rule of energy and karma. The only choice you have is to learn voluntarily or otherwise be forced to learn. I can tell you that voluntarily learning is much nicer. You will find the dark side of yourself, your less nice, repressed side, but also your hidden possibilities and talents. When I had intensely ploughed through and emotionally digested my last past life where I had died in Auschwitz, my hidden need to write came to light. This book is one of the rewards. When you do not go forward to meet your shadow, it will bother you, and you will have to learn through the trials and tribulations of life. Ursula LeGuin wrote a wonderful book about this.[1]

Once when I was abroad, I was attacked in the street by three men. One threw me on the ground. The other covered up my eyes, and the third ran off with my bag. Although I emptied my bladder from pure fright, I got up and ran after them. A passer-by who bumped into one of the thieves was warned by my hoarse shouting, and this brave man grabbed my bag from him without thinking. I have thought long and hard about which meaning this attack had for me. I was, in any case, happy that I had immediately stopped myself becoming a victim; I had changed that into successful decisiveness and had not allowed myself to become paralyzed with fear. And yet, there was a message there. I had always had a naive view of the evil in the world. I always wanted to see the good in people. Therefore, I was not on guard when someone wanted to play a nasty trick on me. Often, I could and would not be able to see it. It was the little girl in me saying, "Mamma, why do they do that?" when children wanted to fight. I had to experience that there is light and dark on this planet. It is true that dark is light which has not yet been kindled but nevertheless, it is darkness. Not closing my eyes to what happened and fully learning about reality was a good experience. As I already knew about the use of the carpet beater, I had emotionally digested the experience after a couple of weeks. It gave me a more realistic view of life while I did not loose my general trust in people.

The advantage of learning voluntarily is that you become the manager of your own life. By stepping forward bravely to meet and investigate everything that is within you, you receive more "light switches" and everything in and around you becomes lighter. If you decide to do this, you will learn to focus on it more and to see everything you do in the light of this Work. This focus helps you see what is important in life. It helps to make a hierarchy of values and to act accordingly.

Step Three: Experiencing Underlying Emotions

The third step is about setting the emotions that underlie the guilt in motion and awakening them. We usually see guilt as the result of wrong behavior: "I have done something wrong." I distinguish four types of guilt:

Existential guilt;
Instilled guilt or indoctrinated guilt;
Neurotic guilt: this is often a feeling of guilt that is not guilt but hidden feelings; and
Subconscious guilt from previous lives.

With regard to all four types of guilt, I will describe how to set your feelings of guilt in motion and liberate yourself from them.

1) Existential guilt.

This is, in effect, the result of not meeting the basic standards of respect for another person. It is about crossing certain limits and the violation of the right of the other to be who he/she is and as he/she is. In the most extreme case, it is about denial of the other person's right to exist. This can degenerate into murder and manslaughter or sexual abuse and rape.

The only way to liberate yourself from actual guilt is by acknowledging the guilt, living through remorse, and gaining an insight into your own motives and emotions. After all, behind all existential guilt, there is neurosis, a contorted feeling that needs to be worked out. Finally, we will arrive at neurotic feelings of guilt.

This reminds me of the man who, as a boy had a dream in which a selection was made between "the good and the bad." He was assigned to the bad and taken to hell by the police. In the following years, he leaves home because of problems there, starts taking drugs, becomes a criminal, and does everything God has forbidden. Now at fifty he is in therapy for the first time, and he thinks that the dream was a kind of prophecy. He still feels very guilty about the people he has robbed and is frightened of dying and going to hell.

In this case, the breakthrough in his guilt and fear was not the living through of his guilt emotionally, but the insight that the dream had not been a prophecy but an expression of his feeling of badness before he had really done bad things. When I asked about his youth, he told me that he had forgotten a lot, but he remembered that his father had often beaten him. If he had been naughty, he had to stand with his arms up in front of a big cross on the wall of the living room. If his arms became tired and he let them drop, his father would stand behind him and beat him.

However, this man did not have the slightest idea that such mistreatment had given him the imprint that he was bad. I am often astounded how adults frequently see the mistreatment that they received as "normal." I only see emotions being set in motion when I express my horror at child abuse and show my compassion with the child. People are so used to it. This subconscious imprint that was far too painful to be aware of and for which there was no loving reception, led him, as a teenager, to subconsciously showing how bad he was. Only when emotions are allowed in, can you break out of your habituation and emotional imprints. The solution to his guilt and fear lie with the awareness and healing of his anger towards his father.

Remorse.

If you have overstepped the limits of another person and made a mistake, feeling remorse is not only a way to change your behavior but it is also a way to reconciliation with yourself and the other.

My former teacher Osho said in his commentary on the Gospel of Thomas and on the subject of remorse: "Remorse is beautiful if it comes from the heart. If that remorse wells up from the heart, it will cleanse you. Nothing cleanses as well as remorse."[2] Being remorseful means waking up from your stupor and stupefaction. Being remorseful means gaining insight into the foolish things you have done in the past and present, so you can then say, "I'm sorry." These three words are essential in social intercourse where people have truly overstepped bounds. They offer the possibility of reconciliation. A mother, whose only daughter was murdered, said the following in a newspaper interview about the probable murderer who had been found nine years after the murder:

Sometimes I hope the day will come when I can forgive him. But he will have to talk first. I want him to wholeheartedly say 'I'm sorry.' I can go on then. Everybody makes mistakes, but take responsibility in heaven's name. He must tell us what happened. Punishment is not really important then.

Victim-Offender Mediation is a fantastic initiative where contact between victims and offenders is mediated and supervised by a professional social worker. Often mothers of victims seek contact with the perpetrator, but offenders sometimes want to meet the victims and their families.

Neurotic feelings of guilt (more about this below) often make it very difficult for people to say "I'm sorry" when it is really applicable. This is because neurotic guilt is really anger turned inwards. When neurotic guilt has not been resolved, both types of guilt, neurotic and existential, are entwined and prevent each other from coming to light. The more you heal your neurotic, unreal guilt, the easier it becomes to face your mistakes and to say "I'm sorry" where it is appropriate. As long as we have not healed our neurotic guilt, remorse can only be felt with difficulty. Is this the reason why it is so difficult to solve conflicts and transform these into reconciliation?

2) Instilled guilt.

Guilt is the trade secret of all so-called established religions: create guilt in people, make them feel bad about themselves, don't let them be respectful of their own lives, let them feel condemned, let them feel deep down that they are ugly, that they are not of any worth, that they are dust, and then, of course, they will be ready to be guided by any fool. They will be more than ready to become dependent, in the hope that: 'somebody will lead us to the ultimate light.'.
~Osho

When I think about indoctrinated guilt, I always think about the story of the woman who was brought up to be Dutch Reformed and had a children's book with the following poem by Jacob Revius (1586-1658):

> *It was not the Jews, Lord Jesus, that crucified you*
> *Nor those that traitorously brought you to justice*
> *Nor those that humiliated you and spewed in your face*
> *Nor those that bound and wounded you.*
> *It was not the soldiers with their fierce fists*
> *Holding up their staffs and hammers*
> *Or erecting the cursed wood on Golgotha*
> *Or playing dice, quarrelling about your robes.*
> *It was I, O lord, I who did that to you.*
> *I am the heavy cross upon your back*
> *I am the heavy rope with which you were bound*
> *The nail, the spear, the scourge that flailed thee*
> *The bloody crown you carried on your head:*
> *Alas, all of this happened for my sins*

179

And that was put in a children's book! The sentences that she had remembered well were: "It wasn't the Jews that crucified you, Lord Jesus; it was I who did that to you." This woman was, thank goodness, very critical and obstinate as a child, and she had secretly burned her catechism book at the back of the garden. Such theories are stamped in thoroughly during a Christian upbringing. Dogmas such as original sin, the "through my own fault, my own great fault" (*mea culpa*), in the Catholic Mass, the emphasis on sin, guilt, and confession in almost all Christian worship have all led to guilt being an important theme throughout our whole Christian culture. This has evoked a lot of fear of life, constraint, and self-hatred in many people. In The Netherlands suicide was, for a long time, the highest in strict Protestant areas, such as the islands of Zeeland.

The only way to be rid of this indoctrinated guilt is to set the anger that you have in motion and express it. Imagine putting your educators, priests, vicars, and God Himself on a cushion, in your own home or in a safe therapeutical setting, and telling them everything that pops into your head. Beating with a carpet beater and scolding helps not only to verbalize the anger but to let it come to the surface from every fiber of your being. Everything is permitted on that cushion, as long as you do not harm other people or yourself. Within that safe agreement, you can let it all out and bring the anger to expression unchecked. It is possible that you will feel sad after such a burst of anger because of all the years you have been weighed down by such a nonsensical load of guilt that smothered your spontaneity, made you afraid, and on top of all that, stopped you loving and accepting yourself. Let your tears flow...and comfort the inner child with loving acceptation.

Religious imprints are stronger than other forms of indoctrination, such as social and political ones. With religious imprints, guilt is mixed with love and also with something that is often felt to be beautiful and good, such as a service of worship. Moreover, it is not only the parents that are part of the indoctrination but also figures of authority, such as priests, vicars and teachers. And how are you supposed to cope with that as a child? You just had to stomach it. All that guilt lies heavily on people for years; what should you do when you have eaten something that is bad for you? Correct—just put your finger down your throat and throw up!

We often do not realize that we have been brainwashed. Our whole culture, our whole planet has been poisoned by this. We have perhaps changed our ideas and theologies and many have turned their backs on the church. In some churches things have changed. But what remains is the habitual stomaching of certain things because of subconscious guilt. I will give some examples. How often do you feel guilty when you say no to somebody's suggestion? How often do you listen to authorities more than you do to yourself from a deeply rooted feeling that the other party knows better? How often do you have guilty feelings (which stem from indoctrinated altruism) when you choose for yourself? How difficult do you find it to say "I"? How difficult is it to love yourself and to see yourself as fundamentally inclined to all good when you have been taught that you are a sinner and "inclined to all evil"?

3) Neurotic guilt.

This covers the largest part of guilt and lies at the basis of the two formerly mentioned types. After all, lack of respect for another, as found within existential guilt, has its origin in a distorted mind. If you rape another person, you do that because something is very wrong within your psyche. But also lighter forms of disrespect, and everybody knows these, stem from neurosis, from where we are not yet light. The problem with neurotic behavior is that it leads to really wrong behavior, which makes us feel guilty again and again. It works as a vicious circle—because you feel guilty, you do the wrong things, and then you feel guilty again.

A friend of mine, who does not want to work with himself, feels guilty every time he visits his old mother. He did his best in the beginning. He loved her after all. After a little while, he started to get irritated with her nagging and with her meddlesome behavior and started to be nasty to her. He always leaves with a guilty feeling and tells himself that he will be nicer to her next time. He does not succeed in doing this because of the undigested anger towards his mother that he subconsciously carries on his back.

Guilt really means accusing yourself because you do not dare to accuse others, who are usually parents, educators, and God. Essentially, you are frightened to blame people who are important to you. A lot of people will now say, "Yes, but my parents meant well." Yes, they did.

- Our parents have given us the best they had.
- They have really done their best.
- They received the baton of human shortcoming that was passed on by their parents.
- They did what they did or did not do from ignorance and neurosis.
- They often had a difficult time of it and had to learn parenthood, too.

As an adult, you can probably accept how your upbringing has been. And yet, to your inner child (your true feelings), that is of no concern as it feels that it has been wronged and unjustly or foolishly treated.

The five above mentioned arguments are often used to stop your feeling what the child in you feels. The following sentences are used so you will not feel your true feelings: "They did it because they loved me," "If I become angry with them, I will lose them," "They are so old. I can't reproach them anymore," "It won't do me any good," "Every man has his cross to bear." Blaming parents is highly taboo. If I broach this subject during a lecture, there is always a part of the public that furiously starts to defend parents in general. During the discussion afterwards, it turns out that people have not heard the above-mentioned arguments. It seems that people are defending the parents, but underneath they are protecting themselves against the true emotions of the inner child— because that is where the pain is! And the anger! This anger was not allowed to exist because of the great power imbalance.

Power imbalance.

When you are small you look, not only literally, up to your parents. "They are big and I am little." Parents are gods to a child; they are dependent on them for their lives. This original imbalance of power can be exaggerated by parent's problems with power or the lack of it. I remember, for example, that my mother did not dare to go against the doctor who told her that he thought you should not spoil a baby by feeding it at night when it was crying. In a case like this, the baby's feeling of powerlessness is only strengthened, and the feeling of "they decide for me" enlarged. Authoritative behavior of parents, who find it too difficult to listen to children's points of view, strengthens the natural imbalance. There are thousands of examples that you could give from your own upbringing, too.

A child acquires a certain habituation because of the sheer amount in volume and time of power imbalance; you have to eat, when "they" want you to, you have to go to school because "they" expect that of you, you have to go to church because "they" think that is proper, etc., etc. You only know that "they" know best and that you have got to learn and listen. With this, you learn to accept what you feel you cannot accept. Depending on the extent of the power imbalance and on that of respect for your feelings, you learn to suppress and deny your real feelings and wishes.

Anger is one of the first things to let go during the process of upbringing. The difference in power is too big to do what you want and follow your own insight. Moreover, many educators do not know the difference between emotion and behavior. For example, it is of essential importance to allow the feelings of the child to exist in their entirety but not to accept that the child kicks you.

I remember the story of a little girl of four and her mother. I do not know what the quarrel was about, but if mother could not think of anymore arguments, she would put a suitcase with clothes next to the front door and threaten: "One more cheeky answer and you're out." The only thing the little girl could do was to suppress her anger. An extreme story? No, the little girl lived in a nice neighborhood in an ordinary town. Because of our missed chances to freely form an adventurous life, we have all become hugely adapted but with a volcano of anger underneath. How often were you told: "Shut your eyes. What you see is yours," or "It's not about what *you* want," or "Hold your insolent tongue"?

If anger is suppressed, it will turn inwards and will cause retroflection. The energy that was originally aimed outwards returns like a boomerang, and you become angry with yourself. If this gets stuck chronically, it becomes self-hatred from a deep sense of being to blame for everything. Underneath this there is a repressed feeling of worthlessness that is pushed far away. When you are grown-up, you often do not know that you are angry or at whom you are actually angry. You only know that you are not good enough, not nice enough, not beautiful enough, and whatever else you would like to fill in. Often that is too painful to feel. If you ask ordinary people if they love themselves, 80% will say, "Yes, I suppose so." Really feeling hurts, and we would rather not feel pain.

However, what is done is done, and we cannot change it. You can choose between chronic pain and temporary acute pain. It is like a sore; if it festers underneath the skin, it cannot heal. If you lance the skin, you can clean the sore; that can be painful for a moment, but it will heal! This also goes for feelings of guilt: a chronic feeling of guilt, conscious or subconscious, chafes and gnaws at your life energy. Transforming feelings of guilt into acute anger not only frees you from your past but also gives new life energy. Moreover, anger helps you to stand firmly on your own two feet.

Pitying parents.

This brings me to a second aspect of neurotic guilt: children often spare their parents because they can see that they are having a difficult time. Especially sensitive children have a finely tuned antenna for this. Children want their parents to be happy because, of course, they also have a need for it. By sparing their parents, these children stand on the parent's side instead of relying on themselves and their own needs and feelings. Especially if parents have clearly had difficulties because of poverty, a large number of children, illness, or death or depressions, it is very difficult to transform feelings of guilt into anger at what happened to them. I often see this pattern in children from large families that have had a lack of affection. It is often very difficult to be angry with mother as she, for example, is often seen as the victim of old Christian morals.

The anger is aimed First at the church system that encouraged large families, often under moral pressure. It takes courage to aim your anger at your father and mother who let themselves be led by religious authorities. There is no point in aiming the whole of your child's anger at your real parents, and it is not very beneficial or very loving either. Expressing anger for you own sake should be done in a therapeutic setting or in your own room. It is a fact that you have chosen these parents as a mirror and as a learning school. This is your own work of liberation under your own responsibility.

Pitying your parents is understandable, but does not help you to become a free person that stands firmly on his own two feet. Only when you rely on yourself can you rely on others, and this includes your parents, who have given all they had, even if it was not good for you and not enough to develop into a free human being.

Greatest anger with the one/s you love.

This paradox is the cause of much inner imprisonment. Those people from whom you expected the most have disappointed you the most. It is difficult to permit yourself to be angry if you subsequently see that your parents have worked hard for the family. Rather than that, you feel guilty because you want something more. You start to judge yourself: you want too much, you are never satisfied, you are spoiled rotten, etc. This is, in other words, self-hatred and guilt. We often become imprisoned in a chain of guilty feelings which keep on intensifying one another if we do not work through this anger. This can express itself in irritation and in catty and cynical behavior that just seems to come from nowhere. Later we feel guilty about this behavior.

Why is it so difficult to be angry with the one you love? Fear of loss plays a large part in holding your true feelings back. That might have had a legitimate reason when you were a child, but as an adult that does not count anymore, especially if parents have died a long while ago. Yet this pattern of denial of anger continues in later life when you have become an adult, as if it is still possible to be abandoned. As long as you are not conscious of your emotions, patterns will repeat themselves as if you were still a child. Ambivalence is a theme that came up in Freud's early work. He formulated, certainly for that day and age, the shocking hypothesis that it is the rule rather than the exception to have feelings of love as well as hatred towards our siblings and parents. His famous theories about the Oedipus complex and the Electra complex stem from these observations.

Accusing and being accused.

Transforming guilt into anger is difficult for most of us, certainly in the beginning of Spark of Light Work. And yet we constantly move between guilt and accusation. These two are closely entwined. When it is within you, it is guilt. When you project it towards another, it is accusation. We are usually not conscious of this, but if we look at our human society, we see it as a central theme. Just think of all the reproaches that are made in relationships between parents and children and in working relationships. How many reproaches do you think fly back and forth there? And what about divorce? If one partner wants a divorce, there are bound to be reproaches. It is very difficult to just listen to the feedback of another person without feeling guilty, defending yourself, or going on the offensive. It is very difficult to not directly accuse someone yourself and take the road of "an eye for an eye and a tooth for a tooth."

When we look at society or at the political arena, we see that a culprit is always sought as soon as something happens, an accident or a mistake for example. If mistakes have been made within a Ministry, the guilty party is in trouble and has to resign. A culprit has to be found and punished. Just owning up to mistakes and rectifying them is apparently exceedingly difficult. Heads must roll to give the masses the feeling of justice and to transfer the collective guilt neurosis. Accordingly, people feel their own guilt less. It is one big game, played subconsciously and, therefore, according to an established pattern. Yes, there is a word for it, namely scapegoat mechanism. When a political murder took place in The Netherlands, it was not enough to imprison the murderer. A whole chain of accusations started; the media, the politics, and the police organisations were all told off. Everybody was guilty.

Essentially, we all suffer from a collective guilt syndrome. So every now and then we change roles: sometimes you feel guilty and sometimes you accuse. It seems to be an illness we all suffer from on this planet. Some people will fundamentally develop more feelings of guilt (and depressions) and others reproaches. All these patterns have their origins in our past and in past lives. There will never be an end to the stream of accusations if we do not become conscious of the underlying emotions. We must find where our emotional charge really belongs. There will never be an end to it if we do not learn to express it under our own responsibility.

Of old, anger was number one on the Roman Catholic list of seven deadly sins. We really find it difficult to reproach our parents (becoming angry with them) because we know that many things were done with good intention. There is really just a huge pool of ignorance from which we have all drunk. Here, too, it is important to distinguish between the adult and the inner child. The adult in us can see that things were done for the best; the child has experienced the behavior. So let the child rage and accuse. On the path of emotional digestion, you temporarily need accusation to reach your emotions, but you must now do it with awareness. You must do it as Work with a capital letter, with your own responsibility, and under your own supervision. Later, sadness and insight will come and then real love for these parents who have made it possible for you to incarnate in this time and on this planet. Then, when all wounds have been brought to the light and emotionally digested, guilt and accusation will dissolve and be transformed into love. Only then can we wholeheartedly forgive and forget. But before we get that far, there is a lot of healing work necessary. Let us free this earth from the old tale of guilt. And we can only do that if we keep our own house in order.

Reproach is a longing.

For most of us, expressing a reproach is easier than expressing a longing. When you express a longing you show yourself in all your vulnerability and neediness. And we usually find that scary. Yet a reproach is nothing but a longing that is expressed in an angry way. In fact, they are two sides of the same coin. Only the effect is different. Often, it is only possible to transform your reproach when you have set your inner anger in motion. It is important to disentangle the two aspects with a view to the Work. If you let longing and anger in at the same time, you will become paralyzed and imprisoned. Longing is approach, and when you are angry, you push away from you. These are two contradictory movements. Deep down inside you, you feel both.

What we see here is that if you do not bring your emotions to the surface and express them properly, you will actually stay imprisoned in your contradictory feelings. We have all become ambivalent in our feelings. You love the stick that you are beaten with because your father holds the stick, and you love him. You hate your mother's manipulations, but it is your mother. You have been in her womb for a full nine months, and you were never that intimate with anybody. You hate the way your husband makes love to you, but you long for intimacy and contact, and so you say nothing. You hate your wife's frumpiness, but you long for homeliness and coziness and so you say nothing. You reproach in silence and you have longings in silence, and you just live your everyday life. Is there another way? Disentangle your feelings! Bring them to the light! Express your rage under your own supervision and management on a cushion. The sting of your irritation and anger will then be taken out of it.

Subsequently, go to your partner and express your longing. Not the reproach! If you reproach, almost everybody on this planet will either go on the defensive out of guilt or counter-attack out of anger. This is a vicious circle we must break out of. If you express your longing, there is a chance that the other person will really be made to feel responsible and can break out of his/her own pattern of guilt and reproach. When you voice your longing without anger, it works wonders. In this Work with yourself, you can see how much this Work and responsibility belong together. Do not wait till the other takes a step forward and changes his or her behavior; do your Work, keep your house in order, and then go for fulfilment by expressing your longings: "I would like you to treat me like this, I feel respected that way, I need this in a relationship with a partner, and I need that in our sexual contact."

The Work is slightly different with regard to your parents. As an adult you have usually left your youth and living with your parents behind you. That lies in the past. Yet the relationship with parents is, for most of us, not over on an emotional level. This goes on in a profound way in the relationship that adults have with their parents. The ambivalence of attraction and rejection stays.

Parents are deeply unhappy when a child, after some therapy or other, severs all contact. They cannot understand it. Their experience is different from that of the child. They have done their best and have usually stayed unaware of their background. Moreover, it is very difficult to admit that you have not done it right as a parent. It is no easy task making sure that children grow up to be happy adults.

Not long ago, we had a mother and daughter together in a Spark of Light Week. While both worked on their emotional history, they discovered and went through their shared pain of lack of affection. They felt and saw the passing on of the baton of human shortcoming and felt closer because of this. After the week, the mother went to *her* mother and noticed that their contact was better, even though she could not say everything. The relationship changed favorably because she herself was changed.

Your parents do not have to change. They have their own path to travel. More important is to set yourself emotionally in motion so the anger, guilt, and pain of loss melt in softness and real understanding. Perhaps this is the difference between therapy and Light Work: we always Work on ourselves *because of the Love* we want to realize. That is why it is not advisable to go to your parents with your old emotional charge in the here and now. Do the Work for yourself with the help you choose.

Sometimes it is possible to share things with them. This depends on the relationship you have with your parents and the amount of awareness and openness. But you must first digest your emotional charge for yourself. It will then be possible to transform reproaches into longings. It is not necessary to literally speak them aloud if that feels threatening. There are many creative and loving ways to be found. If you have experienced that your mother never left you alone with your father because of subconscious jealousy, and you really want contact without your mother now that you are a grown-up woman, you could suggest an outing which especially your father would enjoy. Or perhaps your husband can do something nice with his mother-in-law, so you have your father to yourself. This is a better idea than confronting your parents with your mother's jealous side. If your parents are also on the path of awareness, that is wonderful, of course; they can learn and develop further thanks to your growth work.

When you do your emotional homework, you can become emotionally independent of your parents and, therefore, acquire real respect for who and what they really are: the people who, however neurotic, have opened a gateway, so you could take your place on this earth at this time. You can also feel compassion for your parents who usually did not have the chance to work at themselves as you do now. My ninety-four year old mother said to me, "If I had had the chances you have now, I would have screamed the house down, too." When she was already in her seventies, she tried therapy a couple of times, but she no longer had the vitality to digest and integrate it all.

The conflict between duty and longing.

A theme that must not be forgotten in this chapter is the inner struggle many people have between their duties and their responsibilities on the one hand and their longings on the other. Everyone knows the feeling—a family, a job, an expensive house, high mortgage—and the huge amount of energy that it costs to keep it all going. We all heave a sigh of "and what do *I* really want" sometimes. Inner dissatisfaction and burn-out are possible consequences because it all gets too much, and you cannot do everything... Our society has become very complicated. You have to work so hard to meet social standards that your own deeper wishes do not stand a chance.

Guilt can go in two directions: outwards and inwards towards yourself. There can be feelings of guilt towards your children because you do not have enough time and cannot give them enough attention. Many men and women only see their children in the morning when they get up and in the evening when they go to bed. Do you feel guilty when you take them to the day-care center? Do you feel guilty with regard to your work because you need a few days off because your tiredness has caused yet another bout of flu or a cold? Your feeling of guilt can also be aimed at yourself because you are not doing what you really want to do in your heart of hearts.

There are many questions that you push away because you do not see a way out. You are too firmly tied to the system. A burnout can then be a blessing and a chance to radically change direction. It does me great pleasure to see that a lot of people who have had a breakdown in their forties, those astrologically important years of possible change, go through a difficult period and ultimately find creativity in themselves and decide to take a new course in life. The latter is possible to the extent that you do emotional work well. Your emotions are the driving force of change. Your deeply felt indignation and sorrow at the way in which you have been caught and mangled

192

in social systems and fixed structures becomes your motive for a new direction and a new life.

I did my change direction, of course, in two stages. When I was twenty-eight, an astrologically important age, I had a break down within the structure of the Mental Health Care where I used to work. During several months away from work due to burnout, I experienced great satisfaction in learning to put my own wishes first. I resigned and started my own private practice. The second stage came ten years ago when an inner voice asked me if I would enjoy living in nature and if I wanted to follow a new path. I was told that somewhere in the south of France there was a house for my life companion and me. It was a mill, and if we got into the car, we would be led there. That is exactly what we did.

Within a week we had found a little piece of paradise on earth. Next to the mill stood a wonderful dwelling house, part of it could be lived in without any problem. We sold our house in the Netherlands, and I stopped my practice. I asked the voice, "What are we going to live on? The wind?" We did not have all that much money. The voice said, "Just go and live there, and everything you need will come to you."

That was an excellent exercise in trust! But it worked! When we needed new curtains or a shower cabin, we soon found them in the local rubbish dump. The new poverty, which was really richness, made us creative and deeply satisfied with what we were given and found. Slowly we built up our work in this new place. By this, I just want to say that if you really do what your heart or inner voice tells you, you will receive whatever you need. It is necessary to openly conduct your struggle between what you feel is your duty and your deepest wishes and not to push it away as impossible. Realize that "For whoever believes, everything is possible," and life is too precious to waste on matters that are not important and do not have a connection with your soul. It is always possible to change your course of direction, sometimes radically, sometimes gradually. Making your intentions clear to yourself is the first step. The courage to begin an exercise in trust is the second.

Promise makes debt.

Be careful about what promises and vows (such) situations may induce you to make because they are more binding than you think, even from life to life.
~Ceanne deRohan

"Promise is debt" is a saying familiar to many people. And yet we all take many vows and make many promises. Once somebody wrote to me:

> *Most of the feelings of guilt I have are linked to promises, oaths, or vows. I did a confession of faith, a vow of chastity, poverty, and obedience as a member of the lay order of St. Francis, and I promised to be faithful to several partners. A lot of guilt is attached to that. Even now, the solemn vow of chastity, poverty, and obedience (to my vocation) plays a repressed role in my acts. Guilt still gnaws at me.*

We take vows when we are too insecure and when we do not have enough self-assurance to be able to stand by our ability to give an answer to the reason for our existence. We give power to an institute, such as a church or a monastery or convent because we do not stand firmly enough on our own two feet. Vows are disastrous to your freedom and bind you. A vow is a bond for the future and does not give room for you to organize your future in a different or new way except if you break it. As vows are usually burdened with divine or religious authority and connected to rituals, it takes courage to set yourself free from such bonds. Such a vow can become deep-rooted, especially if it has been long-lasting, and you are sensitive to authority.

It is important to become conscious of the reason for taking such a vow. Deep imprints can play a part that goes back far into previous lives. With regard to the vow of celibacy, you might carry the imprint with you from this or a past life that you are not worthy of love or that you are frightened of being rejected. It is also possible that you carry the burden of sexual abuse in your history or that you associate love with suffering. Especially, the latter is a deep Christian imprint.

With regard to *the vow of poverty*, what does this reflect? Perhaps it reflects your sense of unworthiness? Is there a subconscious need for punishment which stems from old feelings of guilt? Do you, perhaps, feel guilty because you did not share your wealth with others in a distant past? Even if you did not take a vow of poverty in this life, you might have done so in a past life as a result of which the money theme is now a problem for you. These are old emotional imprints at work. In our Calvinistic culture, we subconsciously carry the conviction with us that money is evil, and God is good. God and money cannot go together. While we seek for the connection with Loving Light, we reject money, but we also love it. These old opinions and subconscious dilemmas cause a blockade in our flow of energy and also in the flow of money.

Poverty of the soul is usually interpreted as humility. *Humility* is often enfeeblement and an invitation to be less than yourself. Humility is a blockade in becoming who you are and in the realization of your authenticity. The latter is the only thing of importance. A lot of humility is false due to a lack of healthy love for yourself. When I was young, I decided to become Roman Catholic of my own accord because I had a penchant for mysticism and a longing for guidance on my spiritual path; I became "holier than thou." I gave away many of my possessions; the golden jewelery that I had received from my parents went to my cousins. My mother was not far wrong when she said jokingly, "She is proud of her humility!"

195

An important part of humility is the idea that the "Divine power, the inspiration or the healing energy is not yours, but goes through you." In current New Age jargon people simply call that "being a channel for Divine energy." I know all about that, too. If you are insecure, it is easier to say that a Divine power is working through you, and something is being opened up by another than to recognize that you yourself have healing powers. Tat svam asi" as they say in India: "Thou art that."

With regard to the *vow of obedience*, this can be a way of denying your own power and strength and not accepting your own responsibility. Fear of power plays a big role here— perhaps because of old misuse of power in past lives or from experiences of impotence as a child. Obedience turns you into a robot and stops you from forming your own creativeness and dedication to what you experience as good inside you. A vow of obedience was often given in exchange for safety and care. It might have been a good exchange in the dangerous Middle Ages, but it does not belong to modern adulthood.

And then we have the *marriage vows...* and the numerous divorces...and the numerous guilty feelings. Quite often, from the moment people get married, it seems to them as if they are living in a prison with fixed agreements and established patterns. A lot of people do not admit to the fact that marriage, along with the good things, restricts them.

A relationship based on love because that is what a marriage is, is pre-eminently a free relationship. Without freedom, there is no love. Love and respect need no formal promises. Why tie yourself down with regard to the other. The need for security and the fear of loss are often, subconsciously, the reason our neurotic selves demand a vow from the other. You can enter into a relationship and devote yourself to the other without tying yourself down, for later life could be different then. Your partner can choose to become an alcoholic or to take another path that you do not sympathize with, and it is good not to let another person ruin your life.

Finally, there are the vows we have *given to ourselves.* You can determine the flow of your life by promising yourself "never to have another relationship" because of old disappointments. Or you have promised yourself "never to put any children on this earth" and suchlike vows.

It is important with regard to all these vows to plumb their depths, digest emotional backgrounds, and subsequently liberate yourself. Remember which neuroses lie behind them and for what reason you took those vows. Was it fear, naïveté, or a longing for something else? Imagine holding a pair of scissors, then cut through all the old connections to oaths and vows. Do it with love for yourself, for your freedom, and for the realization of your authenticity.

4) Subconscious guilt from past lives.

Many feelings of guilt are so subconscious and so indescribable that we only see them in their consequences and compensations. There are various *compensation scenarios* that can be an expression of deeply repressed guilt. I shall name a few scenarios/scripts:

- The Show-off Script;
- The I Am Not Allowed to Be Happy Script;
- The Do-gooder Script;
- The Accidents Script; and
- The Achievement Script.

There are other things that play a part in these compensation scripts, but I view them from the angle of guilt. Subconscious guilt can play a part in all these scenarios; it can be pushed far back in the mind but also far back in time. You can be weighed down with guilt that has an unknown content. You may have done something wrong in a previous life about which you feel guilty. A vague feeling of guilt has remained, but the memory of it is lost. This vague guilt, tucked away somewhere in your soul, can result in you begrudging yourself things. It can lead you to living according to one of the above-mentioned scripts which stops you from living a full, rich life.

An example may clarify this: imagine that you have killed your newborn infant in a previous life because it was a girl or handicapped, and that was not desirable in that culture or time. When you died, you gained insight in the cold-heartedness of your deed and felt guilty. You have heard or seen that life with a handicap can be a path of purification for the soul or for its surroundings and that it has a meaning. You should not have made a decision about that life on your own authority. With each following incarnation, life is so merciful that it drapes a veil over your knowledge of previous lives. Yet you carry that guilt with you. It can make you compensate: you want to be a good person and you do your utmost to lead a good life. There is nothing wrong with that, but subconscious patterns can exhaust you and make sure you never allow yourself to be really happy. It is too much of a good thing! The tendency to be prone to many small or large accidents can have its origin in remote guilt. If you wish to live in the here and now and not as a compensation of bygone days, you will have to become aware of the past and cleanse it. That means you will have to remember why you feel guilty and why you begrudge yourself things. You can only feel remorse through memories that are emotionally lived through, digest what has happened, and gain insight in the how and why. In this way, it is possible to transform guilt and self-hatred into love for yourself because you know that everything you have done is now in the past and is part of your learning process of self-knowledge and love.

Summary: Concrete Steps

1. Realization of guilt.

In which way do your feelings of guilt present themselves? Make a list with sentences, such as: "If I say no, I feel guilty" or "If I have a lovely lazy day, I feel guilty" or "If I do what I want, I feel guilty." Remember those subtle, non-verbal guilt imprints.

2. With regard to whom do you feel guilty in the present?

For example, you find it difficult to go your own way and to do things on your own with regard to your partner. This could be a repetition of a pattern you had with your mother. Perhaps she found it difficult when you went out when you were a teenager while she stayed at home suffering and feeling miserable.

3. Where does it come from?

In this case you will have to look at faces, sentences, habits, and atmospheres that are usually from your past. If you say the first part of certain sentences, find out which face, which name, or which words surface. Sentences, such as "If I'm having a lovely time reading a really good book, my mother comes by and sighs because she has so much work to do with all those children" or "If I choose the biggest piece of cake, my father says that I should choose another and not be so greedy." It was possibly not words that made you feel guilty; perhaps it was a surprised or indignant look. It is also possible for a family to have a certain formation of habits which leads to your feeling guilty when you do something else, such as being idle in a very busy and active family. I call this *mother's knee energy*, something that you learned at your mother's knee and seems to be yours but is not.

Guilt has many layers and very many variations. Sometimes they are not easy to recognize. A person who has lost his mother at a young age can feel guilty about it. After all, a very young child still thinks egocentrically which means he/she can only think "What did I do wrong that my mummy left me?" A child cannot think or formulate like that, of course, but deep within him/her, a guilt imprint like this may develop. An important source of guilt is to be found in previous lives. If we regard the history of man in general, we can see how much misery has come out of our collective ignorance. We are all part of this history, and we all carry the history of our own souls with us and the feelings that go with it.

4. Which feelings suggest themselves to you?

Remember, there are only four basic emotions: fear, anger, joy, and sorrow. Like pity, the rest is neurosis, which will not help you any further. Try to reach an emotion; anger will be primary in the case of guilt.

5. Aim your emotions at the person in question (on a cushion) and start a discussion.

Say and do everything that suggests itself to you but within the bounds of safety.

6. Realize that every reproach is a longing.

Give the other side of reproach a chance, that of longing for love and respect.

7. Then look at the way in which you have continued the story of reproach towards yourself.

Look in the mirror and especially at your inner child and talk to it. Perhaps you can now begin a less reproachful and more loving relationship with yourself!

8. *Take back the responsibility that you hid under your reproaches and anger.*

Only when you have set your emotions in motion, can you do this wholeheartedly. Responsibility is not a moral issue. It is the freedom to answer to your existence yourself.

Forgiveness

Forgiveness is a much-discussed theme. Forgiveness is central in *A Course of Miracles* and in Christian religion. We speak of forgiveness as long as we believe that guilt exists. But if we assume that there is no guilt, only ignorance and neurosis, is there anything left to forgive? Talking about forgiveness implies that there is guilt.

A personal story.

I found a lot of guilt in myself on my own path of liberation, especially when I started to remember a lot of my previous lives. I do not have much guilt from my current life: I have not been raised as a Christian, and I received a lot of freedom and respect from my parents. A few of my past lives took me years to digest. They were important lives that are central to the life I now live and the work I do. Remembering those lives meant I had difficulty accepting who I once was and what I had done. Even though I tried, I could not forgive myself for a long time. It was about betrayal, abandonment, revenge, and misuse of power.

At issue was my first life on earth, from which my karma on this planet stemmed. It set a chain of learning experiences in motion, which I remember for the larger part. One of the most important lessons was how to cope with guilt. In my Spark of Light Work in this life, I went through deep processes of remorse. I cried a lot. I could not forgive myself as long as everything was not digested at an emotional level. I prayed for forgiveness but could not receive or accept it. However, by emotionally digesting unfinished things from distant pasts step by step and by getting a clearer picture of the backgrounds and situations, I developed a softness and mildness towards the persons I once was. I slowly started to love the men and women in me, who all had a lot to answer for.

The word forgiveness was not an issue anymore. By learning to feel love for all my personalities, or you could say my whole Self, I discovered that guilt does not exist. There were only undigested emotions and experiences which caused guilt. The guilt dissolved in anger and tears. Where there once was guilt, there is now consciousness and love. Forgiveness and the need to forgive was not something I thought about anymore. It turned out to be a mental category that did not exist in my perception.

And what about forgiving others, you might rightly ask. You forgive together, don't you? If I take my own experience as starting point, I come to the same conclusion. To the extent that I emotionally digested my unpleasant experiences with other people from my past through expression of anger and tears, I could see the people in question as they were and could view and accept the experiences as part of my learning process to become a wiser and more mature person. I saw my ignorance and struggle and also that of others. After expressing anger and sorrow, there was no reproach or guilt. And so, forgiveness was not necessary. Everything was fine as it was, and everything is fine as it is. Proceeding from my own personal perceptions and discoveries, I look at ideas such as those discussed in *A Course in Miracles* with amazement. Even though I feel a lot of sympathy for this Christian revival movement, I cannot agree with their ideas or with those in traditional Christianity about forgiveness. I will begin with the latter.

Guilt and forgiveness in Christianity.

As is well-known, the theme of guilt and forgiveness is important within Christianity. Given that forgiveness is an important word and significant to many people, I shall describe the different views that exist and comment on them.

The Our Father and "Forgive us our sins as we forgive those who sin against us" has a special place in the prayers of Christians. The theme of sacrifice is directly linked to guilt. The other day, both a thought and a question flashed through my mind. I had not allowed them into my consciousness before because of attachment to old thoughts. I realized that, judging by his painful death on the cross, Jesus must have had karma, too. Why should he not have known karma if he is one of us and our brother? He also had to learn and develop.

Later I read in the very inspiring, channeled books by Ceanne deRohan [3], the following: *No matter how much you might want to say that Jesus was perfect, He had guilt mixed with love. The guilt that created His death on earth...* It seemed to be a direct answer to my question. At any rate, we can say with certainty that in Christianity love and guilt have been thoroughly mixed together.

Guilt and love have been mixed together, too, with regard to sacrifice. By sacrificing yourself for someone or something, you imply a negative attitude towards yourself. With sacrifice you give up something essential of yourself. With love you do not have to give up anything. You just share your whole being and your abundance, and you do not have to give up anything or miss anything. You do not have to be crucified for love. At a deeper layer, perhaps that was the mistake Jesus made or rather that was his lack of knowledge— otherwise it would not have happened. Perhaps he came to earth because He had something to learn just like the rest of us. In this way, he was and is our brother. Is it conceivable that because of the subconscious guilt he had, and he is not alone in that, guilt and forgiveness have acquired the emphasis that they have had up until now? Of course, his followers are to blame for this, but Jesus might have unknowingly set a trend. That has not done us any good. It is time to set ourselves free from guilt.

It is not effective to go on thinking in terms of guilt and forgiveness. As long as we remain imprisoned in this theme, we will fundamentally stagnate at the level of the will and the reason. Guilt is nothing but a lumping together of emotions: fear, sorrow, and anger. If these emotions come to light and are digested, guilt will disappear. If there is no longer any guilt, there will be no accusations and hence no need for forgiving or being forgiven.

Guilt and forgiveness in A Course in Miracles.

I will take this book as an example since it deals explicitly with the theme of forgiveness. Many of the ideas of the Course are also to be found in other schools of the New Age Movement. Marianne Williamson, one of the most important teachers of the Course, calls forgiveness "the mental technique with which our thoughts are transformed from fear to love." She also says, "Forgiving is selective recollection, a conscious choice to concentrate on love and let go of the rest... It is a choice to see people, as they are."[4]

Three things strike me: mental technique, choosing selective recollection, and forgiveness as a conscious decision. I have a few things to say about this and will do so point by point.

Mental technique.

There are many people for whom mental access is a good way to begin their path of awareness and liberation. But as the word *mental* already indicates, it is a limited way with the primacy of thinking as its starting point. As my approach will show, I think that the emotional experience is primary and that our thinking is formed according to that. This is a fundamentally different approach. People are of two minds in the Course: on the one hand, they say the ego is allowed to vent its emotions, but at the same time they say in a rather disparaging manner, "Let the ego vent unrestrainedly for a while... for the moment we will believe the ego story about the other being to blame, we will play along with the ego game Shh! Do not tell the ego, or otherwise it will stop immediately."[5] I cannot hear any respect for our hurt inner child from whom this *ego* originated. On the other hand, they say that emotions do not have to be vented: "The most important thing is for the emotions to come to the surface and be present in our consciousness. They do not need to be shouted out with drama and theatrics. Forgiveness is a gentle process that takes place inside us. And the liberating change that forgiveness brings, takes place in our thinking, in our consciousness because it is there that we can make choices." Here too, the subtle contempt for expressing emotions (theatrics) and the equalization of consciousness and thinking. It is also very suggestive to set the expressing of emotions against "gentleness" and does not do justice to reality.

Selective recollection.

This is chosen as a conscious decision to concentrate on love and to let go of the rest. The emphasis on conscious decision shows that they want to give this the power over the subconscious. There is nothing wrong with that. But *how* do you do it? It would be great if our conscious will was able to let our subconscious emotional imprints disappear and then realize love in this way.

However, as every good judge of the soul knows, the power of the subconscious and all its emotional imprints are enormous. As is apparent from our collective and individual histories, undoing negativity and fear cannot be accomplished with one's will. Can you undo the power of the subconscious by not giving it any attention or by not feeding it? Directly after the 9/11 disaster in New York, an email circulated with the story of the two wolves:

> *A native Indian asked his grandfather how he felt after this disaster. He said, 'It is as if there are two wolves fighting within my heart. One is revengeful, angry, and violent; the other wolf is loving and compassionate.' The grandson asked,' Grandfather, which wolf will win the fight in your heart?' The grandfather answered, 'The one I nourish.'*

Initially this seems to be a wonderful story, but when you analyze it, you find out that it is not correct. First, revenge, anger, and violence are mentioned in one and the same breath. Anger is a healthy emotion after such an event. Violence and revenge are not. Second, anger and love are imperceptibly opposed to each other in the fight. As if anger, when expressed correctly, is not part of love. Third, this story gives the impression that what you are not nourished by disappears, and this is not correct, according to psychological experience.

If I generalize I would say that this is slightly similar to what I call *the Oriental way*: just look into the sun, and you will not see any shadows. This is in contrast to the psychological approach whereby the confrontation with the shadow is seen as a pathway to the light. "Confronting someone with his shadow is showing him his own light" noted Carl Jung. I am afraid that the Course in Miracles' approach and many similar ones in the New Age circuit are like new veneer over the old repression of our emotionality. In the Oriental approach, the emphasis is on detachment and non-identification with the ego; in the Course it is called "letting go." Incidentally, in both cases we see a negative attitude towards the ego (more on this subject in Chapter 44).

But here again, we must ask: how do we let go? Our history shows that a conscious and mental exercise of one's will does not work; the power of the subconscious, of everything we have repressed—especially our emotionality—is too great. A conscious mental decision is a good declaration of intent to begin with. It helps you to change course and do your best. But is it enough? I doubt it. Detachment and letting go by the use of willpower and reason is similar to suppression and denial. The consequences of this path are twofold:

> 1. By suggesting that you can make the power of your shadow disappear, people who take this path and are not able to do that, will be confronted again and again by their inability and their accompanying feelings of guilt: "I am apparently not doing it right." This has a ***deflation of the ego*** as consequence, which means identification with not-being-good-enough. In the old school of ethics, this was called awareness of sin.

2. Falsification and an ***inflation of the ego*** occur. You identify yourself with ideals, whereby people often think that *that* is the Higher Self. This makes you forget your shadow which represents your incompleteness and your worldliness. The result is that you seem to be further in your development than you are in reality. An emotional backlog develops in contrast to the mental and verbal progress you are making on the path of love. This is the background against which Eastern gurus and Western priests sexually and relationally make mistakes. We can also see this in the New Age Movement where people strive for enlightenment and identify themselves prematurely with the sought after ideal.

As Erich Neumann already showed in his *Ethics for the Future*, putting the emphasis on the ideal of perfection (in the language of the Course "only concentrate on love") is an important characteristic of the old school of ethics: "The ideal of perfection can and should be realized by the eradication of character traits that are contrary to this perfection. The denial of 'the negative' and its violent and systematic exclusion, is the basic principle of these ethics."[6]

By looking into the sun and not wanting to see the shadow, we do not reach the light, but only a falsification of it.

Forgiveness as a conscious decision.

People who follow the Course of Miracles, even say that the willingness to make another choice is in principle, enough. I believe that this is a good first step. Forgiveness seems to me to be the end result rather than the beginning of a process. "It begins with acceptance" a Dutch writer remarks, when asked if it is possible to forgive the murderer of your child. It provides a good insight in that way of thinking. To my mind, it ends with acceptance which we can then perhaps call forgiveness. This reversal of the end and the beginning is a pattern which we see in many spiritual schools of thought. People want to start with Z while the basic A, B, and C of the spiritual alphabet are preferably skipped. Sometimes people pityingly call this therapy—we should leave this behind as soon as possible.

Marianne Williamson describes a recent experience with her mother in her previously mentioned book. She writes: "When I was on holiday with my family, my mother and I nobly tried to get on together, but we did not succeed. Old attack and defense systems continually cropped up between us. She wanted a conservative daughter, and I wanted a more enlightened mother..."

After Marianne had read through the Course, she worked out where her thoughts were not in accordance with those of God. She discovered: "It is true; God does not look at her and think 'Sophie Ann is a bitch.' As long as I chose to see her like that...I could not be at peace because I did not share God's perception. As soon as I had understood this, I let go of my tense fixation on what I saw as her fault. Miraculously, she was nicer to me, as I also was to her."[7]

In such a concrete situation and relationship, a shift in the way of perceiving things can be a breakthrough in a pattern that has reached deadlock. Friendliness is catching, after all. In the past, people practiced asking themselves: "How would Jesus react?" It is the same exercise. In principle there is nothing wrong with it. A friend of mine wanted to visit a man who had betrayed her trust and tell him what she thought of him as she was wont to do in similar situations. When she saw him lying by his pool in all his vulnerability, she suddenly felt compassion with this poor old man, turned round, and "It was alright." Both women in these examples connected to a layer within themselves that was bigger than the little hurt *self*. One of them made a mental decision, the other a spontaneous one.

Marianne Williamson adds that forgiveness is the choice of seeing people as they are *now*. In its self, this is a very good attitude, for example with regard to your parents with whom there is old pain to be worked through. See them as they are now and at the same time, for your own self, work emotionally through old pain with the intention of *becoming spontaneous and natural*. The latter is lost with behavior that is too mentally thought through and inspired by good will. Spontaneity and naturalness are important behavioral values and expressions of self-acceptance.

As long as you cannot embrace yourself and your shadow side with love, you are still bothered by guilt about who you are and how you express yourself. In that sense, the Course might strengthen guilt rather than enhance forgiveness. The often absolutely negative talk about the ugly ego fits seamlessly here.

The Natural Person

From my point of view, I prefer the natural and spontaneous person who has once again learned to cry when he is sad, to "carpet beat" when he is angry, to acknowledge fear and live through it when he is scared, and to laugh when he is happy. If this natural digestion mechanism works properly, the air will repeatedly be cleared and neither guilt nor accusation will remain. In this natural climate, we do not need moral categories as guilt and forgiveness.

I propose deleting the words guilt and forgiveness from our vocabulary and staying close to direct human experience. Ouch is just ouch, and yes is yes and no is no. There is light and there is shadow, heaven and earth and we, humans, in-between as children of both. As those children, we can find our innocence under dusty layers of old feelings of guilt. There is nothing to forgive and nothing to forget; we only have to digest. What is important to me is to find a way out of the diabolical cycle of guilt. Of course, errors are made. But we must look behind and under the guilt, and then we will find anger and impotence and immense sorrow...and that can be digested.

The Feeling of Worthlessness: The Base of Our Guilt

It is our light, not our darkness that frightens us. We ask ourselves, who am I to be brilliant, gorgeous, talented, and fabulous? Your playing small doesn't serve the world. And as we let our light shine, we unconsciously give other people permission to do the same. As we are liberated from our own fear, our presence automatically liberates others.
~Marianne Williamson

At the base of our guilt, a feeling of worthlessness lies from which we all, without exception, suffer. Many people will deny this feeling they have and say that they are self-assured and have self-respect. And yet, I think that the demon of worthlessness is at the base of our collective psyche. It is a layer that only a few dare to feel because it is too terrible. It forms the basis of our feelings of superiority and inferiority that has been fed for centuries by, amongst others, Christian principles and is expressed in sentences such as "I am nothing; God is all." I will cite from Calvin's *Institutiones*[8] whose ideas underlie the Protestant branch of Christianity: "For I do not call it humility as long as we think there is anything remaining within us...We cannot think of ourselves as we ought to think when we do not exceedingly despise everything that we perhaps find excellent within ourselves. This humility is the sincere submission of a spirit that is overwhelmed by the knowledge of its own misery and wretchedness: because this is its true description in the word of God."

This attitude has deeply penetrated our whole culture although not all churches and Christians will still agree with this self-contempt. Erich Fromm calls this self-contempt the core of authoritarian religion or a worldly authoritarian institution in contrast to a humanistic religion in which man and his own power are central.[9]

The Roman Catholic inheritance is pervaded with the practice of virtue that is based more on self-denial than on self-affirmation. Saint Augustine, who we can place at the basis of Roman Catholic theology, writes in his often read *Confessiones.*[10]

> *The frailty of a child's limbs may be innocent, but not the souls of children; I have personally seen and experienced a child being jealous; it could not yet speak but it looked pale and angrily at its nursing brother. (...) Truly that is not innocence, at the source of milk that flows abundantly...*

The treatises and books that have been written in the same vein about the sense of sin are uncountable. Until now, the sense of sin and self-contempt are passed on from generation to generation like mother's milk. Righteous anger gives you the chance to eradicate this demon inside you with a firm hand. Anger helps you to stand firmly on your own two feet and get back what has been taken from you, namely a healthy feeling of self-respect. As long as we do not find this self-respect underneath our flow of emotions, we shall keep on blaming each other and comparing ourselves to each other in a cold-hearted way. If we find our sense of worth again, we will be able to appreciate each other. There will be love and respect. We will no longer spend time and energy on theories that keep us in our place and that stop us seeing our greatness and the beauty of our earth.

The most extreme consequences of worthlessness are found in two different places: first, in psychopathy and in the world of crime, where there is no respect for other people, and second, in religious beliefs. The concept of Enlightenment is known in the East. In the complete identification with the Light, we see, very subtly, the denial of the human ego and the denial of creation as if it were an illusion. The mystic path is, in the West, also often based on the denial of the natural human and the sinfulness of creation. Both extremes are based on the worthlessness of humans and creation. The starting point of every religion is indeed love and freedom, yet this is corrupted again and again by humans because of their need for power that has everything to do with fear and ends in contempt and restraint ...and guilt.

In this day and age it is important to learn to live our life in full respect of ourselves and the earthly creation without denying anything that is part of human existence. That is the real challenge of the New Age! Loving Light assists us to amend what has to be amended. "Soften the hard-hearted, cherish the heart that is chilled, and lead those who could not find the way." In this beautiful Whitsun hymn, we also see how Christianity, guilt, and love have been mixed together to form a knot that can hardly be disentangled. In the same hymn we read: "Light full of blessing, shine in our darkness, conquer our hearts; without your secret glow, there is no good in us humans and the soul is not pure." We are darkness, unclean, and no good! Now that I write this down, I realize how uncritically I used to sing such hymns, both in my Protestant and in my Catholic period. And most of us do. We have become so accustomed to the intermingling of guilt and love by centuries of collective indoctrination that we do not really hear what we are singing about. It is almost in our genes!

However beautiful this song may be, it is also a kind of loving castration! It is castration of our self-respect in the name of love. Due to this intermingling of love and guilt, we have really become paralyzed and imprisoned in feelings of worthlessness. Or have we become imprisoned in the intermingling of guilt and love because of our basic feeling of worthlessness. What came first, the chicken or the egg? That is perhaps difficult to discover and probably not important anymore. By disentangling love and guilt and no longer mixing them together, by freeing ourselves from guilt and regaining our dignity, we can liberate ourselves. Free from personal and collective neuroses, we are free to lead a life of dignity and respect, for ourselves and for others.

Chapter 16

From Power and Impotence to Strength

There is only one solution to the human condition: for one to face the truth ... to recognize that there is no power transcending him which can solve his problem for him. Man must accept the responsibility for himself and the fact that only by using his powers can he give meaning to his life.
~Erich Fromm

here is a lot of power in this world and a lot of impotence. There is a lot of authoritarian behavior and a lot of helplessness. There is misuse of power, and there is strength, but what is what?

First of all, I shall explain a number of words. Power is sometimes seen as a positive word but usually as a negative one. Here I depict it as negative, as a fixation that belongs in the first phase of our model: in the pool of stagnant water. With this I make a distinction between power and the word "strength" from the third phase. It is one of the treasures we can find at the bottom of our stream of emotions.

Power and Impotence: Two Sides of the Same Coin

You could say that where there is power, there is impotence; and where there is impotence, there is power. As with all polarities, you will find that if one side is fully aware, the other side is unaware. Someone who uses power in contact with his fellow men feels impotent inside. Someone who behaves like a victim, helplessly, is a ruler deep down inside. Power and impotence are both compensations of the opposite. They are really the same but with a different manifestation. Some people feel mainly powerless, and some live mainly from their power. It is more often the case that within one person power and impotence alternate. They swap places. Our bodies clearly show our survival strategies. We will look at the expression of power and impotence in our bodies. I shall describe the typologies although we are, in actual fact, hybrids of various survival strategies. But there is usually one type that is dominant. For a complete typology, please refer to Chapter 34.

Power: The Swollen Body

If you feel powerful on the outside and use power to survive, you often look powerful. It is, however, exaggerated fake power. It is body builder's strength. The muscles are strongly developed and the body is top-heavy. The power is in the chest: "Here I am." It is the survival strategy of the child that has been overpowered one way or another and has not known intimacy. To make sure that does not happen again, you try to be as independent as possible. You are inclined to ignore your own and other people's needs and to repeat what has happened to you.

We see an extreme form of this in the behavior of psychopaths and terrorists. By showing one's power and

216

qualities, the overpowering can be massive and open. This overpowering is sometimes done with more subtle manipulations.

The feelings of worthlessness are so strong that they are too painful to feel and are compensated by the opposite, by showing how good one is "I'm okay, but the others are not." We can see this mechanism in whole sections of the population: people think they are special as compensation for a very painful feeling of inferiority. This compensated feeling of "I am okay, but the others are not" means feeling free to abuse power and take part in criminality, terrorism, and war. It goes without saying that this is an extreme form of the problem of power. Many of us use power as a compensation for feelings of impotence.

Anny comes from a large family: she was the ninth child. Mother was an alcoholic, and father was unemployed and addicted to gambling. Anny never had the feeling that she was welcome. Even worse, she was called 'a nail in her mother's coffin.' She might have been called Queen, but she was never treated as such. She was also sexually abused by her father. At sixteen she severs her ties with home and decides to prove that she is a queen. She ends up in the world of prostitution and quickly works her way up to become a madam. She holds sway over many foreign girls whom she rules harshly and pays little. She vents her anger, which is probably meant for mother and father, on her employees.

Impotence: Slackening of the Body

If you feel fundamentally powerless in life, your body will express that as a slackening and heaviness: the head is positioned forward as if trying to find support. The shoulders are rounded and hang downwards and express a lack of aggression in the original meaning of the word (aggression comes from the Latin *aggredior,* which means to go towards).

There can also be a hollow chest, where deep sorrow and loneliness reside and sometimes tenseness in the stomach so as to not feel the emptiness. Gravity is felt most in a slack body. The feeling that belongs to this type is one of not getting where you want to go in spite of great effort and struggle. The feeling is one of suffering that often reaches further than one's own suffering; you share the suffering of the whole world.

Anger: The Common Denominator

Restrained anger is central in both power and impotence. A powerful person is more likely to show his anger in macho behavior, insolence, and misuse of power. He will not be inclined to work on himself or his repressed anger. A powerless person will try to hold in his anger, in which he is bound to fail from time to time. He will be more inclined to work on himself as the depressive component is felt. The powerful do not feel all that much. They use all their power to prevent themselves from feeling. Setting old anger in motion will help both to dissolve their fixations on power and impotence. The following is an example of a man who has remained trapped in his impotence:

Bill is a nice, kind man of fifty. He is very interested in personal growth and spirituality. He has already done many courses, from Psychosynthesis to shamanism to Reiki, and all have enriched him. Yet he has remained basically depressed. He cries easily and often, and yet he does not feel relieved. The depressions and the unexpected mood changes keep on coming back. Sometimes he is grumpy and short-tempered towards his partner for no reason at all, and he feels guilty about this later. He sympathizes with the suffering in the world and can cry about what is happening to Mother Earth and to the children in his street who are growing up without any spirituality.

Getting in contact with the anger smouldering under his sorrow would fundamentally help him further. How should he go about this? He could begin by projecting the whole world on a cushion and enlarging his wrath. Something in the vein of: "I hate you with all your misery and all your stupidities, with your violence, etc." I imagine that he will eventually arrive at the little boy who could not withstand the emotional violence of his mother or could not defend himself against the bullying by other children. You can deal with anything in this way. Put it all on a cushion, talk to it and see who *emerges* on that cushion. You will peel the onion of your emotions and bring these emotions home. And everything that really comes home, finds peace and quiet. He has to make a connection with his repressed anger. He may then be able to use his creativeness and do something about the spiritual development of children.

An example of somebody who is extremely locked in his power is the murderer of a politician. *He is an environmentalist, a fighter with the small print of environmental laws in the hand. He describes himself as somebody who is not sensitive and says that in his work, he does not act from his feelings. 'I just act rationally; I do not have to be an animal-lover to protect animals,' he says. After his arrest, he remains unbending and silent and fights via a hunger strike for an ending of the camera surveillance in his cell. He seems to be completely hardened in his own power game. Nobody knows what is really going on in his inner self, and perhaps he does not know himself.*

Here, setting anger in motion is the road that should be taken. Contact with animals also helps according to experiments with hardened criminals in the prisons in America. By giving every prisoner an animal as company, which they have to look after, they become soft-hearted and open. The man from the above example might be helped if he had an alley cat to look after. Perhaps that would be the first step to his becoming a friend of animals. The next might be his becoming a friend of humankind. Everyone is a child of God and a fragment of the one Great Spirit and deserves a chance to find a way out of his/her protective shell. That is if he/she wants to, of course, and everything depends on that. People like this have been so damaged in their love that accepting the love of an animal can be the first cautious step on the path to love. It is all about the ABC of love. That is why it is important for children to have animals and to live in nature. They can learn to set the first steps on the road to love.

Mutual Attraction of Power and Impotence

As power and impotence are two sides of the same coin, they will constantly seek each other out; tormentor seeks victim and victim seeks tormentor. They are each other's mirrors and just like Narcissus, we all need a mirror to get know ourselves. A weak teacher always finds a class that bullies him, and a woman who is frightened and has no inner strength will find a rapist on her path. This is not about the despicable "It's your own fault." There is no judgment here. It is about the chance that the mirror of life gives us to get to know ourselves. And, yes, these can be very difficult lessons in life. They need not be repeated for those that want to understand them.

The Game of Power Within Ourselves

This tormentor and victim game does not only exist in the outer world but also in our inner world. There, too, the pursuer and his victim seek each other out alternately. A victim has always got his tormentor at hand, and that is also an important *light switch*. If everything in the outer world is a mirror and if we agree to take that as a working hypothesis, then we have an important lesson in life: seek the inner game of power and impotence. Go and find out in which way you are your own tormentor and in which way you make a victim of yourself. A few examples:

Are you a workaholic that never takes a day off? Then you are your own tormentor.

Do you criticize yourself often because of your appearance, your inabilities, or your fears? Then you are your own tormentor.

Are you a slave of your own perfectionism? You are your own tormentor.

Discover your own inner war in this way. I think that our inner wars are the most important wars on this planet and the cause of those in the outer world. When you make peace with yourself, you are actually contributing to world peace. A good way to make peace with yourself is by letting your tormentor and your victim, the hardened and the hurt part of yourself, talk to each other. Put them both on a cushion and identify with them in turn. Or write a letter to them, so it becomes very clear how you treat yourself. We often forget that the way we treat other people (also animals and plants) is based upon the way in which we treat ourselves. We often forget that the way we treat other people (and animals and plants) is the base of the way in which we treat ourselves. How nicer you are to yourself, the nicer you become towards another. And for that, you do not have to do anything. It will all go automatically.

People with Inner Strength

You are the salt of the earth, but if the salt has lost its flavour, with what will it be salted? It is then good for nothing, but to be cast out and trodden under the feet of men.

Ye are the light of the world. A city set on a hill cannot be hid. Is the lamp brought to be put under the bushel... and not to be put on the stand?
~Jesus

Who has inner strength? There are many misconceptions about this. Somebody told me admiringly about a woman who had transformed her pain from a rape in earlier years to strength by founding a worldwide imperium in the escort branch. She had become exceedingly rich.

In today's world, we imagine she became socially and financially rich because of strength. But do we call it strength when you take the sexual abuse you have experienced into prostitution in this way? Is it strength when you let other women be sexually abused? Is it strength or a sublimated way of working off your own undigested pain of sexual abuse? I expect that it is the latter. Our world is poisoned by such forms of working off undigested emotions. And the terrible thing about it is that we do not even notice it anymore. We do not know the difference between these types of *strength*, between financial and social success and strength. Anger is not annulled by the power or influence she achieved, and it is also not transformed into real strength. The cause still exists and the inward journey has not been made.

True strength has nothing to do with social and financial success. True strength is all about overcoming power and impotence and digesting your pain. With true strength you have explored power and impotence exhaustively, lived through them, and overcome your own inner war. You have been through the mill. You are not familiar with violence anymore, not against yourself or another. You have found your strength at the bottom of your deepest emotions and at the bottom of your deepest weakness. Somebody who struggled with the acceptance of her strength had the following dream:

> *I am sitting with my son on the floor. He has a salt pitcher, spills the salt, and makes a little hill of it. I tell him to be careful with the salt, but he just goes on. Then I'm at a Spark of Light Week and Riet tells me, 'Identify with the salt.' I say, 'I am the salt of the earth' and become confused. I wake up crying.*

222

A person with inner strength had the following dream:

> *I am walking on the beach with my dog. On my right is the sea, on the left, moorland and bushes. At a certain moment a big green snake glides out the bushes. I know immediately that it is a poisonous one. It comes towards me and wants to attack me. I am holding a cane that I point at the snake; it rolls over on its back in surrender. When I wake up the next morning, I know that I have conquered evil and now have inner strength.*

Strength has everything to do with taking full responsibility for your life. You are no longer a victim, and you do not have to blame yourself or anybody else for anything. *Problems* are seen as challenges and as a chance to learn something.

The Body That Is Set Free

Let us look at the body of a person with inner strength. It is a body that has been set free. It radiates strength and spirit but also vulnerability and flexibility. Relaxation is the basis of the body. Gravity no longer makes it heavy but links it to the earth from which you can grow, light-footed, towards the Light. The body rests in its center, in the abdomen. Here you can find what the Japanese call "hara" and the Chinese call "chi." When you *rest* in your abdomen, you are connected to power that makes you strong in the world, but not in a defensive or offensive way. You have finished with that. You are just yourself, and you rest in your own strength.

Chapter 17

From Pride to Being Proud

Everyone who has any pride will feel torn apart by the feeling of being worthless.
~Carlos Castaneda

We can distinguish between being proud and pride. Being proud is positive and goes together with feelings of happiness and admiration. You may be proud of yourself after achieving a difficult goal or proud of your children.

Pride, on the other hand, is a hindrance to growing and flourishing. This chapter is about pride which profoundly masks anger. It belongs in the first phase of our model, that of stagnant water. It is a fixation that does not help you further in life. Pride is often seen from a moral viewpoint. We have to learn to *bend* although this only helps to strengthen pride. To liberate yourself from pride, you must regard it with love and from a psychological viewpoint.

We will have a look at the various layers found in pride and how to set them afloat in deep, flowing water.

What is pride? There is no univocal answer to that question. The following is compilation of a number of aspects:

- Some people have a proud, aloof attitude. These are usually shy people who have covered up shyness with the opposite. In reality, they are people who are scared to make real contact and for that reason show an aloof pride. Anger is often found under pride, too.

- Pride is assuming you are better and more special than another person. Pride is also the disguise and reversal of an inferiority complex. Underneath this, we can find anger again and a feeling of worthlessness lower down and hidden far away.

- The saying "As proud as a peacock" is well-known. What does a peacock do? He impresses by showing off his feathers. If we translate this behavior to the human level, we find that it is about being impressive and showing off rather than showing who you are. Underneath is an inferiority complex with anger lower down. Of course, we use the expression, as "proud as a peacock," in a positive way when we are proud of an achievement. There is nothing wrong with that!

- Sometimes people are too proud to accept something from another person. It is linked to being cocksure, stubborn, and tight-lipped. It masks anger. Here we see the angry child in the grown-up that says, "I will and shall do it all on my own."

- We also talk of pride when we feel proud of our descent, our country, our children, etc. That this can cover up restrained anger is shown by the following story:

Kate was born in The Netherlands and has an Indonesian father. Because of her skin color, she was discriminated against even though the Indonesian community has been in The Netherlands for years and is reasonably well-integrated. She was sometimes called 'darkie' and was rejected by the local supermarket when she tried to get a holiday job. Whenever she came home sad, her father would say, 'You should rise above it and take pride in your descent;' the Muhammed Ali syndrome of 'Black is beautiful.' When Kate took part in a Spark of Light week, this message was screwed down like a lid on her anger. By becoming aware of this, Kate could liberate herself and scream and beat out her old anger.

Now that we have mapped the manifestations of pride to some extent, we can see that pride usually masks something else. Pride is like a frozen layer over deep undercurrents. If you want to liberate yourself from this negative pride, you will have to melt and discover the underlying layers. You will only be able to melt when you have fundamentally felt and expressed old anger. To allow ice to melt, you sometimes have to light a fire! I think that anger is the common denominator of all the above-mentioned examples. Under this anger lies the feeling of worthlessness, which we already discussed in the chapter about guilt. That is the deepest underside of all our neuroses.

I often see pride in action during Spark of Light Work. Pride expresses itself as the angry child that tells the parents, "I don't need you." It is often the only way out for a child that cannot express its anger. It is, ultimately, the underside of pride. If you remain ignorant of this child's pride, pride will stay lodged inside you and express itself in many ways.

Jane trained herself to be independent during her teenage years. What she wanted was not to need anyone.

She carried the deep, subconscious imprint that the need for someone had not been beneficial to her as a child. She went to outside cafes on her own, went out on her own, and went on holiday alone. She had a slightly unapproachable yet friendly attitude because of which she remained alone. During the Spark of Light Work, she discovered not only the pain of her loneliness, but also the intense anger underneath her pride. During breathwork, she felt she had the choice between growing stiff with pride or stepping over her pride and transforming it into anger with regard to the abandoned child. She chose the latter and liberated herself from the proud attitude, which was not really who she was.

Pride as Found in Mythology

If we look at old mythological tales, we see that pride is often the keynote of the hero who lands himself in all kinds of difficulties because of it. We shall examine a couple of those stories from the viewpoint of inner growth. We shall tell the story of an unsuccessful individuation and the story of one that was successful. We shall also see where the difference lies.

The story of Icarus.

According to the story, Icarus was the son of Daedalus. From a psychological viewpoint, the son is the underdeveloped, young side of Daedalus, the greatest master builder and sculptor of his day. Nobody could equal him. At a certain moment, he had a pupil who threatened to surpass him. Because of vanity and pride, he killed him.

He fled from Athens to escape punishment and landed up in Crete with his young son. Of old, Crete was the place of goddesses and inner growth. After long years in Crete and after having, among other things, built a labyrinth, he became homesick and longed for his fatherland (which is his inner home). The labyrinth with its many secret tunnels and chambers symbolizes the inner quest for one's own core in the tangle of motives and emotions. However, he was stopped from leaving by the powerful king Minos. Together with his son, he thought of a trick to enable them to leave Crete anyway. They made wings and attached these with wax to their clothes. Daedalus warned Icarus not to fly too high, but this fell on deaf ears. Icarus flew close to the sun, the wax melted, and he fell into what is now called the Sea of Icarus. It is the classic story of pride that literally comes before the fall. Daedalus went on his way, broken and lonely, reached the Italian coast, and died in those foreign parts.

The story of Odysseus.

In Odysseus' case (his name means 'the hated') misfortune, but also inner development start with hubris, with pride. He, the proud macho, the conqueror of Troy, was pursued by Poseidon, the sea-god. The sea is the symbol of emotion, and this means that he is pursued by his feelings. He did not become engulfed by the sea as happened to many of his fellow warriors. This means that he is not totally engulfed by his emotions, but manages to keep his head above water. He was protected by Athena, the goddess of insight and transformation at that time. This means that Odysseus has managed to keep in contact with his inner female aspect. Because of his longing for home, he persevered during his voyage which was full of ordeals and strange meetings. We would now call that inner Work. But then he arrived back home in Ithaca, in his own land, where his partner Penelope, waited for him. The inner marriage with his female aspect is crowned by finding his earthly love again.

The crucial difference with the story of Icarus is the presence of the female, the world of feeling and emotion, in the story of Odysseus. In the story of Icarus and Daedalus, the female aspect that symbolizes emotion is completely absent. For that reason, the story of Daedalus-Icarus is one of failure. His pride is not followed by an inner process of growth and ends in a catastrophe. The wholeness of our male and female traits is crucial to our inner growth and to the possibility of transforming pride into a homecoming within ourselves.

Being Proud of Yourself

Being proud of yourself is an accomplishment that you can find at the bottom of your pool of emotions. When you have set your stagnating pride in motion by means of your repressed anger, you will stand firmly on your own two feet. Being proud of ourselves has to be learned by most of us. You learn to be proud to the degree that your qualities and the person you are have been acknowledged as a child. Being proud makes you straighten your back and walk tall through life. This stems from a healthy awareness of who you are and what you can do. You can then face many difficulties and overcome them. Being proud becomes your hallmark when you stand firmly on your own two feet and are happy with who you are. Being proud comes about when you have released your old pride and healed yourself of feelings of worthlessness. At the bottom of your feeling of being good-for-nothing lies the pearl of your divine nature. We are really gods in the disguise of pride and worthlessness! We must liberate ourselves from our disguises. Being proud will then become a definite part of your personality, and you will have a happy self-confidence.

Chapter 18

Bringing Shame to Light

Bringing shame to light is the quickest way to get rid of it

Shame is a significant obstacle. Not only in your life, but also in the Work on yourself. First of all, we shall look at what shame is exactly. Shame is a struggle between your "self" as the *feeling* of who you are and your ideal self. It is a subconscious fight. You feel shame when you think that you have to be different from the person you really are; you are ashamed of yourself. Your ideal-self consists of all the messages you have received since your early youth about how and who you should be according to others. You were brought up with these messages. You have made them your own as it were. Shame is the consequence of your inner struggle between your own definition of who you are and who other people say you are. The more the scales tip towards the ideal-self, the more you feel ashamed in this, usually, subconscious struggle. Shame has to do with external matters that you can perceive. The following areas are found the most:

- *Your appearance.*

  If we open a magazine at random, we see that nowadays the emphasis is on looks. Famous people are put under continuous scrutiny. It is not about what they do but about what they look like. Hair, make-up, and

231

clothes are constantly put under the microscope—women, especially, have to take the rap. After all, women are more emotionally involved in their looks. Women have definitely received more imprints with regard to their appearance than men, although men seem to be catching up. There are more men now that go to the hairdresser regularly, have their hair dyed, and have facelifts. Magazines of the worst kind, but sadly with a wide circulation, allow their readers to put together a top ten of the "worst cases." A make-up artist or a hairdresser has the first go. Somebody has to do something about her eyelids or her "wildly growing eyebrows;" another has to do something about her hair that looks like a wig. Yet another is such a disgrace that she "should come by soon." This is all under the guise of "helping." The hairdresser *does not want to make a fool of the ladies; he wants to help them. In any case, the people in the Top Ten now know what the world thinks of their looks.* How malicious! Such an emphasis on appearance in the media is, on the one hand, the cause of the manipulation of women who are uncertain about themselves and their looks, but at the same time it is the consequence of an almost collective uncertainty. It is the result of being ashamed of your looks. All that emphasis is one big disguise of our inner uncertainty and shame. It is time to liberate ourselves so we can devote ourselves to more meaningful things in life.

- *Ways of expressing ourselves and spontaneity.*

Being ashamed of the way you express yourself is a significant obstacle in your spontaneity. There are so many judgments! "Act your age," "Don't be so childish," "a...doesn't *behave* like that." Shame comes to the fore when you are frightened of showing yourself as you are. Spontaneity comes from your core, uncultivated and uncivilized. As we have all been made neurotic and have become damaged in our natural qualities, we have to dig spontaneity up from under layers of shame and rejection. It has to do with finding your natural, spontaneous, inner child again. We have learned to play so many roles during our life, and we have learned so many virtues and morals that we have lost the knack of being ourselves. Spontaneity has also got to do with living fully in the here and now, and we can only do that if we have fought ourselves free of idealized images from our past.

- ***Expressing emotions.***

This is where we find a lot of shame. Shame can be present in every emotion in which you have been rejected. That is the reason why people put their hands in front of their faces when they cry or grit or grind their teeth when they are angry. There has been great damage in your life if you are ashamed of your natural emotions. After all, emotions are life and movement. They are, for example, the zest in your relationship and the truth in your religion. Being ashamed of emotions means restraining yourself more than is good for you. We have seen what pent-up emotionality means in this book.

- ***Achievements.***

Some people are ashamed of their capacities because they have never been affirmed by significant others in the important years of their youth. Generally speaking, we can say that it is more usual to say what is wrong than what is right. We can see that in our newspapers where news is usually a selection of bad news. It would be fantastic if somebody published a "good news" newspaper. We have all heard the remark "Stop boasting" or "You are getting too big for your boots" when we said something good about ourselves. Jesus said, "Do not hide your light under the bushel." The influence of Calvin and company was usually stronger than the original message of their Teacher. How paradoxical for a child.

- ***Certain subjects can be full of shame.***

  Subjects, such as sexuality or other taboo subjects, may fill you with shame. Blushing is a symptom that may occur in these cases. Blushing is, in fact, fear of showing your vulnerability or a sign of a hidden vulnerable issue. A woman, who had been a frequent visitor of the Moulin Rouge in a previous life, blushed every time the subject of sex was broached. She was a biology teacher at a Secondary School, and this blushing almost made her work unbearable.

The Ways Shame Hinders Us

Shame is an obstacle in your development when it becomes the reason to avoid things. In extreme cases, there can be an atmosphere of keeping silent, denying, and lying. The core of shame is after all, something that is not allowed to come to the light. The most important obstacle for inner growth and development is the shame for expressing emotions. The rest is mostly a derivation. When you do not allow your emotions to come to the light, your life will eventually come to a standstill and be dull. When you keep things that you are ashamed of hidden away, you will not be able to solve them. Your problem-solving ability will thus be damaged. You may become passive. The most important step with regard to shame is to do what you are ashamed of. It will speed up your liberation. After all, the cause is usually in the past and the present does not have to mean a repetition of the past.

Methods of Conquering Shame

To conquer shame, your 'self' must become stronger, we have, after all, seen that "the ideal-self" predominates. To do this, you must become aware of the following:

1. *What does your ideal-self look like?*

   Make a list with traits you would like to have. Do you want to be prettier, more intelligent, tidier, or less chaotic? Can you show your true colors? Can you express the way you feel? You will gain clarity by making such a list.

2. *Which experiences lie behind this?*

   When were you made to look silly when you showed your vulnerability? Were you bullied, or did they laugh behind your back when you expressed something that was really "you"? Did people point their finger at you when you had to wear your sister's old clothes?

3. *Which hidden messages are to be found under your shame?*

   I think that hidden, indirect messages play a major role here. Shame has a lot to do with secrecy. Think of messages in the above named areas.

4. *From whom are those messages anyway?*

   Who gave you the message that you were, for example, not pretty enough? It does not have to be a direct message. The most effective messages are the indirect ones. Were you compared to your sister? Or was your mother insecure about her appearance, and did she sneer at you every now and then? Or was there a competition going on at school about who could please the boys or girls the most? Or was your father not interested in you because you were a girl? Who gave you the feeling that you were a sissy or a softie because you cried? Or did your mother need a strong little man because your father was away a lot? Who secretly gave you the feeling that it was not right if you were angry? Or where did the feeling of being ashamed of sexuality come from?

5. *Accepting emotions.*

Set your emotions in motion in the way that has already been described in this book.

6. *Do and say things you are ashamed of.*

Leave your cloak of old neurosis behind and take the risk of being laughed at or rejected again. Neurosis is only fear of repetition. It can be completely different in the here and now. I overcame my blushing as a young girl by saying laughingly, "It makes me blush." In that way I brought what was hidden to light and felt sure of my ground. The blushing went away quickly. Blushing goes hand in hand with shyness, the fear to step forward.

Shame is unpleasant because it gives you an "unfree" feeling and restricts your life. During the Work with emotions, shame can be a difficult obstacle to proceeding further along your path. We have learned to be ashamed of emotions, such as fear, anger, and vulnerability. It works wonders if you can show for once (in a safe environment) what you have been ashamed of all those centuries! Safety is one of the most important conditions of this Spark of Light Work. Shame is, as all neurosis, the consequence of a learning process and can be overcome with some inner Work. The device is "What you bring to light, becomes light."

Chapter 19

From Victim to Creator

We either make ourselves miserable, or we make ourselves strong. The amount of work is the same.
~Carlos Castaneda

When we have a good look around us, we see how much our way of speaking and looking at things is poisoned by the language of "victimhood." We all seem to be victims of each other in one way or another. Children are victims of their parents; civilians are victims of war, of traffic accidents, of criminality, and of health care; farmers are the victim of legislation; animals of people; children of educational systems, etc. Psychological problems are also described by using the language of victims. We read in a leaflet from the Dutch foundation for mental care: "It can happen to anyone: one in five Dutch men and women are out of circulation due to psychological problems. That is three million people. They are depressed, suffering from stress, have a relationship that is in a rut, are scared, or are still mourning the death of a loved one." Psychological problems are also described elsewhere as an illness, as something that just happens to us, and as something that we are apparently at the mercy of. Where is our own responsibility in the sense that we are able to give an answer to our existence?

237

I will not describe the things that are wrong in our society. I will try to shed some light on our sense of victimization, victim mentality, and victim behavior. The one stems from the other, whereby the sense of victimization is primary.

When you were a child, you knew how the imbalance of power felt, how it felt that "they are big and I am small." Depending on the way the powerful treated this imbalance, you started to feel like a victim. When I say something like this, people often react in a trivializing way and say, "It was for our own good." Of course it was, yet others determined that you had to be at school the whole day and that is not enjoyable for a playful, lively child. Of course, you did not know any better and you adapted. But if you could have listened to your own feelings and have had a say in the matter, you would have organized the way you learned differently. A healthy child does not need to know about earning a lot of money or about other worries for later. A child needs lessons in life and an initiation to life on earth; it needs guidance. Our school system has become a factory where children are indoctrinated and adapted to a world in which economy and financial matters are of first importance.

We sometimes have to dig deep down into ourselves to find the call for liberty under the layer of indoctrination and adaptation. Proceeding from that call for liberty, you can discover to which extent you feel victimized by others who lay down the law for you. This can start early and depends on you whether you had an authoritarian upbringing or not. You had to go to bed when your mother and father wanted you to and not when you wanted to. Yet a child that has the freedom to live from its own center and needs will certainly tell you when it needs to go to bed; it will find its own natural rhythm. You had to go to school when the government thought you should. Your parents determined when you had to go to the day center. You had to behave nicely, not put your hands under the blankets, and not put your elbows or your feet on the table. These are all rather trivial matters when seen from a natural point of view.

All this *having to* is one side of the sense of victimization. The other side is specified by the presence of essential matters such as respect, attention, and affective connection. You did not have any power over these things either. It did not help when you tried to force the love you needed as a child. You cannot receive what is not there.

Children will try in all manner of ways to get what they miss. One child will adapt very well just to get a compliment or a pat on the head. It will think that that is love. Another will behave defiantly and make sure it gets attention in that way. Another will withdraw into its own little world and become *an easy child* for the parents and get a lot of positive attention. Achieving at school and later at work is a strategy a lot of children keep up till far in adulthood! "If I just...they might love me." Our achievement-oriented society developed in this way. Everyone has to be the best. Just take a look at all the advertisements. Even a Calvinistic Dutch newspaper calls itself "probably the best newspaper." It is a good newspaper, but why do they need to be the best? Cities want to be the most beautiful, sports men and women the best, and businesses want to be the greatest. It is no wonder that children lose their natural needs and take part in the race to be the biggest and the best. It is all a cry for love: "See me, love me!" Our true sense of victimization is hidden under all those cries for love and attention.

Complaining and Dissatisfaction

We do not only try to do our best, but we also complain about all manner of things, and this stems from our sense of victimization. Complaining really means not taking responsibility for our life. It is often an unspoken accusation towards others. We see, yet again, a generalization of anger here. The repressed anger of the restricted and neglected inner child will be aimed at anything or anyone that can function as a stepping-stone in adulthood. Does this mean that we cannot complain about criminality or noisy neighbors? Of course, I do just that in this book! It is more about a subconscious and chronic pattern of behavior that is spreading like a cancerous growth in us and in our society. It is about generalizing an old emotional charge which found its origins in the past. It is about chronic dissatisfaction that may be aimed at the doctor or the neighbors or at other times at the children, etc., etc.

The feeling you had when you were a child was right. You were left to the mercy of adults, after all. The problem that many of us have is that we never got over the sense of victimization. We give free rein to repressed emotional charge far into adult life in the form of complaining and dissatisfaction. This complaining is like an oppressive thundery wind blowing through our society. This kind of basic dissatisfaction is not good for our coexistence. It is important to dig up your original dissatisfaction and the feeling of being unfulfilled so these can be digested as old pain. Room for satisfaction and your own responsibility as a true grown-up will then come. You will realize that you create your own life and that neither your past nor your present makes your life what it is. *The light switch is the moment you understand that the cause of your dissatisfaction is not having coped with your past, your traumas and want.* To cure yourself of chronic dissatisfaction, you have to go back to where you really did not have enough in life. It is painful to feel this need again, but on its own, it is not the reason for our neurosis of dissatisfaction. The essence of the story is not having digested the pain caused by this need. It is not only the essence but also the light switch! You can still do your backlog of digestion Work by making use of the device *better late than never.*

Gratitude

It has struck me that there are hardly any people who can really say "Thank you." From a subconscious, undigested feeling of want, many people cannot distinguish between what is there now and what once was not there. Many people do not know what thankfulness is due to being neurotically unfulfilled. I have also noticed that a lot of people have difficulty expressing their gratitude. It is as if they cannot utter the words "Thank you" as if anger or pride are part of expressing gratitude. As we have already seen, pride is hardened anger. The annoying thing is that it is old anger which is aimed at people in the present. I remember a friend of mine who really minded not being able to say "Thank you." Really minding about something is an important step on the way to gratitude. Her respectable upbringing was to blame for this; as a child, she was always made to say thank you while she could not feel thankful inside. She had to say thank you for the clothes her mother bought for her, but she was not allowed to choose them herself. She was forced to be dishonest, which made her rebellious and angry which was justifiable in that case. Gratitude became blemished. Gratitude should have come from inside but was enforced from the outside, which resulted in not feeling real gratitude anymore.

When the cook is not thanked for all the work after a delicious meal, I see that as a kind of poverty. I remember once journeying through Denmark with my swimming club; we shared meals and stayed overnight at the homes of our fellow-swimmers. It was the custom for children to say "tak for mal" to their mothers after every meal. Grace, spoken with conviction, is a good habit and teaches children that everything is a gift. It is a kind of poverty when people complain about what they *have not*, but cannot see what they *have*. It casts a shadow over a party when after the host and hostess have done their best to make it enjoyable, everyone goes home without showing any signs of appreciation and gratitude.

The realization that life is a present is lost in our affluent society. Everything becomes a matter-of-course. Everything can be bought after all! Only health cannot be bought, and people complain bitterly about that. I shall examine that subject further in Chapter 42. I shall stop discussing this now, as it will otherwise become complaining about complaining!

The important thing is to realize why you cannot be grateful. Which feeling of anger or being unfulfilled has caused this? If the reason lies in your past, it is best to Work on it. If your anger and feeling of being unfulfilled are in the present, see if you can change your life in such a way that there will be room for contentment and gratitude. Gratitude is a solace for the soul and a blessing for our coexistence on this beautiful planet. It is important to know that you hold the light switch even if a situation is difficult. Everything depends on your willingness to see how you created that situation and your life and on how you handle it.

This might sound like a harsh statement, but I know that it is not only true but that it works as a wonderful guideline for a fulfilled and grateful life. True gratitude is an aspect of our essence when we have overcome our neuroses.

Helplessness and Requesting Help

The feeling of helplessness is part of the sense of victimization. You often felt helpless when you were a child, and that was not a pleasant feeling so you pushed it away quickly and hoped to be grown up soon. Now that you are grown-up, you can still feel helpless while that feeling does not really fit the adult you are now. You still push it away as it is still not pleasant. We usually compensate feelings that have been pushed away, in this case: "I don't need anybody" and "I can look after myself." This is the proud voice of the disappointed and angry inner child that did not know what to

242

do with its sad feelings of want. This pride is one of the biggest obstacles on our inner path. Most of us have decided early on in life, deep down within us, to manage on our own—not because we enjoy doing it but because it was once too painful to need help but not to get it. That is the reason why it is still very difficult for us to request and accept help. At the same time we constantly visit the doctor with all manner of complaints and ailments. Really asking for help means accepting your helplessness and that conjures up memories. You can learn to ask God or other people for help if you are prepared to remember old hurt, let it go, and then finally cry about it. When there are no old charges involved in asking for help, you can feel free to ask for anything you need and accept it! After all, when you do not have to do it all on your own, life becomes easier. What you cannot do yourself, perhaps someone else can. In this way, we can all become the one body of God because that is what we really are. We are all part of the one great Light and the one great Being that once began to create this universe. Together we stand strong and can create our world. If we learn to create again from within our inner child who has digested its pain, the world will look different. There will be more naturalness and more harmony with nature. There will be more playfulness and contentment, and everything will become simpler as we do not need much when our inner child has been healed.

Things I Must Do/Not Do or I Want to Do/Not Do

The constant use of the word "must" is, in fact, an indication of victim behavior. Make a list of all the things you *must* do. Here are a few examples to get you started:

I must help . . . (fill in the blank) as much as possible.
I must go and do the shopping.
I must read those books.
I must stop smoking.
I must not eat so much.

243

Now fill in "I want to" or "I don't want to" in place of "I must." Can you feel the difference? By using "must," you become a victim of your own demands and live on autopilot. With "want to," you take responsibility for your own behavior. This is where freedom of choice and life begin. To "want to" means believing in what you want and is an inner impetus.

Weakening: The Jelly Feeling

A physical characteristic of the sense of victimization is muscular tissue that has become weak. When you have a sense of victimization, you literally let yourself droop. It means suffering and enduring, and the pattern consists of weakening and not fighting. I recognize this from the family pattern of my youth; I was a late arrival and could not compete with my older sisters on physical, mental, emotional, and verbal level. I hid behind my mother's skirts, and she protected me, which was very pleasant, but left me feeling socially inconvenienced. I did not learn to stand up for myself, and I could not fight, not even with children of my own age. I felt the victim of my sisters and later of others. I only learned what assertiveness was and how to stand up for myself in a healthy way and take my place in this world when I came in contact with my pent-up anger during a scream therapy. My muscles became suppler, and the weakness almost completely disappeared. You can recognize weakening mainly by drooping shoulders that express a lack of aggression and by the inability to hit out with the arms. The body often has the tendency to lean forwards and looks like it is having a hard time in life. Somebody once jokingly called this the "jelly feeling"!

Feeling Guilt as a Victim

People who feel a victim of something, often feel guilty although they are not guilty at all—especially people who experienced a violent crime, such as rape, who feel guilty although they realize rationally that they could do nothing about it. Often they do not understand why they feel like this. I think that there is only one answer possible—the feeling of guilt is an accusation turned inwards. Liberating yourself from this feeling of guilt can be done by expressing anger with the method we already described. A series of talks is often used as victim assistance, but that is not enough for the digestion of this kind of trauma. Expressing anger and other emotions intensely by shouting and beating a cushion will make guilt melt like summer snow. It will also help you to stand firmly on your own two feet again. After all, such guilt is a sign of hate that is aimed at yourself. You can turn it in the right direction by aiming it at the person who has used violence against you.

The other connection between the sense of victimization and the feeling of guilt is when you as the victim, give another person the feeling that they are guilty. This is closely connected to the above-mentioned variant. We treat others as we treat ourselves, after all. If you feel chronically guilty, you can cause someone else to feel guilty. The overburdened mother with many children can serve as an example here. She has a lot of work and has not learned how to stand up for herself. She feels a victim of the life she leads. She will silently vent this sense of victimization and give others a guilty feeling. She does not, of course, do this consciously. The subconscious is once more the evil demon of our behavior. If you realize this, you hold the key to changing the situation. A second step is changing the situation creatively and to your own advantage.

If parents decide to bring children into this world to compensate for their lack of fulfilment, these children may feel guilty about the mere fact that they exist. When parents still say "me, me, me" deep down inside themselves, children will often be a burden and will receive this message early in life. The consequence is a feeling of guilt. Liberating yourself from the sense of victimization is essential in ending the story of guilt as no good comes from it.

The Rescuer

When you feel guilty in regard to a person who has victim behavior, you will perhaps feel that you want to save that person. A lot of children have tried to make their parents happy and "help Mummy." Many have carried on with this pattern of exhaustively helping others. Helping each other is worthwhile and loving, but, in this case, I am referring to help that is based on guilt and on people's own neuroses.

I am talking about help that finally exhausts you because it is not based on love or pleasure but has the same pattern as the small child that wants to help and rescue mummy and daddy because they are not happy. Circumstances like this are difficult because our behavior is simultaneously influenced by a multitude of things: neurotic or healthy, straightforward or not so straightforward. We are very complicated beings! Every helper in the mental health-care, who says that therapy is a piece of cake, underestimates his own complexity and that of those he is trying to help. It is important to get rid of the neurotic part of your help by awareness and digestion. It will then be great to help another person a bit further! We cannot save each other. We may try to do that from a subconscious feeling of guilt, but it is bound to fail and will lead to exhaustion. The motivation of the person in question is necessary for real rescue. Help is only possible when motivation is present, however difficult it may be to accept this. You can only give responsibility back when you know your own responsibility.

The Pursuer

There is a third player in the game of victimhood, and he is called *the pursuer* in Transactional Analysis. The three players (victim, rescuer and pursuer) are inclined to swap places. That is the most important rule of this victim game. An example may elucidate this game:

Trudy and Hester are friends. Because of a traumatized youth, Trudy is inclined to give up every now and then and not take responsibility for her present life situation. She feels bitter and a victim of her horrible past. She is inclined to lean on Hester. Hester is sorry for Trudy and really wants to help her. She advises all kinds of therapies and gives her good advice. Trudy does not really want to be fundamentally helped and prefers her victim behavior. After years of help and advice, Hester starts to become impatient and angry. She cannot keep her irritations to herself any longer. She feels that Trudy and all her problems are forever bugging her. She now experiences this behavior as moaning. Her position switches from rescuer to victim and subsequently to pursuer. Trudy is now also a pursuer, as she feels abandoned and unjustly treated. She starts to snap at Hester who gets all her angry charges which really stem from her past and are meant for somebody else.

A lot of people are caught in this contact game because it is brought about subconsciously and from a repetition compulsion. Hester was a prisoner of her role as rescuer because she probably had a similar history with her chronically depressed mother. Because she had not coped with her mother's depression, she felt compelled to save and help Trudy. This will ultimately lead to anger, the position of pursuer, or to exhaustion; the position of victim. Real help is always done freely; free of repetition compulsion and neurosis and free of expectations and results. Many people, myself included, have become helpers due to, among other things, a neurotic background. It is important to clear this for your client's sake and for your own. Therapists and helpers should always keep working on themselves, especially those in the mental health-care. The best therapist is always the one who is the best client!

Responsibility: The Capacity to Answer to Your Existence

Responsibility means being prepared to say: 'I am who I am' and 'I am what I am'.

~Fritz Perls

The only way out of this disastrous three-cornered game is to become aware of it. We should realize that it is a game and accept that the way out is by accepting our own responsibility. In our everyday vocabulary, responsibility has become a word that has been linked instinctively to duty, guilt, and seriousness. When someone says, "It is your own responsibility," many people feel troubled and abandoned. It has acquired moral connotations. If we look at the word itself, we see that the word *response* is central, followed by the word *ability*. It is about your ability to respond to your existence and to be the answer itself. This ability is part and parcel of the gift of liberty, as we know it on this planet. Responsibility is accepting the challenge to shape your own life as you see fit. This does not mean that we have to do everything on our own; we can help one another. If we do not know something, somebody else might; and when we cannot feel, another person may do so. Brother- and sisterhood is another challenge. Together we can take responsibility for our existence, each in our own way.

Being a Creator

There are of all kinds of tips and advice on how to become the creator of your life. A lot of books are being written about this subject at the moment. They are about motivation, intention, and visualizing what you want to realize. They discuss activating latent possibilities, using positive thinking and affirmations, using the spiritual laws of success, and such like. They are all great aids in helping you organize your life as you see fit. And yet, I feel that all that exercise and mental realization is not enough if you do not fundamentally free yourself from your story of victimhood. When you change your pool of stagnant water into a stream of emotions, you will automatically become more creative and create your life to your own taste. Transforming your sense of victimization into anger helps you to stand firmly on your own two feet and makes you strong. It helps you to choose what is important for you. This transformation helps to make weak muscles supple again. The anger you have vented gives you the courage not to weaken again or to do things that you do not want to do. It gives you the ability to make your own choices. The digestion of anger helps you to come bravely out of your shell and exchange your petty life for larger and more abundant living. Your discontent gives you a motor with which to do whatever is important to you in life.

The digestion of underlying sorrow makes you feel compassionate and soft towards yourself. It helps you to choose what your heart longs for. You want this, but not that. You chose what gives fulfilment. You become the creator of your own life. At the bottom of your stream of emotions you can find creativity as one of your greatest treasures.

Chapter 20

From Wishing Death to Loving Life

*As long as a person gets in his own way, it will seem that
everything gets in his way.*
~Emerson

Suicide and the attempt to commit suicide are themes that
should not be omitted in this book. It is a subject that
needs some clarification. First and foremost, I would like
to state that I do not have an opinion about the fact whether
suicide is permissible or not. This planet is a place of free will,
and that is a precious and important part of the "experiment
Earth." This means that we are allowed to do what we want
with our lives. I believe that there is no judgment and certainly
no condemnation in the cosmos. Suicide and the attempt to
commit suicide are an indication of much human suffering
which needs help and clarification.

If people try to kill themselves, it is usually a sign of
obstructed emotionality and life energy. The reason for having
a death wish is often sought in existing life issues. However,
the present problem is the result of the path through life
whereby denial and repression of emotions are central (again).

251

By focusing on present life issues, we do not go to the heart of the matter, namely the death wish. Taking your own life is usually self-denial rooted in self-hatred. Self-hatred is hate that is wrongly directed and which should be transformed into anger and grief. Suicide, certainly when it is committed in an aggressive way such as throwing yourself in front of a train, is usually retroflection, a boomerang of extreme aggression directed at oneself. Even if depressive behavior and despair are demonstrable on the surface, we will have to search for the original anger and the beginning of sorrow. It is also possible that a flood of emotions from the subconscious play a role. The self is not strong and integrated enough to steer the emotions in the right direction.

If we cannot find the cause in the present, where should we look? In the past, of course! Despair and self-hatred do not just come into existence; they have their roots in the past. To find a cure, you must go back to where it went wrong in your life because that is where you take the sting out. That sting is called undigested experiences. It is never the trauma itself! This is a misconception that often leads to a sense of victimization and to victim behavior. As soon as you realize that these undigested experiences are the reason for your misery, you can start with the Work of digestion. During sessions I found that many people have a hidden death wish. In actual fact, many discovered a suicidal child in themselves. Sometimes it was even a suicidal baby, who was, of course, not able to articulate that feeling. Arthur Janov, the founder of the primal scream therapy, claims that a hundred per cent of his clients have been confronted by suicidal feelings during sessions.[1] Most of us have forgotten those feelings because they were once too painful. Remembering these feelings is very difficult because our perception of reality was vague when we were a baby. We had difficulty focusing, and that is the reason why we have more difficulty remembering the time we were a baby than we do later years. But it is possible to let this suicidal inner child come to the light in deep emotional work as an adult. Suicidal tendencies are a generalized "No" to life and also generalized anger against life and the whole world. The light switch in this work is directing and localizing the "No" in time and seeing which life you are really saying "No" to. This "No" has usually got to do with an old history that you have repressed. You have forgotten the story, repressed the feelings, but the subconscious "No" as expression of pain and anger has stayed and been generalized to the whole of life and directed at the here and now. It is, therefore, very important to always place your feelings and emotions correctly in time and place.

I remember a young woman who, during emotional work, started to feel how she once lay in a cradle in a room with many doors where she felt very unsafe. She experienced her parents as being emotionally distant. In her perception, she did not have a warm emotional bond with her parents. After she had felt emotional coldness during breathwork, whereby she started to shiver, her suicidal inner child started to speak: 'I want to go back' and 'I don't want to be here.' By completely experiencing this 'No' in an eruption of anger after which an intense and helpless grief came out, her "Yes" to life could grow.

If you want to be able to say "Yes" to life, you will have to find all your "No's", experience them again, and specify them; by digesting the "No's" in your past, your "Yes" will become bigger in the present!

Besides this experience of emotional coldness and disappointment in the childhood years, you may perhaps carry a so-called incarnation refusal on the basis of past lives. This often happens when you died in a traumatic way in a past life, during a war, for example. The same Work applies here as with the "No" from this life. By experiencing the old trauma anew and by working through it in an emotional way and by remembering it, energy will be released that will help you to live fully in the present and to say "Yes" to the possibilities life on earth offers you. I know the incarnation refusal from my past life. I died a traumatic death in Auschwitz in my past life, which meant I had now a lot of trouble coming to earth. As a child, I always used to walk on my toes, and I remember my mother encouraging me and saying "Heels, toes!" I did eventually learn to put my feet on the ground, but my soul had more trouble with earth. Only when I relived that past life in therapy did life start to become really nice. Your "Yes" will always be unsatisfactory if your "No" is repressed. Your "Yes" will become more complete to the extent that you bring your "No," which has many layers, to the light. The following is the story of a forty-year-old woman and her liberation from depression:

> *During a number of months, I felt myself becoming more and more depressed and tired, and I had a flat feeling as if dark clouds were hanging above me, and all lights were going out inside me. I desperately wondered where all my cheerfulness had gone. I was sure that it had nothing to with my current life and situation. I had a great relationship, beautiful children, and nice, interesting work. The depression felt like an ancient part of my soul, but I could not place it. When I started Spark of Light Work, memories started to surface: when I was a child, I wore a button with the text: 'I wish I was dead'. Everybody laughed about it, I did, too. But I did not wear it for nothing. I remembered lonely, sleepless nights. My teenage years followed. I withdrew; I thought I was stupid and uninteresting. Alcohol helped me to feel a bit better.*

> *Through intensive breathwork I reached emotions that I once could not express, but now could, thank goodness. I experienced this seemingly endless loneliness and cried for weeks. When I had worked through this painful period, images surfaced from a past life in which I had committed suicide as a young woman. Here, too, intense breathwork aided by music*

helped me to remember and to digest. From my emotions came the image of losing my mother as a young child and being lodged with family by my father. As a grown-up, I could not find my niche in life and felt very lonely. During the reliving, I felt how alone and desperate I was. It defies description. I felt less and less life energy and was pulled towards death as if it was the only solution. I cut my wrists then. In the reliving I could feel how the blood and life slowly drained out of me. I was happy that there was someone there to supervise this process. In talks I started to see the connection between that life and the depressions in my current one. After all this deep Work, I started to recover from this 'dark night of the soul'. I started to gain energy and what I had wanted so much, happened: I regained my pleasure in life.

If you have remembered and digested the pain of your past, in this life or in the past one, you can feel compassionate about your inner child or the other person you once were. You straighten your back and meet the challenges of life with courage and pleasure.

The Work in Steps

Here are the steps to move from moving from wishing death to wishing and loving life:

- Going from the realization of a general "No" to a specific "No." Starting to remember where the "No" belongs in time, place, and relationship.
- Expressing the "No," the anger, and the sorrow in a therapeutic manner.
- Embracing the inner child and granting it life.

Chapter 21

Self-mutilation: A Contorted Attempt to Feel

I cut myself, so I'm in pain. Pain is feeling. I can feel again, so hurrah! I'm back again, even if it is for a little while. I am in contact with reality for a little while

*T*here are many forms of self-mutilation. The most direct form is wilfully cutting yourself, scratching, burning, hitting, or pulling out your hair. The official term is auto-mutilation. In addition to this, we find anorexia, excessive drinking and smoking, or the extreme use of drugs. In the first instance, I will discuss the first mentioned and most direct form of self-mutilation. There are no known statistics of the numbers of people who mutilate themselves. Research shows that especially women choose this form of self-mutilation and that many were sexually or physically damaged in their youth. Andries van Dantzig, the well-known Dutch psychiatrist and founder of an organization against child abuse said: "It happens more than we realize; at least fifty thousand children are abused in the Netherlands alone. At least fifty die. One in five wrestles with psychosocial problems. We do not know how many children receive adequate help and neither do we know what happens to them. We do know that undigested experiences lead to numerous problems at school, in relationships, at work, in health matters, and in the upbringing

257

of children. Child abuse leads to extensive personal and social problems."

It is important to eradicate self-mutilation utterly, and we have to start with child abuse. The organisation against child abuse recommends taking on a law that forbids parents to hit their children, as has already happened in Sweden and other countries. I agree with this wholeheartedly. Hitting children is misuse of power and should be eradicated by means of a law, proper information, and courses in education. Not very long ago, I read a newspaper article in which a Dutch conservative Minister advocated giving children a clip round the ear in class again—and that as part of bringing back values and standards! I agree that children have to be taught respect, but if that has to be done with physical violence, then something is wrong with the authority of adults. It would be good idea to train teachers in loving, distinct ways of showing their power and authority.

The young man who wrote the following demonstrates a clear link between abuse (and mental abuse) and his self-mutilation:

> *I grew up in a loveless family. I was not really wanted by my father. Very much wanted by my mother who assumed I was the perfect son. When something happened, they told me much too often: 'thought so' or 'there he goes again.' When something goes well, I still hear: 'Golly, can't believe that went right'. In other words, you can't really do anything right and if you try, there is hardly any chance you will succeed--'I'm so disappointed in you'. If I did receive any love from my mother, it was quickly stifled in the problems between her and my father and in her perfectionistic expectations of me.*

> *Cuddles? I can't remember them. I try to find traces of intimacy in my past. But they are usually not there, and I often lose my way. My father openly*

committed adultery with the rear neighbor. My mother did not want to be left behind. It was the early seventies after all; feminism, free sex, partner swapping. As revenge, she committed adultery with the husband of that self-same rear neighbor. There was a lot of tension in their relationship. Now why doesn't that surprise me? My father vented his emotions on me—physically. He knocked me straight into hospital the very first time. If you want to do something, why not do it properly? The damage was physically and mentally irreparable. I still have an earache almost every day. According to the doctor, there is nothing to be done about it.

Oh, God, I wish I could cry. Cry because of the pain in my stomach, I feel so much sorrow. I'll try anything to be able to cry: boozing, sex, smoking dope. The only thing I wrote in my diary, page after page, was 'Please help me.' I feel lonely and abandoned. Hidden away in a small room, a small, frightened kid, abandoned by mummy. I need you, mummy. Hold me. I'm scared to be on my own. In all the confusion, I read a book. The main character cuts himself. I don't find it shocking. It gives me an idea. Then, a few evenings later, I cut myself. I hardly felt anything during the cutting. The only thing I feel is a knot, deep down beneath my self-control. I want to cry, scream. I don't really feel anything during the cutting. I can see that I'm doing it. I look at my arm, but my arm isn't mine, not joined to my body. Not feeling has been so drummed into me that I don't feel a thing. Just a moment—I do feel, but it seems that it is not happening to me. Exactly like it once was.

Bullying and being bullied.

People, who were bullied in their childhood by other children, are another group that may start self-mutilating.

259

Bullying at school and in the street is a widespread problem. There is a lot of suffering in silence. When children do not receive a loving reception for their pain at home, self-mutilation becomes an option. It is important to completely stamp out aggression between children. It is usually not anger towards each other; children often vent their anger at each other because anger is not tolerated by parents and educators. It is turned inwards or is vented at other children "that they are able to deal with."

Self-mutilation has various aspects:

1. Pent-up emotions;
2. An attempt to feel;
3. A call for autonomy;
4. A need for punishment;
5. A cry for help; and/or
6. Addiction.

Pent-up Emotions

I just had to do something, I had the feeling I would otherwise explode.

The most important background of self-mutilation is the inability to express anger. The anger is unemotional and is not allowed to penetrate into the awareness because of fear or because of a taboo. For this reason, anger returns like a boomerang, and every time the inner emotional tension becomes too much, the need to mutilate and hurt oneself comes into being. From the website of a self-help group:

> *Cutting yourself, scratching, burning, pulling your hair out, or the intake of harmful substances not as a suicide attempt but rather as a survival strategy. Self-mutilation is a taboo that people do not know how to cope with.*

Anna: I wanted to feel. I could not cry and did not know what to do with my emotions. If I had not cut myself, I would have gone mad ages ago. I started three years ago, after being assaulted by a colleague. I have been the victim of assault, rape, and abuse since my early youth.

After the last 'event' I went bananas. I had been able to keep a lid on my feelings, but I couldn't suppress them anymore. All my traumas came to the surface. I could not cry and didn't know what do to do with all my emotions. I had eating problems, suffered from sleeping disorders and panic attacks. I wanted to run away. I worked 12 hours a day, I had a morbid passion for sports, and my house was immaculate. Nothing helped. In my despair, I started to cut myself. That was an enormous relief. It gave me peace, a breathing space. If I hadn't been able to cut, I would have gone mad, long ago.

Auto-mutilation is a way to handle extreme tension. We also see this in animals who find themselves in pitiful situations, such as laboratory animals and animals in captivity. The psychological pain is worse than the physical pain. Sometimes the person who inflicts the wounds feels temporarily less because of the heightened adrenalin levels in the blood that numb the pain.

Jane explains, 'You express the pain that you feel inside that you cannot deal with. You are in a mist when you cut. Your sorrow and anger are temporarily gone because of the pain of the wounds. You only realize what has happened when you come to your senses. And then you have to concentrate all your attention on looking after your wounds.'

A young girl relates:

> *I have not been not neglected, physically mistreated, or abused, and yet I started auto-mutilating at a young age. In my case, it has to do with expressing tension, anger, and powerlessness. Emotions, especially negative emotions, such as jealousy and anger, were taboo at home. I was not allowed to have those emotions. Everything had to go well with me. Severe sanctions were imposed on expressing those emotions. If I threatened to show something of my 'evilness' in a moment of weakness, I was told that other children were better than me and that I had to be careful if I still wanted my parents to give me love. Because you are dependent on your parents or educators, you try to do your best for them. Often at a cost to your identity! I was not allowed to have the anger I felt, let alone express it.*

The carpet beater is a simple aid in this case. Every time you feel the urge to mutilate yourself, start hitting a cushion and try to 'warm-up' the unemotional anger. Allow emotion again. Aim your anger at a cushion and imagine that the person at whom you are angry is there. You will not hurt anybody in this way, not yourself or another person, but you will get rid of your old charges of anger because that is what is important.

An Attempt to Feel

Hurting yourself is an attempt to feel something—a relocation of the physical pain that you dare not feel. It is a pity that a lot of help remains at a verbal level and does not answer the deeply felt need to feel. The young man from our first example found, after years of searching, a haptonomist/bodyworker, who brought him in contact with his tears by touching him. It is really very simple; a safe environment, a helper who is not frightened of intense emotions and a sincere touch and a few simple techniques as described elsewhere in this book.

> *At last I find the help I went without all those years. A haptonomist's/bodyworker's touch makes it possible for me to feel—inside, without the endless flow of words. She touches the damaged places. I cry for hours after all those years of searching. She slowly lets me feel who I am, and the tears come—tears that had never came with all the help I've had. I'm very good at covering things up with words. What an emptiness I found in that sea of tears. She let me be, tears were okay, silence was okay, and I didn't have to do anything.*

Searching for Autonomy

For some, searching for their own autonomy is an important aspect of self-mutilation. It is a way to have control over something, in particular your own body.

> *Self-mutilation gives me the feeling that I have a say in what happens to me. My parents lived my life for me. They wanted to make me a model daughter, and I did everything within my power to make sure they were not disappointed. What I wanted was not taken into account. By damaging myself, I could do something, secretly, that I had power over. I decide when and where I will have a bruise! It gave me the feeling of autonomy I needed, but that kind of freedom is fatal. It was my friend, first of all, but became my enemy.*

The Need for Punishment

When a child receives the message that it is not good and cannot be loved, it will take over that attitude. It will think it is bad and punish itself. Most people have a veiled need for punishment. They do not allow themselves to have anything, or

263

they live a petty life of misery. In extreme cases, negative feelings about oneself can be expressed by the need for punishment in the form of self-mutilation. Especially feelings of anger can be a reason to punish oneself.

A Cry for Attention

'Receiving attention has also become an aspect of my self-mutilation. Asking for attention by hurting myself originated in my not being able to express myself in less destructive ways by talking, for example. For me, self-mutilation is a way of communicating, a way of saying, 'Help! It's going very badly.'

The cry for attention is often hidden and has fear or a taboo attached.

Addiction

If self-mutilation has become part of your life, and you have found no other way to express your emotions, it can then become addictive, just like alcohol and drugs. Self-mutilation becomes a recurring attempt to keep the real pain at a distance. Self-mutilating gives you a kind of high that numbs your real feelings. One person alternated self-mutilation with excessive masturbation. Both methods helped to feel no emotions at all. An important characteristic of addiction is the fear of feeling.

The Work

As the aggressive component is, first and foremost, it is obvious that anger should be mobilized first and that people should be taught to aim their anger properly with a carpet beater and a cushion. The intense sorrow underneath should be released. The Work is really quite simple. A self-help group works well; acknowledgement, mutual solidarity, not beating about the bush, and no pressure are important ingredients.

> *There was such recognition; everybody was interested in my story, everybody accepted me, and there are no taboos. That we self-mutilate is our bond. We call it self-mutilation when talking to others; amongst ourselves we do not mince words and call it cutting, scratching, burning. Together we try to discover patterns. It can happen that somebody feels the need to self-mutilate during a session, we discuss that then. Of course, you try to stop each other, but if you really must, you go home. The agreement is to keep in touch.*

Another member of the self-help group writes:

> *Cutting has shown me that there really is something wrong with me. I have gone into therapy and because of that, I have gained a lot. I have started to take myself more seriously. I have started to gain more self-assurance, and I understand that I have all the reasons in the world to be angry and sorrowful. I can cry for the first time. Cry! That was something I didn't dare dream of. I am not scared to feel my grief, and I discover that the world does not stop turning. Sorrow is slowly disappearing.*

Cosmetic Surgery: A Luxurious Alternative?

When you randomly open a newspaper or a magazine nowadays, there is usually an advertisement from a commercial medical clinic offering breast implants, breast reduction surgery, tummy tucks, face lifts, hair replacement, lip enlargements, labia corrections, penis enlargements, nose, chin, or ear surgery, etc., etc. Is this a new form of self-mutilation? It is done under anaesthetic, but what about scar formation? Our body has energy pathways, meridians, and scars disturb the energy balance. It seems that this kind of self-mutilation is very popular among middle-aged women and men. Is it another case of repressed anger against oneself? Is this modern craze, a form of self-hatred? I am afraid it is but disguised under a layer of coquettishness, vanity, fear of growing old, and fundamental insecurity. It would be interesting to see in how far the six aforementioned aspects also play a role in this group; pent-up and denied emotion, an attempt to feel, a call for autonomy, need for punishment, a cry for attention and addiction.

A certain person, who is now following the Spark of Light Work path, felt the need to have a 'nose job' but she had not yet decided. During a Spark of Light week, somebody said to her, 'You have such a lovely face'. She reacted in surprised way and could not allow the remark to sink in. A little while later, she started to cry and remembered her elder sister saying hateful things about her nose when they were in company. While she was telling this, she grabbed hold of the carpet beater and beat all her aggression out of her system. A few weeks later, she rang me up to tell me that her sense of smell was much better!

We can do it like this, and that is the Work.

Chapter 22

Jealousy, Longing, and Fulfilment

Jealousy is one of the most prevalent areas of psychological ignorance about yourself, about others and more particularly, about relationships.
~Osho

*T*he only Bible story I remember from my childhood days is the one from the Old Testament about Joseph and his jealous brothers. Father Jacob had many sons, but Joseph was one of the youngest, and he loved him most of all. Moreover, Joseph was very special because of the dreams he had. One of his dreams was about binding sheaves of wheat with his brothers in the fields; his sheaf stayed upright while his brother's sheaves stood in a circle around his and bowed.

As a child and a late arrival, I loved that story. On a subconscious level, I recognized myself in Joseph and my elder sisters in his brothers. They were also jealous of the late addition to the family. I cannot recollect any concrete deeds that were done from jealousy; I was not thrown in the well or sold. I have discovered through reliving the past, that jealousy did have an effect on me on an energetic level. Jealousy means, ultimately, that others begrudge you life and light. My sisters did not do that because they were nasty people but because they apparently did not get enough of what they needed in life and had the impression that their little sister did.

And that is what jealousy really amounts to: 'Me, too, please'. If you feel jealous, it is always a signal of your own unfulfilled desire. It is a longing for something that the other has. Jealousy is often swept under the carpet of respectability because it is not right or not really permitted. I think it is a good thing to allow yourself to feel jealousy and to learn from it. Of whom and what are you jealous and what do you long for? You will keep the jealous energy to yourself in this way and not allow it to go to another person who will feel it one way or another on an energetic level. Jealousy can become your teacher on the path to fulfilment. It shows you the path to what you long for but have not brought to fulfilment yet.

Of course, the next question is how are you going to fulfil yourself? That can simply be done by becoming aware of your longing; it is just a question of "going for it." Just go and do what you long to do. If you, for example, are jealous of people who can play music beautifully, learn to play an instrument or take singing lessons. '

"Going for it" takes effort, discipline, and perseverance. That is where it often goes wrong; people want their fulfilment handed to them on a plate. The longing inner child does not come in contact with the adult will. But that is the second step.

Let us take as an example, the jealous feeling you have when your wife pays attention to another man. Your message is "I want a lot of attention, too." You do not usually want more attention from your wife but have just discovered the bottomless pit syndrome. These longings usually stem from your inner child that did not get enough love. What you should do is go to your wife like a small child and ask her if she can pay attention to the inner child. You should not go to each other as adult men or women but as the little children that you still are sometimes. The latter is very important. A shortage can only be supplemented on the level at which it belongs, and that is usually at the level of your inner child. You must do this consciously. You do not really have to change anything; you only have to ask consciously for what you usually demand from each other subconsciously. This not only allows you to become aware of your inner child but also allows that child to catch up. If you can also acknowledge the feeling of sorrow that you have because your mother or father were too busy to give you much attention or they were perhaps ill or dead, then you are on the right path to healing yourself and having adult relationships and fulfilment. If you give your inner child a chance in a relationship, it will become fundamentally richer. We think that we are grown up, but our unfulfilled child regularly emerges in all kinds of ways. The subconscious child makes us demanding in relationships and especially in our married relationships. We all demand subconsciously that our partner fills the hole that we have felt since childhood. The subconscious child is usually the cause of marriage problems.

A person who is fulfilled is never jealous. If you feel jealous, it is time to get to Work! Just get on with it! Your life and that of others will become much more pleasant!

Jealousy, the Urge to Possess and the Fear of Abandonment

There can be a subconscious nagging fear of abandonment in relationships where jealousy plays a major part. The tendency to regard the other as your property stems from this fear of abandonment.

Eric and Anne have been married for years. Subconsciously they have a complementary relationship; she is his mummy, and he is the undernourished boy who never grew up. When she goes into town to do shopping, he looks for her after a couple of hours. When she wants to visit a friend, he

269

makes nasty remarks over that friend. When she wants to follow a course, he advises her not to, and if she does anyway, he sits and sulks like a child. This goes on, year in, year out. Finally she gives up her mother role and says that she feels stifled in their relationship. She wants freedom and space and wants to divorce him. His answer is to threaten to commit suicide.

With this threat, he shows that he wants to leave her but stop her from leaving him. He thinks he can defeat the same with the same. He ought to realize who it is he actually feels abandoned by; it is logical to think of his mother here.

This does not mean that his mother literally left him by, for example, dying when he was young. Such a fear of abandonment and the ensuing urge to possess usually stems from affective neglect. The only way out of such a dilemma is for him to realize that he is trying to get his wife to make up for the absence of his mother. That is not what she is for, and what he is doing will not work as it is a never-ending story. Because this is happening at a subconscious level, he will not become fulfilled by her motherly care and attention. He can only make up for this absence by becoming aware. It would be better and more effective if he was prepared to work at it on an emotional level.

Comparing and Self-acceptance

I was planning to write that jealousy is also a product of our deeply ingrained tendency to compare. I was building on what my former teacher Osho used to say—comparing is the basis of our inferiority and superiority complexes. But I now think that there is probably nothing wrong with comparing in itself. Comparing is a good method to becoming acquainted with the relative dependency of things. It is also a good way of getting to know your own merits and building up your own identity. By seeing the consequence of another person's behavior, you can draw your own conclusions. You can learn by observing somebody who is doing something in a totally different way than you would. By comparing, you can see good and evil, light and darkness. We live in a world of polarity, and that is our school of learning.

And yet, there is something wrong with our way of comparing as it often does indeed lead to feelings of inferiority and superiority. The old emotional charges are prevalent here, and this causes comparing to deteriorate into something negative. We are compared to each other from childhood. We learn to compare ourselves with others in this way. It begins in the cradle: "He has his father's nose" or "She is smaller than her sister." That goes on, but it is of no real importance as long as there are no old emotional charges connected to these remarks, and they are loving or even emotionally neutral. Comparing becomes ugly because of unfinished histories and accompanying subconscious emotional charges. I think that the word "achieve" plays a major role in this case. Achievement thinking stems from deep feelings of worthlessness. Comparing that stems from subconscious feelings of worthlessness leads to comparing combined with emotional charge. I think that we all suffer from a feeling of worthlessness on this planet although we usually do not realize it (I have already covered this subject exhaustively in the chapter about guilt).

For centuries we built a culture based on an achievement-orientated form of comparing from this extremely subconscious layer. This achievement-orientated form, which originated from feelings of worthlessness, has become mixed with the neutral and enquiring form of comparing, which is geared towards learning.

We must perceive as purely as possible. It is often said that objective observation hardly exists; we all have our own way of seeing things subjectively. A healthy way of seeing things means cleaning our doors of perception. That is what Emotional Work is all about!

There is nothing wrong with us establishing the fact that Mary is better at abstract learning than John, who is better with his hands. However, it does go wrong when we generalize and say that Mary is more intelligent, stupid, pretty, or uglier than... We have all developed preconceived cultural notions about intelligence and beauty. I remember a former childhood friend of mine who was ugly according to the usual standards of the day. She had a large head, a big crooked nose, and unruly hair. But I remember her as a very lively, generous girl with whom I loved to play. I could not see her ugliness; to me, she was a wonderful person. And what are we to think of our culture of slimness? Or our culture of intelligence where we ask, "Who is the most intelligent?" Thank goodness the concept of emotional intelligence is finding its way in our culture. But there are a lot of cultural measuring rods taking our measure, and that is not good for us. The appreciation for the miracle called *uniqueness* is lost. For me, a very special aspect of Creation is that nobody is the same, except for identical twins. But even in this case, there are differences. God is very creative. However, it seems that we cannot cope with enormous creativity and diversity, and for that reason, we often use measuring rods and compartmentalization to keep a hold on all that beautiful abundance. Perhaps admiring Creation instead of trying to keep a hold on it is part of our training here on earth. Perhaps it will also be possible to learn to admire each other in all our colorful diversity.

In schools, comparing also reigns supreme. This is expressed by figures, by stamps, and by favors from the teacher. The joy of learning together is pushed to the background for the purpose of obtaining good marks and passing exams. This is the way to obtain a fear of failure. Sport is all about competition and scoring points rather than about taking pleasure in playing a game together. It is no wonder that feelings of inferiority and superiority play a major role in our mutual relationships; sometimes you feel like a giant and sometimes like Tom Thumb. These are not extremes but two sides of the same coin; the achievement-oriented comparison coin. If you feel superior, you have a feeling of inferiority within you. If you feel inferior, there is a need deep within you to be superior. The common denominator is a feeling of worthlessness. In both cases, you have a tendency to prove yourself through your deeds, your words, or your appearance. You often do not realize that you feel inferior because of these compensations. These compensations have become so ordinary and so much part of you that you imagine that they are part of your authenticity. The only sign is the continual tension under which you live. Eventually you may have a burnout. You are, after all, not living peacefully from your own strength and authenticity. This is doomed to fail sooner or later.

The consequence of compensation behavior and comparing yourself to others is not having the slightest notion of your own uniqueness and because of this, not loving yourself. If there is no acknowledgement of your beautiful distinctiveness, then jealousy will rear its ugly head and play a nasty trick on you and on other people. Jealousy means living in competition with others and comparing yourself to them; it is a road that leads nowhere and deviates more and more from who you are. If you have learned to observe objectively in a clear emotional daylight, you will no longer compare yourself to others but love your own matchlessness. There will no longer be any jealousy. There will be love! Where there is jealousy, there can be no love… for yourself.

Longing

Knowing your true longings is an art that all of us, more or less, have lost on this planet. As we have all been trained by upbringing and socialization to do the things that are expected of us, we no longer know what we really want. You

273

may have vague dreams of love and happiness and about finding yourself and maybe God. But how do you go about this? Why do you have difficulty achieving what you long for deep down inside yourself? I see five reasons:

1. *Adaptation.*

As you have become well adapted to your surroundings and are very much part of what is expected of you, you have little connection with your own vocation—the reason for which you are here on earth. Perhaps you were planning to do something for children. When you were a child, you dreamt of becoming a teacher just like that nice teacher in fourth grade. However, your father has a thriving business and high hopes of you carrying on his work. Your father is always very busy and works hard for his family. You do not want to disappoint him and succeed him in the business. Moreover, you earn a lot more. You forget your childhood dream and your soul's path.

2. *Losing the connection with your needs.*

This is the direct consequence of the above-mentioned adaptation. You do not know what you truly want. Perhaps you really do not want to know because then you will have to admit that you miss something, are unhappy, or made the wrong choices.

3. *You have become stuck in neurotic, unfulfilled needs.*

If your basic needs have not been fulfilled and emptiness and pain have not been digested, you will remain stuck in those needs, and there will be hardly any room for other needs and desires to develop. Longings are, as it were, a rung higher on the ladder of basic needs. Maslow developed a great theory about this in the nineteen sixties. He distinguished a hierarchy of five basic needs: physiological needs, the safety need, the belonging need, the esteem need (respect and love), and finally the self-actualization need. A need must be fulfilled to a certain extent for the next need to be given a chance. A lot of people have become stuck in the first four basic needs, so self-realization is hardly given a chance or even not given one at all. After all, as long as your basic needs are not fulfilled and the pain of this is not digested, you will subconsciously repeat your patterns. You may, for example, remain oriented towards receiving compliments and having success because you once did not have enough recognition. For this reason, you choose those activities and things which render applause, and you do not choose what your soul is searching for. Another example is that you will be inclined to stay in your safe, enclosed world of suburban bliss if you were not given enough basic security in years past and did not digest that emotionally later on. The adventurous side of your soul will then perhaps not be given a chance, and you will not be able to realize what that side has in store for you.

4. ***You use your head too much instead of your lower chakras.***

A lot of education is geared to what is sensible and not to your needs. Especially in times gone by, a need was a rather tainted word, or it was an egocentric one. One of the participants of a Spark of Light week once said angrily that the only need you were allowed to have was "the need to go to the bathroom."

5. ***An old taboo rests on need.*** Listening to your own needs was once called egocentric. Living according to your own will was not right according to Christian morality. The word longing has a different meaning, but longings stem from our basic needs. If you do not know your needs, you will not know your longings. They are higher on the ladder of needs. Longings faired

badly in religion, too. Buddha said that longings are the reason for all suffering. In almost all religions, detachment is of the utmost importance. Many desires or longings should be sacrificed for the benefit of the one longing for God.

Being Fulfilled

When you deny your basic needs and emotions too much, the flow of life becomes restricted and shut off in two different directions: from the inside to the outside and from the outside to the inside. You do not express yourself sufficiently or accept life's gifts because of fear and control. Both your ways of expressing yourself and your ability to receive become affected and minimal, and you have the feeling that you constantly lack something. And you do! It will, however, not help if you subconsciously try to fill this lack from the outside. Our consumer society developed in this way, and as everybody knows, it is never enough!

Our emotional dependency on each other also developed in a similar way. Take a look at our marriages and relationships: we say implicitly and usually subconsciously that the other must fill our gap. This is what most marriages are based on, and they may also be ruined by it. It is the story of the complementary relationship: the man and woman complementing each other beautifully. After a little while, if we learn that the other is not able to fill the hole we have inside us, we become disappointed or keep to our petty ways or look for another person with whom we try out complementarity again. This happens if we do not become aware of our hole and realize why it is there. Because of this, power plays such a major role in our relationships. It is our subconscious demand "Fulfil me."

How can you fill your gap in a healthy way? Or perhaps we should not fill it at all? Or perhaps it is impossible anyway?

These are the questions people will ask on this path of inner growth when they encounter what they lacked in their childhood. The Spark of Light Work has two fundamental aspects: digestion of old pain and learning to accept anew what you went without and shut yourself off from. I know people who, in therapy, only worked through the first aspect. They have expressed a lot of anger, cried a lot, and faced their fears; yet something is missing, namely the feeling of fulfilment. I will illustrate this with an example:

Mary-Anne had followed a therapy course, which included a lot of emotional work. It had done her good. She had become sturdier, more assertive, and independent. She had also learned to embrace her inner child and comfort it. Yet she remained unfulfilled in her contact with others and in love, and she was not really happy because of this. She soon found out during Spark of Light Work that she had embraced this child, who lacked a lot, too early. When she was emotional, she noticed that she, in all reality, hated her inner child. She hated it because it needed so much. It turned out that behind this self-hatred, there was another hate, especially aimed at her mother who did not give her what she fundamentally needed. But this was not all there was to it. The next step was opening up to others again. To this end, she had to become aware of and overcome the pride of her inner child who had decided to do everything on its own.

This means that you have to learn to ask once again, this time consciously and with people who can now help you. A colleague of mine always said, "You were once dependent on that one woman who was your mother and on that one man who was your father. Now every man can be your father to some extent and every woman your mother." So receive, knowing that it is not about the quantity of love, which does not even exist, but about the quality. It is not about the person but about your willingness to receive. It is important to receive it at the level at which it belongs, and that is the level of your inner child. This means that you ask as a child and not as a grown-up. It is good to distinguish between the child and the adult that are within yourself. The child has, after all, other needs than the grown-up. If you have a partner, it can enrich your relationship if you can be a child with each other. With this, I do not mean just playful children but also Work with each other alternately as needy children. If you feel uncertain about certain things even though you have done various form of therapy, "ask your partner, "Am I doing this right, mummy, or daddy?" or "Do you love this little girl?" or "Will you hold this little boy?"

This is perhaps new and unfamiliar to you; yet we do just this in our relationships with partners although it is then subconscious. The only thing you have to do is do it openly and consciously. This is the path of bringing everything to light. And one day it will be enough, and you will be fulfilled, content, and thankful for what there is.

Chapter 23

Addiction: A Cry for Love

Addiction means that you deny yourself real healing and nourishment.
~Marcy Foley

*T*here are many kinds of addiction: food addiction, alcohol and drug addiction, nicotine addiction, shopping addiction, gambling addiction, work addiction, sex addiction, and the most recent version is a computer addiction. As I do not want to discuss all types of addiction separately, I will reduce them to their common denominator: not wanting to feel your cry for love. Addiction is a way of coping with emotions that have not been digested and so keeping your head above water. It is, in fact, a survival strategy, a defense of the layer of feelings and emotions. Addiction is a form of trance behavior, wanting more of the same so as not to feel the pain.

An important aspect of addition is that it is a misguided form of seeking happiness and well-being. You try to feel pleasantly relaxed in the hope that it will bring you happiness. As it is too painful to admit your longing for love, you direct your longing towards *feeling pleasant*, towards having things, towards money, achievement, sex, or sweet things. Every addiction is, in actual fact, a cry for love. The reception of this cry and aiming this cry in the right direction is what it is all about. If you learn to receive this primal scream step by step, you will encounter many emotions on your path. It can become your path of liberation from the chains of addiction. By focusing on this deep layer of addiction behavior, you have a better chance of success than when you address yourself to your behavior and symptoms. If you are too fat because you are addicted to sweet things, it does not really help if you focus on your eating habits. That becomes an addiction on top of the original addiction and a vicious circle of being tolerant and being strict. You are better off concentrating on your longing for the sweetness of love and discovering what you lacked in your past history. You will, of course, encounter your pain and the bottomless pit of your lack of warmth, tenderness, and respect. It might sound strange, but in living through your pain, the bottom of your endless longing will be found. Your longing has become endless because it has never been acknowledged. In the loving reception of your longing and your want, your salvation and your base lie. You can only prepare this loving reception for yourself when you have mobilized the emotions of anger, fear, and sorrow. Somebody with an eating disorder, told me about her experience:

> *When I went to the kitchen to get something in-between meals, I was in a kind of trance. I felt something coming, apparently. I then went directly to the kitchen to get food. I did not even know what the feeling was. I was often not even conscious that there was something I did not want to feel. The food gave me a 'good' feeling, but if I stopped, I felt rotten and guilty and depressed. I told myself off, 'You are so weak' or 'You are a big fat pig.' Lately, I realize earlier what I am doing and can prevent it happening. I stand in the kitchen, for example, (I sometimes have something in my hands or I am searching for something) or I am on my way to the kitchen and realize suddenly, 'I am doing it again.' I then fill a feeding bottle with orangeade, or*

I go back to the room and try to find out why I wanted to go to the kitchen.

I often recommend a feeding bottle to reduce the addiction to the original need to suck. A feeding bottle is also an effective method of getting rid of a nicotine addiction. As always, it is about regressing to where it went wrong, so it is possible to progress to the next stage.

Recently, I received a letter from one of my students who suffered from a shopping addiction for years. By doing intensive emotional work, she transformed suffering from addiction, which reveals a victim attitude, into liberation from her addiction. By not focusing on the behavior itself—she had tried that in vain for years—but by transforming her excessive cry for love into Spark of Light Work, she could write the following to me:

I was in Amsterdam with a friend today. For the first time, I felt the contentment and peace of not having to buy anything. I could go into all kinds of shops without feeling rushed. Even eating just one sandwich was enough for me. I could really enjoy it without having to think of a third or fourth. Of course, it can all go wrong next week, but this experience feels like a victory and nobody can take that away from me again, and that's the truth. I just wanted to let you know.

Central in her message is the sentence: "I could really enjoy it." When you can prepare a loving reception for your neglected child that has wanted for so much, you can receive everything. Fundamental in this process is being able to receive and really accept; a base will subsequently be created by expressing emotions. Contentment and real well-being will then come into existence. Then enough will be enough.

From Fighting Symptoms to Liberation

A lot of people who are addicted and many helpers, too, still address themselves to what they see on the outside, namely addiction behavior. As we have already said, addiction is really a survival strategy. You will encounter a lot of resistance by focusing on a survival strategy and wanting to undermine it. It is threatening. It is like trying to take away somebody's only lifebuoy at sea. Nobody will thank you for doing that. I saw a good example on the website of a self-help group for people who are addicted to self-mutilation:

> *Preceding the group therapy, I had to sign a contract saying that I would not hurt myself; I had to tell them every day if I had done so. If I had hurt myself, the counselor would tell me that I really must not do it. I could have hit her. I am not a little child that you can tell off. Her reprimands had the opposite effect.*

In the self-help group, people understood very well that they could not help each other by focusing on cutting. They started to talk about their backgrounds and supported each other. That turned out to be the right way. If they had also made use of the carpet beater, such self-help groups would have taken another step forward. My message is simple: focus on whatever lies under the behavior and symptoms; it will be, as always, old pain. Expressing your emotions about that old pain is the way to transform your addiction to more of the same into creative ways of living. A person who had just started this Work exclaimed,

I can cry for the very first time. Cry! I never dared dreaming of doing that. I now have the courage to feel my sorrow and have found out that the world does not stop turning.

282

Once you have taken that first risk, it becomes easier, and you will say, "Was that what I was scared of? It hurt, but by crying, I started to feel happy again.

Part III:

The Work

Chapter 24

The Spark of Light Work Methods

Know thyself, the reason for being here

O ur consciousness has two important functions: awareness and memory. If we want to get to know ourselves, we will have to appeal to both functions. We can perceive what is happening within us by means of our five external senses and also with the help of our internal senses: a feeling, a pain, or a mood. But it is often the case that we do not know the meaning. You may feel, for example, vaguely unhappy, yet there is nothing in your momentary field of observation to give a meaning to that unhappiness. For that you will need memory, the second function of consciousness. In your memory, memories are stored of all your experiences. If you combine both of those, you may find out that a remark your friend made yesterday is still simmering and has made you feel unhappy in the here and now. This is a recent event and easy to interpret.

It becomes more difficult if the reason for your unhappiness lies further back in your memory, may be years ago or (taking past lives into account) perhaps even centuries ago. The problem of our self- knowledge becomes apparent with this gap between a current experience and a distant causal effect. Everything depends on having remembered or having forgotten. The more we remember, the better we know ourselves and all the bigger and more spacious our consciousness becomes. Therefore, memory is a very important function, more important than momentary awareness. The latter is fleeting and limited. Our memory or you could say, our consciousness depot, is much more extensive. It includes the memory of all our past lives on earth and also the memory of times and places that are not on this earth but are in different cosmic dimensions. That is an immense depot of forgotten knowledge. Great mystics of all time have always said, "Know thyself; that is why you are here—to remember who and what you are. You have forgotten. That is a real pity.

On the path described in this book, it is all about remembering who we are and to that end clearing up all the mess that hinders our view. As we have forgotten a huge amount, it is good to know a few things that will serve as handles and accelerate the pace of our learning process. Real life is, of course, the best school. However, by supplementing the *normal* learning process with conscious learning methods, we can get to know ourselves faster. Life will not only become more fun in this way but also more interesting and less problematic. You will reap the benefit of that extra, voluntary, learning in daily life.

Spark of Light Work has five important tools which lead to the speeding up of self-knowledge and inner growth on our path:

1. The use of muscle tests or biotensor/pendulum;

2. Breathwork;

3. Gestaltwork;

4. Bodywork; and

5. Regressionwork.

All five are geared to increasing your current awareness by joining this to your consciousness depot, i.e., your memory. All five offer the possibility of the connection between both consciousness functions being established more rapidly. We shall look at them, one by one.

Chapter 25

Muscle Testing: Access to Your Memory

Everything you ever experienced is stored in your memory.

*P*sychological kinesiology is what I call Spark of Light's diagnostic acceleration. The chiropractor Dr.Goodheart, founder of applied kinesiology, discovered that you could find the possible causes of physical, emotional, and energetic ailments with the help of muscle tests. It is easier to find out what is wrong when you use a muscle test. It has greatly speeded up my work with people. I used to need ten sessions, whereas now only five are necessary to give the same result. The use of muscle tests is based on two facts:

1. Everything we have ever experienced is stored in our organism. Our whole memory is to be found somewhere in our organism.

2. When we sense a positive, emotional, reaction within ourselves, it strengthens our muscles. If we have a negative reaction to something, it weakens our muscles. When asking a question, a strong indicator muscle means *yes* and a weak one, *no*. An indicator muscle is a muscle that we use as test muscle. It can be an arm

muscle or the muscles of a few fingers. With this we have a measure with which we can really test everything. It is important to know that you can only test what is in the joint knowledge packet of the person who is testing and the person who is being tested. You are, as it where, one energy during testing. A simple test to experience the way it works is to let somebody think of something beautiful: he or she will then *test strong*. In reverse, when he or she thinks of something unpleasant, he/she will *test weak*. You can use a biotensor/pendulum in the same way. This consists of a handle with a strong thin thread of about 25 cm to which a round marble or disc is connected.

We can set to work with these two facts. The trick is to ask the right questions. Second, you must not undervalue the importance of being completely disengaged from the results of your test. If you do not have an open mind, you will test what you, as a tester, are thinking. In that case you could unwittingly manipulate the response results. I focus on the psychological-spiritual aspect in my work because I believe that to be the basis of all other aspects and because it is my field and sphere of interest. Muscles tests can be used in all disciplines and all fields. I know of dental surgeons who check which molar is involved by using a muscle test.

One day, a young woman came to see me in my practice. After many medical examinations for neurological complaints, she was told that her complaints were probably the onset of multiple sclerosis and sent home. I had heard that multiple sclerosis is sometimes related to amalgam poisoning. Amalgam is the material used to fill our molars, half of it is mercury. Her subconscious knowledge showed a connection between her complaints and the amalgam when I tested her. I detected a high quantity of mercury in her organism; mercury builds up in the central nervous system, in the liver, and in the kidneys. When I tested if a certain molar was perhaps responsible for the poisoning, one molar tested weak. Nothing seemed to be wrong with this molar, and neither did it hurt. She went to the dentist, but there was nothing to be seen in the photo. Because she trusted me and my tests, she asked the dentist to open her molar up. It turned out to be completely rotten inside and as leaky as a sieve. After having her molar extracted and her organism detoxified with homeopathic remedies, her complaints all disappeared like melting snow.

However, I usually concentrate on emotional issues in most of my work. I have reduced and adapted the kinesiology I learned to my specific work. As you can test almost everything with applied kinesiology, its structure has become unnecessarily complicated and technical. A lot is done without the client's knowledge. The client is not actively involved enough and this encourages dependency and the idea that somebody else can cure you. It would be a good idea to have simple courses in the use of muscle tests during which everybody, friends, partners, and children could try things out. It is a great tool with which to test the cause of a headache or stomach-ache in children as that is often the way they express emotional pain. It can also bring more clarity to emotional work.

Sometimes, at the beginning, people cannot be tested. The only real reason you cannot be tested, as far as I know, is the fear of entrusting yourself to what your memory wants to tell you. By talking about that fear, it will enter into your consciousness and will not have to be expressed subconsciously through a muscle. It is important to focus on what is really important if you still want to see the trees and not just the forest. I will not give a whole course on psychological kinesiology but sketch a few outlines:

- We test by using a few finger modes (certain finger positions that have been agreed on) if we have to do with a regression in this life or a past one. With simple yes/no questions, we can sift through further information.

• We have agreed with ourselves that only what is important at that moment will come to the fore in the test. This agreement is of the utmost importance.

First, because many things in the memory play a role by, for example, present complaints of a depressive nature. We assume that the subconscious knows precisely and that it will indicate, through the muscles, what the sequence should be in the process of liberation.

Second, the sequence is very important, as you cannot always reach your feeling. That is also the limitation of what clairvoyants sometimes tell people. It is possible that your fears stem primarily from a past life; however, you may have to digest things from this life before you can get in touch with those feelings. After all, it is about emotionally reliving what went wrong in your past and not just about mental knowledge.

Fundamental in our Spark of Light Work is the testing of what can possibly now be brought to the Light. Work goes very rapidly because of this, and everybody reaches emotional reliving quickly. It would be wonderful if couples could learn to do the test together; they would then speed up their emotional Work and make things clear. The content and background of emotions are, after all, not always clear.

The real work starts after the testing, namely reliving what we have tested. Kinesiology is a diagnostic system and not a therapy. After the muscle test, breathwork or gestalt work is used so we can live through the memory in the here and now. We will discuss this in the next chapter.

Chapter 26

Breathwork, the Acceleration of Your Growth

Your own breath is the motor of this work of liberation

When people speak about expressing emotions, they often mean talking about emotions. Somebody wrote the following:

> *When I read about your work, I wonder if I have a motive to do something with it. When am I going to give myself the chance to use the carpet beater? What is stopping me? Perhaps it's the idea of not wanting to do something out of the ordinary? But also: why should I use the carpet beater? I'm letting my motives and fears enter my consciousness, isn't that enough?*

Expressing your feelings and *bringing them into your consciousness* is a good thing but absolutely unsatisfactory with regard to detaching and liberating the deep imprints and emotions which are stored inside you. Feeling means feeling deeply with every fiber of your being. Emotional liberation

295

means a complete liberation and includes the cells in your body. Feeling is also a chemical and hormonal process. This means that healing becomes possible not only on a mental level but also on a physical one. When the process of emotional liberation is done thoroughly, there will be a detoxification of the neurotransmitters in the brain, beneficial changes in the hormonal system, and a deep relaxation in the muscles and inner organs. Your breath is the motor of this liberation work. Breath can revive and loosen everything within you that has become rigid and stiffened, weakened and fouled. Breath is life and by working at your breathing, you can optimize not only the quality but also the length of your life.

Important: Please note!

Breathwork is very powerful work. It is important to be very careful, especially in the following cases:

- When you have had a heart attack recently;
- If you have a history of psychosis; and
- If you are a diabetic, it is essential to have some food in the vicinity

Breath and Emotions

We will have a look at what happens to your breath when you repress your emotions. You can see this most clearly with reactions of fear and fright. In the case of real danger, your system shows a flight-or-fight reaction. In that case, holding your breath and being as quiet as a mouse is a good reaction. You can see this *pretending to be dead* survival strategy everywhere in nature. When one of our cats had caught a large grass snake recently, it lay as dead next to the proud cat. He lost all interest because the snake remained motionless. As soon as I had laid it out of the cat's sight near the stream, it quickly glided away.

The snake could get away, but what about you as a child? If you had a safe home, you ran home quickly. But what happens when there is no safety at home among the people you should really feel safe with? And what happens when your country is occupied by brute force? Your healthy flight-or-fight mechanism will be discontinued if fighting or taking to flight is not possible. If there is nowhere to go, your fear will go inwards, and you will become petrified or frozen with fear. First of all, fear seizes you by the throat and your breath stops short. Then it lodges itself in your muscles, your organs, and last but not least, your soul. If there is no loving reception for your fear, you will repress it as not to feel it. The best way of doing this is by making your breath shallow and less deep. *You instinctively know that you feel less if you breathe less.* Your inborn capability works in this way to allow you to survive in an unsafe environment. In this way, you not only learn to repress your fear but also all emotions connected to it, such as anger and sorrow. All emotions and feelings that are not given a loving reception, starting with from your parents and moving later to yourself, are kept under the lid.

Mixed and Minimal Breathing

When this is something that happens chronically and remains subconscious, you will develop certain breath patterns, muscle patterns, and living patterns. Life and real life energy will become restrained and restricted when you live your life according to fixed patterns. Your breathing that was originally meant for breathing in air and inspiration now becomes mixed together with defense patterns that limit you. Energy used for defense cannot be used for growth. All the energy you use to defend yourself cannot be used for the growth of your organism. Thankfully, we have received enormous energy reserves with which to compensate for such a loss of energy, but our defense and survival still take their toll. As a consequence of essential survival in the past, you breathe

297

incompletely, irregularly, and shallowly. This has not only consequences for your body but also for your psychological well-being. If you chronically breathe too high up in your chest, you will not only feel short of breath but also live fearfully or hurriedly.

We can distinguish two types of superficial breathing. There are people who breathe mainly from the chest area and with some difficulty from the diaphragm (often wrongly called abdominal respiration) and the flanks. Women especially breathe from higher up. Men can generally breathe more easily from the abdominal region but with rather more difficulty from the chest. This has to do with the fact that men live less easily from the emotional area around the heart than women. That is also one of the reasons men have more heart attacks than women do. In our achievement-oriented society, women are increasingly becoming more masculine which, in terms of percentage, means that they are drawing level with regard to heart disease.

Emotional Imprints in the Breath

Now thatwe know how our breathing has become mixed with patterns that are not natural, we can see how we can undo this destruction because that is what it is. If you want to remedy something, you must find out where and how it went wrong. It is clear from the above mentioned that emotional repression and denial cause breathing to be minimized. Recovery should lie in maximizing breathing; this is indeed the case but how we go about that needs further explanation.

There are many schools and methods that teach techniques for better breathing: yoga, various relaxation techniques, and meditation. These techniques are indeed helpful to learn to relax at moments that you are looking for that. You learn to breathe more from your diaphragm and your flanks so as to acquire more complete breathing. You can *relax* a bit more and release tension and feel more at ease. Many of these techniques, and certainly yoga, are based on a new control of your breathing. As I have written before, control is an old story that has limited value and needs supplementation if we want to learn what liberation is about. As long as your deep emotional imprints have not come to light, e.g., in your keenly sensitive consciousness, breathing will not fundamentally change. As long as fear remains in your organism, your breathing will travel upwards again as soon as you forget to think of the techniques. As with many things, techniques are handy and helpful, but transformation and healing will have to come from within. This means that we should liberate emotional imprints in breathing so the defense mechanisms can release, and only the liberated breathing remains. If you wish to liberate yourself fundamentally, you should liberate your breathing from old imprints of fear and denial. The next question is how to do that.

Spark of Light Breathwork: Consciously Hyperventilating

The best therapeutical results are reached when both the therapist and the client have no ideas or expectations about the desired progress of the process. They will have to have an open and adventurous attitude and simply follow the energy flow and the experiences with a deep trust that the process will automatically benefit the client.
~Stan Grof

Breathwork, as used during Spark of Light Work, does not primarily aim to bring about relaxation but to bring the emotional imprints in the breath, in the body, and in the psyche to light and so to liberation. It is about the fundamental liberation of old emotions and the awakening of repressed memories.

We do not use relaxed breathing to this end; instead, we use breathing that is stimulating whereby the organism is overloaded with extra oxygen. In the case of relaxed breathing, the emphasis is put on exhalation. In the case of stimulated breathing, the accent is on inhalation. The chemical composition of the blood changes due to the extra supply of oxygen. The concentration of carbon dioxide in the blood lessens and the degree of acidity, the PH value, changes; this causes the muscles to become more supple and accessible. It becomes clear that as our emotions are mainly stored in our muscles, this process activates our emotions. Although midriff breathing or diaphragm breathing has a relaxing effect, in our work high chest breathing is stimulated (during the Work!).

This type of breathwork is, in actual fact, the same as *conscious hyperventilation.* Subconscious hyperventilation, which catches us unawares, is a natural reaction to chronic minimal breathing, also called subventilation. Our body and soul are protesting against the minimal breathing and the retaining of emotions. *Hyperventilation is, in fact, a spontaneous attempt to recover.* We start to breathe quickly and more completely; as our body is not used to that, the well-known hyperventilation symptoms, such as dizziness and tingling begin. During breathwork we hyperventilate consciously. We do not wait until tension has become so great and breathing so minimal that our body spurs us on to have a hyperventilation attack as a matter of course. On the contrary, we initiate the work of liberation by consciously hyperventilating. We do this in a safe environment so we can really express emotions. We will begin to breathe consciously more in than out so a more connected breathing occurs; in this way we can make contact with repressed emotions and memories. Everything is stored within us; nothing is lost. After all, energy does not disappear but just changes form. In this way old memories change into subconsciousness, but are still very much around. We can never digest or let go of things that remain subconscious.

Those of us who know this subconscious form of hyperventilation are sometimes frightened to hyperventilate consciously in the beginning. They soon experience that consciously hyperventilating (intensive breathing) dissolves hyperventilation problems. By continuing the breathing, we give ourselves the chance to let repressed emotions out. As soon as emotions come to the light, hyperventilation symptoms disappear immediately. I have already described the various symptoms of hyperventilation in Chapter 10.

Spark of Light Work: Breathing in and Expressing

Spark of Light Work is aimed at breathing in, at breathing quicker and deeper than you normally do; breathing out goes automatically. Old pain is awakened just by breathing intensely—after all, breathing in means feeling again. You also breathed in with your original reaction of fear, but you held your breath then. Now you will release your breath and start to feel what you once had to repress because there was no loving reception for it. With this kind of breathwork, expressing repressed emotions is first and foremost. Due to this kind of breathing, your consciousness becomes heightened and deepened. It becomes easier for you to gain access to repressed experiences from your youth or from past lives. Forgotten, joyful memories can return to your consciousness. Some people also have experiences from other dimensions of existence and feel the comforting presence of guides or angels.

Evocative Music

Music is an important part of Spark of Light breathwork. Music that recharges and activates is used at the beginning of a session. Later more evocative music is used; this is music that has the ability to summon all kinds of experiences and emotions. In this phase, we use certain classical music, such as Verdi's *Requiem*, Mozart, or Orff's

Carmina Burana, but also Lloyd Webber, marching music, church music (to trigger old anger with regard to religious upbringing), and many kinds of folk music from all over the world. This can be helpful by reliving past lives. In the last phase, quieter music is offered to help integrate experiences.

Group Setting

Breathwork is done in a group, where we work in pairs. We take turns in sitting next to one another in order to assist each other with the Work. Spark of Light workers are present and encourage where necessary. We assume, basically, that every one can reach his or her inner healer and that the breathing itself will do the Work. When you breathe intensely, energy goes to where it should go to at that time, according to your own inner need. You could also say that the breath *tackles* whatever ought to be liberated next. The trick is to allow your breath to lead and to trust it; a breathing session then becomes a wonderful liberation. The most important effect is having a better connection with yourself.

A Different Kind of Breathwork

Spark of Light breathwork is closely in keeping with so called *holotropic breathing* as developed by Stanislav Grof. There are various other techniques, such as Rebirthing and Transformational Breathing, that are geared to the liberation of breathing and that often serve a certain goal, such as reliving birth or experiencing ecstasy. An often mentioned goal is putting an end to the mental talk in your head. People breathe through emotions that come to the surface, and these are often not expressed. The focus is more on breathing than on the expression of emotions. They expect repressed traumas to automatically be cleaned, emotionally and mentally, at a cellular level if you breathe completely, and that your consciousness will become broadened in this way. Complete breathing *through the emotions* often gives a feeling of being high. In the case of *Transformational Breathing,* the emphasis is put on the fact that by intense and deep diaphragm breathing, the endorphins, responsible for a feeling of well-being and euphoria, are stimulated in the brain. It is propagated as *the fast lane to enlightenment, health, and peace.* I believe that continual breathing, crucial to this type of work, cannot go together with complete expression of emotions. When you express yourself emotionally, your breathing changes, and you cannot follow a technique at the same time. It is important to consider which type of breathwork you choose.

Chapter 27

Gestalt Work:
From Emotion to Clarity

Our Work is to emotionally complete what has not been completed.

*A*fter using muscle tests to find out what is wrong and to see which themes should be worked on and after breathwork during which especially the emotions are set in motion, it is time for a different approach; emotions have to be given a place in our lives and integrated in a wider perspective. By fully experiencing emotions, much can become clear and "pennies can mentally drop,"a realization after a period of confusion or misunderstanding." And yet, other ways are often vital to gain the necessary clarity.

Gestalt therapy, as developed by Fritz Perls, is a good method. Perls warns of using therapy as a technique. "A technique is a trick. A trick can only be used in exceptional cases."[1] In the first place, people need people and not techniques. Safety is essential and is realized by someone who knows the depth of Working on oneself. Expertise based on one's own experience is subsequently necessary. The basic principles of Gestalt Therapy are wonderful aids to introducing form and structure to the Work and to finding emotion through verbal channels. I shall outline a few practical main characteristics of Gestalt Work.

Uncompleted Gestalten and Emotion

A 'gestalt' is a unity of energy that moves on the boundary between yourself and your environment. For example, you are hungry, and there is food within your grasp. Your need and the food form a gestalt together. However, when the energy flow is broken by a frustration, in this case the absence of food, we have to do with an uncompleted gestalt. Only by eating can you complete the gestalt. When you frequently do not receive something you fundamentally need in childhood, for example love, an uncompleted gestalt will develop, too. Your need for love becomes frustrated and blocked. Gestalt Therapy work is geared towards opening the flow of the blocked energy. This is done by adding the missing link: emotion.

Again we arrive at emotion's core meaning: "that which sets in motion." Emotion sets the blocked energy in motion. When you complete a state of affairs (an old or present gestalt) by emotional digestion, you allow the energy to flow again, and you can concentrate on other things. Emotionally completing unfinished affairs helps to let go of the old and grow towards new points of interest. All the old emotional layers that you carry with you and which weigh you down in your present life betray "unfinished business," as it is called in the world of Gestalt. The Work is about becoming aware of these uncompleted energies and completing them with emotion and awareness. Subsequently, you will be able to heal and grow and give your life momentum.

Identification and Dialogue

The subconscious is integrated into the conscious by means of a dialectic process.
That is to say, by the dialogue between you and the subconscious characters.
~C.G. Jung

The core of Gestalt can be found in the ground rule of identifying and communicating with everything during the Work. You will find your own message by dialogue and not by interpreting or talking about things. This will give directness and the possibility of intensely feeling what you are talking about. With whom or what will you communicate?

1. ***People.*** You do not talk about your parents or whomever, but start talking to them via a cushion on which you put them in your imagination. This gives a directness that brings you more straightforwardly to your feelings and emotions than when you talk about them.

2. ***Your body.*** As your body often speaks to you in a more *honest* and direct way than your mind does, it can be helpful to listen to your body and to understand it's *language*. You can identify with a certain part of the body, talk to it, and try to understand its message when you experience certain bodily sensations that you do not know the meaning of. For example, you notice that you have a clenched fist—ask the fist what it has to tell you. Identify with the fist and answer. Or perhaps you swing your leg when you are seated. A lot of sayings can help you with this. A headache can mean "you are banging your head against a brick wall." When you have a stomachache, you can think of "It turns my stomach," and you can discover the message of a restless leg by exaggerating the movement—by

307

walking away or kicking, for example. Exaggerating and making something stronger is a good method. Everything you do has a meaning; nothing is pointless or meaningless.

3. ***Your dreams.*** Dreams are the messages from your soul to yourself. It is important to understand them but that is not always easy. The clear messages from your soul have to go through the filter of your limited personality. This filtering and translation causes messages to come to you in all kinds of images. All images and characters in a dream are part of yourself. Dreamwork within Gestalt has several different aspects:

    *   ***Identification***: By identifying with different parts, in turn, you can let them talk. Imagine that you have a dream about a crocodile emerging from a mole hole, and you are standing there, watching it. By identifying with the crocodile in your fantasy, you can find out which part in you he represents. You play the part of the crocodile and allow him to talk freely.

    *   You allow all parts to enter ***into a dialogue*** with each other. Perhaps you, as an onlooker, have something to say to that crocodile coming out the earth—and what has the earth got to say? Another example: you are dreaming about being in a boat at sea. You are at the helm and holding it tightly, and then you notice that somebody has thrown your dog overboard. You dive after the animal and save it from the waves. In this case, you should not only identify yourself with the sea, which usually represents the unconscious but also with the ship, the helm, the dog, the unknown person that threw your dog overboard, and eventually with yourself.

- It is important to describe the dream *in the present tense.* It will be made direct in that way. Feel what happens if you describe the following dream in the past or present tense. "I was in an uncompleted house. There were stairways without banisters." Now describe it the present tense and identify with it: "I am in an uncompleted house, etc." Doing inner psychodrama with your dreams is nice work and often very enlightening. It is also very direct and confronting. A friend once told me, during breakfast, that he had dreamed about a soft-boiled egg. He could still see that slimy egg in his mind's eye and shuddered. I said spontaneously (we were both doing the Gestalt Course), "Go on then. Identify." He became hopping mad!

- Another dream technique is *completing your dream.* An example will illustrate this:

A young woman dreamt she had a little being hanging on her leg. It was a cross between a little animal and an ET, an extra-terrestrial being. By identifying with this being, tears soon flowed; the little being represented her neglected and denied inner child. While she is describing the dream, she unconsciously stroked her leg. By focusing on that, she felt her love for her inner child. By talking to that little child hanging on her leg, she felt compassion and could take it off and hug it.

By practicing identifying and using dialogue in your dreams, you are less dependent on therapists and books about dreams. Books about dreams can be handy to inform yourself, but explanations are very general while your own meaning is often specific and unique.

How Instead of Why

Gestalt work is especially about looking at and listening to *how.* It is not about finding out why you have a headache, but how you brought that about. If you are lonely, the question is "How did you happen to become lonely?" If you ask a *why* question, you will be ruled by your head and a *because* answer will follow which is always mental and restricted. With a *why*, explanations will follow but not necessarily, understanding. The *how* question is practical and addresses your whole awareness and responsibility. In the example about loneliness, you can consider the ways in which you shut yourself off from contact. By observing the question "How do I do that?" you take responsibility for your loneliness and search for ways to change it.

Your voice is also an important tool to becoming aware. It is often more important to listen to *how* you say something than *what* you say. Listening to your own voice can help you to become conscious of what you feel more quickly. How does your voice sound? And where and when does it sound toneless, without energy, high or low, hoarse or pinched, monotonous or melodious?

Here and Now

These three words are often wrongly understood in therapy country. Understanding incorrectly means that the present is important, and the past is over—over and done with—only *now* is important. The consequence is that many kinds of therapy stay superficial, e.g., behavioral therapy and cognitive therapy. Understanding correctly is about *experiencing* the *here and now*. Perls calls this theme of the *here and now*, a kind of koan, a puzzle that seems insolvable. "If you remember or run ahead of things, you do that now, at this moment."

When something in the past was emotionally finished, it became assimilated within you; it became part of you. But if the past was not digested and remained, in the language of

Gestalt, "an uncompleted gestalt," it can be digested as yet and completed as gestalt.

Only when the past has been digested, can it be let go. Only when something has been completed, can something new begin. The *here and now* is, indeed, the only place you can really live. The question is, however, *how* to accomplish that. As long as your past has not been finished emotionally, you will carry your past with you and will not be able to live in the here and now completely but only to the extent that your past has been digested. This means that it is not important to speak *about* the past in the here and now, but to *relive it* in the here and now and so heal it and leave it behind you.

Games Played on the Path to Authenticity

Before we dare to become ourselves in all situations, we often make use of certain roles and play *games*. Your authenticity and your emotional outbursts were often not recognized and tolerated. You had to be in command of yourself, but you have also developed methods to hide behind yourself. We are familiar with:

- ***The superficial politeness layer*** with polite questions and answers, such as "How are you?" "I'm fine, thank you" and "What kind of work do you do?"

- ***The role-play layer*:** You play the role of daughter, son, helper, patient, or parent. The marriage relationship caught in fixed patterns belongs here, too. It the layer of fixed routine behavior. It is behavior that has been imposed from the outside. It is programmed unoriginal behavior of the kind that tells you, as do your surroundings, that you have got to do things. You have been chained to your role.

- ***The top dog-underdog game.*** This is another name for the earlier mentioned Tom Thumb-Giant game. You can play this role with yourself and with others. You are not in your core and an enemy of yourself. Your top dog represents all the messages from your parents and educators about having to do this or be like that—those roles that you had to accept. Your underdog is the little child within you that still listens to these messages.

To find your authenticity, you have to become conscious of this avoiding contact. You start to realize that you are not your roles and games and that something essential is missing in this role-play, namely warm-heartedness, contact from heart to heart. In the Gestalt theory you have to go through the layer of deadlock and implosion whereby your energy feels as deadened, via your explosive layer to get to your true authenticity. With this explosive layer, I mean the layer of emotions here. Your emotions show your true face to yourself and others. After this layer, in which you make contact with your emotions and work through your old emotional charges, you arrive at the layer of authentically being yourself.

You will not need role-play or games any longer; you will show yourself as you are. Only then is real intimacy with another possible. With this we have a great, although not complete, definition for intimacy: not playing *games* or role-playing anymore. The other positive half of the description can be described as sharing your heart and feelings with another.

Chapter 28

Bodywork: From Tension to Emotion

Physical tension is a symptom of an inner struggle

Spark of Light Work's fourth pillar consists of various kinds of bodywork. To discuss this subject in detail in one chapter would lead too far afield. I will limit myself to the essence. At the moment there is an abundance of types of bodywork: various types of massage, physiotherapy, manual therapy, acupressure, methods such as bioenergetics, Postural Integration, Rebalancing, Mensendieck physiotherapy, the Alexander technique, Haptonomy, Reiki, etc. It is almost too much to still be to see the forest for the trees.

It will probably be clear by now that in Spark of Light Work, emotional liberation is first and foremost. Because of this, some of the above mentioned methods will fit in while others will not. The criterion will be if the therapist has the inner intent to convert tension into the expressing of emotion. This criterion will probably depend more on the therapist as a person than on his or her technique. Without explaining every method, I will limit myself to explaining what it is about in Spark of Light Work.

313

Transforming Energy

Everything is energy and no energy can be destroyed, only changed into something else, as Einstein proved. Water cannot be lost but changes into vapor when heated and into ice when frozen. In the same way emotions transform when *heated,* in other words, when they are expressed into zest for living, creativity, clarity, wholeness, and joy. When emotions are not expressed, they become frozen in our bodies as it were. When we want to work at our transformation, feel more "joie de vivre" or amass more treasures, we must set the *frozen emotions* in motion; that process is called melting. We do not really add anything in the case of bodywork but encourage the transformation of energy. To keep with our imagery, at the very most, we hold a light to it.

The question is what is the best way to melt it? In the first instance, the answer seems to be to have a nice relaxing massage. But what happens then? Will anything be really changed when we go back to our daily routine?

Tension as Frozen or Rigid Emotion

When your emotional ice melts, it is crucial that the emotions are really liberated from your body; you will start to cry or become angry. Therefore, the bodywork within Spark of Light Work is always emotional bodywork. It is about transforming physical tension into emotion. Physical tension, also called stress, is a symptom of an inner struggle between two impulses: one of the impulses is an emotion that wants to come to light, the other a ban on expressing that emotion. Bodywork includes the realization of this inner war. Because of the intensely felt awakening to this struggle, a choice can be made to give up the ban on expressing emotions. It is about surrendering to what our body wants to express in emotions. A safe base is clearly of the utmost importance in this case, as in all types of emotional work. Somebody had the following question in connection with this:

> *Can you give yourself a safe base? I find that difficult, but I do notice that it helps if I imagine (oh yes) Jesus himself sitting next to me. Important is that feeling of love, important for getting ahead with the Spark of Light work...and if I can't do it myself (yet), would it help to ask assistance from higher beings? Or is that just nonsense?*

No, that is not nonsense. Indeed, it is about safety and a loving reception of your feelings, so everyone can be an intermediary. Jesus is, in Christianity of course, pre-eminently *the* Mediator. Why should you do it alone? You have to do it yourself, but not alone. From this point of view, physical complaints and pains will almost always come back when the frozen emotions that are within them have not yet been brought to the light. Bodywork means manipulating the body in such a way that emotions are released and expressed. Clarification and insight are also an important part of this. It is often not very difficult to release somebody's emotions in a safe environment. It takes skill to help aim and clarify the emotions. Expressing emotions without insight is insufficient for growth and healing. Emotional bodywork has many essential components. We could also say that emotional bodywork must be part of a path that includes more elements. For this reason, Spark of Light Work is supported by five pillars. A lot depends on the abilities of the counselor with regards to experience, technique, insight and....love. A loving touch can sometimes be more important than a technically correct manipulation. It is, essentially, about surrendering to your own body whereby bodywork can function as a catalyst. You will begin to feel how you can transform your tensions into emotions and so heal yourself in this way.

Chapter 29

Regression Work:
From Past to Present

Traveling back in time enables us to be better in the here and now

egression work is the last aspect of Spark of Light work. It is not really separate and plays a part in all other aspects mentioned. Spark of Light Work is always about regression, whether people feel that they are going back in this life or previous ones.

As will be clear from the previous, liberation or healing of fixations consists of making a connection between an earlier event and the present. We travel back in time so we can live in a better, nicer, and especially more complete way in the here and now. If this regression or reliving is to be effective and beneficial, it should be of an emotional nature and entered into consciously. A spontaneous, subconscious regression has no point or meaning to it, except if we use this event for awakening.

Regression means going back to another time and place somewhere in your past. By reliving emotions, you start to remember things from the past. Due to the emotion you have lived through, you connect past and present and regard your present behavior, fixations, feelings, and patterns in that light.

In analytic literature, regression is a return to a different stage of life. A child of twelve, that because of the death of her mother spontaneously starts to suck her thumb as if she was a little girl, is an example of this. In our Work we *consciously* relive previous stages of life. It is possible that, within the work, you will feel like a baby who is crying for its mother and who wants to suck. Healing can only occur where it has gone wrong. This proposition is fundamental in this Work and has important implications. It means not only feeling like a child or baby again but also receiving at the level of a child. Trying to regain your lack of love as a grown-up only works partially. It is important for you to ask for what you need as a small child does, for example, from your partner. Because of this, Don-Juan behavior will not work to make you feel more fulfilled. What belongs at a child's level should be experienced and regained at that level.

Spark of Light Work in the Here and Now

Spark of Light Work means that you, consciously, go back in time to connect the present fixations and stagnation in life with an emotional occurrence in the past. It is an essentially different path than that of meditation, for example, where the focus is only on the here and now. I started my path of awakening with meditation, Yoga, Zazen, and various forms of Christian meditation. My teachers were, among others, Von Dürkheim and Lasalle. I noticed during my meditations that I did, indeed, have glimpses of awareness in the here and now, but that I did not fundamentally advance on my path as long as my volcano of repressed emotions did not receive room for expression. It seemed like I was practicing forever. Only when I took the path of emotional digestion did I learn what meditation is and the *power of now*; I felt, through deep relaxation, a sense of homecoming within myself and in what there is now. Only by going back in time did I learn what it is to be completely in the *here and now*, and I sensed that this is the only place where life is. This life must be dug out from your past, where you left unfinished business and lost such things as emotional expression, childlike receptivity, innocent perception, playfulness, and the capacity to enjoy. Most children can really live in the here and now, and that fits in seamlessly with a saying by Jesus: "Except ye become as little children..." which is a wonderful definition of regression. It means that we should become like children again, not remain children, and that is a vast difference. In between those two, you will find the Work of awakening.

Part IV

Liberation from Emotional Imprints and Defense

Chapter 30

Complex Emotional Imprint Programs

The traditional model in psychiatry and psychoanalysis is pure personalistic and biographical, but the modern study of awareness has added new levels and dimensions and departs from a fundamental similarity between the human psyche and the whole universe.
~Stanislav Grof

Imprints are deep tracks carved into our cell memory; they can be compared to computer software. Each imprint is, as it were, a miniature program. There are genetical imprints; karma imprints; physical imprints; social, mental, verbal, and emotional imprints. All those imprints together have made us into the people we are now. They are all messages and experiences contained within a kind of program like a computer. I think that Stan Grof observed this for the first time in his work. He uses the term Coex systems, systems of "condensed experience." A Coex is a "dynamic constellation of memories from different periods in somebody's life/and lives which are all strongly charged with the same emotion and contain a similar intense physical sensation or have other important elements in common."[1]

A Coex is an unintegrated psychological program that drives us towards integration and completeness. This means that it is not just one trauma or conflict that lies at the basis of psychological problems, but a chain of events, emotions, feelings, thoughts, and fantasies. This makes Working on our psychological health not only extraordinarily interesting but also extremely difficult.

Such psychological computer programs or complex imprints predispose us to certain situations in life. This is where we meet up with Jung's synchronicity and the Hermetic law:" so within, so without." My own example follows:

> *I did not know much respect for myself in the past. This had to do with a grave misstep during my first life on earth. When my only child was murdered, I used my powerful position and had all the children in the area killed—the well-known eye for an eye and a tooth for a tooth under which our earth has suffered and still suffers so greatly. The lack of respect for myself that I then developed, expressed itself during many lives in many ways:*
>
> 1. *More deeds without respect (repetition compulsion stemming from unsolved anger);*
>
> 2. *Situations in which I let myself be treated without respect (out of guilt and a subconscious need for punishment); one of these was my previous life as a Jewish woman which ended in Auschwitz*
>
> 3. *A search for respect and what respect means in human society (this stemmed from a spiritual longing for healing and knowledge).*
>
> *From this theme (although I have more, of course) and from this one Coex system of complex*

emotional imprints, I chose this life in a family in which I was a late arrival. I was not really part of the family, and I did not feel much respect for who and what I was. I was the odd one out, whose search for psychological and spiritual things was not understood. One of the biggest insults I can remember was when, as a five year old, I wanted to go to church with the parents of a friend, and my mother told me that I was much too small to go. It was not really very wrong of her, but it was, for someone with an 'inborn' search for respect, a huge emotional imprint. In this example, it becomes clear how relative the events in our surroundings and the actions of our parents and educators are. They are always in relation to a child with certain complex imprints, which are very old indeed.

The Work of Liberation as painted in this book means becoming aware of these complex imprints as much as you possibly can and liberating yourself from them. They are not only in the way of your true liberation, but also stop you from realizing your soul and the person you really are. I am reminded of what my former teacher Count Karlfried Von Dürkheim, always said, "For me it is about how Karlfried breaks through Dürkheim." I would like to go a step further: it is not only how I break free of my family history, but "how my eternal soul breaks free of my temporary identity." To be able to do this, you not only have to become conscious of old imprints but also find ways to get them out of your system. For me, that is the spiritual path of liberation at all layers and levels.

I have experienced knowing that the emotional imprints from former lives and those from my present life are at the base of all other imprints, such as mental, social, physical, and even religious ones. In any case, my line of approach is the Work of liberation. Others may choose the mental or devotional approach. On my own path, emotional work has proved to be the most effective for me. I have followed many different paths, but the ones that have helped me most to liberate the deep imprints from my total organism are, in chronological order: Gestalt Therapy and various form of body work, such as *LeibTherapie* within Von Dürkheim's school of initiation; *Postural Integration;* breathwork similar to Stan Grof's Holotropic breathing. It would lead too far afield to describe all these different paths. He who seeks, shall find the right information somewhere else.

Essential in this Work of liberation is to realize that the path has many layers. You can become conscious of your imprints at a mental level. Examples of these mental messages follow:

- If I cry, they will reject me.
- I am a victim of my fate.
- God has deserted me.
- I am not allowed to be happy.
- I have got this character after all.
- I am not good enough.
- This world is not a safe place.
- If I am vulnerable, they will get me.
- If I am spontaneous, I will be punished.

For many people this is the first layer of awareness—and then? The second layer of imprints lies under these mental messages; they are emotional imprints. To rid your system of these messages, it is not enough to become conscious of the stories and histories that lie behind them although it is a good beginning. This reminds me of a joke about Freudian psychoanalysis.

There once was a man who suffered from wetting the bed. He told a friend, who recommended a good psychoanalyst. They meet again six years later; the friend asks, 'And how are you and the analysis doing?' The man answers, 'Great.' 'Fantastic', answers the friend, 'I suppose you've stopped wetting the bed now?' 'No,' the man says, 'but I do know why I wet the bed.'

The emotional layer is the layer that has the ability to liberate deep imprints from as far as the cells. That is what this book is about in actual fact. In the following chapters we will go a bit deeper into the various types of imprints. Central to this Work is not only the liberation of old patterns and imprints but also the freedom of new behavior and new choices. Our acts will no longer be reactive, but we will be able to answer from our souls.

Chapter 31

Conception, Pregnancy, and Birth: Early Imprints

An adult has time to develop defense mechanisms and find
answers.
An unborn child does not have that possibility. What influences
him is very direct.
~Thomas Verney

The Conception

Our very first beginning here on earth starts with the fusing of the female and the male, the ovum and the sperm. Even then, we already had awareness although we do not usually remember. The awareness and emotion of babies and fetuses has been largely denied in our recent past. Evidence of there really being awareness during conception, pregnancy, and birth is growing. The belief that the baby "doesn't feel anything" and that awareness only starts after the brain has developed, months after birth, has proved to be a myth. Recent worldwide scientific research has, thankfully, shown that babies and fetuses perceive a lot. This has led to a greater understanding of the emotional development in the womb during and after birth. Fetuses and babies know what is happening; by using simple regression techniques, such as breathwork and hypnosis, we can remember everything. Language is not necessary to store experiences and imprints in the memory.

It has emerged from research using echographs that the unborn are equipped with the full ability to communicate and react to sound, vibrations, and especially emotions. This ability is *unrelated to the development of the brain*. This fact corresponds with a study into near death experiences by two Dutch cardiologists which was published in the internationally important medical magazine *The Lancet*. It appears that people still have their complete awareness with the ability to think, feel, observe, and remember while they are brain dead and thus have a completely flat EEG. "This means that there is awareness from outside your body, which you can receive in your body and your brain."[1]

In spite of all these new research facts, there is still a lot of scepticism and the domination of the brain is taken for granted. Brain mass is seen as central and not consciousness.

With regard to conception, people still often deny in the usual jargon that the developing child has awareness, emotion, and feeling. Conception is much more than the story of an ovum and sperm. With the present artificial insemination methods, there is a denial of emotion and feeling. People even talk of "a highly technological surrogate motherhood." The conception of a child is an emotional matter and a natural occurrence. We have come to think of it as fairly commonplace and talk quite technically about it. However, it will always be a great miracle.

It is of essential importance to gain insight into the very first imprints a child receives during conception. It has been said that all good things come in threes; well, conception consists of three things: a father, a mother, and their combined energy of love.

1. Energy is generated when two people have sexual intercourse. If these two people love each other, it becomes the energy of love.

2. Energy is released from the explosion we call orgasm, and it is given during conception to the future child. The child is given life energy by the *orgasm of the father* which is, of course, always part of conception. I believe that not just the quantity but especially the quality of the orgasm of the man is very important. With quality, I mean the extent of the connection with the heart energy and not just if sex was good. Having sex is often just routine or a physical need to feel good or to release tension. How many men are familiar with the connection between their heart and the "sex chakra"? The connection is more naturally present in women, and it is the woman who should teach her husband that connection. She can do that by treating herself carefully, by discussing everything freely, and by only allowing sex when the connection from the heart is there. I have noticed that the same separation between heart and sex is present in a growing number of women. They say, for example, that the relationship with the partner does not amount to much anymore, but that sex is still good. You can only say this if you have separated both areas in your energy. More about this subject in the chapter on sexuality and emotions (Chapter 40).

3. The *orgasm of the mother* makes room for the soul of the child. She receives the child. The orgasmic energy of the mother is also important for the child. Not only does she express her enthusiasm for her partner, but

also her welcome for a possible child. It was certainly quite usual for the generation of older women to not have orgasms. Orgasm would not have been part of many conceptions because of the general feeling of shame and a taboo about sex which existed until recently. Another factor was unfamiliarity with female sexuality and its denial. Marcey Foley[2] believes that the child's imprint will be that it is not really welcomed because of this lack of female orgasm. It will not feel at home in the world afterwards. However, I believe that the emotional welcome by the woman is just as important, if not more important, in this process. With this, I mean the extent of being wanted and also the extent to which a woman can connect affectively with the child. More on this subject in the part about pregnancy.

A child receives these three energies which become imprinted. The child also brings its own soul   energy and its emotional bond with these specific parents. Besides the energy that a child itself brings, a lot will depend on the quality of the orgasm and the collective love energy. Somebody told me recently that he remembered that his conception was not exactly a high point. "But," he added, "I will make my life a high point myself!" The following is an example of the way a young woman's conception was imprinted in her memory:

> *For quite some time now, I have wondered why I was so scared of boys during puberty. As soon as a boy made advances, I ran away and even panicked. Because of this, I did not have a 'normal' puberty with dates and courtships. Later on, in the relationship with my husband, it no longer played a part; I think that was partly due to him having a very soft energy. During the reliving of my puberty, a lot of sorrow connected to loneliness surfaced. During Spark of Light work, shortly after this reliving, emotions and a strong feeling*

*of knowing about my conception came to light. I felt,
whilst crying a lot, my father's aggressive way of
making love. I felt that I was disgusted by it. I suddenly
realized that my fear of men and sex is based on this
mixture of sex and aggression (my father always felt
very jealous about my mother).*

If it is true that these three energies are of essential
importance with regard to conception, what are we to think of
children who are conceived with artificial insemination and in
a test tube? This is, of course, an area about which nobody can
say anything for certain. However, I do believe that it is
important that these aspects, that have more to do with emotion
than with technique, are taken more into consideration when
making decisions.

I read about the customs of an African tribe[3] whose
habit it is to not to use the date of birth as the day the child was
born, nor that of the conception, but the moment it comes into
the thoughts of the mother. I cannot guarantee that this is a true
story, but it is a meaningful one. It would be wonderful if it
was really like this! The story goes as follows:

*When a woman decides that she wants a child, she goes
and sits under a tree and listens till she hears the song of the
child that wants to be born. After she has heard the song, she
goes to the man, who will become the father of the child, and
she sings the song to him. When they make love, they sing the
song together to invite the child. When the mother becomes
pregnant, she sings the song to the midwife and the other
women of the tribe so they can sing it as a welcoming song
when the baby is born. When the child grows up, other
villagers learn the song, too. If the child falls or hurts
him/herself, they sing its specific song. When the child does
something good, they sing the song to honor it. And that
continues throughout his/her whole life. When he or she
marries, the collective songs are sung and finally the song is
sung at death.*

In our modern society, there are also people who are open to such experiences and who catch a glimpse of their unborn child before conception or receive a message from their future child.

There is, for example, the story of the film star Richard Dreyfuss. He talked in an interview about being addicted to alcohol and drugs for twenty years and how he changed his life completely after being in a drug and alcohol rehabilitation center again. He saw, in a vision, a little girl of about three years old wearing a pink dress. She said to him, 'Daddy, I can't come to you if you won't come to me. Please sort your life out, so I can come' and then she was gone. But what stayed was Richard Dreyfuss' motivation to bring his life in order. Within three years his daughter was born, and she was the same as the little girl he saw in the clinic.[4]

Becoming more open to similar experiences of the awareness that every child carries with it, will hopefully make our way of thinking and acting less technical and more respectful of life. It is time to develop a type of parenthood that is more aware and broader and which begins before conception.

Pregnancy

Study shows that a child in the womb has a rapidly developing sensory system from two months onwards. Thomas Verney and John Kelly relate many stories of unborn children reacting to voices, to music, and to the moods and emotions of parents in their book *The Secret Life of the Unborn Child*[5]. They narrate the story of a conductor who was asked in an interview how he had become interested in music. He was quiet for a moment, and then he said that he had been amazed when he was young that he could play compositions without having seen them before. He said:

When I conducted a piece of music for the first time, I knew before I had turned the pages of a score how the cello would sound. One day I talked to my mother, who is a cellist, about it. I thought that she would be fascinated as it was always the cello part that I could hear so clearly in my head. She was, indeed, fascinated, but when she understood which parts I was talking about, the mystery was quickly solved. All the parts I knew, without ever having seen them, were the ones she played when she was expecting me.

What an imprint! We will now look at the imprints that can play a role at an emotional level. Not only regression experiences but also echography studies show that the unborn can experience emotion. Fetuses react to a puncture of the stomach with reactions of fear, fluctuations in the heart rhythm and withdrawal. Not every emotion will leave a remaining imprint in the child. What matters are the constant emotional attitudes of mothers, such as how much she wants the child, serious depression or fear, and serious events, such as violence and rape.

Emotional Imprints

There are four important emotional imprints during pregnancy.

1. ***The importance of a symbiotic connection***
   In my work I have noticed that one of the most important factors is the extent of emotional connection with at least the mother. This is about forming the first emotional bond that will be a basis for the rest of our lives. There are questions, such as Am I welcome? How much? Are they looking forward to my arrival? Are they curious about me? Are father and mother emotionally connected to

me? Do my parents love each other? Is mother able to attach herself emotionally to me?

Symbiosis is an emotional perception of the unity between mother and infant. The infant cannot yet function as a separate individual in the womb or for a certain amount of time after birth and has a very fundamental need for the energy of the mother.

In practice, I have noticed that the experience of being attached to the mother is of crucial importance for the following three reasons:

- The symbiotic bond is the basis of a child's feeling of security. The developmental psychologist Erik Erikson called this **basic trust.** This trust lays the basis for all further developmental stages of the child.

- The intimacy with the mother forms the basis with which you can enter into an **intimate relationship later on.** It forms your ability to connect emotionally with someone else in the future. The mother is, after all, the first person on earth that we actually meet and with whom we reside for nine months. That starts a trend. The following is an example of how a marriage that was not working, started to work again after both partners had made a regression to the womb:

> *Annie and Peter have been married for thirty-six years and have become trapped in a lack of contact. He did not know much about emotional contact, and she did not know much about sexual contact. This is how it looked on the surface of things. During Spark of Light*

work where we work in a small group, we did not work primarily at their relationship but at everybody's own soul history. During the week, both arrived at the lack of connection during their time in the womb. Both cried at the lack of intimacy with mother, and they could comfort each other with this. Because of this experience, their eyes were opened. They began to understand that their inability to share intimacy was rooted in this early lack. Where there was once reproach and anger, there was now compassion for each other because of the child that had not received enough bonding.

- In this symbiotic bond of love, the ***love for yourself*** is established. It is important that the mother-to-be is emotionally mature and capable of such an experience of unity. I see two variations of the incapacity of women to connect symbiotically with their children. I see this incapacity in women who have rather a cerebral disposition and who have hardly any connection with instinctive maternal feelings. They have often not known this basic motherliness with their own mother. On a fundamental level "What I have not known, I cannot pass on" applies; with the exception that this *hole* because that is what it is, is lived through and dealt with.

I find the other variation in people who come from very large families where the mother, after giving birth to a certain number of children, is not emotionally able to connect to a child anymore. In regards to this this last possibility, here is an account from the Spark of Light Work:

One of our Spark of Light weeks was almost completely about the earliest experiences with parents, especially with mother. By coincidence, the participants all came from large families whereby hardly anybody had been given the feeling that they were especially welcome; they were one in a row of many, and mother had not had the time or energy for every new child. The care and goodwill were there, but the most important aspect of a healthy basis for self-acceptance is the inner ability of the mother to bond emotionally with her child and to welcome and confirm it completely in her inner self. Outwardly, the child was accepted as something natural, but in the subconscious of many mothers of the generation of 'ten children families' something completely different was felt. Those mothers hardly had any time to themselves and were subconsciously and unwittingly angry and rebellious, although this was very seldom allowed to come to the surface. However, as we know only too well, everything in the subconscious will eventually come to the surface by way of a detour and will be projected and directed, unsurprisingly, towards the children.

This is the reason we did a lot of work about early childhood loneliness and pain. Sometimes we went back to the womb, which felt more like a nine months isolation cell than a warm nest. After all, if the consciousness of the mother is not directed towards the child in joyous expectancy, the womb will not be a nice place to be. By reliving the painful loneliness in the warm nest of a Spark of Light group, it is

338

possible that the adults we are now will discover the ability to welcome the child within us and learn to love it. This is where the ABC of love and acceptance of us begins. There is a lot of chaos in the world because we do not accept and value ourselves. As a consequence of our experiences in childhood, we have not developed sympathy and gentleness towards ourselves, and because of this, we radiate very little towards others even though we do our best to be friendly and helpful. Seeing that we can only recover where it went wrong, we must return to the source of the hardening towards ourselves, and in this case, that is the womb.

2. ***The extent to which a child is wanted.*** The second important factor with regard to emotional imprinting during pregnancy is how much we are wanted. The following is David's story:

> *I was always unsure and timid, really. I never understood it. My parents were good to me. I was allowed to study, and my parents supported me very well. They were proud of me. I had a successful career, and yet I stayed fundamentally insecure. Even though I did my work well, I always felt that somebody could do it better. During Spark of Light Work, it became clear that I would have to travel a long way back to find out about this undermining uncertainty. It was as if I was back in my mother's womb during breathwork. I felt safe with her, but at the same time I felt a gnawing uncertainty in her about... me. I had the feeling that she wanted me, but at the same time, she did not. It drove me up the wall and made me angry, too: "What is it you really want, woman,*

yes or no!' My mother was already forty when she was expecting me, and she felt very dualistic about it. When I was born, I always felt very much loved by her. But that fifty per cent, imprinted there in the womb, caused me to always doubt myself. I have the feeling that now I have experienced this history from within, I can really leave the doubt behind and build up self-assurance.

It is clear from this story how important the first imprint is. The doubt in the beginning remained in spite of the love and acceptance later on.

3. *Depression and fear during pregnancy*

A deep imprint in the mood of the unborn is certainly created when an expectant mother is chronically depressed or fearful. I can imagine that a baby in the womb of a chronically fearful or depressed mother, distances itself from his feelings, as there is no other escape. This means that he learns, early on, to make a separation between himself and his feelings. This dissociative behavior can lead to psychotic behavior later on.

4. *Traumatic experience*

It will be clear after the above mentioned that when there are traumatic experiences during pregnancy which are linked to violence or rape they will not go unnoticed by the unborn. Much will depend on the love and attention of the parents and the ability to bond with the child. The following is an example of a person who experienced bombing during the Second World War while she was in her mother's womb.

Annette is a rather nervy woman. She has been on the path of inner growth for years. She follows all kinds of training and courses to become a freer person. She wants to get rid of those nasty fears that she cannot place. She comes in contact with an acute fear of noise during breathwork where we sometimes use intense music. She hears bangs as if from a bombardment. She has the feeling she is going to suffocate; however, she pants out her fear as it were. After the session, deep tranqulity descends upon her, and she has a strong feeling that she has experienced the war... from the womb of her mother. She also has the feeling that her own fears are mixed with the fears of her mother.

Pregnancy Education

In the West we have advanced so far in our collective consciousness that pregnancy education has become quite accepted. Many people do pregnancy yoga or follow a course of Haptonomy/bodywork. This smooths the path to emotional communication with the unborn child long before birth. This means that there is and will be more prenatal contact with the child than ever before. Only ten years ago, doctors told parents that talking to an unborn baby was pointless and unrealistic; no doctor will say that now. Because of good anti-conception, the theme of not being wanted will also reduce. What remains is work at the deep layers of the personality where it concerns developing emotional maturity and the ability of making fundamental contact. The "relay baton" will be passed on from generation to generation as long as the theme of bonding is not worked through emotionally.

The Birth

Birth is, next to death, one of the most important experiences in a person's life. We carry the memory of our birth with us in our soul and in our body even though we are not conscious of this.

The imprints received here are crucial for the rest of our life and for our emotional development. It will not determine everything; later experiences can make up for where it went wrong during birth, but the experiences during birth set a trend. In reverse, if the birth process goes well, it is not a guarantee for the rest of our lives.

From the beginning of our collective history, babies were born at home with the help of other women or a midwife. From the twentieth century onwards, this situation changed: children were born more and more in hospitals under the supervision of men. Women had to give birth lying down, instead of in a natural sitting position. Slowly women not only lost their influence over the birth but also their natural knowledge and trust in a natural birth, and a lot can go wrong due to this. Not everything used to go right in the past, of course, especially because of unhygienic circumstances and inadequate medical knowledge. Nowadays things go wrong for a very different reason; it is usually rather for a psychological reason than for a medical one. This is still not acknowledged and recognized enough. The influence of highly technical delivery rooms with bright lights and a cold routine atmosphere should not be underestimated. Separating mothers and babies and putting them in different rooms also has consequences. In my mind's eye, I can still see the sweet rows of cots, all of them conveniently together in one ward in the hospital where I worked. But how *sweet* was it for those babies? And how efficient are those nursing bottles? The opinion that a baby did not feel or experience anything because the brain was not fully developed, held sway for a long time in the medical world.

Thankfully, much is changing thanks to the emancipation of women and to books, such as that of Leboyer.[6] Fortunately, in the Netherlands, more and more home births are taking place under supervision of well-trained midwives. However, in The United States the birth is specially adapted to the schedule of work and the appointment with the hospital. On the day you have agreed on months before, labor is artificially induced if the time is right for the baby or not.

The more unnatural a birth is, the more that can go wrong. Ronald Laing, the Scottish psychiatrist who did pioneering work in the field of schizophrenia in the 1970's, wrote the following:

> *The preference for unnatural birthing practices that is becoming more and more prevalent in the whole world, despite contrary reactions, has led to birth becoming a major psychological catastrophe area where exactly the opposite is done of what would happen if things could take their natural course.*[7]

In his book *The Facts of Life,* Laing has collected poems of people whose current problems in life are put into words that are very much reminiscent of experiences in the womb and during birth. It is said that a person's birth is mirrored in his later life. If somebody becomes stuck in the birth channel, he or she can develop a phobia later on. People born with the umbilical cord wrapped around their neck could later develop a fear of suffocating, have speech problems, or not be able to bear wearing something around their neck. The use of the forceps, or anaesthesia, a Caesarean birth, and the cutting of the umbilical cord are all experiences that can reverberate in later life.

There are many theories and experiences with regard to the effect birth has on later life. However, there is great danger in making generalizations from your own experiences; in the field of human psychology, nothing is simple and nothing has just one cause. Moreover, a person's own experiences are unique. We can say, however, that the imprint during birth is significant and that remembering your own birthing process is important, especially if your intuition or dreams point that way.

Emotional Imprints During Birth

The Czech-American psychiatrist and researcher Stanislav Grof[8], who first introduced me to Breathwork, which is described in this book, regards the human psyche as an individual blend of imprints of four fundamental perinatal matrixes. These are imprints that have to do with the birthing process.

Perinatal Matrix 1:

The period of pregnancy

Perinatal Matrix 2:

The beginning of the birth. This is the point where the cervix is still closed, but labor has started. This gives a huge pressure from all sides. The child is literally under pressure. There is no way out yet, no opening. Due to the contractions, the blood vessels become constricted, and the blood supply is hindered. It can mean confrontation with death. There are not only near death experiences in adulthood but also at birth. Babies cannot, however, recount it. Feelings of timeless pain belong in this phase. The fetus has no sense of time; people who have relived their birth often report hopeless feelings of "there being no end to it." Later, despair and suicidal feelings can originate from a birth experience like this.

Claustrophobia and fear of narrow spaces can be a consequence of having spent an extremely long time in this phase. It is also possible that you will have difficulty dealing with stress if you have problems in this phase. The following is a young woman's experience of the world; yet it could also be the experience of her birth.

> *the world is crushing me*
> *the world is collapsing down on top of me*
> *I am under lock and key, imprisoned, locked away*
> *I have no room*
> *no room to move*
> *no room to turn round*
> *I am being suffocated*
> *I am being throttled*
> *pressure is coming from all sides.*[9]

It will be evident that it is best if this phase is as short as possible. Grof believes that if you have only been in this phase for a short while, you can later withstand physical or psychological limitations because you carry the imprint that this situation will be over quickly.

Perinatal Matrix 3:

The opening of the cervix and the struggle through the birth canal. It is a fight for life or death. If you come through this easily, it seems that you also come through the struggle of life easily. You are then, literally, "a born winner." Surveys show that children born by Caesarean section have more difficulty fighting for something. A long struggle in the birth canal leads to the imprint that life is a battleground. Imprints of war may already start here.

Perinatal Matrix 4:

The transition from water to air. From "an existence in water to an organism that breathes air" is a tremendous transition, and breathing problems can occur. The first breath is an enormous effort for the muscles and lungs.

Life as an independent organism begins when the umbilical cord is cut. According to Grof, manic-depressive imprints could originate in this transition from deepest depression and struggle to relief and liberation.

Much depends on the way you are welcomed in this phase. Was your birth a forceps delivery? Whose hands received you, and how did they do that? Were you exposed to the glaring lights and noise of a cold hospital room, or were you born in the safe shelter of a bedroom or in a warm bath? Were you immediately mechanically washed and weighed, or where you given to your mother? Were you perhaps put in an incubator? Traumatic circumstances, such as war, for example, can bring birth trauma's about.

Furthermore, it is of utmost importance that you had an emotional bond with your mother and father during birth. Did you have the feeling that you had to do it on your own, or did you experience it as a collective event? When I relived my birth during Stan and Christina Grof's training, I felt angry directly after birth. I felt that it was mostly my mother's anger towards my father because he was not really emotionally present during the birth but had been talking to the doctor about other things.

Reliving One's Own Birth

It would go too far off the subject and take a whole book to study all these possibilities in depth. It is important to obtain your own experiences and to examine what this chapter does to you emotionally and in which direction your feelings lead you.

The sensory observation of a baby may be diffuse, but its awareness is not. With its awareness, a baby observes fully.

346

The fact that we can remember so little is because that large awareness narrows down to a restricted identity during our earthing. However, you can rise above the boundaries of the restricted self during Breathwork and remember your birth. It is only possible to heal the memories and traumas stored there by going back to your birth through a process of reliving. Emotional reliving and developing a corrective experience are both important, whereby you will learn to be a nurturing parent for the little infant that is within you.

In Spark of Light Work, experiences of reliving one's own birth are treated the same way as all other traumas and events. I agree with Arthur Janov of "Primal Therapy"[10] that reliving one's own birth should take place as it did in reality if it is to have a therapeutic effect. Reliving is sufficient for imprints to disappear and heal. There are therapies where a good ending is artificially staged, e.g., a client has to crawl over a mat whereby the therapist receives him or her at the end of the tunnel. It is a superficial and naive way that has little to do with healing the old birth trauma. Reliving means living through and letting go of old pain and cannot be symbolically played out. If the original birth did not go well, the cure consists of being able to digest and integrate as an adult what you could not do as a child. It is evident that the comforting presence of a therapist or fellow member of the group will be beneficial to you.

Chapter 32

Emotional Imprints from Childhood

Not only is what we experienced in the past important, but also how we pursue it now.

*I*mprints from our childhood are innumerable; many have been discussed in previous chapters. Everything that you are in your subconscious thinking and in your existence is caused by old imprints. When you become aware of these imprints, you can begin to write a new life story that will stem from regained liberation and consciousness.

Without repeating the whole range of emotional imprints from shame to guilt in this chapter, I would like to discuss the subconscious ways these imprints are expressed in your life. By this, I mean the subconscious replaying of childhood drama's in adulthood. Just as a child who is bullied by her sister will quarrel with her doll and "shoot" it, we concretize our childhood dramas in our adult life.

If you have hardly experienced safety with your parents, you will be inclined to seek partners who cannot give you that safety either. If you have been abused, you will seek a partner who abuses you again. If you have been sexually abused as a child, you may tend towards prostitution. If you have received the message that you are no good, you may become a criminal. At a more subtle level, if you have received the message that nobody is to be trusted, you may find it difficult to be intimate with someone.

The imprints with regard to your possibilities and qualities can determine your profession. This is possibly contrary to your soul's choice. When you have received the message that "if you are born poor, you remain poor," you may not tend to strive for better possibilities and a better social position. When you have been brought up with the idea that you ought to earn a lot of money, you may disregard the path of your soul that recognizes how important it is to devote your self, body and soul, to something.

All these subconscious imprints cause a lack of freedom in your behavior, your choice of partners, relationships, your work, your profession, and even your whole life.

The Work is to become aware of these old emotional imprints and to scrape them off; this will then change your life. It will not be an automatic continuation of your past then; you will break through old patterns and tread new paths that are more in harmony with your greater soul. You will transcend your past and realize your soul and your destiny in this way. This means that you will no longer walk the beaten track but will give shape, in an original manner, to your life from your own source.

Chapter 33

Emotional Imprints from the Solar Plexus

I want to open. I do not wish to remain closed anywhere
because where I am closed, I am insincere.
~Rainer Maria Rilke

The emotional Work that has been described in previous chapters is fundamental work with the emotional body, which is situated in the solar plexus/third chakra in the stomach area. In this area the exchange takes place between your energy and your surroundings, as well as between yourself and others. In this manner you are energetically connected to your environment. The emotional digestion of all that you experience, takes place here. The solar plexus is fire and digestion, analogous to the physical processes of detoxification by the liver and digestion by the stomach. It is your fire of life, your vitality, and your emotional openness. As a child, you are open, and your solar plexus is vulnerable. You are totally dependent on your environment, and you reach out, as it were, from your solar plexus. Everything depends on the way this vulnerability is treated. If you are respected and welcomed, you will be able to keep your solar plexus open and full of vitality. You will grow up in an emotionally healthy way, be able to digest events in life and remain full of vitality. This is the ideal scenario. Usually something goes wrong with our emotional development because humankind has, as yet, a lot to learn; the solar plexus then tenses up and becomes closed off.

Solar Plexus and Emotional Health

Emotional health is a continuum of many measures. The measure of your emotional health after childhood depends on the way in which people reacted to your emotional expressions. Were you allowed to cry when you were sad? Were you allowed to become angry when you felt indignant or when people over-stepped your limits? And were you allowed to laugh exuberantly and act crazily when you were happy? Or were you told not to show off? Were you comforted if you were scared, or did you have to be brave and were you told "there was nothing to be frightened of"? How was spontaneity channeled into do's and don't's? Did people trample on your vulnerability?

How did people react to your vitality? Were you allowed to be energetic and make noise? Or were you too lively? With this I refer to children growing up in thin-walled flats or children in large families and small houses. And what kind of imprints do babies receive who are, once again, tightly swaddled up? Especially babies who cry a lot receive this treatment; I have already heard a number of mothers say that it really helps, and that the child is much quieter.

If the emotional reaction of the child is not heard or seen, it will go inwards. The solar plexus will then slowly become constricted and hardened. You become shy and "clam up." You withdraw into yourself and become more and more cut off from your environment. You learn to control yourself because of this fear and cut yourself off emotionally while you still go on functioning and doing what is expected of you. But emotionally you are not there anymore...

The Mechanism of Emotional Digestion

According to Freud and to most psychologists who came after him, the first six years of a child's life are fundamental and determine the rest of his or her life. This means that the emotional imprints in the solar plexus have almost been completed by the sixth year of our life. I do, indeed, believe that the first basis is laid then, but that experiences in later years of childhood and especially puberty are very important for further imprinting.

We will assume that the solar plexus is already formed and deformed in childhood. This means that the quality of our digestion mechanism is determined in our childhood, depending on the extent of emotional closure and tenseness. A lot depends on your mechanism of emotional digestion, more than you probably realized up till now. It is usually thought that the tribulations of life, its shocks and blows, determine the condition of your emotional health or well-being. However, this is not the case; the state of your emotional health or the extent of your happiness depends on the extent to which you are able to *emotionally digest* your life experiences. It is, of course, true that some people do receive more blows and traumas, e.g., the death of loved ones, ill-treatment, or rape, and yet our mechanism of emotional digestion is fundamental.

This means we have a light switch! We now have an opportunity, a switch, with which to repair our lives as adults and make them freer, lighter, and happier. The only thing you have to do is to make sure you improve your digestion mechanism. This is done through emotional Work in which your solar plexus can let go of its tenseness and closure step by step, and you can open up again and trust fully. This means gradually daring to take the risk of being hurt again. This

353

means slowly leaving your armor of neurosis behind. Neurosis is, after all, just the fear of being hurt again, and there was a time when you armored yourself against that happening. When you let go of your neurosis, you can become a natural person again and cry when you are sad, beat the carpet when you are angry, and laugh when you are glad. It means regaining what you have lost; your natural child and your natural way of reacting.

Regaining Expression and Creativity

In the case of closure, not only will nothing come in, nothing will go out either. We lose our ability to express ourselves. People may talk a great deal in our society and make a lot of noise about all kinds of things, but talking about what is in our heart of hearts is much more difficult for most. It means that you become vulnerable, and that is frightening to the neurosis within us. You could get hurt if you stuck your neck out! So you keep quiet and well-adapted and make sure not to attract attention. You take care not to be special and unique, perhaps because you can hear that old record playing over and over again in your head: "Behave yourself." In church you may have heard about Jesus who told people not to put their light under a bushel, but in daily life it is often forbidden. This creates a lot of confusion about what you ought to do, about what is fitting, and about what you can or cannot do.

Due to all these imprints and messages, you have learned to look outwards towards that which is expected of you, instead of inwards where you can draw from that completely unique and original source that you are, so you can emerge and create your life and world in your own way. Going your own way really means trusting your own wisdom. Creativity can only come from within, from your own unique individuality and originality. Digging this individuality and originality up from under the emotional debris of contorted adaption and mediocrity is certainly worth the effort for those who want to drink deeply from the cup of their lives.

Emotional Digestion and Receptivity

Because you have had too many indigestible *bits and pieces* in the emotional sphere, you have closed yourself off and find it difficult to receive. We could also say that when your mechanism of emotional digestion fails, your mechanism of receiving is damaged, too. Both mechanisms are part of the solar plexus. As you have closed yourself off because of all the hurt, positive energy cannot be let in, and thus old negative experiences are confirmed again and again. History repeats itself.

Carry grew up with an authoritarian, quick-tempered father. She is a calm, shy woman, who likes to please others. She quietly goes her own way. She married Peter when she was a young girl because he seemed so different from her own father; Peter was a quiet, shy boy. However, during their marriage, Peter turned out to be a restrained man who was domineering and quick-tempered. She also shrinks in fear from him and once again she does not receive the safety and intimacy she needs from a man.

There will only be room for a new experience whereby love can be received when the story of Carry's father has been emotionally digested by her. To that end, Carry will have to connect with her anger towards her father, and that will lead to her not shrinking from her husband again. Her anger will allow her to stand firmly on her own two feet and to enter into a confrontation with Peter. The anger can initially liberate her from her escape behavior. The next step will be to sorrowfully accept what she missed in her father; if she is able to find that in Peter and then work through it will depend on his willingness to "work on himself." Many men and women give up the path of self-realization at this point. People are often scared of a real confrontation with the partner; they do not want to lose the other.

The more the past is emotionally digested, the more room there will be for new experiences and the desire for a new balance within the relationship. You can become more receptive and accept your vulnerability when you have the ability to become angry and not allow yourself to be led by fear of loss.

From Massive Closure to Selective Openness

It is important to rectify the massive closure and learn to become selective when you become an adult. It is not about absolute openness. You can make the choice when and where you open up. It is important to take good care of yourself and to only open up to the degree that feels right. It is not good to open up in situations that are violent or with people you feel are too coarse to be allowed into your "china shop." As an adult you can choose where you to open up and where not, and to what extent. Feeling safe is an important criterion to not being unnecessarily hurt again. It is not advisable to do emotional work in the marketplace; you would instantly end up in a mental hospital! The Work must only be done in a safe and suitable place.

You can also choose *what* you want to let in. It is simply about letting nourishment in and keeping poison out of your solar plexus; this is also a light switch! You will, however, have to know where to find it and also dare to use it.

We often subconsciously hunger so much after contact that we do not choose carefully between what feels right or wrong to be allowed in. We often settle for some poison just to satisfy our emotional hunger. Experiencing going back to the real source will help to emotionally digest the old hunger; in that way your hunger for love will not become a stumbling block in the present. How often do you swallow what is unacceptable because you do not want to lose the other? How often do you weigh nourishment and poison against each other because you feel dependent on his or her love? Choosing what nourishes you means having the courage to stand up for yourself and to enter into confrontations.

It is, in the end, about regaining your inner freedom that was lost due to emergency measures in the past. Everything revolves around awareness and freedom of choice here. Nothing is ever lost; all the energy is still there. It only has to be transformed into freedom and joy; that is what Spark of Light Work is all about. It is about choosing fulfilment, learning to express emotions, becoming aware of old imprints and blockages, and by becoming receptive again to what you really need: love.

That last aspect is what it is all about here. Receptiveness can grow again when you have made room within yourself. You make room by expressing repressed emotions and become receptive to the extent that you do this. Receiving love is the core of all work of liberation; "Love is all you need." Love as the source and core of all Being is always there.

The Work is opening up to this source of loving light that can be found everywhere but especially within you. What you essentially are, is hidden, repressed, loving light that yearns for disclosure and realization.

Finding the Connection to Your Source

When you become emotionally closed off and are no longer able to receive, you become fundamentally detached from your source. You become a closed system and are not really nourished anymore. Our source is twofold:

1. Horizontal: nourishment from fellow men

2. Vertical: nourishment from your soul and the world of your soul. I not only refer to the connection to your soul and higher self here but also to guides, helpers, angels, and God.

If you are locked in your emotions, nothing can really affect you anymore, and nothing can nourish you. This is never completely the case, of course. Everybody will be somewhere in the continuum of open and closed. Perhaps being turned adrift from our real source is the reason for our consumer society where *nothing is ever enough*. And perhaps this is the reason for our contactual problems. When you are cut off from your source in this fundamental way, you can feel lonely even when you are surrounded by people because essentially you cannot let very much in. You can feel deserted by God and everyone.

The path to connection is once again deep emotional Work that slowly eases the constriction of the solar plexus by crying and expressing anger. If you de-tense and let old pain come to light, you will feel lighter inside, and there will be room for connection. The power of emotions will heal you and will make you open and free to accept nourishment. In turn, this nourishment will strengthen you. We need nourishment from the horizontal and the vertical source. Your emotional healing is not possible without a deep connection with other people. Most of your hurt lies in your relationship with other people. Only in the restoration of the relationship with people (and they do not have to be the same people) can healing take place. However, a vertical opening is necessary at the same time, one that goes into the heights and depths of your own soul. You can connect there with your own soul, your angel, and your God. You will then feel tranquility, satisfaction, and gratitude.

From Survival Strategy to Life Energy

If your life energy has been lessened by this whole process of emotional destruction, only survival strategies will remain. When the healthy life energy which leads you moment by moment through the jumble and abundance of choices and possibilities no longer flows, you can only think of what you will do or will not do. That way you're no longer following your gut feelings and basic needs but your rational thinking instead.

You lose your natural steering mechanism and use one you have devised. You lose your natural spontaneity, put on the mask of a well-adapted person, and seek ways to survive emotionally. Naturally, this usually does not happen consciously.

Survival strategies are subconscious ways of not feeling and yet keeping our head above water. I can remember how I quickly became a completely different child from the third grade in primary school onwards. I could not live as the sensitive and fearful child I was anymore. I did a U-turn and became a cheeky, bold child that liked nothing better that to raise hell in class. I survived for a couple of years in that way until I found a new strategy; I withdrew into my books and became a studious pupil. I only became aware of these strategies later in life. The only thing I did realize slightly was that I was not happy.

Perhaps another example is the girl who feels very unsure and cannot live with it because it feels uncomfortable and then tries to find certainty in outward appearances—in fashion and in pleasing behavior. A survival strategy is really a camouflage method to mask real feelings. How often do you do what is expected of you instead of living and answering spontaneously from your origin, from your own source? How adjusted are you in daily life? Do you live according to fixed patterns? How seriously do you live? How respectable and proper is your life? Can you still live according to your childlike passion for life, or do you use your brain for everything? All of these questions are part of this theme, and it is worthwhile asking yourself about them.

Finding the Love for Yourself

The end of this solar plexus drama is losing respect and love for yourself. As a child, you cannot understand why there is no loving welcome for your emotions and feelings. A child cannot understand that parents are restricted in their love and possibilities. Parents are godlike to children: I am just little and they are big. The only thing a child can *think* (although it is not consciously) is: "There must be something wrong with me if the grown-ups treat me like this and don't touch me tenderly. I can't be any good if my qualities are not seen." The conclusion is usually this: "I am not good enough, not pretty enough, not intelligent... not lovable." A destructive process has started with this doubt and uncertainty about yourself which lasts far into adulthood. The consequence is that you do not feel much sympathy for yourself or tenderness or compassion.

You start to do your best and succeed, gain points, make a career for yourself, be a good mother, a fantastic husband, a good father, and on it goes... till you wake up one day and look in the mirror and say to yourself: "Hello, dear. How are you? How do feel? What are you really living for?" The light switch is next to the mirror in this case! As an adult it is possible to realize that you are not guilty, bad, or wrong. You can start to realize and feel that although your parents usually tried to make the best of it, you did not get all you needed and were damaged, as they once were, too.

You can see through the relay race of human shortcomings and opt for not passing on the baton. Then you can make a U-turn and choose your inner child that yearns for love and respect. From that moment on, you can take the path

360

back, as described in this book—the path to undo what has been done. You cannot change reality or your past, but you can change the way you treat yourself. You learn the path of true love and start with yourself. You do not have to worry about the love for others then. That will follow naturally. You do not need an exercise in virtuousness or in altruism then. If you love yourself in that way, you will love everybody and everything.

Exhaustion: Burnout

In the beginning of this chapter, we saw that the solar plexus also stands for vitality. Exhaustion will soon come knocking at your door if your emotional body has become tensed up, has lost its potential to digest, is no longer receptive, cannot express itself and has broken way from its source. This is burnout! You are literally burned up. You do not have enough energy to emotionally digest anything. I was already burned up at twenty-eight due to an excessive need to perform, idealism, eagerness to learn, and success. Driven by fundamental uncertainty, there was not enough room to listen to my gut feeling and my need for rest and relaxation. Until things went wrong, and I could not do anything for eight months, except listen to myself and my own needs. The scales had to be balanced again. Thank goodness that it happened! It forced me to reflect on the how and why of this crisis. Crisis is also a chance to grow, leave old patterns behind, and win back life.

Chapter 34

Emotional Imprints in the Body

These physical patterns are ultimately the chains that imprison
the soul of man.
They isolate us painfully from each other.
~Ron Kurtz

*I*f you really want to get to know yourself and the state of your emotions, you will have to get to know your body. Your mind speaks the language of your awareness, but it lies sometimes. Your feelings can become mixed with your fantasies, and your intuition may become confused with desires or fears. But your body never lies. Your body is the perfect expression of your subconscious and conscious state of being. It tells you how you are doing in life. Although you may think that you are full of self-confidence, your body can tell you if this is really true. Your mind is not always aware of your feelings and sometimes takes you even further away from them with splendid reasoning. You may feel strong and powerful, but your body will tell you unerringly if this is real or compensated power. The latter means that you hide your powerlessness with the opposite. A good example is macho behavior and a bodybuilder's body.

Chronic patterns of emotional denial and tenseness are slowly imprinted in the body—they even become embodied. They are carved into us, just like a river without enough room will carve its way through rocks and stone. Certain body patterns originate in this way, drooping shoulders, a hollow chest, a heavy or light step, feet that point inwards or outwards, a head held high in the air, stiffened or slackened muscles. We express ourselves through our bodies. We are used to seeing our bodies as the result of genetic factors and, of course, certain characteristics are inherited. You may have inherited the drooping shoulders from your father, but you express who you are through them and that determines if your shoulders express slackening or relaxation—especially our muscles and their amount of tension or relaxation tell us how we are doing in life.

Muscles and Emotions: Our Physical and Psychological Locomotor Apparatus

First of all, we should us ask ourselves what muscles really are. Our muscles form the active part of our locomotor apparatus while our bone system and connective tissue form the passive part. Muscles have the ability to literally set us in motion. We have seen that the central characteristic of emotions is movement. We could call our emotions *our psychological mobility* and muscles *our physical mobility*. They are clearly connected! They are brother and sister. Emotional movement is expressed in the movement of our muscles and emotional stagnation in lack of movement. The degree of our emotional mobility is indicated by the degree of mobility that our muscles have. With this we have a good criterion with which to understand our emotions. It is possible to make a classification[1] of a number of basic patterns on the basis of this criterion. This classification is not used to label but to clarify. You will probably recognize one or two of these patterns, but there is often a mixture of different basic patterns.

Stiffened Movement: Fear

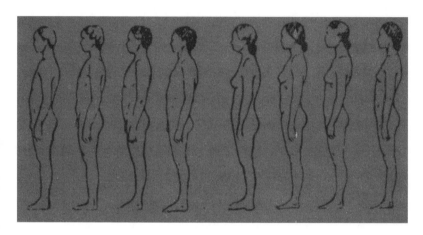

We all know the saying *paralyzed with fear*; fear is the most important restrained emotion here. As this fear has been denied and repressed, the fear expresses itself at the back of the body in a stiff back, shoulders, or neck. The fear has literally been left behind. The body sometimes leans backwards. The restrained fear is compensated at the front by a certain aggression in the original sense of "proceed towards." The willingness to enter into challenges is shown here; the chest is forward and the chin is up in a defiant and proud way. You love activity, but relaxation is difficult with this pattern. *Restraint and self-control* are central characteristics. Being on the alert and waiting to see which way the wind blows are part of this picture. Enthusiasm and exuberance are not easily shown because of fear. When are you scared? You are scared when you do not have enough support. This is the reason that stiffness usually occurs in the back. From this observation, it is fairly easy to connect the lack of support to the father figure. That is an important role for the father after all. While the mother should give a sense of basic trust, the father should give the child enough support to be able to move freely in the world.

The pelvis becomes unbalanced because of the tense back. The pelvis is usually tilted backwards due to a hollow back. Reserve and *holding back* may also be expressed with regard to intimacy and sexuality. It is possible that the emotions of the heart and the sexual emotions are unconnected here. Fear of surrender is a theme.

> ***The imprint***: "I am doing my best, so I exist."
> "If I am independent, nobody can hurt me."
> "If I surrender, I will be hurt."
>
> ***The work***: Deep massage, such as *Postural Integration, Bioenergetics,* and *Reichian Body Work,* whereby stiffening is transformed into emotion. Learning to let go of self-control through Breathwork.
> Learning to accept longings.

Slackened Movement: Anger

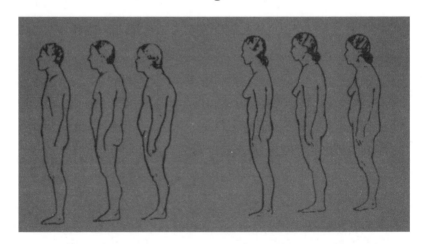

A feeling of hopelessness and giving up is expressed in slackened movement. You have given up. It is as if you have lost, and gravity has won. The body expresses heaviness and has lines that hang downwards. Drooping shoulders and a stooped and forward leaning posture are part of this. Feelings of inferiority play a major role, and the feeling that everything is an effort. Nothing ever happens of its own accord, and hard work is necessary. Characteristic words are "suffering" and "enduring," and the fundamental feeling is being a victim of something. Restrained anger and sorrow are characteristics, for movement that has become slackened. Restrained anger and sorrow accumulate in the diaphragm and stomach.

> ***The imprints***: "I suffer, so I exist."
> "If I let go, there will be nothing left of me."
> ***The work:*** Working with anger to develop power and the feeling of being proud. Intensive Breathwork to loosen the tenseness of the solar plexus by expressing sorrow.

Blocked Movement: Longing

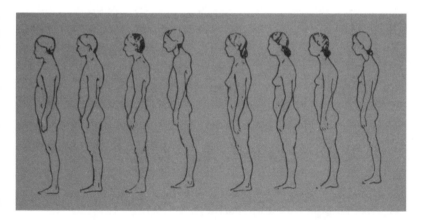

Being cut off from the source can be seen in blocked movement. Fundamental needs have not been satisfied, and, as a result, the body gives the impression of being somewhat weak and young. The muscles have a tendency to be underdeveloped. Tiredness and exhaustion are all part of this. Undernourishment is a basic characteristic of this pattern whereby thinness as well as fatness can be observed as compensation of *affective undernourishment.* Because of this, there is often a hollow chest with the head leaning forward as an expression of having trouble keeping one's head above water. You will seek support from others because of this affective undernourishment and easily end up in dependent relationships where the fear of being abandoned will play a major role. You tend to ask for the undivided attention of others due to this fear. It is possible that jealousy will also play a major role. Yet the round shoulders indicate an inability to give and to receive what you need. *Feelings of emptiness and deep sorrow* are the analogous psychological characteristics and reside especially in the chest and stomach. Breathing will have a sucking sound, like a hungry child's does.

> **The imprints**: "I long, so I exist."
> "I am too weak. I need you."
> **The Work:** Becoming aware of affective hunger; allowing suck and bite impulses. Grounding. Learning to receive. Digestion of sorrow.

The Confused Movement: Swamping

The confused movement stems from confused feelings where an individual is swamped/engulfed by emotions, and the ego does not have enough strength to integrate those emotions. The body's energy will be located mainly in the head so as to remain in charge of the many emotions that are not integrated. The consequences are a tendency to intellectualize and have very little contact with the earth.

The body gives the impression that the energy is going all over the place, as if there is not enough coordination ability and not enough combined coordination. There is not enough identity at hand to keep all the energies together. The body seems to be fragmented. This expresses itself in a somewhat lanky posture. There is a lot of movement in arms and legs. Physical contact with others is difficult because it can lead to swamping. Breathing is minimal because intensive breathing carries here the danger of getting swamped/engulfed by too much emotion. Breathwork as described in another chapter, is usually too threatening for people for whom this pattern is dominant. A great amount of safety and grounding are necessary to be able to open oneself up. Isolation plays a major role and stems from the need to keep others at a distance. Insight, clarity, grounding, and a slow build up of therapeutical contact and work are important in this category. This pattern is difficult to capture in a drawing because it does not express itself in posture but in movement.

The imprints: "I keep myself together, so I exist."

"If I open up, I will be destroyed."

The work: Grounding and strengthening of the self. Insight. In safe surroundings step by step becoming accustomed to the emotions.

Enlarged and Diminished Movement: Domination and Temptation

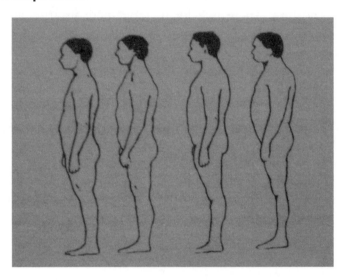

We see an imbalance between the upper and lower part of the body in this pattern; one is enlarged, the other diminished. There are two variations in this pattern:

- In the first variation, the upper part of the body is enlarged, and the lower part is diminished. We can call it top heavy. It is the body builder variation that we usually see in men, but increasingly in women. In our western culture it has become *the* image of beauty in the male: broad shoulders and narrow hips. The enlarged chest and broad shoulders show muscle power and arrogance and reflect a compensation mechanism whereby the feeling of smallness has been changed into the behavior and outward appearance necessary to create an impression of importance. The theme of power and powerlessness play a major role here. Characteristics are the need to impress and dominate, as well as the urge to control. The will and the power of reason are strongly developed to the expense of the emotions. The attitude presented to the outside world is often one of being independent and carefree and masks the deeply repressed need of dependence and being cared for. Those with this appearance will frequently have the urge to deny their own needs and emotions and those of others. They are often helpful because they need a helpless person so as not to feel your own helplessness. The upper part of the body may express compensation; the lower part shows the truth. We often find thin, tense legs without any energy that express that the powerful and carefree person "has not got a leg to stand on." The energy in the stomach and pelvis is weak, which expresses fundamental emptiness. The lack of fundamental support, speaks volumes here. The sexual experience will be minimal or accompanied by compulsive acts to discharge surplus tension. Performance and conquest are more important than pleasure and contact. The connection between the heart and sex chakra will be minimal. Blocked anger and the fear of being crushed dominate in the legs and stomach.

> *The imprint*: "I will, so I exist."
> "I have power, so I exist."
> *The Work*: Becoming conscious of the weakness in legs and pelvis. Finding the meaning and expressing it. Accepting the need for support. Melting and becoming soft in the diaphragm and heart.

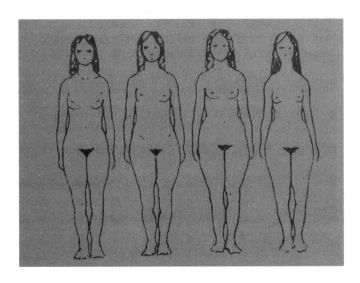

- The second variation is especially to be found in women. The upper part of the torso is diminished and the lower part, enlarged. This can be called *under heavy* or pear-shaped; it is the woman with a so-called Rubens figure, broad hips, and a full stomach. Just as the first variation is seen as the height of manliness, this type is seen as the height of femininity.

The lower part of the body is full and feminine, but the upper part slight and girlish. *Femininity and relationships* are often central in this pattern. Femininity is used and emphasized here to obtain acknowledgement for *the hurt girl that* expresses itself in the upper part of the body. The lack of acknowledgement by father is not felt and changed into an attempt to please the male. Themes: outward appearances, clothes, fashion, and eroticism belong especially in this category. A lot of life energy is poured into this.

The imprint: "I please, so I exist."

The Work: Working with the hurt girl and the relationship to father.   Breathwork to develop inner independence.

The Supple Movement

A supple movement can no longer be called a pattern. It is the liberated movement of those who have shed their emotional tenseness and in whom the life flow moves freely. There is relaxation where there was once tenseness. There is coherence and connection in the body. There is a balance. The body will rest in its core, and that is the lower part of the body. We can call the heart our complete middle and our stomach, the physical middle; it is called "hara" by the Japanese and "chi" by the Chinese. It is central in many Oriental martial arts. In the Western world, we have learned to carry our center in the chest. As a result there is tension in the shoulders and neck, our back becomes hollow and our knees overstretched. The weight of your body then rests on your knees for which they are not made. Your feet are built to carry your weight. It is not surprising that we have so many meniscus problems, here in the West. Your knees can be relaxed by bending them a few millimetres. You will notice that your stomach will protrude slightly, that your weight will shift to your feet, and that your back and shoulders relax. With this change of posture, which you can learn, you will not only prevent meniscus problems but also feel more firmly rooted. When I was taught this way of standing by one of my first teachers, Karlfied Von Dürkheim,[2] I noticed that I felt fundamentally stronger in life. I also became less afraid and defensive in contact with others. You can sometimes take the path from the outside to the inside!

The supple body, as you will understand, is not very easy to find although it can be found in small children.

When you do emotional work well, you are on the way to relaxation, suppleness, power, and a body that is in balance. Your body will express that you have conquered fixed patterns where possible, just as you have transformed your emotional patterns into essential being. You will then truly inhabit your body—you will be free.

Chapter 35

Emotional Imprints from Previous Lives

*Every soul comes into this world strengthened
by the victories or weakened by the defeats of its
previous life.*
~Church Father Origenes

A subject that should not be missing in this book is the influence and meaning of past lives. The memories of past lives have been of crucial importance on my path of liberation.[1] I did not search for them intentionally, but on the path of awakening they presented themselves sometimes quite fiercely. My most intense emotions originate from past lives. These emotions brought old, deeply hidden feelings of guilt to light, as well as deep despair and long forgotten depressions. In addition, they also revealed new "old" talents and new significance and meaning in my life here on earth—too much to mention here. I have the discovery of many lives to thank for the richness of my consciousness; they have helped me find my origin.

Working with past lives offers the possibility of extending your consciousness far beyond the boundaries of your current personality and life. What you now call "I" is only a sub-personality of your greater soul. What you call "I" is only the tip of your own personal iceberg. The rest is under water, concealed in your great sea of unconsciousness. If you do emotion work properly, this path will lead to your encountering many fragments of emotions, images, and memories from other times and places. The work you do on your emotions will take you there sooner or later. After all, emotion does mean to set in motion. So just let yourself be taken along by your flow of emotions and experiences, and everything will become clear, step-by-step. But why should you let yourself be taken along by your flow of emotions and not, for example, by your flow of thoughts or interests? The reason is that it is not always beneficial to find as many lives or memories as possible. The important thing is your liberation in the here and now. The finding of past lives should be beneficial to your present one. Emotions make the connection with what needs clearing up. Emotions tell you what is getting in the way of your being totally in the here and now and reaching your strength. Because of my work with muscle tests, only those experiences that are important at that moment come to the fore. They are then emotionally accessible. For this reason, a real emotional experience is possible. I am always surprised by how quickly we can move to other times and places. It is possible because we all carry our histories with us. Understanding those histories is the trick. We can then tidy them away and really say: what is done, is done. I live now!

Physical Imprints

Robert had a difficult bowel movement from baby onwards. He was chronically constipated, and going to the bathroom was always painful and full of shame. School trips and staying over became problematic. When he was about thirty, he started with the Work of emotional liberation. He quickly came into contact with all kinds of feelings that had to do with desertion by his mother. He could, however, not place these feelings in his current life. Even though the affective relationship with his mother was not all that good, she was always there for him and had not actually ever left him. The fragments of feelings and images he received during breathwork had to do with real desertion in a dreadful situation. He had images of camps and frightened people, and he felt like a little girl during the Work. Within a few months the images and feelings became clearer; he was a young girl of Jewish descent. During her stay in the transit camp Westerbork in the Netherlands, she was put on a different transport to Auschwitz than her mother because she had been in the sick bay. She had to make her last journey to the gas chambers of Auschwitz alone, amidst strangers.

Since this reliving, which took a couple of months, Robert has not had any constipation symptoms. He has regular bowel movements and the pain and shame have disappeared gradually. He has let go of a major trauma.

I always like to tell this tale because it has such a real result and shows that it is possible to release deep recollections in the body's cell memory through emotional reliving. I once wrote a little Christmas story that stemmed from old karmic memories. A small lopsidedness between the left and right hip had a major background.

A Christmas story.

There once was a man who was born with his left leg quite a bit shorter than his right. It was a signal from a previous life that his emotional side had remained underdeveloped compared to his more active right side.

He was a disappointment to his parents and became the object of derision. Only his grandfather loved him but died when he was about eight years old. As an adult he was so bitter and sour that from pure frustration, he took the gun he had *inherited from his grandfather from the cupboard and started to shoot haphazardly at animals. He shot at everything that moved; a horse or a stoat, a cat or a dog. He did not hunt animals for food for himself or his family because he did not have one. He shot from the enjoyment of power and from embitterment as well. He felt like a failure and because of this, he behaved like a failure and made sure that everything in his life failed.*

Centuries later when his lameness no longer manifested itself so prominently in his body and could only be seen by clairvoyants in his energy, the animals visited him in his dreams, and he remembered his sins against them. He threw himself on his knees in front of the angel of animals and cried with remorse. He begged for mercy. He realized that since his cruel acts towards the animals, he had cut himself off from his own vitality and instinctive powers. He remembered his grandfather who did love him and for whom his lameness was of no importance. The memory of his grandfather made him melt and find love and respect for himself again. But most important of all, was that he remembered his name: Christoph which means 'he that carries Christ.'

From that day onwards his equilibrium was restored. He found his center between right and left, between action and feeling. And in that center, he found his heart and knew that he was loved and forgiven.

Life Scripts

The physical imprints are clear in the previous examples. Imprints from past lives often have to do with the coming into being of certain scripts, certain scenarios.

I remember that long ago, I gave guidance to a brother of a religious order. "Previous lives" was not something that had a place in his vocabulary or in his way of thinking. However, he very spontaneously "shot"' into a reliving during emotional bodywork without me saying anything about past lives. He saw images of himself as a young wastrel during his life at court in France. He was a real whoremonger and felt really guilty about that in the here and now. He immediately saw the connection with his current oath of chastity within a religious order.

All kinds of vague feelings of guilt and shame can be traced back to old experiences of overstepping the mark, which we have all done at one time or another. We are often not conscious of these guilty feelings; they have, however, an influence on the life scripts we write. The following is an example of an over-zealous, burnout script:

Marilyn is following Spark of Light Work intensely because of a burnout. She can no longer do her work as a teacher and because of extreme tiredness is not enjoying it either. After Working with much unfinished business in her present life, she suddenly, during breathwork, came into contact with her life as a Russian woman who lived long ago. She could feel that she was fleeing from a war situation and that she was dying at the roadside. She cried bitterly because she had to leave her children unprotected and neglected along the roadside. She died with the feeling that she had woefully failed in her duties towards her children. And that last realization was a connecting thread in this life. She had the feeling that she failed and did not do enough which led her straight to an exhaustion script. This expressed itself mainly through her work. If she had had children, it probably would have expressed itself through them.

I do not profess to give a complete picture of the work with previous lives in this chapter. There are plenty of good books on this subject. There is not really a difference between traumas in this life or in previous ones in Spark of Light Work. They are approached in the same manner; it does not make any difference to the experience. A trauma of four thousand years ago will, when it is its "emotional turn," be just as emotional and lifelike as something that happened ten years ago. In our personal Akashic records, the place where memories are stored, there is no difference in time. Experiences, thoughts, and emotions are stored there from all ages, often jumbled up together but arranged according to theme. Your soul knows which experiences need liberation and makes sure they come to light....that is, if you wish to listen to your soul. You have a built-in motor that drives you towards growth and awareness. You can choose if you want to learn the hard way or voluntarily. The latter is done by meeting your darkness and inviting it to come out into the open, so it can become light within you. If you choose the latter, the motor will go at top speed, and everything will turn towards the light as a flower does. Then what needs to come to light will come to light from whichever time or place it originates, so that your consciousness becomes more complete. My experience is that emotional digestion is an effective road to experiencing this light of awareness.

Karma and Emotion

Finally, a short explanation of the concept of karma about which there are many theories. Karma is often explained as the law of cause and effect: "As you sow, so shall you reap." You have built up *good karma* by good deeds and *bad karma* by bad deeds. In this school of thought, you are murdered because you murdered in a previous life, and you are raped because you have been a rapist yourself. My experience of karma is the following: nothing happens in this life, rape for example, because you were a rapist in a previous life but *because you have not emotionally finished with it*—because you feel guilty, you attract a dreadful occurrence like rape at a later moment or in another life. It is not the overstepping of the mark itself, but the emotional not coping and guilt that makes you the victim of another person's *overstepping*. Deep inside, we feel that we deserve such experiences. The universe does not judge and moralize. We do that ourselves.

Chapter 36

Defense Mechanisms and Survival Strategies

*D*efense mechanisms and survival strategies are two aspects of the same phenomenon. These are ways to protect that which you experience as vulnerable—or believe to be vulnerable in your inner self—from danger. On a fundamental level, it is a healthy protection from something that does not feel right for you. Your defense mechanism helps you to fight or take to flight in case of real danger. It is, on a fundamental level, an instinctive reaction. Biologically speaking, we have an immune system that protects us from germs. Our lymph system has an obvious role but also our hormonal system and particularly the thymus. Lesser known is the fact that the tonsils and the appendix play a role in our defense. Nothing in our bodies is superfluous, even if we do not know its function very well. Next to this, or perhaps even under this, we have emotional defense as a basis that helps to keep our heads above water in times of trouble when there is no loving reception for feelings and emotions. This emotional defense very simply states: "I do not want to feel now." This emotional defense is mirrored in the immune system, whereby especially the hormones as physical bearers of emotions, play a mediating role. Hormones are the body's chemical messengers which are, amongst others, secreted by the endocrine glands. The brain sends a signal to the adrenal glands to produce adrenalin in case of chronic emotional tension. Adrenalin is a hormone that prepares the body for a threatening situation. The fatty acids that were meant as fuel remain in the bloodstream, which causes a rise in the level of cholesterol. The muscles are primed, the heartbeat quickens, and the body is ready to fight or take to flight. This fight or flight reaction can boomerang and affect the immune system. Under influence of the stress hormones, the immune system produces signal chemicals that can influence the brain, causing tiredness, concentration problems, sleeping problems, and lability of the autonomous nerve system.

Emotional Defense: Fear of Feeling

In this section, I will categorize the various attempts at not feeling.

Defense Mechanisms

Since energy is never lost but only transforms into something else according to Einstein's law, we can change our defense and transform it into positive energy that is not used against things but for them. Being against something costs a huge amount of energy while being for something, gives life and energy.

Introjection and differentiation.

"Introjection" is "swallowing or suffocating." During your childhood there were many unacceptable things that you had to swallow. Many of the messages you received at your mother's knee did not really belong to you or were not good for you, e.g., "Big boys don't cry" or "Girls don't do things like that" (climb in trees or play with cars). Or perhaps: "Hurry up! Stop whining." You swallowed deep imprints, such as "I am not good enough as I am" and "I am not lovable" because you were only little, and you thought that your educators knew everything. Not only did you swallow down emotionally laden messages, but also your emotions; how often do you literally have a lump in your throat when you feel sad? How often do you sigh deeply so as not to feel your anger?

The consequence of this introjection mechanism is that emotions pile up in your solar plexus. The feeling of being full of old rubbish that is not right for you is part of it. As the solar plexus is in the stomach area, various complaints of the liver and gall, pancreas and spleen may result. Another consequence is that you tend to accept things before you have really found out if they are right for you. You stray from your path easily when you chronically swallow things. Choosing the wrong study, profession, partner, or the wrong path through life, is all part of this.

The way to liberate yourself from this mechanism is to become aware of all these messages and to spit them out. Spitting, vomiting, and finally expressing yourself are the opposites of swallowing. To rid your system of the tendency to swallow things in life, you may often have to literally vomit. You will have to learn to make contact with your disgust. In any case, literally setting your peristalsis in motion helps you to undo the swallowing motion; you do this by putting your fingers in your throat and just letting your reflexes do what they do naturally. You will not really have to vomit, except if you do this just after a meal, which is not advisable. Quite often you will bring up some phlegm which you should spit out so as to literally learn not to swallow things that are not right for you. The peristalsis motion is often sufficient to express and ease away emotions that sit heavily on your stomach and that is what this is all about. You will notice that it not only gives your consciousness more room, but also brings back your memories, which is also good for your organs in that area. You will literally unburden those organs from many things that are indigestible. These indigestible *bits and pieces* are the cause of many of the discomforts and illnesses of our mechanism of physical digestion.

You will develop ***the ability*** to differentiate between what does or does not feel good and between what is or is not right for you. You learn not to overstep your own limits. The basis of healthy living is letting nourishment in and keeping poison out.

- You can, for example, practice with *food*. What kind of food is right for you and does you good, and what kind does not? Break through old food patterns that do not belong to you, but have become fixed. Here we can think of slogans we were brought up with or old advertising slogans such as "Drinka a pinta milka day." Thinking about it carefully may show you that milk is not good for you at all. We have become used to cooked food, but does it agree with you? Tasting our food properly is very important!
- Another area is our *encounters*. Which encounters are nourishing and good for us and which "poison" us? Which feelings and messages from others do you let in, and which do you keep out? Properly experiencing and feeling is here, once again, very important.
- Which *ideas and theories* suit you and which do not? Critical differentiation, based on your own experience, ensure that you do not overload yourself and that you only let in ideas of others that resonate in your emotions. Do the same with this book!
- What kind of *life* suits you and which does not? Which profession should you choose? Which study? Do not forget that energy is never lost but can be used for something else. Whose messages are you still following? Perhaps it is time to change

your course and go in a direction that really suits you. It is never too late to change your direction. A lot of energy and creativity to do what you always wanted to do deep down, will be released when you really liberate the energy of defense.

Retroflection and no longer being cramped.

Retroflection literally means "bending backward" and was used for the first time by Fritz Perls, the founder of the Gestalt therapy. It has to do with the boomerang effect; when you do not express your emotion, it can boomerang back to you. Guilty feelings are a good example; when you are not able to angrily express your original accusation towards your mother, it may boomerang back to you and become your problem. It is then called a feeling of guilt. You may feel guilt if you go your own way, for example. When you transform your feeling of guilt into an accusation and aim it towards the party intended, you may find out that your mother was very moralistic and made you feel you were an egoist.

The consequence of retroflection is cramping, especially in muscle tissue. This cramping can lodge itself in the organs, depending on how massive the retroflection is. When the energy of rage is not expressed, it is stored in your body as a cramping. The most apparent characteristic are muscles that are tensed up. Being cramped can express itself in your behavior as a "staying put" syndrome. Cramping is literally staying where you are in life.

The road of liberation is setting your tensed muscles and your static life in motion. A good tool is emotional bodywork, including breathwork and bodywork, which is geared to loosening the muscles, as previously described in this book. You will learn to liberate yourself from messages and burdens which you carry on your back but that do not belong to you. Liberation means expressing what does not belong to you.

The ability that is formed by bringing the boomerang back home is distinction between you and the other. This ability is, in actual fact, the same as with introjection—only the learning process in different. The locomotor apparatus is at issue here. Introjection is about the digestive system.

Projection and good perception.

Projection as defense is a way of *sticking* onto another person what you do not want to know about yourself and thus deny. It is also called shadow projection. If you do not want to see that you nag, you will have trouble with people who show the same kind of nagging behavior. When you deny something that is inside you, an urge, a longing, a characteristic, or an emotion, it is just as if that emotion comes from outside and is aimed at you.

- An example of a denied ***impulse*** is you may think that someone is keeping you on your toes and pushing you around while you are really denying your own drive. Here's an example of the latter:

  Anna-Marie is a rather chaotic woman who has trouble keeping her house tidy. Things lie about all over the place, and she has trouble getting things done. One morning, she decides to spring-clean her house and wants to get started. Then she remembers that she wants to record a certain television program. She fetches the television guide and forgets all about cleaning up and loses herself in the reading of the guide. Then her husband comes home and asks quite innocently, he is used to her mess, if she was planning to spring-clean today. She erupts in anger and tells him to stop pressurizing her.

  She does not recognize her own drive anymore and experiences it as pressure from outside. It is the projection of an impulse. A person, who is very inhibited sexually, can think that somebody else is a sex bomb while she is not all.

- An example of a projection of **longing**:

  Charlie hates people who like to be prominent. He loves to rant and rave at politicians, artists, and anyone who receives public attention. His own longing for attention is denied and projected towards others.

  I remember a boy who used to do odd jobs in our house. I felt that he needed acknowledgement, so I regularly went to have a look at his work and told him that it was great what he was doing because it was. However, after a few months, he threw in my face that I never came to have a look at his work and that I did not really appreciate him. His own denial of himself, which stemmed from the denial of his parents, made him project the denial onto me which was not true or fair.

- The following story is about a person who was not aware of her denial of herself and is an example of denied and hidden **emotion.**

  Mary quickly feels attacked and rejected by others. She has the feeling that nobody really cares about her. She has the perception that she likes everybody. She puts herself out to be nice to others. She does not understand why others are so critical of her.

  This is typical of projection: you do not have the tendency to reject, but others do. The denial of your own "criticaster" makes you oversensitive to criticism. Denied anger is to be found underneath.

- Finally, we may deny a *characteristic* of ourselves and assign it to another person. You think you are stupid because your sister had slightly better marks at school, and you were compared to her all the time at home.

389

Later you have the idea that intelligent people find you rather stupid.

The consequence of projection is above all, troubled perception, troubled communication, and troubled relationships. You do not perceive the other or reality properly due to denied emotional charges, and this leads to many unnecessary conflicts. All war and discrimination stems from this projection mechanism. The denied shadow of social undesirability is stuck onto other population groups. We have talked about the scapegoat mechanism since biblical times. You will estrange yourself from things that belong to you and make yourself dependent on your environment because of this attitude.

The road to liberation from this socially disastrous mechanism is becoming aware of your own shadow, your own repressed emotions, and needs. Your emotions will clarify for whom your emotional messages and emotions are meant. Rectifying projections has to do with finding the right address for them.

The ability you will hereby develop has to do with the right perception. When you let your emotions come to light, everything becomes clear step-by-step. Your perception becomes clearer, your communications more pure, and your relationships cleaner. You take away the emotional charges. You know, from within, what emotional management in relationships means. The better you manage your emotions, the less you will project them. However, the more you control your emotions, the more you will project them.

Dissociation and individuality.

Dissociation literally means "splitting" and "alienation." It is a very strong way of not feeling anymore.

You split yourself off from your feelings by withdrawing from reality and locking yourself away in a fantasy world of your own. Elnora van Winkle[1] describes her psychiatric past as follows:

> *The fantasies in which I lived for almost sixty years were subconscious attempts to recreate the traumas of the past and to relive them in such a way that I could vent my anger against my parents. I withdrew into my fantasy world when I was about four or five years old...the human brain is beautifully equipped to create inner dramas to heal the psyche, but the brain cannot create new experiences. The imagination is deformed memory. What the brain does do is make new mosaics from old fragments of experience.*

As children, we all withdrew into our own little world from time to time. And as adults we also need peace and quiet from time to time. Not feeling very much for a while helps us to survive in turbulent periods. But if you do withdraw chronically and frequently, you run the risk of being even worse off. If the outside world is emotionally very threatening, a child can dissociate and live more and more on automatic pilot without having any connection to the layer of emotions. You become more and more alienated from yourself in this way and also from the inalienable core that is you.

Dissociation is sometimes consciously used as a way to become detached. In many religions, *detachment* is considered to be of paramount importance with regard to spiritual virtues. Freeing yourself from the layer of emotions and feelings and consciously aiming them at higher goals is part of this strategy that, as a rule, is not called a survival strategy but does certainly build on it.

The Freudian concept *sublimation*, whereby an impulse or an emotion is lifted to a higher plan, builds further on the

391

mechanism of dissociation. Freud talks about transforming vital drives into culturally and morally acceptable impulses. An often used example of sublimation is the butcher who becomes a surgeon. Sublimation has been compared to the damming and taming of rivers to make reservoirs whereby they are then used to generate electricity. Sublimation also belongs to the list of defense mechanisms that make life easier, but does not liberate from emotional imprisonment.

Nowadays, the word *transcend* is used in the New Age Movement. With this, people often wrongly mean that we should not dwell upon the ABC of emotions and feelings for too long but should rise above them. However, it is important how the word "trans" is translated—as "through" or as "over." In the case of "through," it is about the path that is described in this book: we work through the layer of undigested emotions to get to that other layer in ourselves, the layer of essence, which is who we fundamentally are. This is a healthy path whereby we omit nothing. The second meaning refers to going over the layer of emotions as "something we have dealt with" or "the time for therapy is now over." Something has been skipped here. Here, defense mechanisms are at work in the service of a weakened and floating spirituality that does not have a worldly basis.

The consequence of dissociation is, that on the one hand you lose more and more contact with the external reality, and on the other, the connection to your emotions and internal reality. You do not belong anywhere anymore. When you lose the connection with your emotions, the bottom falls out of the structure that is you. This means that your identity has not come out of the battles of your childhood strongly enough. When your "ego" is not strong enough, you cannot cope as well as you should with all the variety of life and with different kinds of relationships. It is possible that you suffer from mood swings, fear, and depression. When your "self" is not strong enough, your *"Sitz im leben,"* your setting in life, is not strong.

Your base is not sufficient. This means that you do not function as well as you could socially. Making use of autopilot does not help a great deal with regard to communicative and relational skills. This is called the borderline syndrome nowadays. It can lead to a psychosis in extreme cases. A psychosis is being swamped by the contents of the unconscious and by the emotions that go with it. The "ego" is not strongly developed enough to integrate the emotions step by step.

The road to liberation from this defense system consists, in the first place, of "ego" strengthening measures. How do you strengthen your self? This can, primarily, be done by seeking the connection with your feelings and emotions again. Those who feel quickly swamped by their emotions should do this, step by step. After all, if you are not very strong, you will quickly feel swamped not only by the outside world but also by your own emotions. Haptonomy/bodywork is a nice, soft method to explore your emotions and to receive them once again. Seek help from somebody who knows a lot about emotions. Subsequently, loving care and attention help the most in strengthening your identity.

The ability that can be developed if you surmount your dissociation has to do with your pureness. A person with dissociation as a main defense has protected his or her vulnerable child in such a way that it has hardly been corrupted by contact with the outside world. You could say that you have put your child in a freezer so you can take it out again in better times. And, as you know, whatever is kept in a freezer comes out fresh!

Second, the development of identity is an important achievement if you have stopped unconsciously dissociating. By digestion and integration of old emotions, you create a basis which consists of your feeling of "self" and your realization of being a unique human being. "Individual" literally means "being undivided" and that is contrary to being dissociated and split.

393

Survival Strategy Themes

We have already seen that survival strategies become concrete behavior patterns that make sure we do not feel our real emotions and pain. Characteristic of survival strategies are the following:

- They are subconscious;
- They make sure the real trauma is avoided;
- They do not give the hoped for fulfilment.

These strategies go round and round like a hamster in a cage. Survival strategies are, in actual fact, *ways to repeat the past drama with your parents.* You subconsciously hope to become fulfilled, but because of the high degree of subconsciousness, this drama is repeated. It is as if you want to tell yourself the truth about your emotional history in a subconscious way. You repeat the same theme but with other people who stand in for your parents in certain ways. This is why people find out, after many years, that they have married somebody just like their father or mother. A woman who received marriage therapy after a relationship of fifteen years, only then found out that she had married the same kind of surly, taciturn man as her father. She had met him at a party where, aided by drink, he had been an easy-going, friendly man. Our subconscious fools us when we think we are paying attention!

In the following, we will have a look at defense strategies that have to do with certain themes. There are really only three themes that play a role between people: love, power, and brotherhood and sisterhood. The others are mostly variations on these three themes. We shall have a closer look at love. Everyone will recognize something in all of the themes. But perhaps you will recognize yourself especially in one theme. It all depends on your personal life history, and all of us have developed a personal emotional "make-up." For this reason, it is impossible to put someone in a psychological box.

We are all very complex and unique. Outlines are only meant for clarification.

Love.

Love is a theme whereby survival and strategy play a major role. On this planet, most things that go wrong have to do with love. Somebody once said, "There are only two things: love and a cry for love." In this story, it is about that cry. Our first encounter with people and love is enormously important for the rest of our lives and also for the rest of our experiences in love and with love. There are three important imprints that can give you the feeling that you are lovable. These three forms are, as it were, the basis of your ability to love. If something is wrong with one of these three, you will become crippled in your further experiences of love. However, everything can be restored and healed; that is what this book is about. But first, let's examine the following about the three areas of imprinting:

The feeling of oneness and merging with your mother
If my memory serves me well, it was Litaert Peerbolte who called this the oceanic phase. This is the phase that you chiefly experience in your mother's womb and the first days after birth. It is of utmost importance that you know the feeling of merging with a loving person who awaits you and welcomes you to mother earth before you go into the world as an independent little "ego." It is very important in the beginning of your life to know the feeling of being cradled and to feel that you do not have to make your way alone. In our Spark of Light weeks, where we work as described in this book, the person that has emotionally gone back to early childhood is cradled and rocked by the group. It is one of our "hits:" the feeling of being cradled and rocked is an essential corrective experience after an expression of emotions.

Which survival strategies arise when this experience was unsatisfactory in the beginning of your life?

- An important way of surviving is ***searching for oneness and merging together in relationships.*** Merging is different to contact. An adult relationship consists of two individuals who find it pleasant and inspiring to spend some time together in life. A lot of people do not look for contact but for merging. They are looking for the lost, perhaps never experienced feeling of oneness with mama. I call this jokingly "we-soup." When you are looking for merging instead of contact, it means that you are unfulfilled at this level of love. Only when you have been fulfilled in a certain phase of life, can you grow healthily towards the next one. You can, of course, feel so united with your partner that you feel as "we" during intense emotional contact or during love-making. However, this "we" and this merging together is the *consequence* of a good contact between two independent individuals. The neurotic longing for merging is premature and happens *before* contact that then does not really take place because you remain in your original longing for merging. You may wonder if there is anything wrong with that. There is a huge amount wrong with that because if you get stuck in this neurotic search for the first form of love, you will not grow towards love, and you will remain an unborn baby. You will keep on getting love whilst adult love is about sharing, and giving and taking. As this merging is usually subconscious, you will not grow or become fulfilled by it.

- Another survival strategy has to do with the opposite; ***the avoidance of intimacy.*** Due to the subconscious feeling of a lack in the experience of oneness with mother, an intimate relationship is avoided at a later age. You cling to your mother as it were, not because contact was so good, but because there was something lacking fundamentally. This does not mean that you do not have an intimate relationship or that you are not married. There are many people who have lived together for years and are so-called intimate with each other (with which physical or sexual intimacy is usually meant) but who are not intimate at an emotional level. Intimacy of the heart is avoided with this strategy so as not to feel the pain of the early childhood lack of intimacy and oneness.

- Another area where people search for merging and oneness is ***religion and mysticism.*** Mysticism is pre-eminately suitable for searching for a higher unity with "all that is." It is, in itself, the best thing we can search for on this earth and stems from the deep knowledge that everything is essentially one. The neurotic longing for the unity with your mother can be a major motive in this but does not have to be. Perhaps finding unity with all that is is the greatest expression of health. But this is also the end result of a path in which all stadia of childhood have been passed through and the emotional wounds have been healed. Exactly as with searching for merging in human relationships, it is about adult individuality being present before we take the path of the highest mysticism. Mystic longing can only be healthy and have a healthy result when it is not the replacement of an early childhood longing for oneness. Religion will then be a childish, stagnating business. Religion will then be in the service of survival. True religion serves life on earth and should not bypass life.

- We can also see the longing for merging and oneness at work with ***mass manifestations*** that are of a political, religious, or sporting nature. Singing together, cheering together, and spurring on your favorite football team or fighting together for a good (or bad) cause, can let you forget your bottomless and subconscious loneliness. Anything that allows you to lose yourself may point to this longing for basic oneness. If it happens consciously, then there is nothing wrong with it. When you need such oneness experiences to feel good, then you should look at the neurotic background. And remember, we are all more or less neurotic and have all had our knocks because we were all brought up once.

What can be done when we notice that we are not fulfilled in love?

First, an important step is becoming aware and seeing through this pattern. Remember that everything that is subconscious is a disturbance, but what is conscious is like a lamp before your feet, not only for yourself, but also for others.

Second, you can now receive your longing for oneness and merging at a conscious level (which is crucial) and explore it within an intimate relationship and catch up a little with what you have missed.

Third, it is important that you let emotions in when you begin this process with yourself. Your partner, friend, girlfriend, or therapist will play the role of mama with whom you can be little once more. You can only catch up in a way that really helps you further and lets you grow when you are conscious of what is happening and when you catch up at the level where it belongs—in this case, at the level of a baby. Jesus once said, "If you do not become as little children, ye shall not enter into the kingdom of heaven." We could take this saying literally. So now and then, imagine going back to where it went wrong in our emotional development—this is called regression. Restoration work is always possible for those of us who want to travel this road with heart and soul. You will notice that it will be beneficial to your relationship if you do this work with your partner. You will get to know one another on all levels and experience the full richness of an intimate relationship.

Touch.

Lovingly touching the skin of a baby is a very important imprint and gives him/her the feeling that he/she is loved. It is the baby's first encounter with another person's love for him. On a very basic level the touch imprints the, for a baby, an understandable message of love...or lovelessness. There is a whole range of variations in quantity and quality in between these two. The Victorian age may have long passed, but there are still large numbers of people on this planet who have hardly ever been touched as a child because of old imprinted taboos, fear, and prudery. Parents may say that they love their children, do everything for them, or spoil them with material things, but the feeling of being loved will be unsure if skin contact was lacking.

Which survival strategies arise if you were not lovingly touched in your youth?

- A possible form is excessively seeking physical contact, often in the form of *sexual contact*. This is called the Clinton-syndrome nowadays. As we have already seen with regard to merging, real fulfilment will not occur if the backlog of work is not undertaken consciously and at the level of an adult. I will clarify this with an example:

Pete is a man of fifty who has such a need for sexual contact that his wife has given up. She has the feeling that she is being asked for too much and does not fancy the frequent love-making which is always 'the usual', namely 'the gratification of hubby' as she says angrily. They otherwise have a good relationship and nice kids, but the frequently recurring quarrels due to his sexual needs, draw heavily on their relationship.

If we investigate his need for sex more deeply and look at his background, we see a little boy in a large, busy farmer's family who was hardly ever cuddled or touched. He did not realize that he had fundamentally lacked being touched. It was so ordinary and he was so used to it. Only when he started to shake with cold during breathwork, did he feel what he had missed: warm physical contact with his mama.

A lot of people try to make up for their old lack of warmth and being caressed by means of sexual contact. This does not happen consciously and, therefore, it repeats itself. Especially men will have to learn that in this way, they avoid being fulfilled and caressed. Everything has its own level of experience. A lot of things get mixed up due to pure ignorance. Parent's love is different than adult sexual love. In our previous example, Pete had to learn to allow himself to be caressed by his wife as if he was a little boy.

They can, in addition to this, make love as two adults who wish to lovingly "dance". These two kinds of touching should be unravelled and distinguished properly for the sake of healing the old childhood lack. The old childhood lack of warmth and being touched by parents cannot be solved and made up for by sexuality. Only by consciously accepting touching as a child does and with emotion can the old lack be healed.

Clinton, the former president of America has, besides other qualities, the honor of having put sexual addiction in the limelight. Many people suffer from sexual addiction, it stems from the evasion of real pain, and that is the lack of love and caressing. Addiction always means not feeling and more of the same. The intended fulfilment will never be found in this way. An orgasm is wrongly seen as fulfilment.

- Another strategy to avoid the lack of being touched lovingly, is *avoiding being touched* and not becoming intimate with another person.

What can be done?

First, it is important to learn to feel via the skin. All kinds of loving massages are a good way to do this. You could massage each other without sexuality when sex plays too great a role in your relationship. Sex that follows fixed patterns and has become a routine will become playful and engaging when you have learned to feel and play as children do. Sexuality will no longer function as a venting of one's tension or as a covering up of the inability to feel, but it will be what it is, a dance of love between two people. It will then be a celebration, full of feeling, passion, and emotion.

Also, it is important to become connected with the little girl or boy that longs for a tender caress and set the emotions in motion that go together with this, as described in this book.

The need to suck.

In addition to touching, nourishment from the mother's breast is also an important imprint of love. Mother means nourishment. Not only milk, but also the honey of love (if everything goes well) is felt during suckling. The dependency on your mother is a matter of life or death. Sucking or not sucking is of vital importance. When something goes wrong, and that has usually to do with honey and not with milk, a so-called oral fixation occurs. You will subconsciously seek the mother's breast and keep the tendency to suck in later developmental stages.

Which survival strategies play a part here?

- Compulsive *thumb sucking* as defense against feelings of loneliness. I imagine that there are many adults who secretly suck their thumbs in bed, hold a cloth, or a cuddly toy. It is nothing to be ashamed of. It would be a good idea to let this need come to light and find out which feelings are disguised by it. I do not advise you to stop but to do thumb sucking very consciously and to feel what you experience. Comfort, of course, but for what? For what child's sorrow or fear? When children are still sucking their thumbs when they are older, it is a good idea for you as a parent to invite your child to be a baby again and hold him or her against your breast again or to let the child suck your hand.

- *Oral addictions* such as nicotine addiction, alcohol addiction, and food addiction are ways of not feeling the original pain that had to do with love. Addiction is a form of trance behavior; more and more of the same kind of things so as not to feel the actual hunger for them. Work can also be an addiction so as not to feel or live. A lot of people do not have the slightest idea what to do if they cannot

402

work. I advise people with similar addictions to get a nursing bottle with something nice in it and to lie on the sofa and drink like a little baby as soon as the urge to drink, eat, smoke, gamble, or buy things is felt. If you have a partner, ask him or her to hold you.

• Another major form is ***dependency behavior.*** Some people get in a panic or become angry if their partner is absent or comes home late. There is a constant searching for safety in the presence of the other or in fixed patterns. Subconsciously, the loved one functions as mother's milk. Jealousy and possessiveness belong to this survival strategy. There is a tendency to want to stick to your partner from fear of loss. But what you are scared of has usually already happened. Your mother has already left you, one way, or another. Perhaps she died when you were very young, or a new sister or brother was born and you had to be *big*. Perhaps the warmth of the breast was just not there because your mother did not have that warmth or the patience or because she was scared. Perhaps there was a war when you were suckled. There are a thousand and one possibilities, each of us should remember his or her story and recount it to themselves, step by step. Feeling this story intensely with all the accompanying emotions is an effective way of getting over your fixations and growing towards real adulthood.

• Searching for safety also belongs in this list. Subconsciously remaining emotionally connected to the oral development phase can mean that you primarily choose safety in life. Life will then not easily be seen as an adventurous journey with many challenges and possibilities.

What can be done?

- Oral fixation means that there is often literally tension around the mouth. The mouth is rigid or slack and weak. Emotional work that has to do with loosening or activating the muscles of the mouth can be a good way of awakening the deep sucking reflex and enclosed emotions and setting them in motion. It is possible that besides the need to suck, the need to bite will occur. The old baby anger that is within you will primarily express itself through the mouth. Biting a towel and screaming can help to loosen the embodied emotions.

- Working with the inner needy child and with the emotions that have to do with not being fulfilled.

- An exercise: Call your needy child to mind when you are lying or sitting in a nice relaxed way. Ask it what it needs from you. Let your inner child answer and see if you can satisfy its needs. Perhaps it wants to be cuddled. Take a cushion and imagine cuddling your inner child. Remember that being an adult means that you are a good mummy and daddy for yourself. Most people want children but forget their own inner child.

Support and respect that have been encountered at a later age also play a role in the development of the experience of love. However, the three formerly mentioned imprints form the foundation of our house of love.

Power.

We shall now have a look at survival strategies that have to do with power. As a child, the feeling of power starts at around two years of age. At last you have gotten up from your vulnerable horizontal position; you can crawl around and even walk. What freedom! And what possibilities! You start to discover that you have control over your body and can decide things for yourself. You can be really proud of it! You gain power over your mother and over others by doing certain things or by not doing them. You start to become aware of your own will.

This does not suit some adults who call these toddlers a nuisance and headstrong. There is even the expression "the terrible-two's." Psychologists and pedagogues, who, of old, have always been more on the side of the educators than on the side of the child, gave it the unpleasant name of "toddler's negativism." These names show just how little chance a child gets to explore its own will and the amount of power it has. Of course, a child of this age needs guidance and limits, but that does not mean that the process of discovering your own power is wrong. Power has not just become an emotionally charged, *nasty* word. Our first problems with authority are born in this period that has not been called "the anal phase" for nothing. The words *power* and *dirty* have become connected in this stage of life. If you look at the anus of a barking dog that is guarding its territory, you can see how strongly power, anger, and the constrictor are connected together. This is the phase of being proud of your own achievements, of limits, and of power struggles between parents and child. It depends on the way you were given guidance if you come through this phase well. Could your parents tell you in a clear and loving manner where they drew the line? Or did they have difficulty handling you and did it all end in a power-struggle? If so, you as a child lost. Depending on the extent of loss, you will react angrily.

The survival strategies that stem from this period are as follows:

- The survival strategy has primarily to do with ***exercising power*** and ***using your will.*** Something is very wrong between humans with regard to power and the distribution of power, as everybody knows.

405

Do you belong to the category of people who have trouble asserting their power and authority? Or does that not bother you? If you were involved in a power struggle with your parents, you will have the tendency to exert power over others. You may also have the tendency to walk over others as you were once walked over. You may be cruel and want to humiliate others as you were once humiliated. You can become sadistic towards others because you feel that you have been sadistically treated. You will have the tendency to treat yourself and others as your parents, brothers and sisters, and other educators treated you. It is a threefold law, a kind of three-stage rocket of passing on emotional patterns. If you were not allowed to define yourself sufficiently, you will have the tendency to define others.

- If your upbringing was so strict that you had little power, it is possible that you cannot draw easily from your source of power and allow people walk over you. You may get stuck in ***powerlessness.*** The following is an example of this:

Ronald likes to meet people's wishes. He is always prepared to help others in all kinds of ways. He helps his neighbor with his tax form and wallpapers the new room of a neighbor who is on her own, and he knows a lot about computers. He is, in brief, a handy man to have around. His problem is that he cannot say "No" and therefore a lot of people misuse him. It is exactly the same at work and eventually after many years of good service at work and in his private life, his energy runs out. The result is depression and bitterness because who will help him now?

- Knowing where to draw the line is an important issue in this world. It is essential to define your own personal space and if necessary defend it. Older people have usually been brought up with strict *limits.* There were clear rules and agreements, and you had to adhere to them. If you did not, you were in real trouble. An authoritarian upbringing was often the rule. Nowadays we see the opposite tendency; educators bring children up in a manner that is not authoritarian probably with their own authoritarian upbringing still fresh in their minds. It is really a step forward that children are allowed to have a say in the matter. However, this goes hand in hand with children not being told where their limits are. I think that people have gone from one extreme to the other due to a dislike of their own upbringing. Drawing a line has nothing to do with being authoritarian or not. You can tell a child in a friendly and clear manner what you allow and what you do not. Being really non-authoritarian means that you do not make use of arguments which stem from power and from the imbalance of power that exists naturally between parents and children. But it also means you can draw the line at a point where it feels right or wrong from your own authority as a parent, and that is fundamentally different from being authoritarian. You do not draw the line because you are the parent but because it feels right for you as a person. To be able to do this well (and not just in situations that have to do with education), you should have gotten over your survival strategies with regard to the problem of power or at least be aware of it. When you have emotionally worked through your problem of power, you will have inner strength and be able to draw the line in a natural, clear, and friendly manner. You should set your old anger from the said phase (and from later on) in motion when you have problems with power. This *limits* theme is hugely important at the moment in the education of children, and also in giving guidance to them. Children who have not received enough guidance or been taught about limits are being heavily drugged with medicine, such as Ritalin at the moment. Children are even given them to take to school as *sweeties.*

- You have power when you can hold on to something (remember the analogy of the anus) or can hold something back and use your own will to decide when and how you share it with another person. ***Collecting money*** and ***the means of making a living*** belong in this phase. An anal survival strategy is certainly involved if you keep your money to yourself and have difficulty sharing it. This survival strategy is certainly present if money is used as a means of exercising power over a partner and keeping him or her in check because he or she has to ask regularly for house-keeping money. It is a compensation for the lack of power in childhood. Money has, pre-eminently, become the means for exercising power. It is no wonder that there are expressions such as "Money is the root of all evil." There are people who collect things, whether they are relevant or not, and can throw nothing away because "it has to be kept for a rainy day."

Somebody I know has a whole house full of nails, bicycle wheels, planks, and especially books he hardly ever reads. Such people collect compulsively because they do not want to remember that they have lost so much. They try to hang on to what they once lost as a child: the power over themselves and their lives.

What can be done?

Setting the anger of your childhood powerlessness in motion is the most important thing you can do. If you learn to express anger in the way that was described in chapter 10, you will develop the following abilities:

- You will stand firmly on your own two feet;
- You will develop inner strength;
- You will have authority without being authoritarian;
- You will be able to draw the line in a healthy way and define your own personal space; and
- You will be able to let go of things that should be let go of.

Brotherhood and sisterhood.

Realizing brotherhood and sisterhood has always been one of the biggest challenges on this planet. Our relationships are more about rivalry than about brother- and sisterhood because so much has gone wrong with regard to love and power for so many of us. We are so used to looking at what is different about us (that we can hardly see) than at what is the same. We can no longer see the essential symmetry. That is exactly where the opportunity is to see each other as brothers and sisters. Of course, there is *functional inequality* in contacts. One person teaches the other, one person is in charge and the other takes the orders, etc. However, this should not exclude acknowledgement of *essential equality* or equivalence.

What is the reason that people hardly experience the latter in our society and that as a consequence, brother- and sisterhood is one of the most difficult things to realize? We shall have to take another look at our neurotic unbalanced growth from which we all, more or less, suffer. As long as we still have the neurotic need to be somebody's child, we cannot be brothers and sisters.

There is hardly any room for freedom, equality, and brotherhood if we take turns at playing Tom Thumb or the giant, however noble our objective is. These inner psychological mechanisms are to blame for the fact that the world is as it is, in spite of the League of Nations, the UN, and well-meant attempts to shape this fundamental brotherhood and sisterhood.

We must, in this day and age, take our depth work seriously, and as real Spark of Light workers, start with our Work of inner clearance. I would like to launch a movement of this Work in many areas. The beneficial use of the carpet beater should become common property, not only in a therapeutical setting but also in schools, in prisons, and in living rooms. Brotherhood and sisterhood with the carpet beater at the ready? Yes, but not to beat each other over the head with but to help each other to liberate ourselves from old emotional charges.

There are also many lessons in brother- and sisterhood to be learned in the sphere of spirituality. In almost all religions, the priest, the imam, the minister, or the guru has a special place as mediator between God and the people. There is nothing at all wrong with that. There will always be people who have developed themselves further emotionally and spiritually than others. But here, too, the Tom Thumb-giant-syndrome has taken its toll at the cost of brotherhood and sisterhood. Being a guru or a priest is the easiest way of being a master. He sits on a throne; there is distance and adoration from his followers. True "masterhood" means brotherhood.

The Path is to become a true brother and sister for yourself. You can only do this when you have become a father and mother for yourself and are no longer dependent on another person who has to make up for everything you have missed.

What are the ***survival strategies*** that prevent this brotherhood and sisterhood?

The third survival strategy is called the Oedipal defense by the astrologist Liz Greene, and she extends the rivalry between parents and children to the rivalry between people.[2]

- ***Rivalry and competition*** are survival strategies that prevent brotherhood and sisterhood. If we have not been confirmed in our uniqueness and worth as individuals during our childhood, we will have the tendency to measure ourselves against others. Our measure is constantly taken with regard to intelligence, achievement, skill, outward appearance, strength, and power. Sometimes we are Tom Thumb and sometimes the giant. Sometimes we play "Mirror, mirror, on the wall" and sometimes Russian roulette. As long as you are not aware of your old pain and insecurity about who you are and what you are, this "measure" game will go on being played with all the consequences that go with it. You will be injured again and again, and it costs, moreover, a huge amount of energy. The great "measure" game has become so great because most of us play it without realizing that it is one big game, a game of survival. An advantage of survival is that it challenges us to use creativity and give our best. However, this is not really how it should be done; you should not develop your creativity and qualities in comparison with and sometimes at a cost to others. There are better methods to get your creative best out of life, and they are based on a healthy understanding of your possibilities and unique qualities.

411

- ***Feelings of inferiority*** also belong in this list. Feelings of inferiority as well as feelings of superiority (their compensation) are both big obstacles to "freedom, equality, and brotherhood." They lead to comparing and condemning on a small scale and to war and racism on a large scale.

- ***Jealousy and envy*** are survival strategies that stop brotherhood and sisterhood. They are neurotic attempts to impose your own qualities and stem from uncertainty of your intrinsic worth. There is more about this in Chapter 22.

- ***Ambition*** also belongs in this list. Ambition has two sides; it can be a healthy motive to devote yourself to something that you find interesting or that really touches you, but it can also be a neurotic survival strategy, stemming from inner uncertainty, to prove yourself. The latter prevents you realizing brotherhood and sisterhood. I would prefer to call the first type of ambition, devotion.

What can be done?

The Work that has to be done at this level has to do with healing your fundamental uncertainty. It often has to do with repressed anger and with a child's anger against those stupid grown-ups who could not see what a great child you were, who had ideals about the way you should be, and expectations about what you should become. As I was a late arrival, they used to jokingly say to me; "You'll be something, one day." Of course, you had to become something. But who you really were, just you, was often not noticed. So let your child's anger loose on a big cushion and do not forget the teachers who kept you in at playtime because you could not write proper commas. Or perhaps that awful teacher who made you look like a fool because you could not read properly. Everyone has his or her own

412

experience. Unearth them. They are more meaningful than you think. Do not forget the employees of "God and Son." There are many imprints there for your present uncertainty. As a horrible illustration, a child's hymn that somebody with a Dutch Reformed background found in her record collection. The text is as follows:

I wish to be as Jesus
So meek and so mild.
His words were friendly.
His voice always sweet.
Alas, I am not as Jesus.
Everyone can see that I am not.
Oh, Redeemer, help me
And make me as thee.
Oh, no, I'm not as Jesus.
My heart is full of evil.
How can I ever become as Thee?
Where can I find guidance?
My Savior, help me.
Make me free of evil.
Then one day I will behold thee
And become as Thou.

The Spark of Light worker wrote under this text: "Well, I did a lot of carpet beating thanks to that!' The well-known game of improvement has been deeply carved into many a child's soul. It is important to get rid of the neurotic deposits of your religion, so the pure core remains which is love: "Love thyself as thy neighbor."

Part V

Frequently Discussed Subjects

Chapter 37

Perception and Emotions:
A Path to Freedom

If the doors of perception were cleansed,
everything would appear to man as it is, infinite.
~William Blake

*A*n important source of conflict is the misconception that only one reality exists. In actual fact, there are only experiences and perceptions of reality. This is what we mean when we say that there is no objectivity but only subjectivity. Something is red because you perceive it to be red. Another person may call it orange whilst another is colorblind and sees something completely different. If, as a therapist, I was present when couples were quarreling, I often used my teacup and asked whoever was opposite on which side the handle was. The realization that somebody else has a different perception of things, only registers slowly. With our power of reason, we do know, of course, but because of emotional charges, we do not want to know.

What do we mean by this? Our perception has been colored from a young age by the way we emotionally experience reality. The word "mother" is a completely different

417

word to somebody who has a really loving bond with his mother than to somebody who was only "fed and watered" by her. Everything has gained its *emotional coloring* from the experiences we have had. You could say that as long as we see everything in an emotional light, our perception will be unclear or at least highly personal and subjective. This way of viewing things is a summary of all our subconscious emotional experiences and has become enormously charged because of it. The least we can do is become aware of this fact. We should realize that everything we perceive is relative and always stands in relation to ourself and is a reality that has been colored by us. A thing is only real and true for you. And that applies to everything from various things and events to God. We can do two things if we wish less conflict and long for peace.

With this first step on the path to peace, you must be constantly alert and keep an eye on yourself to see if you are paying attention to relativity. After all, as long as you have a lot of emotional charges, good resolutions will slip easily through your fingers. That always happens when something is only understood on a mental level.

The second measure that we can take is doing the Work that we have been singing the praises of in this book, namely working on your old and subconscious emotional charges. It is the most fundamental and effective path to peace. It is about the *cleansing of the doors of perception* about which William Blake and Aldous Huxley spoke. The big question is, as always, the *how* question. My answer is "by purifying all your repressed emotions." When you have had an affective deficit, you will see deficits everywhere. When you are scared, you will see ghosts everywhere, and when you are feeling depressed, the weather will be miserable when it rains. If you feel guilty inside, your God will be an angry, punishing God. We always take what goes together with our inner feelings. We call that projection. Only by freeing ourselves from old emotional charges can we see what is. "Infinite" is what Blake called it. By purifying your emotional charges, you purify your perception and see the common denominator of all that is, and that is light. There will then be peace between people. But before that happens, there is work to be done!

Projection and Perception: Making Contact

The Work is about becoming aware of and taking back projections. As long as you carry your emotional charges with you, you will place the experiences and images that belong to these emotions between you and reality, between you and the other, between you and your God. The way in which you place them is called projection. Because of projection, you cannot see the difference between your image of another person and that person's reality. It is really always about your subjective, therefore, colored perception. Maslov, the humanistic psychologist, made a distinction between an interested perception and an altruistic perception. "Because the last is so much more concrete, less abstract and selective, it offers the chance to see through the essential nature of the perceived."[1] The interested perception is driven by our neuroses and by our affective deficits. We need to keep our house in order if we want our doors of perception to become cleaner. You will notice that when you cleanse those layers of old emotional charges step by step, you will start to project less. You will not stick your own contents, charges, and images on others so much but will then see them as they are. *Not projecting anymore has a lot to do with contact and knowledge,* with knowledge of the reality and with knowledge of the other person. When you become free from emotional charges, you gain more knowledge. And you learn more about yourself! And when you get to know yourself and your dark sides and possibilities, you will get to know others better and contact will improve.

Chapter 38

Thinking and Emotions

There can be no knowledge without emotion. We may be aware of a truth, yet until we have felt its force, it is not ours. To the cognition of the brain must be added the experience of the soul.
~Arnold Bennett

O ur thinking and our emotions have never been great friends. The history of the western philosophy is a history of rationalism. Especially feelings and emotions were suspect and neglected. People have always assumed that truth or knowledge could be acquired via the ratio. People forgot that truth could also be felt, sensed, seen, and heard, with the senses as entry point. The neuroscientist Antonio Damasio describes in his book[1] how our consciousness is not primarily formed by our thinking, as Descartes thought, but by our emotions and our bodies. How did it happen that we became so rational at the expense of our feelings and emotions? I think that it is because of an ancient accumulation of denied emotionality, and the further you stray from home, the more difficult it becomes to find your way back again. We started to live more outwardly, more technically and more rationally in order to survive.

Now, at the beginning of the twenty-first century, we face the challenge of balancing our thinking and feeling and our hearts and minds. Hearts and minds are both just as important, and balance is what it is all about.

Feeling: Not a Mental Process

Now that we are moving towards this balance and are giving more attention to denied emotionality, it is important to bring a few misconceptions to light so a genuine balance will really become possible. One misconception is that feeling is a mental process. Perhaps this has to do with the fact that the verb *mind* can also signify a feeling. This misconception is expressed by the fact that people often think that feeling means putting your emotions into words. Feeling does, indeed, have a connection with the intellect, but it is also a completely individual ability. Many therapeutical and spiritual schools are based on this misconception, whereby talking about emotions and awareness of feelings is wrongly seen as feeling. Feeling is, however, a different ability that does not go via the intellect.

Positive Thinking and Affirmations

Many people work with affirmations in this New Age which is essentially geared towards balancing heart and mind. Affirmations are sentences with positive thoughts that can help you to define what you really want and in which direction you wish to go in life. If you do not like yourself, you can, for example, say to yourself, "I am lovable." If you are frightened, you can tell yourself that you are not scared. Affirmations remind you of how rigid or negative you think and of what you want to realize. However, they can easily be used to deny emotions. Affirmations can never be substitutes for emotional Work. They cannot undo what has been stored in the emotional body. Affirmations can only make you aware of mental imprints and alter them. We cannot reach the emotional imprints in this way. These are to be found on a completely different layer all of their own where the power of reason cannot reach, neither with positive thoughts nor with negative ones. If you only work on one level, the mental level, for example, and neglect the emotional and physical level, the affirmations will not work, and you will not change. When you only work on an emotional level and deny and neglect the clarity of the mental level, you will not get far either. In Spark of Light Work we combine both.

Finally, people often say that affirmations should be repeated frequently. This repetition is, according to me, nothing but an expression of your fear, your lack of trust, and probably your intuitive knowledge that affirmations are not enough for you to become whole.

The Mind's Need to Re-learn to Trust the Heart

The fact that reason must once more learn to let emotions run their normal course is one of the greatest challenges of this Work with balance. Reason has been misused so much by the fear of emotions that it will have to learn to let go of its fears, step by step. It is the same as with men who have underestimated women for centuries and have to learn that they have a lot to offer. To do this, the mind must learn to let go of its prejudices and trust and listen to the heart. Then there will be an open connection between the heart and the mind, and they can help one another on the only road to liberation. You can really change your thinking when you have eliminated enough emotional charges. Much of this thinking has to with emotional themes, after all. You will not have as many fearful and negative thoughts about your body when you have, for example, successfully worked with your shame at an emotional level. And, in reverse, your emotions can receive a positive impulse when you have different thoughts. When you let go of the thought that it is weak to show your tears, it will be a stimulus to your heart to let those tears flow. We can say that a mutual loving reception is a blessing for everyone and for this collaboration. We can only heal when heart and mind become friends, and both make a contribution. This means that we cannot simply use affirmations and think, "I am free of anger" or "I am free of fear" as we often see in New Age schools. The mind is speaking before its turn and shouting down and denying the heart. The consequence is that anger and fear come back at a less mindful moment.

Limitations of Cognitive Studies of Emotions

Most scientific studies of emotion have been done with the mind and from the mind. This is a great limitation. This is clarifying the world of emotions rationally. Before I started to write this book, I browsed through other scientific work because I thought I should also honor my colleagues. I could not get through it; my head started spinning. I am too used to working closely with emotions to understand and value the scientific mass of cognitions. The emotional experience cannot be explained with words of the mind. It can be understood in the direct experience of heart and mind together.

Everything in Its Own Layer

Many therapeutical and spiritual schools attempt, with the aid of one method, to *manage* all the layers people have.

Meditation schools mostly try with various methods to find liberation in one fundamental way: by shifting the focus of attention. To find pure consciousness, identification with the ego should stop. However, the emotional layer cannot be liberated by meditative or mental methods. That has never worked and will not work now. In his book *The Power of Now*, Eckhart Tolle[2] gives various psychological and meditative exercises to liberate the emotional body. He invites his readers and pupils to see through and replace the mental and emotional layer with the power of pure consciousness in the here and now. No matter how good it sounds, it will not work. Tolle also denies that the emotional layer is a layer with content—especially identification with the contents is seen as an obstacle.

Deep emotional imprints with old pain will not allow themselves to be pushed and reasoned away by appealing to the will and the freedom of choice. It is, of course, about not identifying with old pain layers from the past anymore. However, the question is how to do that without denying anything. The only way I see, after years of intensive searching on all levels, is to do justice to all our layers, possibilities, and resources: body, mind, heart, and spirit. This is the way I have taken. By this justice, I mean that everything in its own particular layer should be healed and cared for. If you break your leg, you look after your body; if you have suffered from emotional pain, you heal your emotions; and when there is something wrong with your mind, you train your mental capacities. If you find it difficult to enjoy the here and now, then advice from somebody like Tolle is a great tool to help you become aware of the power of *Now* and to be more present herein. As long as our emotional body has not been healed, this presence in the here and now will retain its nature of......being here now and again. When we have healed and lovingly embraced all our layers, our focus of attention can fundamentally shift so we are able to stay more often in the sacred, healed here and now with full consciousness of all that is.

Cognitive therapy schools do something similar: they penetrate the layer of emotions with the aid of thinking. This does help to some extent because insight diminishes the fear of the emotional level as I have already described above. But the emotional layer does not fundamentally become liberated. You cannot solve emotional problems with reason. That can only be done if this emotional layer has the chance to be what it is, namely: emotional, angry, frightened, sad, and eventually also happy. In this book, I concentrate on emotional Work, as it is still being dominated by mental and meditative methods.

Releasing Thinking

Tolle puts the emphasis on the mind becoming empty and still, like all Eastern-oriented methods do. He says, "The road to being is beyond the mind and only attainable when the mind is still." I agree with that, but how do we go about it?

I have noticed that the flow of thoughts intensifies when you focus on letting go of these thoughts. What is the reason for this? One important reason is that the mind has not only a thinking function but also a defense function attained over the centuries. This defense is meant to keep the emotional layer quiet. Everything tries to keep everything quiet; the meditative layer tries to keep the mind quiet, and the mind tries to keep the heart quiet. And eventually everything starts protesting because it all wants a say, and in this subtle way a war is going on. But what controls what, and what keeps what quiet? My conclusion is clear: exercise and control do not work. What can we do about this? Once again: do justice to everything; let everything have a say about its own territory. Love will then be the bond between all our layers and capacities. Growth and healing is only possible with love. Only in love is there Being.

Meditation is an important training to become aware of how much you *live* in your mind. During meditation you can become aware of the amount of self-talk, inner dialogue that there is in your mind, and how little you live according to your senses. The best way of *getting out* of your mind is by *going into* your senses: listening, looking, feeling, tasting, and smelling will all bring you more into contact with reality than your mind does.

The premature *letting go* of the contents of consciousness, such as thoughts and emotions, is the great

limitation of the meditative way. As you do not identify with
them, you do not get to know them, and this means that you do
not get to know yourself completely.

Judgments and Emotions

A judgment is an approving or disapproving statement
from the rational mind. It is the ability to choose between what
we like or do not like. Judging is choosing, and choosing is
excluding other possibilities. The possibility to choose is a
great gift in this world of free will. It is essential in a world
where good and evil are mixed together. However, judging is
an emotionally charged concept. The imperative "Do not
judge" plays an important role in many spiritual teachings. It
has been said that judgments hold back our stream of
experiences, cut off our emotions and feelings, and lead to
conflict and struggle in interpersonal relationships. The story of
Adam and Eve who lost their innocence by eating fruit from
the tree of the knowledge of good and evil (or of judgment), is
the source of this taboo on judging.

How should this be understood? It is about the
fundamental right of free will and yet, at the same time, there
seems to be a taboo attached to it. I think that it is about using
our ability to judge in the right way and this has, yet again, to
do with subconscious emotional charges, such as fear and
anger.

So, it is not really about judging in itself in the meaning
of differentiating between what does or does not befit us but
about our emotionally charged negative Judgments.

A lot of spiritual literature, from the Bible to Zen,
advises us not to judge. "Judge not that ye be not judged" and
"by becoming the silent witness of all, you stop judging and
allow the stream of experiences to flow and let everything be
as it is." The big problem with imperatives, commands, and
bans is that they often do not work. Even if you count to ten

and swallow your judgment, you will, nevertheless, pass judgment in a roundabout way by your facial expression, the sharpness of your voice, and even more by breaking contact. Moreover, the judgment is already there even if you have swallowed it in time. Saying that you should not judge, does not help us to judge less. What does help?

In the first place, judgments do not appear out of the blue. They are anchored in us, and this anchor is made up of emotions. I will clarify this with a number of examples: if you call Islam a backward culture, this will not only be based on your observation that women have an inferior role, but also the negative wording *backward* also says something about your anger with regard to the position of women. Your emotional charge with regard to the position and the treatment of women is the reason you have a negative judgment. If you do not have a personal emotional charge about your own position and treatment as a woman, you will be able to see that the position of women within the Islam is one of subservience and then decide if you want to live within such a culture or help women within that culture if they so wish. Your observation has no emotional charge in that case, and there will be no chance of having a conflict with people who think differently.

If you are scared of spiders because your brother used to tease you by dangling big ones in front of your face, you will have a negative opinion about spiders and tend to kill them. If you are not afraid of them, you can just observe them and let them live their lives as they let you live yours.

When you think that something is beautiful, that is a judgment, too, albeit a positive one this time. Is this something that is not allowed either, by some Eastern religions, for example? Many meditation teachers say, "No, it is not allowed." By judging something, you lose the stream of observations and experiences and close off the connection with what you observe. I agree, but what I see in many spiritual teachings is a tendency to reverse the aim and the outcome.

428

The aim is, in this case, a connected, non-judgmental attitude which people try to achieve through meditation. I have noticed that many people tend to have an opinion about judging; they say that it is not allowed while they are not yet inwardly ready to be wholly and heartily non-judgmental. In the first place, if you ever come this far, you will no longer have any negative opinions. This is not because you can meditate so well but because you have emotionally come to terms with yourself, which means that you no longer harbor any negative thoughts about yourself. After all, as I treat myself, I will treat others. In the second place, you will now be as one with everything and able to say, like God: "I judge nobody; everything is okay, even if mistakes are made. Mistakes are part of the learning process we all go through." The outcome will be that you will not judge and can let everything be as it is.

After the murder of the Dutch politician, Pim Fortuyn, I caught myself not only examining but also looking judgmentally at the photo of the suspect. That evening I heard a voice inside me saying, "I am also that young man with the tense feeling inside" and "Can you love me?" It made me cry for this young man, and I was able to wholeheartedly send him my love.

If you do not allow yourself to judge prematurely anymore because it is not spiritual or does not answer to your idea of love, you will break the flow of contact with your surroundings. It is healthier and more natural to become aware of your true feelings and to express them when desirable. An example may make this clear:

One of my students thought that I was too judgmental about certain matters in the spiritual New Age circuit. He thought I was arrogant but said he did not want to judge me. Later on, there was a conflict because of a small matter, and I found his way of reacting baffling. Thankfully, he started to do breathwork for himself and became aware of all kinds of emotions, such as anger and sadness of which the emotional charges belonged elsewhere; he expressed the rest of these charges in my direction. I reacted by telling him why I am so critical with regard to so many spiritual matters and what I find important. By really giving me his opinion, we could share what was important for us on our spiritual path. In any case, we had a better contact than ever before. By not judging, while you secretly form an opinion, means you break the flow of experiences and contacts anyway!

To not make negative judgments, you need to clean the doors of perception; intensive emotional work is necessary for this where you not only become aware of subconscious fear and anger but also direct them to where they belong, and that is usually in our past. In the end, all negative judgments are based on fear and anger. If your observation is clean, your judgment will be clean and there will be love.

As long as your observation is not clean, it is important to carefully look at your judgments before you express them, especially if these judgments go together with emotional charges. It is important to count to ten once in a while before expressing your opinions! After that, it is a good idea to tackle the emotional charge under your own supervision so you will less emotionally charged next time.

Thinking and Feeling: Who Is in Charge?

Struggles between therapeutical and spiritual schools are almost always about the question to which does real power belong: thinking or feeling. Does negative thinking determine illness in our bodies? Or do unexpressed emotions determine the measure of illness and health? I tend to think that the world of emotion has been so greatly suppressed and denied for so many centuries that it now demands power. And it deserves it. Studies have proven that at critical moments, the emotional reaction counts. If heart and mind are friends, they will not have to struggle but acknowledge each other for what they are.

430

But it is our ancient broken hearts that cry for attention and justice. Our broken hearts make us look in broken mirrors and see a fragmented reality. What we primarily have to do is heal our hearts. Then our perception will become whole and positive.

Chapter 39

Partner Relationships and Emotions

*One day there will be girls and women whose name will no
longer mean the mere opposite of the male, but something in
itself, something that makes one think not of any complement
and limit but only of life and reality: the female human being.
This progress (at first very much against the will of the
outdistanced men) will transform the love experience, which is
now filled with error, will change it from the ground up, and
reshape it into a relationship that is meant to be between one
human being to the other, no longer one that flows from man to
woman. And this more human love (which will fulfil itself with
infinite consideration and gentleness, and kindness and clarity
in binding and releasing) will be a love between two solitudes
that protect and border and greet each other.*
~Rainer Maria Rilke

Without a doubt, the area where most emotions *play* a
role is the relationship between partners. In a
relationship, people tend to project back and forth

and expect too much. We will have a closer look at a number of relationships and see that there are two ways of reacting to the same experience. One is then the opposite and the compensation of the other.

Subconscious Expectations Due to a Lack of Love: Dependency and Independency

We come, more or less, fulfilled or unfilled out of our childhood and start to look for a new nest with high expectations of doing things differently and finding our great love at last. Of course, there is nothing wrong with longing for love, but subconscious expectations are a problem. What are these subconscious expectations? We can roughly say that we all hope that our partner will give us what we did not receive or did not receive enough of from our parents: safety, love, attention, and respect. These are the fundamental needs of a child. The more unaware you are of the emotional history of your childhood, the more your experiences will continue to play a disturbing part in your relationship.

Anna had always been mad about her father. He was a charming, easy-going man, who had social standing. He was not at home much. When he came home, Anna was showered with presents. When she became adult, flirting with men and pleasing them had become an important part of her behavior repertoire. When she got married, she constantly went out of her way to keep her partner's love. Her husband, an older man, felt devoured by her, and after five years decided to leave and a divorce followed. During a Spark of Light Week she came in contact with the little girl who had missed daddy so much. She saw that her behavior was, in fact, the cry of a little girl, 'Daddy see me, stay with me. Daddy, do you love me?' From under her tears of deprivation came anger towards her father, who was hardly ever there and who bought off his absence with presents. 'I don't want your presents,' she shouted in anger. 'I want you!' By allowing this explosion of anger to happen, she started to feel more independent of men. Her anger made her stand firmly on her own two feet and straighten her back. This gave her the power to lead her life as an adult woman and later to have an adult relationship with a man.

This is an example of a woman who remained a little, emotionally hungry girl, but there are also many examples of men who are still little boys emotionally. We often cannot see it as clearly in men because, in our culture, they have learned to function in the outside world and "be a man." Yet there will be many women who recognize their husbands in the following example:

Edward is a successful businessman. He is the father of two daughters and has a nice wife who does everything in the home, brings up the children, and manages family life. When Helga reaches forty, she starts to become discontented with their relationship and the division of roles between them. She is fed up with taking care of everything and looking after him. During their marriage, she has felt more and more as if she is his mother. 'I'm not your mother,' she sometimes snaps when he expects her to pour him a cup of coffee or lay out his clothes in the morning or when he sulks if she is not at home when he comes back from work. He does not understand what she is [going] on about. He brings in the money and has made sure they live in a beautiful house.

Men especially find it very difficult to become emotionally adult. Men have often a strong mother bond because they are doubly bound to mother—not only was she the first human in their life but also of the opposite sex. This is also the case (and quite frequently so) when the relationship with mother was not good or unfulfilled.

A recent study by the University of Utrecht in The Netherlands in which men were asked about their physical and psychological well-being, showed that "men's health starts to deteriorate if 'mother' does not squeeze out the oranges or has no time to make her husband's sandwiches." The more women work outside the house, the worse men feel. A fifth of men, whose wife worked 32 hours or more, did not feel all that well. They had more stomachaches, headaches, and backaches and felt more depressed. They paid less attention to their diet, started drinking more, and went to bed later. An American study in 2001 confirmed the results of this study.

Socially mature and emotionally immature—it happens more than we want to admit. Nowadays there are many well-trained, emancipated young women who cannot find a suitable male partner because they refuse to play the role of mother. It is often not easy for a man to see his immaturity. It does not tie in with the idealized picture of the successful, well-functioning man, but whoever wants to become really mature, will want to unmask false self-images and get to know himself in his entirety. He will bite the bullet and learn to untie the knot between past and present. Anyway, when you have found yourself, you will not need a self-image. Images are usually illusions and used to camouflage the lack of *being*. It is exactly these self-images that keep you away from yourself... the ones you started using to make people love you. In the end, it keeps love away from you.

The following example shows how Spark of Light Work works in practice:

> *I woke up this morning feeling angry and impatient. I felt irritated towards Gerard and he felt irritated and abandoned by me; in other words, there was Work to be done. And what is really great is that we both worked at our own piece and gained clarity about it. No carrying on about remorse or saying sorry, just Work and then it all becomes clear. Viva Spark of Light Work!*

Affective want does not always have to express itself in dependency behavior. It can also express itself in behavior that is too independent. The child that has been hurt says subconsciously: "Contact was not good for me. I do not need anybody anymore." Often a dependent and an independent type seek each other out. They form a perfect complementary couple. Perfect as supplement, but are they also perfect in their contact? Everything goes well as long as they are not conscious of their survival strategies, but the problem starts when one of them *wakes up*, and consciousness is alerted. The pattern then starts to slide, and the first conflicts often begin.

Subconscious Repetition Due to Fear: Fight or Flight

Want and longing not only continue to play a part in your relationships, but also your fears and the connected patterns are an indication that history repeats itself. Freddy, who knows Spark of Light work from his own experience, wrote the following to me:

> *I have noticed that a lot of the history I have with my mother continues to play a part in my relationship with Careen. The fact that my mother 'farmed me out' when I was six years old and sent me to a boarding school for the children of bargees goes much deeper than I thought. I have always 'excused' her behavior because she suffered, too, but my part of the story is feeling fundamentally rejected by her, which resulted in a fear of being rejected by women. All kinds of questions are going through my head now: Why haven't I ever had a proper relationship and why haven't I ever really been in love? Damn, that's why! I notice that while I'm writing, I'm getting really angry about it (alas, no carpet beater at hand). Because of my mother's rejection, I have been robbed of a lot of healthy human feeling and development. I felt deeply*

437

unhappy and lonely in secondary school because I was unable to go about with girls and handle sexuality in a 'normal' way. Why did I accept so much from Careen all these years? I know why now because I was scared to death that she would reject me. I always thought I did it because I was such a nice, sensitive young man who understands everything and can be so patient. That element is part of it, and I'm still proud of that. It is not easy, however, to face up to my own responsibility for my own situation. It means that I have to get down from my self-made pedestal and modestly enter into the world of those that are hurt. And yet, it offers immense pure prospects for Careen and myself. I see that my brother has exactly the same problems and is also caught in a relationship that completely drains him. I think that this is a good point of contact, I must stop playing a role here, too, namely that of the big successful brother.

Fear of loss and fear of rejection play a gigantic role in our relationships whether we are conscious of this issue or not. You take your early childhood attitudes towards your parents with you into relationships. There can only be room for really adult relationships when you have not only become aware of the story of you and your parents but have also emotionally digested it. This emotional digestion is really important. Just mental awareness is hopelessly inadequate to unravel your closely-knit old and new relationships.

Next to being petrified by fear, as in the example mentioned above, we see the reaction of the flight into fighting. It will not surprise us that Freddy's wife has *chosen* this form of survival. She has primarily compensated her old fears by defying and by testing other people's limits. Her fears are hidden under anger, as his anger now emerges from under the fear. Relationships are almost always complementary with regard to survival patterns. This is not for nothing. You subconsciously search for a chance to let the snowed under part of you come to the surface because you see it mirrored in your partner. That is the background of being in love; it is primarily determined by these subconscious search mechanisms. Perhaps you think that you are pulling the strings when you chose a partner; sadly that is far from the truth! The true determining factor is your subconscious emotional needs and longing for completeness.

Subconscious Repetitions Due to Conflicts of Power: Power or Powerlessness

Power also plays a more or less open role in most relations. That is not surprising if you realize that childhood is per definition characterized by an imbalance of power. A lot has gone wrong around the subject of power depending on the fact to which extent power and power struggles were prominent. When power was more important than love in your childhood, you will taste the bitter fruits of this in your future relationships, and this means power struggles in all shapes and sizes. Another example:

Anne and Gerard are both primarily people who repress anger. They are both full of old, bottled up charges that try to find a way out of their bastions of suppressed emotions.

Relationships often have complementary patterns: somebody who primarily represses sorrow will seek safety by somebody who represses anger and visa versa. These two patterns will keep each other better in balance than two people who both repress anger or sorrow. But this is not the case with Anne and Gerard; their relationship consists of constant fights about anything and everything. It is, in actual fact, about who determines what. Both have a background of childhood powerlessness against parental dominance without love or respect.

It is possible that you withdraw into powerlessness from old experiences of   misuse of power. People who have primarily repressed their sorrow, often with anger underneath, will tend to have a pattern of powerless. It is, as it were, the Yin side of the same hurt

Jealousy

Jealousy is a phenomenon that plays a major role in relationships and has also spoiled many of them. This reminds me of a couple who, years ago, came to see me in my practice: they were both desperate because of her morbid jealousy. In the evenings she investigated every hair on his jacket, she listened in on his telephone calls, and sometimes she sent a detective after him. He looked like a dog with his tail between his legs, and he did not know which way to turn. All three of the above mentioned relationship patterns play a role in jealousy: fear of loss, possessiveness (power), and being affectively unfulfilled. As you can see, putting something into a framework is difficult, especially life.

Repetition of Habitual Patterns

We often tend to subconsciously repeat the marriage patterns of our parents, or we offer resistance to them. You may have the tendency to do things exactly as your parents did, or you want to do it in a totally different way. Before you marry, your parent's marriage is the only reference you have. As a man, you will tend to be often absent if your father was often absent. If your mother cleaned compulsively, you will have the tendency to do the same or oppose this behavior. In either case, you are not free.

Part of your relational liberation process is becoming conscious of what really belongs to you and what comes from one of your parents. Repetition always means standstill and is not original. It is role behavior that has been learned. If you take that behavior out of your relationship and place it where it belongs, your relationship will be much livelier.

Relational Therapy: To Encounter or *In*counter

From the previous, it will be clear that we often think that we have married Mabel or Abel, but in reality we have married mummy or daddy. These subconscious *marriages* are always part of our so-called adult relationships. These subconscious marriages with father or mother determine a great part of the fortunes of our intimate relationships. Yet we often do not want to know! After all, that realization would encourage us to take responsibility for the relationship and Work at it. I often hear of people who have grown apart because they have been in relational therapy. If I continue to ask questions, it turns out that patterns that have originated from the relationship with the parents have not come up for discussion. The therapeutical work was then mostly "horizontal work" or encounter work, whereby it is just about the conscious meeting of two people. This work is, in part, fruitful when people learn to express themselves towards each other and make new agreements. But, as has already been said, subconscious mechanisms play a major role in relationships, and as long as these do not come to light, the effect of a therapy will be restricted to *doing one's best again* or separating.

Without *in*counter there will not be a good encounter. Plainly speaking, this means that horizontal work will not flourish without vertical work *into* the depths of the subconscious. When I started my therapeutical work in mental health institutions in the Netherlands, I was often at my wit's end as an arbitrator between quarreling husbands and wives, whereby one said "white" and the other "black," and they took turns in shouting, "Yes, it is" and "No, it isn't." And it was all about events that I had not witnessed! When I had had my own practice in later years, I started doing things in a fundamentally

441

different way. I did not go into current conflicts but went straight into the depths and worked, in turn, with the man or woman while the other was present, too. That worked—a new commitment to each other and insight into the deeper backgrounds of both them and their partners developed, particularly because of being present at each other's depth Work and at the unraveling of childhood pain—because of this depth work "pennies dropped" with regard to their relationship. Because these insights originated from emotional work in the depth, seeing their own less pleasant behavior was not a threat anymore. My own experience and the experience with many other people has taught me that commenting on behavior is usually threatening. People start defending themselves, or they become complete imbeciles which was my own favorite defense. Suddenly, I could not understand what was going on!

I allow very few so-called feedback rounds during Spark of Light Work even though they are customary in group therapies. It is not interesting or beneficial to know what we think about each other. Of course, you can learn from your projections if you take them back. But the disaster has usually already taken place, which means the group feels unsafe. My motto, in groups and in relational therapy, is keep your house in order and do your own inner Work under your own supervision. That is healthy emotional management.

Spark of Light Work and Your Partner

Now that we have had Spark of Light weeks for some years, a phenomenon occurs with regards to the partners of those who take part. One of the most important consequences of participation is that you acquire a taste for clearing up everything that stands in the way of the light. The joy of "clearing up" is an important part of our weeks. It is also a revelation to see how intense, frank, and revealing contact is between people who did not know each other beforehand.

When they return home, people have an intense need to share such an experience with the family, usually the partner, but then notice how difficult it is to put the experience across. There are a certain number of partners who feel the need to take part, too. This happens more and more, thank goodness, and it is wonderful to see how old relationships that were usually bogged down in habits and patterns receive a new impulse because people not only gain insight into those patterns, but also because the deepest pain and need come to light in each other's presence. By sharing each other's pain, people are often able to become children together again with all the accompanying butterflies in the stomach!

There are, however, also partners who find it threatening that their partners change. Becoming *more like yourself* often means that you will want to change the patterns that have crept into your relationship. Many relationships are, as we have seen above, complementary. Where one is active, the other is passive; where one is dominant, the other is more obliging. We often see the pattern of the giver and the taker. If you discover the neurotic background of your behavior of *giving* and *going out of your way* and want to change this within your relationship, your partner may not like it because it forms a threat to his or her position within the relationship. "I won't be able to be the Princess anymore," the partner of a Spark of Light worker once exclaimed honestly. Two things are then possible: your partner opens himself up to the change from neurosis to a more real, complete, symmetric relationship and starts to work on himself, or the partner refuses to change and to grow. In the last case, you can do two things as a Spark of Light worker: you remain faithful to your own growth and development and risk losing your relationship, or you adapt again, to your old, familiar, situation and to the complementary relationship and end the Spark of Light experiences. I have seen both reactions and it is, of course, everybody's own free choice. However, how free is such a choice? Fear of loss plays

443

a major role. After all, all change is accompanied by fear and the old, familiar patterns are, however unpleasant, appealing.

The Work we do in the Spark of Light weeks is no small matter; it is about the basis of your existence: about the choice for light or dark, for freedom or false security, for depth or superficiality. This choice should be checked again and again and perhaps also accentuated, depending on how serious you are about your inner Work.

Of course there are relationships that have such a good, solid base that intense Spark of Light Work can be shared without the partner feeling the need to take part in such an experience. It will be different for everybody. The nicest road is the road you take together. It is wonderful when, especially on this road, you can stimulate each other to drink deeply from the cup of life. And surely that is what a relationship is about: challenging, stimulating, and helping each other to become whole.

A Few Ground Rules for a Relationship

Here are some ground rules for maintaining a healthy relationship:

- Give as many "I" messages as possible instead of "you" messages;
- Realize that every reproach is a longing and express that longing;
- If sex has become routine or not pleasant, give each other a massage (without sex);
- Take time for each other: go and sit down with each other, look at each other, hold each other, and tell each other how your day was;
- Undertake breathwork and test work;

- Become children together;

- Differentiate between nourishment and poison, and only chose nourishment;

- Most important: take turns, on a conscious level, in being a good mum or dad for each other's needy, hurt child. Get to know the richness of being sometimes as a child, sometimes as an adult, and sometimes a parent with regard to each other.

- If you do decide to separate, say good-bye properly. This ground rule has three parts: I am thankful for..., I blame you for..., and it is a pity that...

Kahil Gilbran[2] said the following about marriage:

> *Love one another, but make not a bond of love:*
> *Let it rather be a moving sea between the shores of your souls.*
> *Fill each other's cup but drink not from one cup.*
> *Give one another of your bread but eat not from the same loaf.*
> *Sing and dance together and be joyous, but let each one of you be alone,*
> *Even as the strings of a lute are alone though they quiver with the same music.*
> *Give your hearts, but not into each other's keeping.*
> *For only the hand of Life can contain your hearts.*
> *And stand together yet not too close together:*
> *For the pillars of the temple stand apart,*
> *And the oak tree and the cypress grow not in each other's shadow.*

The Courage to Be an Individual

During my teenage years, the Danish philosopher Sören Kierkegaard was one of my favorite writers who inspired me to start on the path of "Know thyself." His plea that I should "Go to the place where the real earnestness is to be found, namely in having the courage to be an individual" appealed to me. I disliked fashion and what is right and proper. I hated the mediocrity of daily life and was searching diligently for a path and a freedom that could take me to that place. Although I was outwardly still quite adapted, inside a different path was taking shape. I felt like I was always on my own from a young age onwards and found in Kierkegaard not only an ally but also a teacher who put the sad "not belonging" on a higher plane and showed me its profound advantages: "Is hunting with the same pack, the meaning of living?" he said to his contemporaries. I lapped up these words. Later, in the Gospel of Thomas, I read these words of Jesus: "Many stand at the door, but it is the one alone who will enter the bridal chamber."[3]

The realization of the blessed condition of being an individual took years of hard Work at consciousness and liberation. I became aware of how often I ran with the pack because of fear and how I adapted to what is expected in our society. I became aware of how much the expectations of others, especially teachers and parents, were a part of me.

There are so many things that are expected of us from the moment we are born: we have to grow up, be a big boy or girl, do our best at school, be tidy, be nice, etc., etc. In reverse, from birth onwards, we expect all kinds of things from our surroundings: that we are loved, that we are respected, that we are given freedom, food, guidance, and so on. Between these expectancies from both sides, a lively trade by barter springs up. To receive love, we behave in an obedient and well-adapted way. To receive support, we give up some of our dynamic energy and keep quiet and so on. I live according to your expectations and you according to mine, and in this way we have a nice social contract that is based on unfreedom. Everybody survives in this way. But is this life? We are often not aware of how much our behavior is influenced by convention and unexpressed agreements. The influence of fashion and the force of habit is considerable. But even more considerable than the dependency on certain habits is our dependency on that original trade by barter which we call upbringing. To what extent do we live according to the expectations of other people in our relationships? That expectation is, however, always neurotic, a continuation of the childish barter: "If you do what I say, I will love you." Usually, it is the subconscious demand for the other person to amend and fill in what we did not get from our parents. Living according to the expectations of others is always neurosis and thus slavery! Becoming aware of these patterns of expectation, (yours and as well as those of other people) and liberating yourself is Work that will lead to freedom.

Florinda Donner, a colleague of Carlos Castaneda, says in her book *Being-in-Dreaming*, "An iron discipline is needed to become a dreamer [she means a person with a heightened awareness]. With this iron discipline, I do not mean that we have to keep to exaggerated, strict rules, but that we should not pay attention to what is expected of us."[4] I agree wholeheartedly with this definition of discipline. I do not care about other definitions! This is the true definition!

The fear of being on one's own, of being a solitary individual, also within a relationship, is one of the greatest obstacles on the path to becoming light. The realization of light is a unique and individual struggle that everyone must undertake in his/her own unique way. It is the path of becoming true to your own wise heart that knows its own way, whatever people say of you, and how many may walk away from you. It is a dangerous way, not one for followers and hangers-on but for the brave individuals who dare to go their own unchartered way and take risks by letting go of socially esteemed certainties. It is a path for those who dare to be self-sufficient and stand completely, also emotionally, on their own two feet.

Fritz Perls, the founder of Gestalt therapy, once recited the following poem:

I am I and you are you
I am not here on earth to live according to your expectations
And you are not here to live according to mine
I am I and you are you
If we meet each other, it would be nice
If not, so be it

Fear of Swamping

At the basis of all problems between men and women lies the deep fear of being swamped/overwhelmed—the man by the woman and everything she stands for, and the woman by the man and everything he stands for. The tendency to allow herself to be swamped has expressed itself during the last centuries in dependency behavior and being compliant. Women have developed less trust in their power because of what has happened to them during the hundreds of years of patriarchy. It would be getting too far off the subject to discuss this history more deeply. (There will be more about this in my following book). Men have just as great a fear of swamping, but that is expressed differently.

Men tend to distance themselves emotionally and do not really get a feeling for the world of women. The man chooses the bastion of dominance and the benevolent patriarchy to camouflage his fear of being swamped. But deep under this dominance lies a fear of delivering himself up as he once had to do during matriarchy. Under this fear, the anger of old humiliation lies hidden—the anger of being just an errand boy for women.

These deep, ancient, imprints influence us more than we realize. It is good to be aware of them, so the current learning game between men and women can also be seen in the framework of that old light and darkness. It helps to put things in perspective, at least with regard to your own limited story of relationships in relation to the larger story of male and female polarity here on earth. This is what Jung calls the amplification method: looking at the archetypal background of your own personal story so it not only becomes clearer, but also more bearable. You can then wink at each other and say, "Yes, you are a different species, and that is rather scary."

Proceeding from this fact, it is important that women's groups and men's groups exist. In a men's learning group, a man can learn what authentic male power is; and in a women's learning group, a woman can learn what her unique female power is. An encounter with mutual respect is possible when it stems from our own power, but not any sooner. True power carries vulnerability. It is the vulnerability of the pain that has been overcome. True power has to do with the discovery of your unique manhood or your unique womanhood. The man does not have become womanish nor the woman mannish. Because of the mutual encounter and fertilization, the man can embrace his inner woman and become wholly man. In reverse, the woman can learn to embrace her inner man and become wholly woman.

We do not really know what being a man or woman really means at the moment. As long as we do not know who we are ourselves in full completeness, we will put all kinds of images of men and women between us out of fear. It is important to treat each other's fears carefully and with respect from the knowledge that these are very old traces of imprints that carry further than our limited self. It is up to us to learn what real manhood and womanhood means.

Male and Female Partnerships

Up till now, I have spoken about the male-female relationship because the polarity of male-female energies is essential in a marriage. With this, I do not want to deny the value of male partnerships and female partnerships. I, myself, have lived for the past fifteen years very happily together with a woman. What is important in relationships is that we learn to bring the male and female energies within ourselves in balance and integrate them. We can do that in a male-female partnership, but just as well in male or female partnerships. We are all a very unique mix of male and female energy, and sometimes it is more meaningful and pleasant to start this work of balancing with somebody of the same sex. It is also the case that "this Work" should be done with a man at certain times in your life, and in a different phase with a woman—all entirely according to your own taste and choice.

Not having to live strictly according to traditional rules is a blessing of our modern, Western world. There is room for many variations of living together according to taste and preference. The process of liberation has caused people to identify themselves with their sexual preference. "I am a homosexual." I think that this is a limitation just as all identification is. By saying that you are heterosexual or homosexual, you close something off. You can, of course, say that at this moment in your life you prefer to have a relationship with a man or a woman. You then let the door of your heart open for other possibilities and enriching experiences. The Dutch cultural sociologist and trendwatcher Carl Rohde has an interesting view:

> *All kinds of sexual forms have secured a place in our times. The role that the consumer society plays is*

obvious. All impulses that can earn you money should be possible. The consumer society has contributed to the emancipation of homosexuality in this way. Men were really only seen as breadwinners up till the 1950's. They worked their socks off and hardly realized that they had a body. This was the way he looked after his wife and children. In exchange he received care and attention (also sexual) so he could go back to work again. That started to change in the sixties. In the consumer society, men have suddenly learned that they are also allowed to buy things and to enjoy themselves.[5]

I shall outline the various possibilities of male and female partnerships. According to me, there are three backgrounds from which people chose such a lifestyle.

1. There are people who strongly identify with a specific sex from a past life and continue with this identification while they are of a different sex in this one. These are men who look feminine and would like to live as women. There are also women who would like to live as men and also look male. This category likes to identify with their homosexuality.

2. There is, subsequently, a very large category whereby problems with father and mother play a role (just as in male and female relationships as described above). It can be very beneficial for this category to live together with a partner of the same sex. It is more difficult for a woman to make up for the lack of mother love with a man than with a woman. It is necessary that this need for catching up is consciously done and that this lack is also made up for in a conscious way. In the first place, this means that you become aware of the differences between your need as a child and as an adult, and that you subsequently approach your partner as that needy little child. It is

also possible that a man has such a great need for a father figure that he prefers to be intimate with a man. The same applies here. For both, the opposite is also possible; a woman can have such negative experiences with regard to her father that she does not want anything to do with men. Likewise a man may have had a very domineering mother or their bond was so strong that he cannot make the transition to the second woman in his life. If you do not become aware of the underlying dynamics, stagnation may occur.

3. Finally, there is a group of men and woman who choose each other because their bond is from a previous life, and they want to continue it whatever the sex may be; they choose a certain person or soul. These people identify the least with homosexuality or heterosexuality. They would rather call themselves bisexual, if they did have the need for a label.

I would, finally, like to remark that life is more complicated and richer that what is captured in this outline, and that people often have a mixture of these three backgrounds. What is really important is that we, through relationships, get to know ourselves and love in all our richness of male and female qualities.

Male and Female Energy

I shall end this chapter with a description of male and female characteristics. These should be seen as completely separate from men and women. It does not matter if we are a man or a woman in this life, what is important is that we find our balance between both energies. Especially if we realize that we were both men and women in previous lives, our womanhood or manhood will be put into perspective. What are female qualities? Marcy Foley[6] has a striking description:

Female energies refer to pure creative power before it has obtained a form and the possibility to produce energy. Female energy is present in our intuition, inspiration, creative impulses, openness, receptiveness, compassion, empathy, tenderness, and in all forms of artistic talent. Male energies refer to the ability to give form to that which the female principle inspires. They give us the possibility to set limits. They are present in our clarity, courage, power, grounding, assertiveness, structure, focus and in our linear, scientific, and mathematical way of thinking.

The aim of the learning process of relationships is to merge both these qualities within ourselves, whatever nature they may have.[7] The school of relationships should be seen in the light of this background. The more we are aware of this learning process and the more courageously we commence this Work of balance, the more pleasant, significant, and fulfilling a relationship will be. Also applicable here is the fact that life will become more pleasant and endlessly richer when you face your shadow of subconsciousness.

Chapter 40

Sexuality and Emotions

Remember: you only have one energy. At the lowest point it is called sexual energy. You refine and transform it. Energy starts to rise. It becomes love, it becomes prayer.
~Osho

Sexuality is often undervalued or overvalued. Where is the center? The heart is to be found in the center. Without the heart as center, sex becomes empty and hollow, a compulsive recurring behavior or a repeatedly returning release of tension.

Adult Sex or Childish Hunger

All kinds of love are sought in sexuality. Much is mixed up together. A lot of the searching for touching and tenderness has its origin in our inner child. At the same time we are grown up and searching for adult sexuality. A lot goes wrong in the sphere of sexuality because of this mixture of childhood lack of love and adult sexuality. This is because the one cannot be supplemented by the other. The child's hunger for love cannot be fulfilled by sexual contact. They are two quantities that we should differentiate between. Something is wrong when you need sex on a daily basis because you want proof that the other loves you. When you subconsciously try to satisfy your subconscious child's hunger in an adult sexual way, sex will never be fulfilling and never enough and your child's hunger will also not be satisfied. This mixing is, in reality, the deepest source of much sexual disappointment, but also of a phenomenon like sexual addiction. In the case of the latter, sexual abuse and affective neglect often play a major role. We can see the optima forma of confusion between adult and child here. Our emotionally neglected inner child does not want sex. It wants parental love and that is completely different.

What should you do if you recognize yourself in this description? It is, in the first place, about making an inner distinction between the child and the adult. Before you become a whole person, you must see and feel your dissociatedness first.

What are the needs of your inner child and what are the ones the adult has? If you have a partner, it is good, beneficial, and enriching to be able to go to him or her and ask for a hug and for attention like a little child. At another moment, you may want to express your love for your partner sexually, but do not mix these feeling up.

Sexuality and Power

Old connecting threads often intermingle right through our current sexual relationships. Power plays a major role in sexuality. With power, you can enforce love, for example, or what you take to be love. An example:

Up till twelve years of age, Harold thought, very purely, that his mother would initiate him into sex. Of course, within our culture, this led to a disappointment. Now that he is an adult, he has nightly power struggles with his wife, with whom he is otherwise good friends. He frequently wants sex and makes a lot of fuss if she sometimes does not feel like it.

Many nightly rows are the consequence. He finally discovers, within Spark of Light Work, his longing for his mother, his huge lack of physical warmth, and his longing for sexual initiation by his mother. He suddenly feels the connection between his anger about the physical contact he did not receive from his mother and the power struggle with his wife, the second woman in his life.

How much old anger about unfulfilled love plays a part as power in our sexual relationships? Two issues play a role here; on the one hand, when there is a lack of warm physical contact with the parents this need will be 'sexualized' which means that it will be taken to a genital level where it does not belong (men especially tend to do this). On the other hand, the mother is the first great love in the life of the boy and the father in the life of the girl, for whom an enormous longing exists. There are many little girls and boys who want to 'marry mummy or daddy.' Freud ultimately based his whole oeuvre on this. When something goes wrong with your first great love, it will have further consequences for your other relationships. Partner therapy or sex therapy without studying and experiencing that first great love, is work half done.

Sex as a Painkiller

The longing for sexual contact can develop when you do not feel good, are unhappy, or feel completely worthless. The 'great' feeling sex gives you, works as an emotional painkiller. The high of sexual excitement is an easy method with which to pep yourself up and drive away feelings of loneliness. But for how long? There are more people addicted to sex than we realize. People talk and write about it more often since Clinton and his sexual affairs. This is a good thing, but is sexual addiction also recognized within ordinary relationships? The way out of this intermingling of sex and defense of emotion is obvious: learn to feel what you feel, pay attention to it, talk about it, or work at it, as described in this book.

You should also make the decision to not mask your feelings in any way again. When you feel vaguely unhappy and long for sex, ask yourself what you really want and which feelings really play a part.: do you feel afraid, unloved, alone, or hurt? By giving that attention together with your partner, you will enrich, and make your relationship more profound in a completely different way. Perhaps so much intimacy of the heart will occur that it will be good to be sexually intimate too.

Sexuality as a Repetition of Old Misuse

It is a well-known fact that if you were sexually misused as a child, you will tend to fulfil your need for love with sex. The compulsive repetition behavior behind this is disastrous. It does not solve anything. The only way to fundamentally liberate yourself from this compulsive repetition is to mobilize your repressed anger and sorrow. Proceeding from there, you can once more start to feel what you really need; sometimes sex, but usually love.

Sexuality and Intimacy

There are people who use sex to avoid real contact. The emptiness of contact has to be filled by sexual diversion. People often tell me that their relationship is 'rubbish' but that 'sexually everything is fine.' There are people who avoid sex because they are frightened of intimacy. An example of the latter:

An average marriage: a long standing marriage but a problematic sexual relationship. He avoids sexual contact in this relationship. He is very ingenious in finding reasons for not having sex. He is tired from working, does not feel well, or thinks that she insists too much. He broods on an idea for months, but is indignant when she suggests that he perhaps does not want sex at all.

The only thing that really helps is to be honest and sincere towards each other. In our modern society, we seem to be very emancipated with regard to sex, but things are seldom what they seem. Our ability to be completely intimate, with heart and soul, lags behind our ability to have sex. Here, we see what happens when sister emotion is denied and oppressed. Sexuality cannot do without intimacy and intimacy does not just fall into your lap. Emotional growth and courage is necessary to start on that road. [1] The ability to be intimate has nothing to do with sex, but with the ability to share your emotions, your heart with another person. Many fears lie in wait that are often not even recognized e.g. fear of attachment, fear of abandonment that may go far back to your childhood. Feelings of inferiority can play a role here and all kinds of imprints that tell you that you will get it or be humiliated if you show your true colors.

Sex remains a delicate subject in many families. Teenagers prefer to consult anonymous information sources. Most questions asked on the children's help phone are about sex and the same goes for the question and answer section of young people's magazines. These candid youth magazines give the impression of a youth for whom sex holds no secrets, but what about the connection with emotions?

Carl Rohde[2], the cultural anthropologist, said in an interview about the sexual development of the past century:

The great thing about the past century is that sexuality was rediscovered at the beginning of it. Sexuality has always been there, of course, but it has been rediscovered. It seems that, since Freud, we all have the idea that our true identity is in our sexual organs. On the one hand that sounds pretty provocating, but psychoanalysis keeps quite a firm hold on that. If you repress sexual energy you become completely depressed is what they say...A society came into being where people suddenly started to think 'I must do something with my sexuality otherwise I will suppress something or other.' On top of that, the twenties and thirties saw the rise of the consumer's society which went together with secularization. The moral 'go ahead and enjoy' came into being. The culture of 'go ahead, enjoy' went against the culture of self-control and modesty of Christianity. In that culture Freud said that you can enjoy sexuality. He not only says that you are allowed to enjoy but that you must enjoy, otherwise you have a problem. That was very new, also because Freud's theory had the nature of a scientific study.'

Together with the rise of Feminism whereby women discovered that they had their own sexuality, and the invention of the pill of course, sexuality was freed from the nineteenth century Victorian Puritanism that was full of shame. It is now time for the next step and that is the connection between sexuality with the possibility of being intimate and for that our work of emotional liberation is vital. Then the pendulum will once more hang in the middle. Sexuality will then be neither overestimated nor underestimated but find it rightful place in our human relationships.

Sexuality as Primal Energy

How would you react if I said that God's energy is really sexual energy? If you are shocked, that means that your idea of sexuality is restricted to what you experience in your relationships. Sexuality is, however, much more. Sexuality is primal energy. Everything came into existence because of the fruitful cooperation between male and female energy. It is the same with God. As we have primarily made God male, we have difficulty seeing that God, the Totality, from whence everything originated and became individual, is also a whole of male and female, electric and magnetic energies. There was a male Creator but also a female Creator. Both created and brought everything else forth with their sexual energy. Sexuality is truly creative energy.

We, in our ignorance and backwardness have forgotten this story. We have also forgotten that we worshipped God as a Mother. It is important in our evolution to bring the great Father and Mother together again and that for us to realize that we came from both, from their sexual energy. If we regain an intensely felt relationship with that energy, we will be able to worship sexuality as a holy, healing, and creative energy. We can then feel that sexual energy is more than erotic or genital energy, but that it has to do with liveliness and the creative urge. Sexuality will then become a sparkle in everything you are and do. Thorough Spark of Light Work is necessary to experience that once again.

Chapter 41

Children and Emotions

If you have a child around you, you have paradise.
Do not force it to melancholy seriousness.
Rather make sure you lose your own seriousness when you are
with children.
Laugh together with them and become as a child.
~Osho

Active Children: The Story of ADHD

*A*s I am concerned about what is happening to children on a large scale, I am adding a chapter about emotional work with children. From a very early age on, millions of children are being drugged on doctor's orders with psychopharmacological drugs. Nowadays children are frequently diagnosed as having ADHD, *Attention Deficit Hyperactivity Disorder*. Since the term ADHD has been added to the DSM manual (a list with what psychiatrists see as abnormal behavior), active behavior and concentration problems have suddenly become symptoms of an illness. There is a lot of money involved in the gigantic industry that has sprung up around ADHD. What has happened? There are an increasing number of children in our stressed society who

463

become over-stimulated, over-active, and who sometimes have aggressive behavior. They have trouble coping with discipline, are not able to concentrate properly, and are seen as difficult. Parents and teachers cannot keep them under control. Doctors prescribe Ritalin as a remedy as it quietens them down. But for whom is this remedy? It is a very controversial medicine. Simply speaking, it strengthens the "restraining function" of the brain. Children do usually become quieter, but at what cost? A stronger restraining function means that children's growth is also slowed down during an important period of their life. In the medical world, people play down this fact. Parents are sometimes told to stop giving Ritalin during school holidays to stimulate growth for a little while. The appetite also becomes considerably less due to this medicine. Little is known about long-term effects, but it is being prescribed in the mean time. What is wrong with our culture that we have taken to giving drugs to our children? What does it do to their brains and their emotions? And which imprints do these children receive? Let's look at a few of these imprints:

- They receive the imprint that they are no good;
- They receive the imprint that something is very wrong with their brain;
- They receive the imprint that emotional and behavioral problems can be "solved" with drugs and that it is better to trust a pill than to trust people; and
- They receive the imprint that they can control themselves with a pill.

How can children learn healthy emotional management when the emotions are chemically weakened? And are they being primed for later drug use? In America there is already a brisk trade in Ritalin and prescriptions for Ritalin among teenagers. Three to seven per cent of American high school children use Ritalin regularly. It is related to cocaine and amphetamines when used in high doses and sniffed or injected. It is addictive.

A father told me recently that his eight year old son, who was standing next to him, was 'handicapped' because he always had to take pills...The son immediately and rightly made an issue of the word 'handicapped.' Dad said soothingly: 'No, handicapped is too strong a word. There is just something wrong inside your head.'...The child looked desperate for a moment and then looked blank and started to speak about something else.

Nothing New Under the Sun?

In the past in an authoritarian society, children's wings were clipped. They were kept quiet with authoritative behavior. There were books about the importance of hygiene, quiet, and order for children. In those days an authoritarian God who delivered punishment, backed up parents and educators and helped to keep children in line. Nowadays the medical world and the pharmaceutical industry back up desperate parents who have not developed enough ability to define boundaries—but who stands behind the children? Are they still the ones to suffer?

Something New After All?

- As well organized as life once was for a child, our culture now is so complicated and full of stimulus. These so-called ADHD children really mirror our over-stimulated society that has gone mad. The number of resources and products and the amount of information and amusement, not only for children but also for adults, is gigantic. Perhaps orderliness and quiet were good for children after all. Television and computer have a gigantic impact. During their lives, adults have learned to close

465

themselves off and armor themselves against a surplus, but children are still open and very vulnerable. This reminds me of a remark of a little boy. He had to undergo a minor operation and when his mother comforted him, he said, "You, you're old. You can't feel a thing anymore."

- Present day children are born with a different consciousness. At the present time, people speak of indigo children who have a different color in their aura than most adults have at this moment. Because they are wiser, they are also bolder. This means that they have more problems with authority and with fixed ritualized systems, such as school. They are more intuitive and creative than rational. It means that their way of learning is different from most school systems.

- To which extent do children still have room to play in this busy, over-organized, and demanding world? I think that there are many young adolescents who spoil free weekends for themselves and their surroundings because they are angry that they have been overloaded with homework. What does this lack of room in which to play do to their creativity and their feeling of well-being?

- In our current system of health care where even the care for children is fragmented, parents have not learned to look properly at their children and have real contact with them. They have not learned to part with their own knowledge and responsibility and leave things to experts.

- Most adults have had a more or less authoritarian upbringing. As a reaction, children are not given many limits. However, love is saying "Yes" to the child him/herself, but yes or no to his/her behavior.

- The current eating pattern with its many luxuries and superfluous products full of colorants and additives is not beneficial to children. Children are often too fat, and there is a definitive link between food and ADHD children. It has emerged from recent scientific study into the relationship between food and behavior of ADHD children that 60% of those who took part in the study had improved behavior after following an elimination diet. The study showed that with regards to foodstuffs, children were often sensitive to more than one and usually to about three products. These were ordinary foods, products that were eaten daily, such as milk, peanut butter, or oranges, for example. Children's bowel functions are not optimal because of all the treatment food undergoes. This means that the liver is overburdened and that they have intolerances and sensitivity for allergies. Food loses 50% of its nutritional value by cooking and baking alone. And what about the amounts of lead children inhale in our world full of exhaust fumes? I, myself, have the privilege of living in the French countryside in the middle of nature. However, when I go back home to the Netherlands, I always take an extra amount of vitamin C which well detoxifies the body of lead. From experience I know that if I do not do that, I become exhausted and really bad tempered, and that is something I hardly ever am.

- The influence of vaccinations, which have been given to babies and children in huge amounts since The Second World War should also be mentioned here. The continually growing number of vaccinations a baby receives is an enormous onslaught on the immune system. The many side effects of vaccinations can vary from tiredness, asthma, autism, allergies, being chronically prone to

467

colds, ADHD, and even crib death (as was shown by Japanese research whereby vaccinations were postponed until children were two years of age and crib deaths completely disappeared.) There are, thank goodness, many homeopaths who can neutralize the effects of vaccinations with Nosodes, often with amazing results.

An Alternative Treatment of ADHD

Aviva and Tracy Romm's book[1] about a natural approach, gives good critical information about ADHD and Ritalin and also good alternative methods of treatment. It gives good suggestions for "successful parenthood," and advice on nutrition, phytotherapy, and herbal medicine. The book highlights the problems from different angles.

In addition to this, it is important that more emotional work is done with children so we are able to pull up the problems by their emotional roots where necessary.

Spark of Light Work with Children

It is time to do more qualitative work on emotions with children. The care sector is often torn between two ideas: control and reliving. I quote Kleber, professor of psycho-traumatology at the Catholic University of Brabant in the Netherlands:

The treatment should be geared to letting children, and also adults, regain control, or command. It is a kind of going back to what you have experienced. You are going to face up to it, relive it. The aim is to talk about it without getting upset, that you can give it a name and fit it into your life, that you can handle it.[2]

Here we have control on the one hand and reliving on the other. How is that possible at the same time? I have experienced that children relive old traumas extremely well. They can say how far they can and want to go. A lot is possible if they feel safe.

The Spark of Light Work that has been described in the previous pages is, therefore, very suitable for children. Children often find it difficult to express their feelings; there is hardly any training in many families or at school. Moreover, expressing feelings requires a certain level of abstraction that children do not yet possess. Spark of Light Work is not primarily a verbal method, but it helps them to receive emotions and to clarify them. At the moment, we help children with individual work within the family. Each child has a session, whereby the parents and other children are present. The advantage is that parents can help to give examples and clarify problems in the home environment from their viewpoint. Spark of Light Work within the framework of the family affords the necessary safety. Within the family sessions, the focus is on the children. For the adults there are Spark of Light weeks. In our Work with children, we have noticed how much children love getting attention for their "stirrings of the soul" and working on themselves. The kinesthetic method of testing is a fantastic tool as children cannot indicate what is wrong. They usually like it and find it exciting.

As an example, here is the story of an eight-year-old girl with a lot of vague complaints, such as trouble getting to sleep, headache, and problems with concentrating at school. Her mother accompanies her. When I test her, I find that something must have happened to her when she was five years old. With a little help from mother, we find out, that her grandmother, who lived in England, died in that year. Her lip starts to tremble immediately, and I encourage her to cry freely, which she does in the arms of her mummy. Afterwards, she says how much she minded not being able to say good-bye to granny because she and her brothers could not go to her funeral in England. It was a revelation for her mother and for herself that the sorrow she had not addressed was behind her complaints. As a continuation of this session, the family worked on the undigested grief by looking at photographs and talking about that time. Making a drawing and writing a letter to granny helped the girl digest what was as yet undigested.

Jeanette, an eleven-year-old girl, is another example. She is a highly-strung, sensitive girl, who was shrouded in sorrow.

Although everything is great at home and at school, she is often sad without knowing why. She often feels alone in spite of being on good terms with everybody in her affectionate family. For quite some time now, she has had the feeling that she has a twin sister. She has inner conversations with her if she has any problems. She calls her Janine. When we talk about this during the session, mother tells us that she had a hemorrhage in the beginning of her pregnancy and that she was afraid of having a miscarriage. The presence of an unborn sister is affirmed when we test her, and it turns out that the sister decided not to come to earth at the last minute. On the one hand, knowing that her fantasy was based on truth gives her a feeling of relief; on the other hand, the sorrow of this loss is set free, and she cries her heart out because of this loss. She tells Janine, through the dialogue with a cushion, how much she misses her but respects the choice she has made. At the end of the session, she is happy that she has certainty about Janine, and she understands her feelings of loneliness and vague sorrow.

This work is also meant for teenagers and adolescents. There is a hunger for real attention and guidance in this age category, too. The enormous pressure and social control that teenagers exert on each other, partly due to television and advertising, is often exhausting. There is a lot of uncertainty and suffering in silence. The possibilities for compensation of this uncertainty (which probably does not differ much from past generations) are countless. Drinking alcohol and using drugs happens at a continually younger age. There are not enough ways to learn how to deal in a healthy way with feelings and emotions. Giving shape to depth work (as described in this book) for teenagers and adolescents is a challenge and a healthy addition to existing youth welfare.

Children and Past Lives

A lot of children's behavior is caused by undigested experiences from previous lives. I know of children who have loving parents and yet show extreme symptoms of fear that cannot be explained by their current family situation. I think that many parents will wonder if they are doing "it" right. There is a lot of uncertainty and feelings of guilt with regard to parenthood. First, guilt does not exist, only ignorance and subconsciously passing on "the baton of human shortcoming." Second, we cannot deny that parents have an enormous influence on their children. You can "make or break" them; the power of parenthood demands a lot of awareness and responsibility. Third, children are not *tabula rasa*, clean slates, when they come to earth. We all carry undigested emotions from our past with us to some degree, and that includes those of past lives. In the following example, I will show you how important it is to provide clarity to parents, as well as to children at a young age. Our behavior and our inner life are very complicated and a result of many factors. Spark of Light Work means looking at ourselves at various levels. Behavior and emotion can be connected to things from this life but also from previous lives, and that can make everything very complicated—time, for example:

Louise is thirteen-years-old. She has suffered from asthma and various allergies since she was two. When I test her, first of all, a previous life reveals itself which wants to come to light. We have been told by Louise's parents that when

471

she was younger, she suffered from extreme separation anxiety when her parents went out and left the children with a baby sitter. She panicked so badly that the parents sometimes had to leave the theater early after a phone call from the baby sitter. She is also disproportionally afraid that her parents or her brothers will have an accident. With testing, we find that Louise lost her mother at a young age due to a fatal accident around the year 1800. We do breathwork with Louise whereby she cries for the mother who died. Her current mother turns out to be the same mother as the one long-ago, and she now helps her to receive the sorrow of the past. Louise has the feeling that she was then taken in by the family of an uncle and aunt together with a few of her brothers and sisters and that she also lost her father because of this. We call this girl Agatha. After the session, the parents say that this reliving was an eye opener for them. Louise not only has separation anxiety, but it can also be quite prominent in her behavior. It seemed as if her need for love could never be fulfilled.

A month after this session, she wrote to me,

> *I often try to think 'Don't be scared, Agatha. It will be all right, and everybody will stay alive.'*

> *I find it very difficult, but it is starting to get better. I have also used the carpet beater a few times when I was angry or upset.*

> *I found it very scary, and, all of a sudden, I didn't know what to say. But I think that that will come. Mama now thinks that it a good idea to be close at hand while I'm beating and urges me to shout loudly. I quite like that.*

I train people who can do this work with children from their own knowledge and experience of emotional work. The latter is an important condition for good help. We are busy forming a network of Spark of Light Workers who not only know the simplicity and complexity of the Spark of Light Work from their own experience but have also been thoroughly trained. They will, moreover, be trained in working with muscle tests, so we can see which kind of behavior is influenced by which factors.

Finally, here is another great example of how Spark of Light Work can be continued in the home environment. The mother of one of the families, who knows Spark of Light Work from her own experience, wrote the following to me:

> *I am writing to you with an example of Spark of Light Work in our home situation. Little Henry and I were larking about and having great fun. We had a number of smacks and tickles to set right. I was winning. Suddenly, Henry slapped me on the cheek--a bit too hard, but that can happen when you're having a romp. I cannot say exactly what happened to me, but in any case, I felt this incredible rage rising in me that I could not stop, and I started to cry. I shouted and screamed at Henry, but knew this was not right and said so immediately.*
>
> *Jeanette who was there, too, said, 'It's something from the past, the smack that nun gave you.'*
>
> *Do you remember that story? When I was seven years old, a nun struck me across the face in the classroom because my handwriting was sloppy. And... it was as if I was reliving it. It was great how Jeanette drew my attention to it. I went to work with the carpet beater and cried at the same time. My husband supported me with words that helped a lot. Little Henry, who had had a fright, used the carpet beater too as anti- shock therapy for the mummy who had been so angry with him but had meant it all for that nun. We cried together. That gave us a feeling of relief. The beauty of it is that this can be something collective for the whole the family without it becoming too heavy.*

This is a wonderful example of how you can bring depth to your daily coexistence as a family and how you can bring about liberation of old pain and old emotional charges. It is fantastic when parents lead the way in healthy emotional management.

Adoption Children: Mobilizing the Anger

Adoption is almost by definition a perinatal trauma.

As the problem of adopted children is distressing and needs a fundamental approach, I will share my experiences in this chapter.

Until now, the adoption of children from abroad has been seen through rose-tinted glasses. Adoption helped both childless couples in the West and poor, disowned children from poor countries. Now after many years of adoption, we are faced with the consequences. Study shows that adopted children, especially from Asian and South American countries, have a major chance of having psychiatric problems and being socially maladjusted. They have a psychiatric clinical picture and commit suicide three times more often than their contemporaries who are not adopted. They have a five times higher chance of becoming addicted to drugs, and they commit crimes one and half times more often.

This was written in the medical journal *The Lancet*[3] by Swedish researchers from the Karolinska Institute in Stockholm. They studied the fate of all the adopted children in Sweden born between 1970 and 1979. There were 11,320 children mainly from Korea, India, and Colombia. The researchers compared their fates with that of their 2,343 brothers and sisters who were born in Sweden with 4,006 immigrant children and with 853,419 Swedish children born between 1970 and 1979. The researchers do not provide an explanation for the many psychiatric problems that adopted children have. A possible cause is undernourishment that already took place in the womb and because of which there was not optimal brain development. Another guess is that genetic factors play a role because parents who are psychiatric patients themselves offer up a child for adoption more quickly. It is also thought that mental neglect and staying in an orphan's home before adoption is a cause. The Swedish researchers did not find that any effect was caused by the care services in Sweden. If the adoptive parents did seek contact with the services, there was no less chance of disorders, criminality, and suicide later on. I would like to react from my experience with adopted children. I have noticed from my psycho-therapeutical work with adolescents and adults who were adopted as children that the gigantic repressed anger towards the original mother who gave them up and abandoned them is the core of their problems (whatever form this may take). As long as this anger does not come to Light and is expressed, assistance will not help as becomes clear from the above mentioned study.

Mark is thirty-years-old and an adopted child. In the orphanage he was 'chosen' by his current adoptive parents when he was four. He pays me a visit after yet another failed relationship. When I test him with the formerly mentioned muscle test, his subconscious says that we should immediately go to a reliving that has to with his birth. It surprises him that he cannot remember anything. When I ask him what he thinks of his real mother who gave him up, he becomes nervous and says that he understands her behavior. I ask him to project the unknown mother on the cushion before him and talk to her. He starts carefully but starts to clench his fists. I invite him to hit the cushion with his fists; an enormous rage is unleashed. He hits and curses and lets his anger that has been repressed for years flow into a healing fury. Afterwards, he understands how much he has aimed this anger towards his foster mother while it was meant for his biological mother. And he felt guilty about it, of course. He felt he should be thankful towards her. It finally turned out that during his first years, he had become attached to a young nun who worked in the orphanage. He was wrenched away again, now by his foster mother. He had to detach himself for the second time. He could not bring himself to attach himself for a third time.

Many adoptive mothers will acknowledge that adopted children test their boundaries. They have had little emotional contact with them or have had to cope with a lot of anger. Nancy Verrier,[4] who is a therapist and also an adoptive mother herself, came to the same conclusion. She wrote:

> *Society had an altruistic vision on adoption: it was about saving children from a terrible fate. Part of this myth was the belief that we could replace one mother with another and that the baby would not notice the difference. In my research and psychotherapeutical work with adopted children, I see that this is not true. Babies know they are being given to strangers, and they do not like it. It is against the natural way of things. As children they were, however, helpless; this helplessness and fury rages on during the rest of their lives. This rage goes further: it is the anger that a child feels in the endless waiting for a mother that never comes back. The adoptive children are scared of this inner rage because they feel that they could blow up the world with it.*

These children react in two ways: with control or acting-out behavior. In the case of the latter, the aggression against the adoptive parents is a subconscious attempt to stay one step ahead—rather reject them than run the risk of being rejected by them. Both ways lead to problems, as is apparent from the above-mentioned Swedish research.

In 1996, the world was shocked by the story of Joshua Jenkins who cold-bloodedly murdered his adoptive parents, grandparents, and sister when he was sixteen. He was adopted and had always wanted to know who his real parents were. His adoptive parents said that they had a letter from his mother but refused to let him see it. After years of aggressive behavior, his adoptive parents placed him in a home for difficult teenagers. He felt abandoned by them.

Here we see the phenomenon that we see in almost all adopted children: the searching for the original mother who becomes a kind of dream mother in the subconscious.

There is a major problem with attachment and entering into new relationships as is apparent from the example of Mark. The only fundamental way that I see, is exposing the original wound and setting the original pain in motion, as described in this book.

Chapter 42

Illness, Health, and Emotion

All things transitory are but a likeness.
~Goethe

Identification with Our Bodies

*I*t was routine far into the nineteenth century for doctors to include the role of emotions when giving an opinion or a diagnosis of illness. Medical literature from that time contains extensive essays about emotional conditions and their influence on sickness and health. Anatomy started to become the basis of pathology from the eighteenth century onwards, and illness was located more and more in the body, especially after the invention of the stethoscope. The body was looked at more precisely, but the contact with the patient became less. The patient's body became the central issue instead of the patient self. In the medical world, attention for the ill person shifted more and more towards his illness; man and his emotions were increasingly seen as being separate from his illness. This is the view the main stream now takes within the Western medical world.

From the specializations of doctors and wards in hospitals, we can see that man is divided into organs. You visit the cardiologist for your heart, the urologist for your prostrate, the internist for your liver and gallbladder, and the psychiatrist for your nerves. This division means that people identify themselves with a certain organ: "I am a heart patient" or "I am an asthma patient." The consequence of this identification with our bodies and the division into parts is that we start to see it as a car that sometimes breaks down and needs repair or new parts. If you have heart complaints, you can have percutaneous angioplasty, a bypass, or have a pacemaker implanted—or peacemaker as it is called in Dutch vernacular.

But which peace are people talking about? If your blood pressure is too high, you have to take pills for the rest of your life. If you cannot use your knee, you receive a new meniscus. If you have emotional problems, you are given pills to suppress your emotions. There are 1,000+ examples. Our regular, modern vision of healthcare has become a mechanical one, and our hospitals are garages for body parts.

If we see things this way, we do not have to go very far before we see illness as something that befalls us. We see illness as a kind of fate, as a punishment from God, or as something that is part of life. A lot of clever technology has been developed, a lot of good treatment of symptoms, and there are many life-prolonging possibilities via medicine, surgery, and radiation therapy. It is all very wonderful for those who can have a longer and more pleasant life. A friend of mine has had a kidney transplant and would not be alive without it. I certainly do not undervalue the blessings of the modern medical world.

But...can we still call this healing? And where is our own responsibility for our bodies and our lives? Who still knows about household remedies and herbs? And who, for example, knows of the beneficial use of clay and onion in the case of inflammation? It is, to put it mildly, strange that when you wear your body out by eating unhealthy food, drinking, and smoking, and then become ill, there are no conditions laid down for care in the form of a contribution. I do not mean a financial contribution—but a contribution in the form of one's own responsibility. I heard the following story recently:

The doctor sends Peter to a specialist because his cholesterol is too high. The specialist prescribes pills. When he comes back after six months, his cholesterol is still too high. The doctor suspects that Peter has not taken his pills, and he is right. 'Do I have to take those pills for the rest of my life, doctor?' Peter asks. "Yes," the doctor says, 'there's nothing to be done about it.' Peter refuses the pills and is written out. He then goes to a homeopath who draws his attention to his eating habits and gives him some good advice. From that moment onwards, Peter takes responsibility for his cholesterol problem and starts to eat differently and exercise more. He loses weight and feels as fit as a fiddle.

Healing can only take place when the whole person is addressed and when we realize that we *are* ill instead of *having* an illness. Our totality is our starting point when we speak of "being ill." When we speak of "having an illness," we think of ourselves as divided into parts. A split occurs, as if there is an "I" that possess a body. We are, however, a whole, a complete organism. When we acknowledge that we are ill, we can take responsibility, have a look at how it came about, and change things for the better.

Illness and Emotions

In my vision, illness is *caused* 100% by denied and repressed emotions; the *mechanisms* along which illness develops are 100% physical. At the same time, our thoughts also play their part 100% where they reflect our emotions. Is this 300% all told? No, every aspect of us plays its own role entirely, next to each other and each on its own territory. In addition to this, we must not underestimate the influence of environmental factors, such as air pollution and nuclear radiation in our modern society. When somebody becomes ill, there is a combination of many factors which all play their parts 100%. A person may develop lung cancer because he has repressed a lot of sadness that has lodged itself in the chest area. At the same time, he may have been exposed to toxic substances as a house painter or smoked excessively. You could say that he did not love himself enough to stop exposing himself to toxic substances. A simple cold or a bout of flu is, in this way, caused by lessened resistance that has to do with not feeling happy within yourself and thus has an emotional cause. At the same time, the flu develops 100% according to the purely physical mechanism of an infection. This is how it works: when emotions are repressed, this leads to physical blockades in the energy and to reactions of poisoning.

Repressed emotions cause the following:

- Poisoning in the brain;
- Muscle cramping;
- Changes in hormones, as bearers of emotions;
- Poisoning in the organs; and/or
- Blockades in the general energy flow.

Emotions that have not been expressed can express themselves as pain. Everything is a form of energy which cannot be destroyed but only transformed into something else. Emotions are also forms of energy. We have the choice and the responsibility to either transform them into pain and illness or into creativity and love of life, to name but a few possibilities.

Stress: A Struggle Between a Natural and an Unnatural Impulse

Nowadays, the word stress is used whether it is relevant or not. People "suffer from stress" as if it is an illness, and it is spoken about as something that comes from the outside. People talk about *stressors* and matters that cause stress, such as the death of a partner or children, divorce, redundancy, pension, pregnancy, changing jobs, exams, etc. In modern psychology, we also see that the attention shifts from the inside to the outside and is less and less about the emotional digestion of what presents itself to us as stressor in the outside world. Real healing is only found in the restoration of the emotional digestion mechanism.

But I am now ahead of my story. We shall talk about stress first. Stress means tension and tension is caused by two conflicting impulses. Which impulses are these? Our body, as expression and mirror of our soul, will always naturally seek balance and wholeness. When our balance is disturbed by an emotionally charged event, one of the above-mentioned stressors, for example, we become "emotional." We start, for example, to cry about the death of a loved one or become angry when somebody thwarts us. It is also natural to cry when we have physical pain or a shock, e.g., an accident. That is the natural, emotional response which helps us to emotionally digest things in life and to regain balance and peace once more. That is nature, and our natural ability to cope with things.

> In my personal process of emotional liberation, I noticed that the more natural I became, the easier it was to cry. I started to cry as a child if I fell down stairs or knocked into something. I noticed that I healed more quickly and did not get any bruises. It took some getting used to in the beginning when someone saw me. We are used to seeing such crying as childish. But now I am more indifferent to what somebody else thinks of it.

But now the other, unnatural impulse, which is the consequence of age-long repression of emotions—this impulse says, "I'm scared of emotions, I'd rather repress them, and I don't know any better." The battle between these two emotions causes stress. Stress is not caused by something that happens outside us but by how we treat it inside us. We can see this battle clearly mirrored in our muscles. Muscle tension is the result of these two impulses. This is a real ray of hope, a spark of light, and a possibility to answer to and take "response-ability" for stress ourselves. In this vision, we are not victims of stress or of stressors, but we take our healing into our own hands. Remember stress is always about battles, and the heart is where peace is to be found. It is the center of emotion and feeling. I suggest that we do not talk about stress anymore but about sad and unpleasant events that have to be digested.

To make things easier, I am going to conform to general linguistic usage, so I can discuss the following studies.

Two Studies of Stress

The young rat experiment.

Within the framework of an experiment into the lack of motherly love, young rats were taken from their mothers for a period of twenty-four hours. The brains of the deprived rats did not develop optimally in comparison to the control group. When these rats were exposed to stress in later life, they reacted more intensely *or* more resignedly than the control group. According to Helga van Oers,[1] who obtained her doctorate with this thesis, these twenty-four hours can be seen as an animal model for child neglect. The study shows that affective neglect and the emotional repression that stems from it can have a lasting influence on later life.

Putman's study of sexual abuse.

The American doctor and researcher Frank Putman who is called the "father of developmental traumatology," has been following the lives of two groups of girls. One group of eighty-four girls was sexually abused between the ages of five and eleven, and a control group of another eighty-four girls was not. The groups are similar in age, race, socio-economic circumstances, education, and family structure. The focus of the study was the consequences of sexual abuse during the rest of their lives. Briefly, his conclusion is "When they become adults, the social and psychiatric problems explode."[2] Addiction to drugs, auto mutilation, anorexia, depression, and suicide take place much more often than in the control group. They were also twice as often victims of rape. Finally, they had more physical complaints, such as asthma, headaches, skin problems, and gave evidence of a general weakening of the immune system.

After his studies, Putnam felt so sympathetic towards these children that he is now working with as the head of a therapy and prevention center for abused and neglected children. "Logically this was my next step," he said in an interview.

Two Stress Routes

The hypothalamus-hypophysis-adrenal gland route.

Besides these facts, Putman also studied stress hormones. The hypothalamus, which is important with regard to emotional digestion, secretes a corticotrophin-releasing hormone (CRH) in the case of stress. This goes via a blood vessel to the hypophysis. This is a hormone-producing gland that regulates fertility and stress reactions on the basis of brain signals. The hypophysis reacts to CRH with the production of the adrenocorticotropic hormone (ACTH) which is released into the blood stream. When it passes the adrenal cortex, the production of glucocorticosteroids, among which the stress hormone cortisol begins. These glucocorticosteroids are hormones that restrain growth and inflammation; they are bad for the brain, disrupt fertility, and eventually weaken the immune system. This stress route is called the hypothalamus, hypophysis, adrenal (gland) axis for stress response. This axis is an important route for sending stress signals which are experienced by the brain to the body.

Putman's study found that the abused children had a higher cortisol level in the beginning and a lasting lower one later. This is in accordance with the study results of above-mentioned study into young rats.

As a general conclusion we can state that people who have been exposed to stress in their youth have a stress system that will lastingly work in a different way.

On the one hand, they will react less strongly to a stressful situation as a result of emotional repression; on the other, they sometimes react strongly to new stressful situations. The latter is nowadays measured with a saliva test. In the case of heightened stress, more of the stress hormone cortisol can be found at the start but significantly less later on. In the United States, studies have been undertaken to see if women had a heightened cortisol level in their saliva after a reported rape. There were women who had a heightened level, but also those with a reduced level. According to Putman, those with a reduced level had a history of child abuse. These women had already emotionally shut themselves off more due to the emotional repression mechanism.

The brain-spinal cord-nerve-muscle route.

Besides the hypothalamus-hypophysis-adrenal axis which works relatively slowly, there is another stress route which works much more quickly. This runs from the brain via the spinal cord through the nerve end of the sympathetic nerve system to the muscles and comes into action in the case of sudden stress. The neurotransmitters, adrenalin and noradrenalin, are freed from the nerve endings in the case of a violent shock, a sudden attack, or a huge challenge. They prepare the body for fight or flight. The digestion stops because the energy that is needed for that can be put to better use. The heart rate goes up, energy is released, and the blood vessels that go to the muscles widen. This accelerated route can save our life because it prompts us to take action in the case of real danger. In adults or children who are chronically overstressed or hyperactive, neurotransmitters such as adrenalin and noradrenalin are chronically activated.

We can conclude, from this and from similar studies that because of emotional factors, an unbalance develops in the whole physical system, probably in this order:

1. The brain;
2. The hormonal system;
3. The immune system;
4. The muscles and from there in the bone structure; and
5. All physical functions and organs, depending on genetic and karmic disposition and environmental factors.

Psycho-pharmaceuticals: A False Impression of Things

Neurobiology, biological psychiatry, and, last but not least, the pharmaceutical industry are enormously popular and successful nowadays. But in what way are they successful? In neurobiology it has been discovered that there is an unbalanced amount of certain chemical substances in the brains of people who are depressed—the above-mentioned neurotransmitters. Acetylcholine, adrenalin, noradrenalin, dopamine, and serotonin are the ones that people know best. Medicine, such as Seroxat and Prozac, influence this route of neurotransmitters, just like Ritalin does. People concluded from the changes in the neurotransmitters that depressions are *caused* by these disrupted neurotransmitters. From that moment onward, it was

487

easy for the industry to bring those transmitters up to the required standard. Success guaranteed. But for whom is this success? In any case, for many overburdened GP's and other helpers who can now tell depressed people that they simply miss a certain substance in their brain. It is now just a question of supplementing, regrouping, and sedating.

The studies of Putman and van Oers lead to a completely different conclusion: because of undigested emotional experiences that express themselves in depressions and fears, our brains become so distressed that many neurotransmitters no longer work. *By affecting neurotransmitters with pills, symptoms are affected instead of causes, which are repressed emotions*—this is a well-known phenomenon in the modern medical world. We should stop calling psycho-pharmaceuticals "remedies." It is a sort of linguistic and medical deception. Psycho-pharmaceuticals do not *remedy* anything. Psycho-pharmaceuticals do the same as their users tend to do, namely suppress emotions. They supplement each other. What people subconsciously and from lack of knowledge do, is strengthened by the use of psycho-pharmaceuticals.

It is a disastrous pact. I can accept psycho-pharmaceuticals as a temporary solution for people who are too bewildered to have a consultation or to do emotional work. But I cannot accept them as they are being used nowadays—to disguise and further suppress the enormous emotional problems from which people are suffering. At the moment, pills for depression and hyperactivity, especially in children, are almost a medical and social hype. Apparently 40,000,000 people worldwide have been treated with Prozac. Prozac changes the serotonin levels in the brain and is prescribed for depressions. It is and was widely prescribed in both the United States and in Europe. It is one of the most successful legal drugs. People say they feel more cheerful and less inhibited. However, Prozac has many side effects, such as apathy, hallucinations, hostility, paranoid thoughts, anti-social behavior, and suicidal tendencies.[3] The American Food and Drug administration registered 40,000 reports of side effects in 1997, of which 10,000 were serious. And all this while only 1-10% of side effects are reported; these had to do with stomach bleeding and psychosis, in particular manic psychosis.

The American psychiatrist Joseph Tarantolo said this about "Prozac and partners": "All these medicines dissociate people from their feelings. They become less empathetic. They do not have the ability to feel and share the feelings of others and develop an uncaring attitude." This means that "It is easy for me to hurt you." The American psychiatrist and author Peter Breggin also thinks that there is a link between the use of Prozac and suicide and murder.[4] There are indications that many of the young teenagers who were perpetrators of shootings in high schools used medicines, such as Prozac.

Seroxat is now popular. It is also based on raising serotonin levels. It is especially prescribed in cases of fear disorders but also for depression. It is also called the *shyness pill*. Side-effects that have been mentioned are feelings of sickness, sleepiness, sweating, trembling, muscle weakness, dry mouth, sexual disorders, constipation, and reduced appetite. A recent study from Yale University in America, shows that 8% of the psychiatric patients in that country are admitted because a psychosis due to such "serotonin pills." How did this happen?

The Psychiatry

The psychiatry has carried the aura of science for years but does not live up to that name. Modern psychiatry bases itself on unproven presuppositions and theories which are subsequently introduced as facts. The DSM IV classification system is, for example, presented as a scientific list of disorders and diagnoses, but is, at the most, a list of so-called abnormal behaviors. The might of the medical and psychiatric order does not only reach deeply into our society but also far into the pharmaceutical industry and vice versa. It is time for people who chose real healing to turn back this tide.

The Conflict of Interest Between Medical Science and the Pharmaceutical Industry

With purity and with holiness I will pass my life and practice my Art.
~The Oath of Hippocrates

Ivan Wolffers, extraordinary professor of pharmacology at the Vrije Universiteit Amsterdam, painted a picture of the enormous conflict of interest between both giants, the medical science and the pharmaceutical industry, in an address of 2001. How is this conflict of interest proven?

- Medical research is increasingly being sponsored by the pharmaceutical industry.

- Sponsored research is the property of the sponsor, i.e., the pharmaceutical industry, and the sponsor determines if the interpretation is to the benefit of their medicines. They also determine if a study is going to be published or not. The truth is often trampled on. Wolffers gives the example of calcium blockers that, as emerged from several unsponsored studies, was not a first choice medicine for lowering blood pressure. Yet that medicine is "thanks to" sponsored study with a different outcome, plus a huge advertisement campaign, now frequently prescribed.

- If, during a study, it emerges that a medicine is not getting any support, the money supply is cut off half way, so there will never be any negative publicity.

- It often emerges from the small print underneath study reports in prominent medical newspapers that the statistical analysis was done by the producer of the medicine.

- Medical specialists sometimes receive a huge amount of money for holding talks or taking place in all kinds of committees to the benefit of the pharmaceutical industry.

- The promotion departments of the pharmaceutical industry sometimes write articles in the name of well-known medical specialists.

- There are hardly any independent medical specialists to be found for medical governmental committees because of the above-mentioned conflict of interest.

- Refresher courses for doctors are sponsored by pharmaceutical industries, and specialists who function as teachers are paid by the industry.

- Pharmaceutical companies try to influence patient's associations and, for example, parent associations of children with ADHD. An American parent association received $5,000,000 from Ciba Geigy in exchange for propaganda for Ritalin.[5]

The amount of power of the pharmaceutical industry is apparent from this list. In itself, power is not a bad thing. It is important that this power is used beneficially. I have grave doubts about that. The medical order should read the Hippocratic Oath again.

Dr. Elnora van Winkle's Theory of the Toxic Mind

The brain cannot vomit, and the stomach cannot go mad.
~Herpert Shelton, physiologist

Mrs van Winkle was a scientist in neurobiology and an ex-psychiatric patient who completely healed herself. Her knowledge and experience have led to "the toxic mind theory"[6] that gives empirical and neurobiological support to the path of emotional healing as described in this book. She writes:

> *Since the days of Hippocrates, people understand that the symptoms of most illnesses (...) are attempts by the body to eliminate toxic substances. Every substance coming from within or without and not being used by the cells, is recognized as toxic and rejected. When the elimination process weakens, the toxins pile up. The cells adapt to a certain level, but when the toxin level becomes unbearable, the body starts the detoxification process. Toxicosis is the real illness and what we call illness is a recovery attempt, a complex of symptoms that is caused by the elimination of toxic substances. When the level of poisoning has been brought to a point of tolerance, the symptoms of illness disappear and health returns. But the actual illness has not been healed.*

> *In the case of constant enervation, the toxic substances pile up again, and the next crisis announces itself. Unless the cause of the toxicosis is discovered and eliminated, the crises will repeat themselves until the functional disorders turn into irreversible organic illnesses.*

When emotions are repressed, the nerve bundles in the brain in which experiences connected to emotions are stored become blocked up with toxic neurotransmitters. When we do not remember our traumas, these toxic substances flood the nerve bundles during periodic detoxification crises and lead to fear, depression, and in serious cases to mania and psychosis. When these detoxification crises are aimed outwards, they can lead to violence.

She writes:

> *Because certain areas become more blocked up than others, anger is, as it were, diverted via the wrong neurons* [and also fear and sadness, RO]. *This implies that the anger can be aimed at the wrong person or aimed inwards in the form of guilt or even suicidal thoughts. These nerve disorders are, however, detoxification crises and healing processes; the opening of the sluices of repressed anger.*

Elnora van Winkle's own story.

> *I was not an abused child by society's standards, but I was left by my mother in my crib at birth to 'cry it out' and listened to my father rage, never at me, but at my mother, brother, and sister. I learned to suppress my justifiable anger very early. I was an autistic child and in my twenties was diagnosed as schizophrenic and locked for four years on the violent ward of a mental hospital. I spent much of the time in the 'mattress' room, where I raged against the tight sheets of a straight jacket, or I turned my anger inward in suicidal rage. One of the shock treatments didn't quite make me unconscious, and I felt pain and panic as the electricity surged through my body. It was like being electrocuted, yet still alive. Over the next thirty years I was confined in more than twenty hospitals, rediagnosed a number of times, and was given every drug known to psychiatry. At age 60 I was rediagnosed with major depressive disorder, then manic-depressive, and had symptoms of Alzheimer's and Parkinson's disease. In my years of hospitalization, only one nurse had a sense of*

what I needed. She came into a room where I was tied to a bed in restraint, untied me, and gave me a tray of plastic dishes.

'Throw these at the wall, dear' she said.

If I had known to mentally picture my parents on that wall, I might have begun to heal. I wanted to be locked up in those hospitals. I never knew why, but it was an acting-out of a fantasy. It was a re-enactment of having been imprisoned in my crib and an opportunity to have my justifiable anger. After making this discovery and with the help of the self-help measures based on this discovery, I recovered in a short time.

The self-help remedies that were used by Elnora are exactly the same as the methods described in this book. In her article, "Confessions of a Schizophrenic,"[7] she says to her former helpers:

To you who so generously tried to help me when I came to you as a patient, I confess I did not really want your help. In truth I wanted to be mad—not 'mad' mad—but 'angry' mad. When abusive parents force their children to suppress justifiable anger, a toxicosis develops in the brain consisting of noradrenalin, adrenalin, and other neurochemicals that store repressed anger and grief.

What I want to show you is that the symptoms of my many psychiatric disorders were periodic detoxification crises. I further confess to you that I am playing amateur psychiatrist, have peeked at the DSM-III-R (American Psychiatric Association 1987), and sprinkled my story with parenthetical diagnoses. So unconsciously eager was I to be mad that psychiatrists found my symptoms listed in most of the three hundred or more disorders described in that manual. As explained by the toxic mind theory all the various nervous and mental disorders are manifestations of the same physiological process of detoxification, differing only because of the location of the toxicosis and the function of the area of the nervous system affected.

She gives another great example of how she expressed her anger, but she did not heal in this way:

One time my psychiatrist, now a principle actor in my dramas, found me well enough to go downstairs for a session in his newly decorated office. He had a beautiful new picture window.

'How do you like my new office?' he said.

'Very nice,' I replied, and I raised my arms as high as I could and put my two fists through the window with a force that smashed it to tiny splinters. I was never allowed to disturb my father in his office, and here was a way to release my anger at that rejection. If the psychiatrist had allowed me to punch a punching bag and encouraged me to redirect my anger at my father I might have begun to heal. I am sure there are psychiatrists who help their patients redirect justifiable anger, but no psychiatrist in my forty years of psychiatric care ever suggested my illness was related to childhood trauma.

Mrs van Winkle is a wonderful example of how you can heal yourself completely. *When she was sixty-seven, she started her self-healing through emotional Work.* She is, except for osteoarthritis, completely healed after forty years of psychiatric care and heavy medication!

I feel a deep respect for this woman, whom I only know through the articles she placed on the World Wide Web. She writes:

My life has become simple. I now trust my own feelings more than those of others. I have become more patient and tolerant. I smile easily and I cry easily. I can feel sad without becoming depressed. I do not suffer from mood swings. I can live in relationships. I can be alone but am not lonely. My face has changed, and I stand and I walk like a child. I can concentrate, and my creative facilities are restored. My body does not accept stimulants or cooked food. I eat in the style of 'The Garden of Eden.' I am content.

She is an example worth following. People like her can pave the way to a transformation of our psychiatric institutions where there will be the possibility of connecting to old traumas in a safe environment and doing deep emotional Work.

After I had written this, I heard that she had recently died quite suddenly.

Finally

Mental and physical health depends on the extent to which you have a healthy fight or flight response and your ability to express your emotions. You will then react naturally: you will cry when you are sad, laugh when you are happy, seek shelter when you are scared, and express your anger in an adequate way when people overstep your boundaries. When you have restored your natural qualities, you can overcome many illnesses. I do not mean that you can overcome them all. After all, sometimes an illness may be too far advanced or a part of our learning process. There are no general rules. Each and every one of us must take our individual path; however, I am convinced that the detoxification of our brain by deep emotional Work, as described in this book, is an important condition for real mental and physical healing. This emotional Work is, in any case, a powerful tool for prevention. We should not only learn it ourselves but also teach it, especially, to our children.

Part VI

Essence

Chapter 43

The Ocean of Essence

Ultimately, we are only worth something because of the essentiality we embody, and if that is not what we embody, life is wasted.
~C.G. Jung

*I*n this sixth part, we have arrived at "the ocean of essence." In this phase, which can take your whole life, you are harvesting step by step. I hope that it is clear that this harvest is a continuous process and not a *grand finale* at the end of your period of growth. You will gain more essence every time you have set a fixation, such as guilt or depression in motion. You will gradually experience more essential power, more ability to love, more creativity, or more courage and trust. Our scheme is a *perpetuum mobile* and not a rigid step-by-step plan from A to C. From the various chapters you will already have an idea of the harvest that is possible. In this part I will go more deeply into a number of essential subjects.

Emotion and Essence

The Russian spiritual teacher Gurdjeff once said that most people do not have a soul but can obtain one through inner Work. When I read this, I found it shocking, and I had the inclination to deny it. Now I know what he meant: if we look around us on this earth, we see a lot of people who have become blunted, are not conscious of things, and live according to established patterns. It looks like an ant heap with directionless, teeming people wandering around. We are just aimlessly doing things. Together we keep a gigantic society going that is mostly based on mass production, mass consumption, and mass recreation. It all looks great, but it is really more and more of the same kind of thing.

Who knows what it is really about? Who is still connected with the essence and the meaning of our existence? I think that we can safely say that there has always been a small minority, just as there is now. I believe that this minority has grown substantially over the last forty years. There are a growing number of people who are aware of their essence or at least of their lack of essence. There is increasing friction in many areas partly due to the increasing complexity of our world. Nothing is matter-of-course anymore. The accepted established patterns of marriage and family have become looser. Many other ways of living have replaced them. Due to the increasing migration, borders have disappeared, and a melting pot of cultures and races develops everywhere.

This also increases the degree of complexity. Because of increased prosperity, everything has become much more complex, and there is also more room for leisure, which everyone can make use of as they see fit. The disappearance of established patterns makes heavy demands on everyone. Emotions increase because of growing friction. This offers a huge chance for everybody to awaken from the sleep of old habits and customs. It is a chance to wake up to the essence! It offers the possibility of our soul being awakened from its planetary winter sleep. I think that there is an important connection between increasing emotions and finding our essence, our soul again.

Every time that we close off our feelings or push away an emotion, we miss a chance to get to know our essence and to connect to it. In our Spark of Light weeks, I ask people to bring photos of themselves and significant others. There is usually a huge difference to be seen in their *radiance* in the photos from early childhood and from those of a later date, especially those from adulthood. We often see a sparkle and a radiance that has usually disappeared after several years. Our soul has difficulty surviving in a corset of adaptedness.

Our soul is energy; it sparkles and is original and spontaneous. These are all qualities that disappear first in the process of education and socialization. A playful and creative child that loves to sing has to sit at awkward school desks and learn arithmetic because that is what society wants. In itself, that is not the problem, but the consequence of growing emotionally rigid and cramped ensures that our essence is lost. This book is about emotions against the backdrop of finding our soul and our radiance.

We lost our soul, so we should be able to find it again, in reverse order, of course. This means that we undo the denial and repression of our emotionalism, which is the consequence of too much pain and fear. It is about rediscovering our soul and its qualities at the bottom of our stinking, rotting pool of subconscious emotions. Under our depressions and feelings of guilt, under our resentment and hatred, under our arrogance, indifference, cynicism and distrust lie the pearls of essence. Every one of us must find for him/herself what they are. I can name a few. They are about your deepest dreams, true love, and "peace above all understanding," about the freedom of the children of God, an intense connection with "All that is," and a life in the power of the here and now.

Only now in this intense time of friction and chaos, but also of development, is it possible for us to truly find the path to our essence. Our pools of stagnant water can be set in motion now and become a stream that finds its way to the ocean of essence. That is why we have come to earth again in this day and age. The choice is ours; we either remain by our pools of stagnant water and old patterns of false security and habit or take the path away from the "Ur of Chaldee" or the "fleshpots of Egypt" to the land we once promised ourselves but have forgotten. What we need most is great courage and motivation to rectify the denial and repression of our essence. But we also need vision and clarity to see how to find and walk this path.

Our essence is composed of love, truth, and energy: the Goddess of love, the God of truth, and the energy that fuses them together in a holy marriage. The realization of our essence is Work with a capital letter. We then become who we really are or who we could be—a Human Being with capital letters!

Essence in the East and West

Psyche forms part of the word psychology and means *soul*. Yet there is a lot of psychology nowadays that is not science of the soul. The words are incompatible. The discipline of the soul has become the discipline of the personality, and that is totally different—a gigantic reduction that still has a lot of nasty consequences for our mental health and our spiritual maturity.

Most of the current **western psychology** is behavioristic and oriented towards the cognitive. It is about behavior, (power of) reason, and emotion—not about the soul. Our bodies and our reason are imprisoned within time. The soul transcends time and our limited personality. The soul develops itself in an individual way in the non-physical reality, but also here on

502

earth in a series of incarnations. The word *soul* has become old fashioned in traditional psychology. Happily we have known someone like Carl Jung, who has many Jungerian and post-Jungerian people in his wake, like Erich Neumann, James Hillman, Edward Edinger, and Esther Harding. Gary Zukav and Robert Assagioli and his psychosynthesis have also contributed to the revaluation of the soul. Jung had an eye for the soul, for that what is eternal within us. He gave his psychology rightly the name, *depth psychology*. Although the realization of the soul is central in Jung's work, which he called *individuation*, his method is still analytical. His therapeutical method is primarily mentally and verbally oriented. In my opinion, therein lies his limitation for many people.

Eastern Psychology is essentially geared more towards the realization of the soul. As a person with practical experience, I am interested in the "ins and outs." The Eastern path was always a path of detachment. People try to realize their souls by learning to witness their bodies, their thoughts and feelings via meditative techniques, but not to identify with them. A great authority on this path was, for example, Osho Shree Rajneesh. He taught his followers to be pure observers without identification. "You are simply the observer along the side of the road" and "Being aware of being eternal, is being aware of being God, or part of God. That is my whole work here: making you aware of the fact that you are gods and goddesses and eternal beings. With this experience of eternity, there will be joy and ecstasy, fear disappears; love comes into being and hate disappears; it becomes light and darkness disappears."[1]

Eckhart Tolle, a contemporary teacher, also advises inner observation:

> *Do not judge or analyze what you observe.*
> *Observe the thought, feel the emotion, observe the*
> *reaction. Do not make a personal problem out of it. You*

will then feel something stronger than all those things you observe: the silent, observing presence behind the contents of your mind, the silent observer.[2]

It is essentially the path of "Look into the sun. Then you will see no shadows." But is it true that there *will be* no shadow then? That is the key question when we look critically at the eastern way of detachment. Is it just a trick to get rid of the ego or at least not to be bothered by it?

As a teacher of many western followers, Osho was confronted by this dilemma. He discovered that his pupils were meditating on an emotional volcano and that for many the path of quiet self-observation did not work. Together with therapists and psychologists, he developed various methods which afforded room for emotional and relational therapy. He saw that meditation and therapy were both necessary on the path of soul realization. A truly revolutionary path for an Oriental!

Enlightment or Wholeness?

I find it important to know if it is true that if you look into the sun and no longer see any shadows, all darkness, such as fear and hate, will disappear like snow in summer. The contemporary, female, guru Shanti May who is inspired by the East, says,

> *You have to realize that Ramana Maharishi died of cancer and even though he had that sweet smile on his face, the pain was in his body, in this illusion, but it was there. Every subtle or terrible suffering is rooted in believing: 'I am this experience.' Suffering only stops when we realize that that is not what we are. But the pain may continue.*[3]

That is abracadabra to me. I can understand that your pain is less if you do not identify with it, but are you liberated from it? This is denial with a gloss of spirituality. Have you really been liberated from it by declaring that body and mind (and emotions) are an illusion? The Dalai Lama knew better. During a conference in New York, people were talking about the two levels of reality: the relative and the absolute. Somebody started to say that the relative, earthly level, is, of course, not real. The Dalai Lama interrupted him immediately and said, "Stop, it is very real. And when you deny this reality, you will create a lot of problems for yourself."[4]

If we look at the teachings of the Buddha, we see that the liberation from the wheel of karma is not the end of karma but the liberation of the inner *hold* that it has on you.[5] And that is where the difference lies. According to the teachings of Buddha and his followers, you can be liberated from the hold karma or the past has on you but not really be rid of it.

When I read that, I understood the difference between the Western and Eastern path of liberation. It is the difference between enlightenment and wholeness. In the case of enlightenment, it is about liberation from the *hold* that the past has on you, without it being emotionally digested. People simply look at the sun, so "the shadow disappears." However, it does not disappear—it is just not seen. It is behind your back. What is the difference between repression and closing your eyes? I see no difference.

The choice for wholeness is about getting rid of the past through emotional digestion. If you have emotionally digested something, it will really disappear into the background, and you no longer essentially identify with the problem or theme. Supporters of the Eastern way often say that if you look at the past, you can go on forever, especially if you involve work with past lives. To me, this is a statement based more on laziness and denial than on truth. Their objection is that you also remain identified with the ego and its past. It does take more time. If we travel the path of liberating healing, we digest the past gradually and let go of identification slowly but surely. To the extent that emotions create room within us, light can come in, and we can connect to something larger and more spacious. It might take longer, but it is thorough.

Detachment: A Story with a Shadow

We shall have a look at the theme of detachment and take sexual detachment as an example. Detachment is based on practice and control in both the East and the West. Meditation, looking at the sun, is used, and repression of what is seen as the shadow according to religious ideals. Virtuousness is also practiced to cultivate the ideal, as well as the denial of what does not belong to this virtuousness—in this case, a sexual need. It did not work in the East or in the West. Yes, it worked as long as people stayed within the walls of the monastery or convent or in the isolation of the Himalayas. It has been reported that there were many sex scandals in the West concerning the Roman Catholic clergy. Some time ago, there were scandals involving well-known, spiritually high-principled teachers from the East. Spiritually high-principled and wise, they were not sexually and relationally integrated and often not morally upright in these spheres of life. As long as they stayed in their monasteries where there were no women, there was nothing wrong. As soon as they came to the West where there were many beautiful female followers at their feet, the detachment, which turned out to be repression, could not be maintained. Of course, it does not have to be a problem if people make different choices in new situations by, for example, entering into relationships with women. The problem with these gurus was that the shadow troubled them subconsciously, so the sexual need was expressed in an almost adolescent and not honorable way. We know that one teacher violated the very young daughters of followers. Another violated young boys.

The detachment from wealth and power through poverty and obedience does not have the desired effect either. I remember spending the summer in a contemplative convent as a young student. A nun looked at my suitcase with shining eyes and asked if she could have it. As long as there was no contact with the outside world, nothing went wrong. As soon as there was contact, the repressed desires jumped up like a jack-in-the-box.

We can conclude that detachment as practiced in all religions up to now is an upgraded, spiritualized form of repression.

Reversal of Result and Goal

There is, of course, a healthy form of detachment, but that is the result of real spirituality and not a goal to strive for. Where there is connection with essential things, other things are not important. Detachment is then a natural process, as with a child that is ready to discover the world and who is then not tied to mother's apron strings anymore. However, natural needs are often skipped and prematurely renounced with the exercise of one's will. In many religions, truth has become corrupted in this way. The results became goals to strive for. Many people strive for happiness, which is also a reversal of goal and result. Happiness is the result of being in harmony with ourself. It is a gift we receive when we do your homework and become who we really are. It is the gift we find at the bottom of our pool of emotions.

Holy Wars

Zen priest Brian Victoria's revelation about enlightened Zen masters[6] should also be mentioned here—not to condemn because as my teacher Jesus once said, "Let he who is without sin cast the first stone..." but to clarify. Brian Victoria researched statements made by the famous Zen master Daisetz Suzuki, who is also famous in the West. He highly praised sword fights *during* the Nanking blood bath where the

Japanese butchered, beheaded, and mutilated 350,000 Chinese and raped 80,000 women. He said,

> *The art of sword fighting (an important discipline in Zen) distinguishes between the sword that kills and the sword that gives life. The technical expert that lifts it can only kill. It is completely different when someone is driven to lift the sword because it is not the warrior that kills, but the sword. It does not have a longing to hurt somebody, but the enemy appears and makes itself a victim. It is as if the sword automatically executes the act of justice, which is an act of mercy. The warrior turns into a first class artist who makes a truly original work of art.*

Harada, who inspired many people in the West through Phillip Kapleau's *The Three Pillars of Zen*, applauds the battlefield and states that what he calls Zen fighting is equal to "the highest form of enlightenment" and is "the king of meditation."

How is it possible that a man such as Suzuki, by whom I was also inspired in my student days, can be brilliant on the one hand and so cold-hearted on the other? Josh Baran, who is a former Zen priest, exclaims, "This total betrayal of compassion [compassion is the heart of Buddha's teachings]. These Zen masters were not enlightened or their enlightenment excludes wisdom and compassion."[7]

In a Dutch newspaper, I read the reaction of Dutch Zen masters, such as Ton Lathouwers, who was deeply shocked: "The most important question is how could this happen? How is it possible that Zen masters with their aura of enlightenment could be so blinded? It teaches us to be alert at all times and to remain critical."

I am afraid that without insight into the deeper background of this discrepancy between spirituality and psychology, alertness will not be enough. These Zen masters are not alone with their holy wars. We have the *jihad,* the holy war of the Islam, and the Old Testament where plundering and murdering was done in the name of Yahweh. And we know about the Crusades where the Pope gave the command to kill "the enemies of God." Christian soldiers murdered 40,000 Muslims in just two days. All traditions are, by degrees, guilty. Let us try to understand what the difference is between enlightenment and wholeness. But above all else, let us learn what love is.

Light and shadow: Not One Without the Other

It becomes evident from these derailments of spiritually enlightened teachers that it is possible to have wonderful spiritual experiences and yet to have a dark side, a *shadow* side. But can we still talk of Enlightenment? Are wonderful spiritual experiences enough to be enlightened? The American Spiritual teacher Andrew Cohen[8] is, in his own way, also engaged in looking into what enlightenment really is. I believe that he cannot solve that question because he does not recognize emotional digestion as a meaningful path. He says,

> *As a spiritual teacher, I have found out, without exception, that if enlightenment is the context and the goal of the spiritual quest, giving room to endless needs, pain, fear and frustration of the Narcissistic ego will only have one result: air, water and food is given to that which is seen in spiritual experiences as completely unreal.*[9]

We see another appeal here, to not have anything to do with the shadow. The shadow is judged negatively in advance: "Narcissistic ego."

The only way I can see it is this: the path of self-realization that is based on detachment rests on denial and repression of the shadow, and thus of the much loathed ego. The shadow is mainly repressed emotionality. We could interpret the path of "looking at the sun and seeing no shadow" as "wanting light but not wanting to feel." It is the interpretation of the male, rational path of the Spirit, without the female path of the heart. This unbalance has existed for centuries. In this time of revaluation of women and of female values, there is certainly a chance that our way of coexisting and our religions may become more balanced: the Goddess of truth and the God of love together in holy matrimony. That must be realized within our own hearts. A lot of courage is necessary, and the insight that without healthy emotionality neither a healthy religion nor a healthy society is possible.

Chapter 44

Ego and Essence

*Soul, spirit, and ego are only words. True
entities of that kind do not exist. Consciousness
is the only Truth.*
~Ramana Maharshi

here is no ego. There is no self. There is only consciousness. We should have listened to Ramana! Then we would not have introduced such a disastrous separation between "I" and soul and between psychology and spirituality. From the beginning of modern psychology, the ego became the territory of psychology while the self or the soul became the territory of spirituality. It is an artificial separation and by using this terminology we run the risk of also remaining separated. They are all attempts at understanding man and his path in life, of course. We need models to clarify the Path and beacons for our consciousness so it can find a way to unfold. Yet it is good to realize that all those divisions are only "thought up" constructions and not reality. There is only consciousness and manifested consciousness and that is who we are. We are entire consciousness, but we have trouble embodying that consciousness entirely. The path we have to take in this life on this earth is to make our consciousness complete in our lives and also within our bodies. Mystics have put it like this: God is trying to realize himself within human beings. Or: we are hidden gods. There is really only one way, and that is from subconsciousness to consciousness on all levels: physical, mental, emotional, and spiritual; body, mind, heart, and soul. After saying this, we can have a look at what is meant by the ego model.

The Ego

That I am a human being, I have in common with all people; that I see and hear and eat, I have in common with all animals. But that I am I is exclusively mine, belongs to me, to nobody else, not to an angel, not to God, except in so far as I am one with him.

~Meister Eckhart [Eckhart von Hochheim O.P.)

Our self or ego is the center of our conscious personality. It is the feeling of identity, apart from others; it is an instrument for living on earth. The words *self* and *ego* mean the same to me. Nowadays it is fashionable to be nasty about this ego. Expressions, such as "ego tripper" and "he has a big ego," can be heard all over the place. People speak of "the need to dismantle the ego which is like a psychological cancer."[1] In a Dutch file of A Course in Miracles, we read, "The ego is a disruptive element, a twister, a doubter, a sharp one, a Gordian Knot, murderous, an ostrich" to name but a few swear words. The ego is set apart from the self in the Course; it is called "the focus of consciousness" that you need as long as you "believe that you live in this world." I do not know quite what to make of the latter. Does it mean that it is an illusion that we live in this world? According to the Course, the ego is an illusion anyway, something which does not exist. "The ego is the wrong identification, namely with the fearful, separate part of our mind...The ego is the thought of separation, of an separate identity, apart from God and apart from the rest of creation."

Do we help each other when we swear at that neurotic ego that comes from our hurt inner child? This is not a very loving way of talking.

First, I suggest that we, completely in accordance with this book, show respect to our egos as center of our conscious personality. Second, it is clear that the neurotic, damaged part of our ego needs help and healing. Third, healing is only possible with love and not with disdain and grumbling and scolding.

As soon as we declare that the ego is an illusion, which not only the Course in Miracles does but also other New Age schools, as well as the Eastern way of thinking, we not only deny the reality of our personality but also the reality of our damaged and hurt children. By now we have seen that we do not gain anything by denial only a piling up of our problems. Our ego is not an illusion; instead, it is our identity, our unique and personal interpretation and expression of our universal consciousness. Its development, however, has been damaged. It has been made neurotic and this creates the problems, not the ego itself. We shall hold the story of Narcissus to the light as we can learn something about the ego from that:

The story of Narcissus and Echo.

Narcissus was an attractive young man who scorned the love of the nymph Echo because he was conceited. Echo was so disappointed in love that she pined away. Finally, only her voice remained, her Echo. Narcissus was punished with an insatiable hunger: he fell in love with his own image that he saw in a clear well but could never reach.

It is remarkable that the part of the story in which Echo plays a part is rather an unknown and neglected element in the story of Narcissus (perhaps this has been a symptom of the neglect of women for centuries). It is, however, of essential importance, as I will demonstrate. We can regard Echo as the

513

female side, our *anima* as Jung called it. She represents our longings, our feelings, and emotions. Narcissus refuses to form a relationship with Echo, his female side. Echo pines away until there is only an echo, a weak and vague remnant of her true voice. The result is that Narcissus becomes only interested in himself. He falls in love with his own image that he cannot reach. We must connect our rational side to our emotional side to become a whole person. The anima and the animus must have a relationship with each other within the human soul. Narcissus and Echo should enter into holy matrimony based on equality. Echo will then no longer be a shadow but a valuable partner.

Narcissus' story is our story: "Here I am!" and "You can't ignore me!" Instead of entering into a relationship with Echo, we become obsessed by her. The consequence of this repressed emotionality is that we become focused on ourselves, involved in ourselves, or egocentric, which are all words for the same thing: Narcissus. If we do not want to get to know Echo, the ego becomes a narcissist. We all try to be altruistic and let another person take precedence, but self-involvement comes in through the back door again by means of extravagant behavior, all kinds of unconscious ways of asking for attention: intolerance, provocative behavior, and being too sure of yourself.

If our self or our personality is to emerge in a healthy way, then it must be emotionally integrated. You can then be the center of interest because you have something to say or do that deserves attention without being loud or entering into a conflict with another person. You will then be a strong personality.

We could say that *ego is only healthy with Echo.*

In the preceding chapters, we have described the path of ego with Echo in many variations. Our Echo needs a lot of healing. On our planet, she has become but a tiny echo of what she really is: our emotion and our sister. She screams from pain and she cries for recognition. When people say that another person has a big ego, it is really Echo who is shouting from within! If we integrate our Echo step by step with a huge amount of emotional Work, our little egos will become less narcissistic and, as a result, powerful. There is nothing wrong with a powerful ego. A powerful ego describes a person who has integrated his or her Echo, and is, therefore, emotionally integrated. He knows what he wants, knows what he is able to do, and knows what he feels.

In other words, only a powerful ego is a powerful person capable of surrender and connection with All that is. The continuing confusion between a healthy ego and one that has been made neurotic makes the discussion about the ego so difficult. It is really so simple: there is individual consciousness which is partly our ego. This is a mixture of the feeling of identity and of neurotic identification. The other part of our consciousness is what I call our Spark of Light that corresponds with the soul or with Jung's concept of "Self." It is the center of our entire soul, our totality. We are essentially that Spark of Light, which is so much more and far greater than our ego, our conscious personality.

In our Work, as I have described it in this book, it is essential to first free the self from its neuroses so only a powerful, healthy, and strong personality remains that can connect to All that is. Without a strong self, we will drown in the sea of the life, and that is not what we want. Surrender is different; I will write more about that in the following chapter. In the second place, it is about realizing our Spark of Light more and more and conjuring it up from beneath the debris of the hurt ego. I speak of *conjuring* on purpose because it does not happen with the will of the self, neither with meditation, nor by practicing virtuousness. It is an alchemistic process; by melting down and transforming our emotional debris, the essence of who we are gradually appears. We have described this as the process of the pool of stagnant water, from the stream of emotion to the ocean of essence. In that ocean of essence we are a Spark of Light of the One Great Light. We gradually realize that Spark of Light to the extent that we purify ourselves of the emotional debris.

Identification

It is important to have a more detailed look at the process of identification when discussing the ego. It is, hereby, about how the ego composes itself into an identity. Our ego, as a separate person apart from others, grows on a base of love and respect. When important key figures, in our culture primarily our parents, give us a name and recognize us as their child, we attain a place on this earth and a safe nest which we can later leave and go wherever we want. Because of our vulnerability, we need such a safe nest. Because of confirmation and respect for our unique presence, we feel safe and become secure and enterprising and do what our soul invites us to do.

A good identity is built with love. And this is where we reach the essence of our story: love and lovelessness. What I have just described is what it should be, ideally speaking. Our ego is, in reality, built with love and lovelessness, and that is where the confusion originates when we talk about our ego. Our ego (or we) grew up in this mixture of love and lovelessness. We did not only identify with love: "I am good and lovable" but also with the lovelessness that we experienced: "I am not good and lovable."

The more love we have experienced, the more powerful our identity will be at the end of our youth. The less love we have experienced, the weaker our ego will be. The path I demonstrate in this book is the path of repair work with which we can lessen the lovelessness for ourselves and increase the love for ourselves. Because of this path of love, we learn to tip the balance in favor of love and build a powerful self in this world that can realize the soul's call on earth. For that is what it is all about: developing a powerful instrument to be and to do what we came here for—to become, each and every one, in his or her own way, a Spark of Light of the One Great Light.

The Spiritual Question: Who Am I?

I am the imago Dei in the darkness of the earth.
~C.G.Jung

Generally speaking, we can let go of something when it is lovingly fulfilled. When our needs as a baby are fulfilled, we can grow towards the next stage. Usually we grow physically and mentally but only partly emotionally. This is because of our emotional backlog. If something is not emotionally fulfilled, we remain *stuck* in it. This has been discussed in previous chapters as fixations. This is the reason why we usually remember the traumatic experiences of former lives; that is where we got stuck. What is fulfilled disappears into the background and transforms itself into strength or a quality. Because of the affective deficit, we get bogged down and identify ourselves with what is only a matter of secondary importance. Because of this, we often identify ourselves deep into adulthood with roles we have played.

I was a late arrival and because I had a powerless role in comparison with my sisters and I was not yet in my strength, for a long time I identified myself with Tom Thumb. In this way you will identify yourself with the fact that you are a child of certain parents (that is your personal neurosis) with your profession, your father, or mother, or with being the wife or husband of your partner. As soon as you identify with a role, e.g., include it in your identity, you lose part of your true identity. You *are* not somebody's wife...it is a role you play in your own film. But what is your true identity? This primeval question is what it is about in spirituality: who am I when I

517

leave all roles behind? Am I the sum of all my roles and qualities? Or am I more? Or am I something completely different?

Within spiritual movements, people have always said, "You are the child of these parents, but in reality you are...'a child of God, Light, a Buddha, a Christ.' By identifying with your self and with its roles, you lessen yourself and become less than you are." True spirituality always confronts us with the question of who we really are *deep down*. It invites us to realize the highest and deepest aspect of who/what we are, and they are both the same! Everybody agrees to this, but now what about *how*! How do we do this? By calling the ego and its roles an illusion or a nuisance because love and lovelessness, light and dark, young and old, are so mixed together? Or by liberating the ego from its neurotic darkness and in this way from its attachment to what are only roles and exterior appearances?

It will be clear from what I have written up to this point that I choose the latter path. This is the path of wholeness, whereby we respect everything and learn to love by means of *digestion and integration.* We do not need to *get rid* of anything. Nothing is excluded on the path of love. If I can love my "Tom Thumb," I let go of the identification in a natural way and grow towards who I really am. I will always carry the story of the late arrival with me, but I do not identify with it. I now love that late arrival. This path of love will then be about fulfilling all identifications through loving emotional work and thus to letting go of them. In this way we arrive step-by-step at who we essentially are. We peel our onion further and further till we get to the core. By loving our restricted ego, it becomes fulfilled and disappears into the background. Light will then eventually come to the fore. The wonderful thing about light is that it contains all colors! These are the pearls that we find in the third phase of our model: creativity, thankfulness, strength, courage, trust, and freedom. Together they form Love with a capital letter.

The Fear Behind the Path of the Ego as an Illusion

Because our ego has been a mixture of love and lovelessness, we have become afraid of it, and it has confused us on our spiritual path. For this reason we have declared that the ego is an illusion and a nuisance that hinders us on our path to God. The fear of pride and the inflation of the self, which developed from lovelessness, are the reason that many spiritual schools chose amputation of the ego. Even there where people make a distinction between the ego as identity or self-awareness and the neurotic ego, we see that the latter is called "the dangerous ego" which is seen as proud and egotistic. And we do, indeed, see many spiritual egos on the spiritual path, all styled according to the above-mentioned story: spiritual Narcissuses.

Premature Identification

Everything is one in origin, but every thing, every element, every being has the task to reveal part of that unity themselves, and it is that special own identity that everybody must develop whilst at the same time, the feeling of the original unity must be awakened. ~The Mother

The ego inflation that, in fact, carries a false identity originates when we identify ourselves prematurely with the Spark of Light which we essentially are. Nowadays people say very easily that you should identify yourself with your "higher self" or essence. Somebody who was suffering from a deep depression was (well meaningly) told not to identify with the depressed part but to understand that she was essentially essence and light. She was told not to focus on the wound but to decide from her soul that she had had enough. It did not work. This woman had to work right though her depressions to

519

liberate herself from them and thus find *Joy* as expression of her essence at the base of her depression.

A temporary identification with the wound is necessary to be able to cope. However, when we do this with consciousness, there is always a part of us that does not become identified with the wound. This clear presence of consciousness helps us through. Buddha did not reach Enlightenment through meditation either but because he had reached his lowest point of despair. When he sat under the Bodhi tree, he despaired of meditation, and then it happened. The formerly mentioned Eckhart Tolle described that he went through deep despair before his enlightenment experience. At the deepest point, he had the feeling that he was flung out of it. He described and interpreted his experience later within the Eastern way of thinking. The way through this deep despair is not an easy one. It is the most difficult path that there is for us at the moment, but it is the most worthwhile. To be able to handle the depth of this Work, the ego must be strong; that is why the many steps of emotional work are necessary. A great temptation on this path is the premature identification with the light. This identification then serves denial. Many people nowadays profess to be "past the ego" or "past therapy." They have yielded to the temptation and the pretense that they do not have an ego anymore or at least no negative emotions anymore. The courageous resist this temptation and go to the bottom of the pool of emotions. Only there, in the depths of your own truth, can real treasures be found.

The Higher Mathematics of Spirituality

We shall have another look at the background of our fear of ego inflation. If the self as the center of our personality is not pure and chaste, but weak, we are in danger of not being an instrument or a Spark of Light of the One Great Light but entirely identifying ourselves with it instead. We are then not able to connect the greatness of the realization of one's essence to a deep feeling of deference for being part of Essence. In my language: a total understanding of the fact that we are light and that we are, at the same time, a Spark of Light as individual. The switch in identification from ego to Self can only be made when we have purified and liberated our personality from its neuroses in such a way that we can understand the higher mathematics of identification a little. The higher mathematics are these:

> *I am Light, but the Light is not who I am.*
> *I am All, but All is not who I am.*
> *I am God, but God is not who I am.*
> *I am earth, but the earth is not who I am.*

These mathematics cannot be understood with reason but can only be received through purifying experience. It is good to have an idea of this beforehand, so you not only understand which path you want to take but also reduce your fear of greatness *and* recognize and avoid the dangers of ego inflation. The wonderful thing about emotional Work is that it not only connects us to our greatness, but also to our smallness. After all, we do Work a lot on childhood sorrow. This keeps us firmly rooted. Depth can then develop in which height becomes possible without it being false. Ultimately, we will realize consciousness in this way.

Chapter 45

Surrender and Submission: A Huge Difference

Relax, let yourself go, do not be afraid.
Only then will the powers that lead us open the path and help
us.
~Carlos Castaneda

On the spiritual path, the theme of surrender is often discussed. People speak of surrendering to a teacher or to God. Expressions such as "Thy will be done" are part of this theme. But what is surrender? And surrender to whom or what? We will have a look at what surrender means. Surrender is the opposite of domination and control. The path of surrender is a path of reducing the power of the self that wants to keep everything in hand. This power is based on fear—the fear of ultimately completely feeling who you are. Restraining and controlling yourself and constantly governing yourself by means of voices in your head is a way of not following the natural flow of your heart. You have to work at your fears if you are to learn surrender. You cannot work at the surrender itself. It is not an action word or something you can do by will power. Surrender is a process and the result of gradually conquering your fears. It is ultimately a state of being. You have given up being self-willed and live in surrender to what?

Surrender to Whom or What?

Below is a personal example of surrender:

When I was twenty-three, I had a peculiar and memorable meeting. As a young and enthusiastic mystic, I was doing an intensive weeklong retreat in a summer cottage in the woods. I meditated a lot and in one of those meditations I met a great white light, in contrast to what I usually experienced in my meditations. This frightened me. It was a blinding light that forced me to my knees with a cold-blooded 'voice' and demanded that I submit. I thought at that time it was Lucifer. Of course, it was the voice of my own harsh side! With the help of the person that visited and helped me every now and then, I was able to interpret the experience and to border off this harsh light by plainly and clearly refusing it entrance. That worked and I never met it again in this form on my inner path. I knew from that moment onwards that I only wanted Loving Light and that the discernment of spirits that I had once learned from the Jesuits was a good thing.

I have, moreover, learned after long-lasting inner Work that receiving loving light is quite a task that cannot only be done by meditating. On the path of meditation, I soon found out that I was meditating on a volcano of emotions that could not find a way out. I could not sit still without becoming fidgety! These signals that I received from my body made me realize that I needed emotional work. I then started doing a whole range of therapies and schooling to transform the restlessness in my body into emotions and clarity. In my long-lasting inner emotional Work, I gradually worked at the blockades that were stopping me from receiving Loving Light. This inner Light did not force me to submit but helped me step by step with a light Hand to surrender to my own stream of emotions and feelings from where more and more clarity arose about who I am, where I come from, and for what reason I am here. This Light has shown me the way to where I belong and my true being.

Actually, much surrender is submission, a handing over of oneself. You are then the prey of another person and have given up your own power. It does not really matter if this other is a human being who has invested himself with worldly or spiritual power, or a spiritual being, such as Lucifer or "God." We all know the deep, almost planetary imprint of "I am nothing and God is all." This imprint means that we have often not understood the "Thy will be done." Our own free will has become opposed to God's Will. We can ask ourselves if that was beneficial for our evolution and our spiritual maturity.

With surrender, it is about Working at the liberation of our self-willed ego that wants to have a firm grasp on life because of fear. We should learn to trust again. The sentence: "Not my will, but Thy will be done" fits here. We are then talking about our neurotic personality, not about our true self.

As long as I had not conquered and digested my fears and thus my self-willed way of doing things, this sentence functioned meaningfully in my process. I notice that this sentence does not play an important role anymore. I noticed that the Light inside me did not want me to submit or surrender but to find my own true strength. I discovered how I, certainly as a woman, carried the deep imprint with me that I should submit and deliver my self up to another—and this time Another with a capital letter. My subconscious resistance to this imprint formed an obstacle on the path of surrender: "I do not want to lose my freedom and individuality." Various ancient images of women play a role in this.

Eventually, because of experience, it became clear that it is about the surrender of our fearful and thus controlling will to our *true will*. This true will we can eventually call God's will, and these are not opposed to each other. It is the liberated will, which is past its fears and past being self-willed. To get to know our true will, we *only* have to liberate our self from its fears. That is the Work. As there is often not enough distinction between our neurotic ego and our healthy identity, a lot of confusion has developed with regard to the surrender of our will. In the Work with my students, I noticed how much first-rate strength has been given to a divine power. Setting old fixated anger into motion is a good way to reclaim your own individuality and "Spark of Lightness." Every power, divine or not, and every guru who asks his followers to surrender (in the sense of submitting) and who wants power and does not have any respect for the unique individuality of his followers is not really of service.

True surrender is the opposite of submission, denial, renunciation, or sacrifice. Surrender is a bow to your self in the most essential meaning of the word. It is extracted from the melting down of fears, anger, and pain until they become strength, the strength to be who you are deep down: light. You are Godlike in this and at the same time an individual—*only* a Spark of Light of a greater Light from which you once sprang.

Masterhood

What about surrendering to a guru or teacher? For a time, I was a sannyasin of Osho. My love for this Teacher did me good and accelerated my process of surrendering to myself. By "falling in love" with Osho, I fell in love with my own unrealized possibilities and went into a state of surrender that was very emotional. When I saw him, I laughed and cried at the same time and danced in ecstasy. He, or better, my own longing for surrender, set a stream of inner experiences in motion. The great thing with Osho was that he was not at all attached to his followers. You could come if you wanted to; otherwise, you stayed away. Osho says, "The teacher is only a window; he opens to God, as a window opens to the heavens. What you see through the window has nothing to do with the window itself. The window is just an opening. The teacher is only a path." When a person is so detached from his masterhood, he or she can be a mediator for you with whom to accelerate your process of surrender. When, after a few years, it was "over and done" between Osho and me, he no longer stood between me and myself, and I could carry on with my development. By my surrender to him, he and I activated my kundalini powers and that gave me enough work for years to come!

Whether it is a good idea to surrender to a Teacher or not, depends on his or her detachment from power. Does he point away from himself to your own Work in the depth and to your own surrender to yourself? Does he allow you to worship him as a "representative of God," or does he behave as a brother who is leading the way on the path that he has trodden before and wants to share with you. Brotherhood and sisterhood is ultimately Masterhood. We are, in essence, all brothers and sisters, but at the same time somebody can function as your Teacher because he already knows the path of surrender a bit better. It is then a gift when you meet somebody in person, who can help you to live in surrender.

The Liberating Power of Emotions

Chapter 46

Emotions and Loving Light

Liberation from "God" to Find God

You cannot feel Me because you have never given Me your true feelings.
~God, as channelled by Ceanne deRohan

*I*n this final chapter, we shall study the relationship between God and emotions. We will particularly look at how the denial of our emotions, also those towards God, stand in the way of the connection to God and the realization of ourselves. I will begin by relating a personal story as written in my diary:

> *I recently found out that my image of God is really quite static as is the case with many people in many cultures. If you ask people what they think God is, they usually say 'God is...Love or Energy, or All that is, or all things that are beautiful between people.'*
>
> *Yesterday I read one of the books by Ceanne deRohan where she paints a picture of an evolving God. When I got to bed, I could not sleep, I felt horrible and rebellious. There was one sentence from the book that went round and round in my head: 'You cannot*

feel me because you have never given me your true feelings.'

I allowed my feelings of rebelliousness to grow and felt an enormous, centuries old anger towards God welling up inside me. I started to speak aloud and to yell. I no longer kept my words under control. I heard myself shout: 'You really abandoned me for centuries!' It felt like the cork of an ancient bottle had shot out of me. 'You Wally, you weakling, you had to withdraw from us. You let us plod for centuries all on our own!' 'These feelings felt very old, in any case not from the present. I recognize them from this life from my teenage years, where I was moved to tears by the words: 'He will never forsake the work of His hands.' But these emotions seem particularly to stem from many lives on earth, also from ancient cosmic times. Anyway I kept on swearing at our Origin far into the night. My pillow became a tool, and I hit God round His holy head with it! That really did me good!

I woke up next morning with the song: 'True Lord, oh true Lord, do You remember me?' Yes, I remember You, God; I am part of You and I remember myself and my origin. And only when I start to remember You by receiving all my emotions can I feel that You do remember me and that You have not forgotten the Work of Your hands and that You also went through a development as I am going through mine with Your help. A few days later God showed his respect for me and my Work by literally whispering many things into my ears.

We probably all know the feeling of "My God, my God, why hast Thou forsaken me?" deep down inside of us. I am not talking about our rational opinion about God but about our deeply repressed emotions. We have usually glossed over these emotions with a veneer of beautiful theologies and theories that are in the service of denial and thus in the service of our stagnation. Is this the reason church services are so rigid according to fixed rituals and dogmas? A fixed ritual may, of course, offer a universal basis where individual experiences can find a place. But they can also be an expression of emotional rigidity.

There is a centuries old taboo on emotions in general and on emotions towards God (certainly on the emotion anger) which has developed into a great feeling of guilt. Can you hear the "Mea culpa," "Through my fault, through my fault, my great fault" and the "Kyrie," "Lord, have mercy," which have been deeply indoctrinated by Holy Mass and church services, reverberating in your ears?

As we have seen in the chapter about guilt, guilt is nothing but anger that has been taken back: you blame yourself because you are afraid to blame the other person. By expressing your true indignation, you liberate yourself from feelings of guilt. Then there will then be motion where there was first stagnation, strength where there was weakness and fear, and above all, love where there was once hate. In this way emotions transform into essence. We regain a part of our essence, our soul with every emotional liberation.

And we can also liberate ourselves from an image of God that is at odds with that of a liberated human being. After all, the problem of pure perception and projection always plays a huge role with regard to the great Absent Present One. Our God will always be as we are inside; if we are full of fear in our inner selves, we will then have a fearful image of God. If we feel guilty, God will be a God that punishes or forgives. If we feel sad, God will be a comforting God. If we are love, God will be love. If we dance through life, God will be a Shiva, a dancing God. It is no wonder that the great mystics and teachers, such as the Spanish sixteenth century St. John of the Cross, saw the path of image purification as the path to God. "To entirely come to All, you must renounce everything

531

completely."[1]   Christianity   has   sadly   translated   the magnificence of this message in outward poverty and detachment. Without sister emotion, a complete path of purification is not possible—at best, only half. Without her it has become a rational path of pursuing virtuousness, morals, and a lot of good will. Now in these times in which sister emotion is taking her lawful place, it is possible that we become fundamentally free people with a liberated God.

Trauma and a Non-religious Attitude

The publicist John Spreyer[2] describes in an article the relationship between his non- religious attitude and an experience during his birth. The power of early traumatic imprints becomes clear from this:

When he was sixty, he came into contact with the fear of death because of a possible brain tumor. As he was familiar with Janov's Primal Scream therapy, he dedicated a number of sessions to his fear of death. He found out during one of the sessions that he had had a very difficult time during birth; he felt he was going to die before he was born, and he felt intensely that he was abandoned by his mother during this difficult birthing process.

In a following session he heard himself suddenly swearing excessively 'I started cursing God by the names He is called in the major religions of the world. I began a blasphemous litany: God damn You, God; God damn You, Christ; God damn you, Jehovah; I hate You, Allah. I sent them all to hell where I had just been. I wanted God to suffer as much as I had suffered.'

He welcomed his anger completely and suddenly felt that he had equated his mother and God. 'My mother was not hearing my pleas for help and, as a fetus, I had drawn the conclusion that she was indifferent to my cries for help. This was the image I had always had of God, uncaring and indifferent.'

He suddenly knew for sure that this was the background of his non-religious and non-spiritual attitude in life. 'It was and is difficult to accept the reality that only this one trauma, even though very early and very severe, was to become the cause of my lack of religious and spiritual feelings that I had for the next six decades of my life.'

Fear of Abandonment in a New Light

As we saw in previous chapters, fear of abandonment is an often-occurring fear in our human relationships. Earlier I wrote that what you are afraid of has usually already taken place. It is a fear of repetition based on real experiences. When you extend your consciousness over the limits of your temporary self, you can feel that your pent-up emotions are not only ancient, but you are also familiar with a long history of hope and disappointment with regard to God, who did not let His presence be felt because you could not feel. But you did not know that. You did not know that the fundamental reason for not being able to experience God, was the denial of sister emotion. You could only imagine and suppose that there was Light. For that reason, there was theology, dogma, and ritual as compensation. In your feelings, you were constantly disappointed in this God of Light who let you plod away in your earthly darkness. Deep down we all carry this feeling of abandonment. It is no mistake that the Cross, with a despairing Jesus who called out, "My God, why hast Thou abandoned me" has become so central in our places of worship. We have been so stupid as to worship that Cross instead of seeing that it is our own inner story.

A Spark of Light worker discovered the relationship between her earthly father and her heavenly Father:

I have, in the mean time, discovered how much I feel betrayed by my father. He who before my conception yearned for me, full of longing, turned out to be an inconsistent father after my birth who alternated violence and love. And that angry dialogue I had with 'God' a few weeks ago has also surfaced: unacceptable all that pain, all that violence in the world; there is not an image of God that can compensate for that. But now I realize that my feeling of being abandoned by my father is mirrored by a deeper betrayal: being abandoned by God. That I needed this father to become aware of the much older betrayal. I suddenly feel compassion for my father: he is also just a pawn in this eternal drama. I also realize that I have not dared to give 'God' what for with the carpet beater. God damn, that's what I'll do. 'All right then, you two, I'll take you both on...!'

The Fear of God

The fear of God has always played a major part in religious experience. God was the authority, whereby respect for him was also mixed with fear. To become free human beings in our religious experience, we need to set the emotions that are traditionally taboo in relation to God in motion; these are especially the emotions anger and fear, the twin sisters as we have seen in the chapter about fear. I think that we need to begin our awakening with our fear for God. I have often noticed that people who have been religious and churchgoing their whole lives, suddenly on their deathbed became mortally afraid and began to wonder if they "had done it right" and if they "will endure 'Judgment.'"

Eventually, theology, the rational knowing, took over, but deep down inside the demon of fear lurked, which was quickly covered up with the "the cloak of charity." But do we call this love? This famous "cloak of charity" is but a mere palliative, a cloaking of deep fears *and* anger which are present somewhere in the dark, hidden, recesses of the heart.

It will not be easy to really feel the fear for God. It is deeply embedded, certainly with those who have had a Christian upbringing. There is, moreover, an enormous taboo, which has been in our "mental genes" for centuries, about emotionally feeling the fear and anger that certainly lies underneath. Becoming aware of the fear is elementary because it keeps other emotions firmly in their place.

Eva had a sickening headache during one of our Spark of Light weeks. Deep fear from her Dutch reformed background wanted to come to light but could not yet. When we started to work at her sickness, it changed into disgust. Disgust is a combination of fear and anger that have a hold over each other, as it were. A quarrel will then start between the twin sisters...She set her disgust in motion by putting her fingers down her throat and then went forward to meet the ball of fear and anger that had been there all her life and had caused many migraine attacks. From that moment onwards, she could clearly feel to which extent the God of her youth had become jumbled up with her earthly father. Her father was a deacon of the church, but he hit his children at home on the principle that "he, who loves his children, disciplines them." This mixture of preaching about love in the church (where her father played a prominent role) and physical violence at home meant that she had stored a load of fear and anger for both fathers.

Finally...

It is, ultimately, important to create space within yourself so Loving Light can find a basis within you. You create this space by clearing away everything that stands in the way of Light: your old undigested fears, anger, and sorrow; and fixations, such as pride, shame, false modesty, and living according to fixed patterns. It is about all your repressed emotions, not only your earthly reality and your relationships but also your vertical relations with regard to God, Jesus, or whomever else you feel a bond with in other dimensions. Everything depends on your motivation here. How much Work are you prepared to do to restore this primeval connection with your Origin, with your God? How many tears are you prepared to shed and how much courage can you mobilize to search the deep recesses of your heart?

The only thing left for me to do, dear reader, is to share with you what this path has given me. My experience is that he who dares all, wins all. It has required a huge amount of effort, but I have become immensely rich. Inwardly, I now know that it is true what Jesus once said, "Seek the kingdom within, and all these things shall be yours as well." This kingdom is the Realm of Love (with a capital) and Wisdom. When we step by step get to know sister emotion, she turns into the Lady of Wisdom who once was known as Sofia. Of her is written:

When God prepared the heavens, I was there:
When he set a compass upon the face of the depth,
When he established the clouds above,
When he strengthened the fountains of the deep,
When he gave the sea his decree that the waters should not pass his commandment,
When he appointed the foundations of the earth,
Then I was by him as one brought up with him and I was daily his delight,
Rejoicing always before him,
Rejoicing in the habitable part of his earth,
And my delights were with the sons of men.
Now, therefore, harken unto me, O ye children,
For blessed are they that keep my ways.
Hear instruction, and be wise, and refuse it not.

Blessed is the man that heareth me, watching daily at my gates, waiting at the posts of my doors.
For whoso findeth me, findeth life and shall obtain favor of the Lord.

This Sofia, our Primeval Mother, is able together with God, our Father, to take us back home again—from discord to wholeness, from darkness to Light, and from hate to Love. They all live within us as strengths that can liberate us. Thus, we get to know the Primeval Parents within us. We shall be loved and we shall love. Finally, everything becomes one: the lover, the beloved, and loving. We will then be a loving Spark of Light of the one great Light. There will not be many words then...

Endnotes

Chapter 3

[1] From *Emotional Intelligence* by Daniel Goleman, Bantam Books, 1995.

[2] Ibid., pp.81, 82.

[3] Ibid., p. 83.

[4] Ibid., p. 86.

[5] From "The EQ Factor," *Time Magazine*, October 2, 1995, Volume 146, nr. 14.

[6] From *The Sane Society* by Erich Fromm, Routledge, 1956.

Chapter 4

[1] From *Emotion* by James Hillman, Northwestern University Press, Evanston, IL, 1961.

Chapter 8

[1] From *The Seat of the Soul* by Gary Zukav, Fireside Ed., 1990, p. 34.

[2] From *The Way of the White Clouds* by Lama Anagarika Govinda, Shambala Dragon Ed., Part 3, Chapter 3.

Chapter 10

[1] From *Love Is Letting Go of Fear* by G. Jampolsky, Bantam Books, 1985, Part I.

[2] From *The Healing of Emotion: Awakening the Fearless Self* by Chris Griscom, Simon and Schuster, 1990, Chapters 6 and 7.

[3] From DSM IV, the abbreviation of the Diagnostic Statistical Manual, a worldwide classification system of mental disorders.

[4] From *A Course in Miracles* compiled by Helen Schucman, Penguin Book Ltd., 1975, H 20, 3:3-7.

[5] From *Emotional Intelligence* by Daniel Goleman, Bantam Books, 1995, p. 217.

[6] Ibid., p. 218.

[7] From *Love Is Letting Go of Fear* by G. Jampolsky, Bantam Books, 1985, Part I.

Chapter 11.

[1] From *Civilization and* Its Discontents by Sigmund Freud, W.W. Norton, New York, 1961.

[2] From *Emotional Intelligence* by Daniel Goleman, Bantam Books, 1995, p.59.

[3] From *The Art of Loving* by Erich Fromm, World Perspectives, 1960, Chapter II, p. 3.

[4] From *Stanzaic Poems II-5. Complete Works* by Hadewijch, Paulist Press, 1980.

Chapter 12

[1] From *Emotional Intelligence* by Daniel Goleman, Bantam Books, 1995, p.72.

Chapter 15.

[1] From *The Earth Sea Quartet* by Ursula le Guin, Penguin Books, 1993.

[2] From *The Mustard Seed Part I* by Osho, Rajneesh Foundation, 1975, Third Lecture.

[3] From *Earth Spell, the Loss of Consciousness on Earth* by Ceanne deRohan, Four Winds Publications, New Mexico, 1989, p.153.

[4] From *A Return to Love* by Marianne Williamson, Harper Collins Publisher, 1992, pp. 93, 96.

[5] From *Het Wonder der Vergeving (The Wonder of Forgiveness)* by Willem Glaudemans, Ankh Hermes Publishing House, 2009, p.37.

[6] From *Depth Psychology and a New Ethic* by Erich Neumann, Shambala, 1990, Chapter 1.

[7] From *A Return to Love* by Marianne Williamson, Harper Collins Publisher, 1992, p. 96.

[8] From *Institutiones* by Calvin and quoted from *Psychoanalysis and Religion* by Erich Fromm, Yale University Press, 1969, Chapter III.

[9] From Erich Fromm, Ibid.

[10] From *Confessiones* by Augustinus, Freiburg Herder, 1955, p. 8.

Chapter 20

[1] From *Imprints, the Lifelong Effects of the Birth Experience* by Arthur Janov, Coward-McCann, New York, 1983.

Chapter 27

[1] From *Gestalt Therapy Verbatim* by Fritz Perls, 1968/1992, The Gestalt Journal Press, p. 6.

Chapter 30

[1] From *Beyond the Brain, Birth, Death and Transcendence in Psychotherapy* by Stanislav Grof, State University of New York Press, 1985, Chapter 2.

Chapter 31

[1] From an article in *The Lancet* by Dr. P. Van Lommel, December, 2001.

[2] From *Illuminating Physical Experience* by Marcey Folley, Holistic Wellness Foundation, 2000, p. 48.

[3] From *How Then Shall We Live* written by Wayne Muller, Bantan Books, 1996, that is related by Jack Kornfield.

[4] From a TV interview in 1996 with Barbara Walters. See also: Sarah Hinze, *Life before Life: A Collection of Mothers' Experiences with Their Preborn Children,* Cedar Fort, Inc., 1993.

[5] From *The Secret Life of the Unborn Child* by Thomas Verny and John Kelly, Time Warner, 1988, Chapter 1.

[6] From *Birth without Violence* by Frederick Leboyer, Healing Arts Press, 2009.

[7] From *The Facts of Life* by R.D. Laing, Penguin Books, 1976, Chapter 6.

[8] From *Beyond the Brain, Birth, Death and Transcendence in Psychotherapy* by Stanislav Grof, State University of New York Press, 1985, Chapter 2.

[9] From *The Facts of Life* by R.D. Laing, Penguin Books, 1976,

Chapter 6.

[10] From *Imprints, the Lifelong Effects of the Birth Experience* by Arthur Janov, Coward-McCann, New York, 1983, p. 243.

Chapter 34

[1] Those who are at home in the character analysis of bio-energetics and Reichian body work will recognize elements of the work of Wilhelm Reich, Alexander Lowen, Ron Kurtz and Hector Prestera.

[2] From *Hara, The Vital Center of Man* by K. von Dürckheim, London, Mandala, Unwin, 1977.

Chapter 36

[1] From *The Toxic Mind, Confessions of a Schizophrenic* by Elnora van Winkle, http://www.redirectingselftherapy.com

[2] From *Barriers and Boundaries* by Liz Greene, C.P.A. Press, London, 2002.

Chapter 37

[1] From *Towards a Psychology of Being* by Abraham Maslov, New York, 1962.

Chapter 38

[1] From *The Feeling of What Happens* by Antonio Damasio, Harvest Books, 2000.

[2] From *The Power of Now* by Eckhart Tolle, Hodder & Stoughton, London, 2005, page 45-46.

Chapter 39

[1] From the Dutch newspaper "Algemeen Dagblad," 9-8-2002.

[2] From *De Prophet* by Kahlil Gibran, Knopf, New York, 1923, pp. 14/15.

[3] From *The Gospel of Thomas*, Harper, San Francisco, 1992, Logion 75.

[4] From *Being-in Dreaming* by Florinda Donner, Harper, San Francisco, 1992, Chapter 3.

[5] From Carl Rohde writing in the Dutch Magazine *Wapenveld*, nr.5, October 1999.

[6] From *Illuminating Physical Experience* by Marcy Foley, Holistic Wellness Foundation, 2000, p.162.

[7] More information about this subject in Sukie Colegrave, Androgynie, Virago, 1977.

Chapter 40

[1] From a good book about love and relationships titled *Lessons in Love* by Guy Corneau, Owl Books, 2000.

[2] From the magazine *Wapenveld*, nr. 5-10-1999.

Chapter 41

[1] From *ADHD Alternatives* by Aviva and Tracy Romm, Story Books, 2000.

[2] From the Dutch newspaper Trouw,10-8-2002

[3] From *The Lancet*, August, 2002 and newspaper NRC, 9-8-2002.

[4] From *The Primal Wound: Understanding the Adopted Child* by Nancy Verrier, Ingram, 1993.

Chapter 42

[1] From *Maternal Deprivation: Implications for the Ontogeny of the Neural Stress Circuitry* by Dr. Helga van Oers, Leiden, 1998.

[2] From *Diagnosis and Treatment of Multiple Personality Disorder* by Frank Putman, Guilford Press, 1989.

[3] From *Prozac and Other Psychiatric Drugs* by Lewis Opler, Pocket Books, 1996

[4] From *Toxic Psychiatry, Why Therapy, Empathy and Love Must Replace the Drugs, Electroshock and Biochemical Theories of the "New Psychiatry"* by P.Breggin, New York, St. Martin's Press, 1991.

[5] *From ADHD Alternatives* by A. and T. Romm, Story Books, 2000.

[6] From *The Toxic Mind: The Biology of Mental Illness and Violence* by Elnora van Winkle, Medical Hypotheses 2000, 55(4): 356-368. http://www.redirectingselftherapy.com

[7] From *Confessions of a Schizophrenic* by E. van Winkle, Ibid.

Chapter 43

[1] From *The Book, Series III* by Bhagwan Shree Rajneesh, Oregon, 1989, p. 250.

[2] From *The Power of Now* by Eckhart Tolle, New World Library, 2004, pp. 45, 46.

[3] From an interview in *The Awakening West* by L.M.Lumière, Oakland, 2001.

[4] From an interview of Jack Engler in *What Is Enlightenment*, issue 17.

[5] From *Handboek van de Wereldgodsdiensten.* (*Handbook of World Religions*), The Hague, 1983, p. 231.

[6] From *Zen at War* by Brian Victoria, Weatherhill Press, 1997.

[7] From Josh Baran, in *Tricycle Magazine*, The Buddhist Review, May, 1998.

[8] From *An Unconditional Relationship to Life* by Andrew Cohen, Moksa Foundation, 1995.

[9] From the magazine *What Is Enlightenment*, issue 17.

Chapter 44

[1] *Soul Psychology* by Joshua Stone, Light Technology, Flagstaff, 1995.

Chapter 47

[1] From Collected Works of Saint John of the Cross, ICS Publications, 1991.

[2] From *Another Piece of my Birth Puzzle: My Mother as God, God as My Mother* by John Speyrer, IPA Journal, Primal community.

[3] From Proverbs 8:27–36.

About the Author

Riet Okken grew up in the Netherlands and completed her studies there at the University of Groningen where she earned BS (Bachelor of Science) degrees in sociology and psychology with a minor in cultural anthropology and a MS (Master of Science) degree in clinical psychology with a minor in psychology of religion. Next she studied multiple forms of psychotherapy, such as Gestalt Therapy, Kinesiology, Postural Integration Therapy, Holotropic Therapy, and Initiatic Therapy (the latter with German Zenmaster Karlfried von Durckheim and Jungian therapist Maria Hippius). Always a lifelong learner, Riet was drawn to share her knowing with others: students of theology at a theological university in the Netherlands and individuals and groups at the Spark of Light Work Center she and her partner founded in France to help others with psychotherapeutical counseling and intense training so they could discover whatever prohibited them on spiritual, mental, emotional, and/or physical level/s from awakening to the fact that they are part of the One Light. In addition, she trained therapists in Spark of Light Work. Riet no longer works with clients and students but continues to blend heart and head in her many books that are available in Belgium and the Netherlands and now here in the United States with this publication of *The Liberating Power of Emotions*: *De kracht van de bestemming* (*The Power of Destination*), Ankh Hermes Publishing House, 1988; *Met de stroom mee* (*Going with the Flow*), Ankh Hermes Publishing House, 1998; *De bevrijdende kracht van emoties* (*The Liberating Power of Emotions*), Astarte Publishing House, 2002, and now in English, Ozark Mountain Publishing, 2012; *Lichtpuntwerk de liefdevolle ontvangst van onze emoties* (*Spark of Light Work: The Loving*

Reception of Our Emotions), Astarte Publishing House, 2004; and coming soon: *Jezus ontsluierd* (*Jesus Unveiled*).

riet.okken@wanadoo.fr

Other Books Published
by
Ozark Mountain Publishing, Inc.

Conversations with Nostradamus, Volume I, II, III...............by Dolores Cannon
Jesus and the Essenes...by Dolores Cannon
They Walked with Jesus...by Dolores Cannon
Between Death and Life.. by Dolores Cannon
A Soul Remembers Hiroshima...by Dolores Cannon
Keepers of the Garden...by Dolores Cannon
The Legend of Starcrash..by Dolores Cannon
The Custodians..by Dolores Cannon
The Convoluted Universe - Book One, Two, Three, Four......by Dolores Cannon
Five Lives Remembered ....by Dolores Cannon
The Three Waves of Volunteers and the New Earth .... by Dolores Cannon
I Have Lived Before..by Sture Lönnerstrand
The Forgotten Woman...by Arun & Sunanda Gandhi
Luck Doesn't Happen by Chance...................................by Claire Doyle Beland
Mankind - Child of the Stars............................by Max H. Flindt & Otto Binder
Past Life Memories As A Confederate Soldier.........................by James H. Kent
Holiday in Heaven...by Aron Abrahamsen
Out of the Archives .... by Aron & Doris Abrahamsen
Is Jehovah An E.T.?...by Dorothy Leon
The Essenes - Children of the Light...............by Stuart Wilson & Joanna Prentis
Power of the Magdalene.................................by Stuart Wilson & Joanna Prentis
Beyond Limitations ....by Stuart Wilson & Joanna Prentis
Atlantis and the New Consciousness .... by Stuart Wilson & Joanna Prentis
Rebirth of the Oracle...................................by Justine Alessi & M. E. McMillan
Reincarnation: The View from Eternity......by O.T. Bonnett, M.D. & Greg Satre
The Divinity Factor..by Donald L. Hicks
What I Learned After Medical School ....by O.T. Bonnett, M.D.
Why Healing Happens..by O.T. Bonnett, M.D.
A Journey Into Being...by Christine Ramos, RN
Discover The Universe Within You...by Mary Letorney
Worlds Beyond Death...by Rev. Grant H. Pealer
A Funny Thing Happened on the Way to Heaven .... by Rev. Grant H. Pealer
Let's Get Natural With Herbs..by Debra Rayburn
The Enchanted Garden...by Jodi Felice
My Teachers Wear Fur Coats.........................by Susan Mack & Natalia Krawetz
Seeing True..by Ronald Chapman
Elder Gods of Antiquity...by M. Don Schorn
Legacy of the Elder Gods...by M. Don Schorn
Gardens of the Elder Gods .... by M. Don Schorn
Reincarnation...Stepping Stones of Life ....by M. Don Schorn

Continue for more books by Ozark Mountain Publishing, Inc.